The Linguistic Relationship
between Armenian and Greek

Publications of the Philological Society, 30

The Linguistic Relationship between Armenian and Greek

James Clackson

Publications of the Philological Society, 30

BLACKWELL
Oxford UK & Cambridge USA

Copyright © The Philological Society 1994

ISBN 0–631–19197–6

First published 1994

Blackwell Publishers
108 Cowley Road, Oxford, OX4 1JF, UK

and
238 Main Street,
Cambridge, MA. 02142, USA.

British Library Cataloguing in Publication Data
A catalogue record for this book is available from the British Library

Library of Congress Cataloguing in Publication Data
Clackson, James.
The linguistic relationship between Armenian and Greek / James Clackson.
p. cm. — (Publications of the Philological Society: 30.)
Includes bibliographical references and index.
ISBN (invalid) 0-06-311919-7 (pbk.) : £19.99 ($25.00 U.S.)
1. Armenian language, Classical. 2. Greek language. I. Title.
II. Series.
PK8014.C58 1994
491´.992—dc20
94-26076
CIP

Printed in Great Britain by
Whitstable Litho Printers Ltd., Whitstable, Kent

ACKNOWLEDGEMENTS

This work originated as a Cambridge PhD thesis prepared under the supervision of Professor Robert Coleman, who first suggested to me the topic of research, and whose unfailing encouragement and readiness to read and correct my work and discuss ideas and details I cannot adequately repay. My understanding of the Armenian language and culture, and indeed of a range of other disciplines from Georgian to the habits of ostriches, was vastly improved by attendance at the Oxford 'Thursday Seminars' of Professor Charles Dowsett who was always ready to offer help, advice and hospitality with warmth and humour. I am also very much indebted to Dr Paddy Considine and Dr John Penney who both read the final draft of this work and who saved me from making numerous errors of omission and commission. Professor Sidney Allen and Dr John Killen have also made a number of corrections and valuable suggestions concerning this work, and I am very grateful to Professor Allen for putting forward the work to The Philological Society for publication, and thereby allowing me access to the excellent copy-editing skills of Dr Max Wheeler, the Publications Secretary whose care and perspicacity seem boundless. Naturally there have been occasions where I have been foolish enough not to follow the advice given me, and the responsibility for all errors must remain my own.

I should also like to thank Dr Neil Hopkinson, Mr Peter Khoroche, Dr John MacGinnis and Nantucket for help and support, and the Master and Fellows of Trinity College, Cambridge, who have enabled me to prepare my thesis for publication in financial, material and culinary comfort, and (the first shall be last) my wife, Sarah, to whom this book is dedicated.

CONTENTS

1

THE METHODS OF RELATING LANGUAGES IN THE SAME FAMILY

1.1 Methods of grouping Indo-European languages: a survey

Throughout the nineteenth and twentieth centuries a number of different groupings of the Indo-European languages have been proposed. Rather than repeat here the different theories of the relationships between individual languages or language families, I shall limit myself to a brief survey of the methods and the developments in methodology which have been used to justify some of these groupings.[1]

The notion that some of the Indo-European languages are more closely related to each other than others has been held since the first recognition of the language family. Sir William Jones, in his celebrated discourse which put forward the idea that Greek and Latin and Sanskrit sprang from a common source, proposed that 'the Gothick and the Celtick' might also be related, thereby implicitly accepting the close relationship between Welsh and Irish and between the Germanic languages.[2]

The first full-fledged attempt to present a picture of the relationships between the Indo-European languages was made by Schleicher, who conceived the idea of the linguistic family tree in the 1850s and drew up an influential model in his *Compendium* of 1861 (Schleicher 1861:7). His inspiration for this model was undoubtedly the Natural Sciences, which, he thought, should include the Science of Language (which was at that date little more than the study of the historical development of the Indo-European languages and their relationship). Schleicher's family tree consisted of a stem, representing the parent language, which split into two branches, each of which in turn split in two; the earliest split represented the division between the Germano-Balto-Slavonic branch and the Aryo-Greco-Latino-Celtic branch, with subsequent splits into Germanic and Balto-Slavonic, Aryan (Indo-Iranian) and Greco-Latino-Celtic, and so on until the individual languages or principal groups were reached. Schleicher gave a number of different reasons for his splits; differences of sound, inflection, vocabulary and culture were all counted as significant. For example, the separation of Germano-Balto-Slavonic was held to be justified by the 'sound-change' of *-bh- to *-m- in the nominal case-endings of this group.

The question which most occupied scholars in the decade immediately following Schleicher's *Compendium* was not whether Schleicher's methods were at fault, but whether his groupings were correct; whether, for example, the first split should be between Indo-Iranian and the other languages, rather than between Germano-Balto-Slavonic and the rest. Scholars joined in the debate with an eye on the methods of textual criticism, associated with the name of Lachmann, using the manuscript *stemma*, which provided an analogy for the linguistic family tree. The reconstruction of the original text (the parent language) proceeded via the elimination of corruption in the manuscript tradition (the daughter languages). The detection of manuscript corruptions entails the grouping of manuscripts into related families which stem from lost archetypes; in the same way linguistic innovations since Proto-Indo-European could be recognised through the construction of a family tree.[3]

The first scholar to spell out in full the problem with the *Stammbaum* method as a model for Indo-European languages was Johannes Schmidt.[4] In a comparatively brief work (J. Schmidt 1872), he pointed out that the contemporary theory that the European languages were sharply separated from the Indo-Iranian languages was untenable, showing that there were close links between Slavic and Indo-Iranian and Greek and Indo-Iranian. He went on to demonstrate the connections between Greek and Italic, Italic and Celtic, and Germanic and Balto-Slavonic. All of these individual groupings had been proposed before, and a large amount of the linguistic data which Schmidt uses in support of these groupings would no longer be considered significant, or even correct. However, Schmidt's compilation of the data led him to an important methodological advance: Proto-Indo-European was not, in his view, a monolithic unity, but like living languages was divided into dialects. Schmidt explained the similarities between languages through the spread of features throughout the dialect area.[5]

Schmidt's picture of the development of the historically attested languages from the earlier dialectal array is quite sophisticated; from a range of earlier contiguous dialects

A B C D E F G H I J K L...

in the parent language, he assumed that not all had historical descendants, but that some, for example B, F and L, had, for social or historical reasons, achieved the ascendancy over the neighbouring dialects, which had eventually disappeared. He paralleled this hypothetical development with the historical development of the spread of Attic(-Ionic) and Latin at the expense of the other dialects of Greece and Italy (1872:27–28). Thus Schmidt models his explanation of prehistoric change on the example of historical change, just as he models his reconstructed language on the example of living languages.

One of the goals of the *Stammbaum*, as we have seen, was a better reconstruction of the parent language; so also in Schmidt's work the new model of language groupings had consequences for the reconstructed language. Schmidt sees the unitary parent language as a linguistic fiction; the reconstruction of individual words or forms is possible from comparison of separate languages (where the languages originate from different dialectal sectors of the parent language), but it is not possible to say whether these forms belong to the same chronological layer of the parent language.

Schmidt's theory at first met with criticism and promoted further discussion of the question of language grouping.[6] The dialectic between the adherents of the tree or split model of Schleicher and the wave or contact theory of Schmidt led to an attempt at synthesis by Leskien (1876) who showed that both models could be useful in a description of language developments. Leskien's ideas appear in a work which examined the relationship between the nominal and pronominal declension of German and Balto-Slavonic. In his introduction Leskien discusses Schmidt's theories in detail and sets out his criteria for the construction of language sub-groups; Leskien's approach was very influential to later scholars,[7] and remains a readable and relevant treatment of the topic.

Leskien relates both the tree and the wave models to known historical developments of languages (as Schmidt had done for the construction of his model), and shows that the two models describe different events. The wave model is applicable to cases where languages have been in contact over a long period, whereas the family tree models tribal movements, especially over geographical obstacles, the emigration of the Anglo-Saxons to England providing a clear example. Leskien also points out that Schmidt's vision of a chain of languages, with each language in contact with its two neighbours, is just one of many possible dialectal arrangements.

Leskien further points the way to future investigation of the interrelationships between languages by his study of the selection and weighting of the agreements between language which may be significant for sub-grouping. He criticises Schmidt for his reliance on agreements between languages which could result from earlier shared inheritances or parallel developments (an argument against Schmidt already put forward by others, for example, Fick), and states that shared developments are the only reliable evidence of close relationship.[8] He also objects to Schmidt's extensive use of vocabulary correspondences which rely on uncertain and personal reconstructions and whose interpretation could be affected by further increases in etymologies. He observes that the creation of new inflectional and derivational formants is the most important criterion for a closer grouping of two languages, on the grounds that the number of possible formations is large, and thus the possibility of chance agreement is small.[9]

Leskien's principles for the investigation of linguistic sub-grouping have, for the most part, remained unchallenged to the present day, and much of the discussion of the issue involves minor refinements to Leskien's methods. Leskien's cautious approach to sub-groups of Indo-European proved especially attractive to Brugmann and the Neogrammarian school.

The Neogrammarians rejected many of the sub-groups constructed by earlier researchers, not because of the improvement in methodology, but because the data which had been taken as evidence of shared innovation was now seen in a different light. For example, the widely-held view that all the Indo-European languages except the Indo-Iranian group had formed an earlier unity was largely based on the assumption that the vowel *e* in these languages had developed from *a*, which was preserved in Indo-Iranian alone. This theory was shown to be wrong, since the palatalisation of velars before *a*, as in the reduplicated perfect *cakara*, could best be explained if *a* was a later development of original *e*.[10] Thus Indo-Iranian was the innovator, and had lost the original distinction between *e*, *a* and *o*, preserved in other languages. There was now, therefore, no justification for the earlier 'European' language group.

The discrediting of the evidence for sub-groups proposed by earlier scholars in this way, together, perhaps, with a desire to distance themselves from the scholarship of the older generation, led the Neogrammarians to mistrust what one might term 'high-level' I-E subgroups of the type 'Germanic-Balto-Slavonic'. Brugmann, in an article which discussed the whole question of the interrelationship of Indo-European languages, admitted Balto-Slavonic and Indo-Iranian as the only likely sub-groups. Brugmann's article also set forth clearly the methodological principles which we have seen originated with Leskien, and which still hold good for the subject. Brugmann improved upon Leskien's method in that he clearly spelt out that innovations are the only reliable criteria for the construction of sub-groups, and he recognises the possibility of parallel, but independent, innovations which may disrupt the picture. This leads to his famous observation that sub-groups could only be constructed on the basis of a large number of common innovations.[11] In this way identical developments that may be merely coincidental are not allowed to distort the picture, because the chance of a number of identical but independent developments is very small.

In the years following Brugmann's article scholars were unable to make any major improvement in methodological principles and so looked for more data to clarify the picture of the sub-groups and dialects of the parent language. The search led to attempts to link archaeological, cultural and ethnic data to the findings of language, and to more detailed investigation of minor and scantily attested Indo-European languages. The Neogrammarian doctrine of the three guttural series of the parent language led to a widespread view that the division between *centum* languages, which showed the reflexes of a velar series and a labio-velar series, and *satəm* languages, which showed the reflex of a palatal series and a velar series, reflected an earlier dialectal division within the parent language, although scholars disagreed on the significance of this division.

The first work to make any methodological advances since Brugmann's articles was Meillet's book *Les dialectes indo-européens* (Meillet 1908).

Meillet, like Schmidt before him, profited from the application of contemporary dialect studies and theories of language to the reconstructed parent language. Hence Meillet, perhaps already influenced by his teacher Saussure's division of *langue* and *parole*, points out that Proto-Indo-European must, like every language, have shown variation from speaker to speaker, although a speech community would have presented a unitary 'type linguistique' (1908:2). Meillet also makes use of the concept of the isogloss boundary line, which distinguishes members of a speech community who use one linguistic form in preference to a competing usage spoken by those on the other side of the line. But Meillet's picture of the proto-language, spoken over a number of speech communities with isogloss lines converging to form fuzzy boundaries between dialects, and his account of the later developments of the separate dialects through periods of common unity into arrays of dialects, amounts to little more than a sophisticated update of Schmidt and Leskien.

Meillet did, however, make some important refinements to the assessment of innovations shared by two languages. He emphasised that the relative chronology of innovations was of central importance. An innovation must be shown to have taken place in the immediate ancestor of a sub-group if it is to be significant for relations with other branches of the language family, since innovations which had only taken place in some of the languages of a sub-group most likely represented later developments (1908:10). Thus, to use an example which Meillet himself adduced in his preface to the second edition (1922:7), the development of a first person singular present active marker -*āmi* for thematic verbs in Indo-Iranian cannot be used to group the Indo-Iranian with other language groups, since in the earliest portions of the Avesta the marker -*ā* is also found. The development of the morpheme -*āmi* must therefore be later than the period of Indo-Iranian unity, even though it subsequently spread to all the languages of the family.[12]

Meillet's other methodological strictures attempt to address other areas where parallel innovations could arise from causes other than linguistic kinship. He is thus suspicious of developments which represent universal traits of languages, or which could arise through contact with other languages. Meillet is wary of reliance on similarities of vocabulary for sub-grouping and dialectal studies, on the grounds, already put forward by Leskien, that the number of truly watertight etymologies is small, and the possibility of borrowing is great.

In the period following Meillet's book the previous investigation of sub-groups and dialects of Indo-European was challenged by the discovery and interpretation of two previously unsuspected Indo-European language groups, Anatolian and Tocharian. Both these language branches were of the *centum* type, and both showed the use of a marker **-r* in the medio-passive which had been a principal support for previous theories of an Italo-Celtic sub-group. The existing accounts of the Indo-European languages could not accommodate the upset of the previous neat array of the language groups, in which, it had been thought, every language group bore approximately the same position relative to its neighbours in history as the earlier dialects had borne in prehistory.[13] Thus in order to explain the position of Hittite and Tocharian, either these two languages, and these two alone, had undergone long migrations from their original homeland, or another explanation of the medio-passive *-r endings had to be found. Dialect studies again provided a possible explanation; innovations in living dialects tend to originate around more densely populated areas, and then spread more slowly to outlying areas, sometimes not even reaching the peripheries. Thus the medio-passive *-r endings could represent archaisms shared by outlying dialects, which were replaced in the innovative central area. Meillet's earlier notion that the relative positions of the Indo-European languages were unchanged could thus be retained. This approach was taken up in Italy by the so-called school of *neolinguistica*, influenced largely by Bartoli's *Introduzione alla neo-linguistica* (Bartoli 1925). The members of the school tried to apply the method to many different areas of Indo-European. They met with intractable problems, however, such as why the most conservative Romance language, Sardinian, in which the Latin velars have not been palatalised before front vowels, occupies a geographically central position in the array of Romance languages.[14] The methods of the *neolinguistica* school, although it retains a few adherents to this day,[15] were seen to be wanting by most scholars. The consequence was that the geographical array of languages was no longer seen to be of central importance for language grouping.

A completely different approach to the problem of sub-grouping was made by Kroeber and Chrétien (1937) who attempted to elucidate the interrelationship of the Indo-European languages by the statistical analysis of a number of linguistic features which were compared across Indo-European languages. This represented, if anything, a step backwards, since the features chosen were not all innovations and the data were not always comparable. Moreover, no account was made of the differing time depth of the languages compared in the survey, nor of the discrepancy between archaic and innovatory languages. However, the methods of Kroeber and Chrétien have continued to find adherents right up until the present day.[16]

The approach of Kroeber and Chrétien was a precursor to the work of the so-called 'glottochronologists', an American school of linguists who attempted to draw up sub-groups in language families on the basis of a comparison of lists of one hundred or two hundred 'basic vocabulary' items.[17] They assumed that the rate of replacement of the basic vocabulary was constant over time, and consequently it was possible for the comparison of basic vocabulary items not only to reveal the sub-groups of a language family but also to decide the date at which language splits had occurred. The methods used by the glottochronologists for selection and comparison of vocabulary items were crude, and their assumption that the lexical replacement was constant over time was never proven.[18]

The reliance upon lexical elements as the principal data for the comparison and genetic classification of languages is also associated with the work of Joseph Greenberg. Greenberg disavowed the methods of glottochronology (1957:54) and, in a sensible essay on the sub-grouping of language families, advocated the identification of shared innovations, especially in morphology, as the best procedure for the discovery of sub-groups. Greenberg also discussed the advantages and problems associated with the use of agreements or innovations in different areas of the language system (phonology, morphology, word order and lexicon) as indicators of a close relationship between languages. He states that common innovation of a new lexeme is extremely unlikely to occur by chance; 'that, for example two Indo-European languages should independently make up a new verb "to take" with the form *nem-* is extremely unlikely' (1957:52). Greenberg is aware of the problems involved with the use of the lexicon as an indicator of close relationship; shared lexical items need not reflect common innovations, they may also arise from lexical borrowing or the preservation of archaic terms. However, Greenberg proposes that 'in case of obvious sub-grouping the results will be very quickly evident from comparative vocabulary inspection' (1957:54).

Greenberg's proposals are not contentious; the recognition that the Romance languages, for example, were grouped together was made in the eighteenth century and earlier on the basis of vocabulary comparison, and so also the Germanic and Slavonic languages. Greenberg's method is hence of little significance for the Indo-European language family, since the 'obvious sub-groups' have long been recognised. I am not qualified to judge Greenberg's application of the method to African and American languages.[19]

For the Indo-European family, therefore, the statistical methods of language comparison have made little difference to the conception of the sub-groups and dialects of the parent language. A detailed lexicostatistical analysis of the Indo-European language family was attempted by Davies and Ross (1975), who considered the survival of 1,857 Indo-European roots in daughter languages. The loudest condemnation of their method is given by the results themselves: the following sub-groups are proposed (1975:93) Germanic/Balto-Slavonic, Italo-Celtic/Greek (n.b. Italo-Celtic and Balto-Slavonic are considered as separate branches *a priori* (p. 87)), Armenian/ Albanian and Tocharian/Hittite. The last four language branches (Armenian, Albanian, Tocharian and Hittite) are shown to have had a particularly close relationship (p. 88). The fact that the four branches of Indo-European which have the smallest proportion of inherited roots are linked closely together highlights the inadequacies of the methods used.[20]

A more significant contribution to the subject was Porzig's work (Porzig 1954) on Indo-European dialects. Porzig's book was very much in the methodological tradition of Leskien and Brugmann, and his chapter on method adds only minor refinements to their work. He emphasises the importance of common innovations, and discusses the problems which arise through parallel but independent innovations. He casts doubt upon the Italian school of *neolinguistica* on the grounds that it is impossible to know which languages continue the earlier innovatory dialects and which the peripheral ones (Porzig 1954:57). He also is aware of the problem of identifying which of two alternative features is the archaism and which the innovation, or whether the two features co-existed in the parent language with a functional difference (the competing morphs for the thematic genitive singular, *-ī and *-osyo, are a case in point). Porzig is also cautious over the use of archaeological, cultural and ethnic data for the clarification of linguistic relationships, on the grounds that language and culture are not always co-ordinate (1954:61).

Porzig is aware of the need to weight isoglosses, and, like earlier scholars, understands common innovations in the creation of morphs to be of the greatest importance, and lexical agreements of the least. In his assessment of the relationships between languages he broadly follows these principles, although he takes special note of phonetic agreements and gives a full account of lexical agreements between different languages.

In the period of time between Porzig and the present day there has been little advance in the methods used for grouping the Indo-European languages (the use of large scale lexical comparison excepted). Cowgill's *Einleitung* to the *Indogermanische Grammatik* initiated by Kuryłowicz (published in 1986, although written in 1973) could thus repeat Brugmann's principle that the only criterion for the reconstruction of linguistic sub-groups was a large number of shared innovations (Cowgill 1986:16). Similarly, Gamkrelidze and Ivanov in the chapter devoted to the method of grouping dialects of the parent language in their momentous work on Indo-European (Gamkrelidze and Ivanov 1984.I.371–373) advocate the identification of shared innovations in the daughter languages, particularly in morphology, for the elucidation of the relationships between the dialects from which these languages developed.

In this most recent period there have, however, been a few refinements of methodology. The most active discussion of the problem of sub-groups and dialects in Indo-European surrounded the publication of a number of papers on the topics in a volume entitled *Ancient Indo-European Dialects* (Birnbaum and Puhvel 1966). Although several of the papers dealt with dialects within individual language groups or languages,[21] and there was practically no discussion of Indo-European dialects in the tradition of Meillet, some of the participants brought new points of methodology into the discussion. Hoenigswald, in an article which dealt with the procedure of sub-grouping, discussed the possible different ways in which three languages could be related using the family tree model, and tried to distinguish how innovations could be recognised as such, and what constituted a significant innovation.[22] Hoenigswald (1966) noted that innovations should be considered in the light of the effect upon the structure of a language; a merger between two phonemes in a previously neutralised sector was therefore not significant, whereas a merger of two contrasting phonemes was.

New approaches to the interpretation of the data were also advanced by Watkins in his discussion of the relationship between Italic and Celtic (Watkins 1966). Watkins reasoned that, although common innovations were of importance for the construction of sub-groups, other developments of the languages under investigation should also be considered. One of these was what he termed the 'negative innovation' (1966:31), which meant the restriction or elimination of a previously productive feature or process. Another was the existence of divergences between two languages; if two languages showed divergences which must have taken place early in their history, this weakened the chance that they once formed a sub-group. Watkins's call for 'negative innovations' and linguistic divergence to be taken into account in the investigation of sub-groups has generally not been heeded by later scholars, probably because of the fact that 'negative innovations' could well arise independently, and linguistic divergence (or convergence) could occur after two languages had formed a sub-group.[23]

Watkins himself, in his appraisal of the proposed agreements between Italic and Celtic, was more concerned with the careful examination of the development of possible shared innovations and their place in a relative chronology[24] than with the other criteria for sub-grouping which he mentions.

In the years following the publication of *Ancient Indo-European Dialects* there has been less discussion of the sub-groups in the Indo-European family, although for other language families different sub-grouping theories are still hotly debated.[25]

A fresh impetus on the question of the dialects of Proto-Indo-European, which, as we saw, was a minor issue in *Ancient Indo-European Dialects*, despite its title, was provided by a new model of the parent language proposed by Meid (Meid 1975), which incorporated the features of both space and time. To summarise baldly, Meid divided Proto-Indo-European into three stages, Early, Middle and Late. At the earliest stage, Meid assumes that the language was spoken by a small and homogeneous group, and consequently that it showed little variation. As time goes by, the geographical spread of the speakers ranges over a wider area, and correspondingly the language becomes increasingly differentiated into dialect areas. The model can be schematically represented as a triangle, or cone, the top vertex of which represents the earliest, unified stage of the language, and the base as the last stage, as in the following diagram:

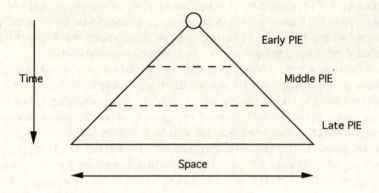

Meid's concept of late Proto-Indo-European is in effect very similar to the picture of the parent language proposed by Schmidt and adopted by Meillet and others. Meid's theory has, however, two major advantages over previous accounts. Firstly it provides a mechanism for explaining competing features in the parent language without labelling one an archaism and one an innovation. The use of the augment in Indo-Iranian, Greek and Armenian, for example, is not seen as an innovation against the absence of an augment in other languages, nor is it seen as an archaism which has been replaced in other languages, but both the use of the augment, and the remodelling of the tense system in Italic, Balto-Slavonic, Germanic and Celtic are explained as dialectal innovations made in late Proto-Indo-European (pp. 214–215).

Meid's model also accounts for similarities between languages which appear not to stem from contiguous dialects of late Proto-Indo-European, and dissimilarities between languages which otherwise appear to have been closely related in their prehistory. For he assumes that the dialects of late Proto-Indo-European do not correspond exactly with dialects of middle Proto-Indo-European; the choice between competing dialectal variants of the earlier stage of the language was made separately by the dialects of later stages of the language. Meid cites as an example the case of the *-r ending contrasted with the *-i ending of the third person singular of the reconstructed present tense middle, the competition, that is, between a form *b^heretor and *b^heretoi. The *-r endings are found in a heterogeneous group of daughter languages: Italic, Celtic, Tocharian, Anatolian and Phrygian, which do not share much outside this particular feature.[26] Meid consequently proposes that these languages had not evolved from the same dialect of the parent language, but that they agree only in continuing the same feature of middle Proto-Indo-European (1975:216).

Meid's picture of the parent language has prompted a certain amount of discussion,[27] and some aspects of his theory remain doubtful, for example, the supposition that the speakers of Proto-Indo-European remained in contact for such a long period of time. However, Meid's model is an attractive and powerful tool for explaining long-standing problems.

The most recent contributions to the methodology which I shall consider attempt to subtract from, rather than increase the methods used by linguists in the discussion of the historical relationships between languages. An article in *Language* by Krishnamurti, Moses and Danforth (1983), working from the hypothesis that sound change proceeds via a gradual diffusion through the lexicon, proposed that cognate words which had not undergone a sound change which had taken place in other words could be used as evidence for the construction of a sub-group. The drawbacks with this method are self-evident; there is a strong possibility that the agreement may reflect chance or lexical borrowing.

Harrison (1986) has even questioned the theoretical credentials for the reconstruction of sub-groups. His objections are basically simple ones. Firstly, he questions whether it is really possible to isolate common innovations. He points out that each innovation made in a language is in some way motivated by the existing language system, and that consequently there is always the possibility of chance independent but similar innovations. Given that there is no method for insuring that when two languages have made the same change in their history they made it at the same time, how can scholars rely on common innovations for the reconstruction of sub-groups? This is the same problem, in effect, which confronted Brugmann, yet Harrison rejects Brugmann's solution, which was that a number of shared innovations eliminated the possibility of chance. Harrison objects that there is no 'metric by which relative quantities of shared changes can be interpreted in terms of the family tree model' (1986:18). In other words, if a language A can be shown to share n innovations with language B, and if language B shares m innovations with language C, there is no way of deciding whether the sub-group AB or AC should be constructed. In practice, of course, if n exceeds m by a large amount (i.e. the shared innovations of A and B far exceed those of A and C) then there is little doubt in the construction of a sub-group AB: an example might be Irish, Welsh and Latin. Harrison's criticisms do, however, highlight the difficulties of reconstructing sub-groups on the basis of a small number of shared similarities, and the need for some method of weighing the significance of isoglosses.

1.2 Method

Much of what will be discussed in this section will not be original. In order to simplify the discussion I shall present the arguments as if they are my own, and refer to other work only where necessary.

1.2.1 The significance of extra-linguistic features for the assessment of linguistic relationships.

Speakers of the same language often share a common culture and sense of ethnic identity and belong to the same genetically related population, and, except in cases of migrations and colonisations, inhabit a limited geographical space. I shall use the term 'extra-linguistic' to cover these three factors of culture, genetic similarity, and geographical situation, although the culture and 'ethnicity' of a people may of course be in part dependent upon their shared language. Similarity between the extra-linguistic traits of speakers of two related languages need not have any significance for the relationship of the two languages, since the connection of the languages is based on linguistic data alone.

The reasons for the independence of extra-linguistic from linguistic facts are straightforward. Firstly, although language and cultural and ethnic identity tend often to correlate, they do not always do so. An ethnic group may adopt the culture of a more prestigious neighbour, while retaining their own language, or they may adopt the language of another group, while maintaining a distinct cultural identity, or they may lose both their language and culture. There are abundant historical examples of these processes and of even more complicated developments. For example, in Mycenaean Crete, Greek speakers aped the artistic culture of the Minoans; while the descendants of the Germanic invaders of the Roman Empire became speakers of Romance languages and developed a distinctive culture.

In the same way the linguistic kinship and geographical proximity of two peoples need not correlate. The location of the speakers of Rumanian and Hungarian in Europe provides a clear example; these two languages are surrounded by Slavic languages, although their closest linguistic relatives are not Slavic.

It is of course possible to draw up a more sophisticated picture of the spread of the Indo-European languages which takes into account the different ways in which language and culture may spread across space and different populations. At present, however, there is no single model which adequately explains all the archaeological and linguistic data. The debate following the publication of Renfrew's book *Archaeology and Language* (1987), in which he proposed to link the spread of the Indo-European languages with the expansion of agriculture, shows how radically different attempts to relate the two subjects can be.[28]

The difficulties in using archaeology to settle linguistic disputes are widely recognised. The use of geographical evidence for the elucidation of linguistic prehistory is perhaps more prevalent. We have seen already how J. Schmidt and Meillet were influenced in their discussion of the arrangement of the dialects of Proto-Indo-European languages by the geographical position of the daughter languages. However, geographical data and archaeological data are equally unreliable as evidence for the close genetic relationship of two Indo-European languages.

This is not to say that the evidence of geographical position and archaeology should be ignored in the discussion of linguistic prehistory; linguistic findings which correlate more closely with known archaeological data and with the relative positions of languages are preferable to those which explain the linguistic facts equally well but are at odds with extra-linguistic material. However, if the only adequate linguistic model is at variance with archaeology, that is not sufficient reason to reject the model.

In this connection it should be remembered how much of Indo-European linguistics and of the discussion of language relationships relies upon basic archaeological and geographical facts, perhaps more so than is generally made explicit. For example, the fact that the Indo-European languages are for the most part spread across a contiguous land mass, without large stretches of intervening water, colours our conception of the spread of the language family. The possibility that speakers of the Indo-European languages spread through the migration of colonies to previously unin-habited areas without ensuing contact with the parent language, and from which in turn further colonies were sent out, is seldom entertained, whereas for Oceanic languages this seems a likely model of their expansion across the islands of the Pacific.

The spread of a language family in this way affects the assessment of the relationships between daughter languages; for the Oceanic languages, the reconstruction of a linguistic family tree, with several intervening sub-groups between the existing languages and the reconstructed parent, appears a reasonable hypothesis. On the other hand, if one assumes that a language family spreads through a gradual 'wave of advance' of settlers over a contiguous land area (as in Renfrew's model), the daughter languages are less likely to fall into discrete sub-groups and the relationship between them may be better described through a model similar to that proposed by J. Schmidt.

Cultural, archaeological and geographical data may also affect the assessment of a similarity between two languages. Shared lexical items, for example, especially those concerned with culture-specific terms or with flora and fauna restricted to certain areas, cannot be fully discussed without reference to their cultural and geographic status. Thus, for example, the significance of the phonetically regular correspondence between the Armenian word for 'panther' and the Vedic word for 'lion', *inj* and *siṃha-*, cannot be considered without taking into account the geographical spread of felids in prehistory and the cultural significance of the lion in India and among other Indo-European peoples. It seems churlish to refuse to give any weight to extra-linguistic considerations in cases such as this.

It may appear as if we are being inconsistent in our use of extra-linguistic factors. Although extra-linguistic data are rejected as evidence of linguistic relationships, they are acceptable for the assessment of lexical agreements. I do not think there is any contradiction here; the reliance upon extra-linguistic data is proportional to the status of the data. Less certain, or debatable, conclusions from archaeology should be accorded little weight, but more secure evidence has more authority. It follows from this that when any extra-linguistic material is brought into the discussion of language relationships, the status of the material should be made evident.

1.2.2 Reconstruction

The reconstructed form of the parent language must play a large part in the investigation of the relationship between its daughters. As we have seen in section **1.1**, ever since Brugmann's article on subgroups in 1884 the existence of a large number of innovations shared by two languages has been understood to be grounds for the reconstruction of a sub-group. It follows that before the sub-groups of a language family can be constructed, one must have a clear picture of the reconstructed parent, since only then will it be possible to identify subsequent innovations. In my later discussion of the relative significance of shared developments in different areas of the language system, I shall pay greater attention to the question of reconstruction and innovation.

It is worth noting here that there is a danger of circularity in the arguments for sub-groups, particularly if sub-groups are assumed during the reconstruction of the parent language. To take an example from the reconstruction of Indo-European case morphology; Italic and Celtic show the reflexes of a genitive singular formant *-ī in the thematic declension, while different formations are found in other Indo-European languages. In reconstructing the formation for the parent language, the scholar may be influenced by a preconception that Italic and Celtic share a close relationship and accordingly judge the agreement between Celtic and Italic to be a sub-group phenomenon and so less significant than that between Greek and Sanskrit, for example. On this basis he may reconstruct *-osyo for Proto-Indo-European, and so justify his previous preconception with the statement that Celtic and Italic have replaced the inherited formation with *-ī, and have undergone a shared innovation.[29] However, this is only one possible explanation of the facts, and the interplay between the genitive singular formants *-osyo and *-ī may be far more complicated, particularly given the appearance of the genitive singular -osio in Faliscan and in an inscription from Satricum.

This brings us to the question of the nature of a reconstructed language. Is it possible to construct a model of the parent language in such a way that agreements such as that between the Italic and Celtic genitive-case marker are not presupposed to reflect a common shared innovation arising from a sub-group, but may reflect a diversity within the parent language itself? Such a model which allows variation in the parent language has certainly been proposed by some scholars, and this goes to show that the nature of the reconstructed language has an effect on the way in which the relationships between the daughter languages are perceived. If the reconstructed parent language shows no variation, then the fact that several different daughter languages agree on a feature which is not reconstructed for the parent language can only be signalled through a sub-group comprising those languages. If, on the other hand, the parent language is reconstructed as a system with variations, then the same agreements can be explained from the fact that the daughter languages concerned have developed from the same dialect of the parent.[30]

The debate over which model of the parent language may be reconstructed has recently resurfaced in connection with the 'space and time' model of Indo-European proposed by Meid and sketched out in section **1.1**. Schlerath (1981, 1982–3 and 1987) and Eichner (1988a) have criticized Meid's model on the grounds that the method of comparative reconstruction does not allow the reconstruction of variant features, nor their relation to points of time and space. For Schlerath and Eichner the reconstructed parent language is conceived of as a point without any existence in time or space. The parent language consists only of those features which can be shown to be common to all the daughter languages; all 'dialect' groupings or developments which do not take place in all Indo-European languages are therefore by definition post-Indo-European.[31] The only certain reconstructable features of the parent language are the phoneme system and a few morphological features and lexemes.

This model of the reconstructed ancestor given by Schlerath and Eichner corresponds with the data which would be produced from a mechanical operation of the Comparative Method on the Indo-European languages. However, a model of the parent language which allows for dialectal variation corresponds more closely to what we know of living languages, and is able to account for features shared by some, but not all, of the daughter languages without presupposing that the languages form a sub-group. It need hardly be added that such a model can only be used as a working hypothesis, and must be judged according to how well it corresponds to the actual data which emerge from comparison of the daughter languages.

1.2.3 Dialect and sub-group

The preceding discussion has touched on the distinction between the relationship of languages which form a sub-group within a language family, and that of languages which stem from the same dialect of the parent language. As I have mentioned, the distinction between dialect and sub-group depends to a large extent on the model constructed for the parent language, but it may be worthwhile considering in some detail whether there is any valid difference between the two concepts.

Speakers of different dialects of the same language will be able to communicate with one another. Their speech will be distinguished by the presence or absence of certain different phonological, morphological, syntactic or lexical features. We have already mentioned the concept of the isogloss line, which divides speakers who use one linguistic form from those who use another. Isogloss lines drawn on a dialect map tend to form 'bundles' surrounding dialect areas, although an otherwise unified dialect area may be divided by a single isogloss line, or a small number of isogloss lines which do not coincide. Speakers of different dialects may adopt an innovatory linguistic feature in common with all or some of the other dialects of the language.

The ideal dialect situation just sketched out can be illustrated from ancient Greece. Speakers of Greek were able to communicate with one another, although they spoke different dialects. The dialects were distinguished by a number of different isoglosses, some of which separated a number of dialects, for example the distinction betwen -*si* in 'East Greek' (Arcado-Cypriot, Attic-Ionic and Lesbian) and -*ti* in 'West Greek' (Doric, the dialects of North-west Greece, Thessalian and Boeotian), and some of which separated a single dialect from the rest, for example the change of inherited *$\bar{e}$ to $\bar{a}$, which took place only in the North-west Greek dialect of Elis. The Linear B tablets have revealed that already at the time of the Mycenaeans Greek was differentiated into dialects, since Mycenaean Greek agrees with East Greek in having changed inherited *-*ti*, preserved in West Greek, to -*si*. Yet between the time of Mycenaean and later Greek, all the Greek dialects had undergone several innovations in common, for example: the loss of -*ei* as an ending of the dative singular of consonant stems; the change of *$k^w o$- to πo-; and the generalization of -*n*- throughout the paradigm of the word for 'one' (thus εἶς, ἑνός) in place of the -*m*- still retained in the Mycenaean dative *e-me*.[32]

If the ancestor reconstructed for two Indo-European languages can be shown to be a derivative of the ancestor reconstructed for the whole language family, then the two languages form a sub-group. The sub-group ancestor is by definition a separate language from the ancestor of any other Indo-European language, and any innovation which occurs in the ancestor of the sub-group will not have taken place in common with any other Indo-European sub-group. The situation is well illustrated by the Germanic languages which form a sub-group in the Indo-European language family. The ancestor of the Germanic languages has undergone a number of changes which separate it from Proto-Indo-European, for example, the phonetic changes associated with the accent known as 'Verner's Law', the creation of a 'weak' preterite formation with a dental suffix, the continuation of the Proto-Indo-European perfect tense by either preterite formations or new present formations. None of these innovations are shared by any other Indo-European language, nor are there any innovations made by Proto-Germanic, or any Germanic language, in common with any other Indo-European languages which do not belong to the Germanic sub-group.

The difference between dialect and sub-group is therefore one of time and degree. The sub-group was a unified language after the end of mutual intelligibility of the parent language, whereas two languages which stem from the same dialect, or proximate dialects of the parent language will not have shared any common innovations following the end of the period of mutual intelligibility of the parent language. Therefore innovations made by languages which derive from a sub-group reflect later developments than innovations made by languages which stem from the same dialect of the parent language.

If two languages earlier formed a sub-group, then at one stage they were in a unique relationship with each other. Thus innovations made in common by such languages are more likely to be unique to them alone. Innovations which were made at a dialectal level during the period of common unity are more likely also to have taken place in other languages.

In practice in some cases it may not be possible to decide with certainty whether a shared innovation made by two languages is due to an earlier sub-group or dialect relationship. The presentation just sketched out is based upon ideal situations and does not allow for some of the very complex linguistic situations which may actually occur, such as prolonged bilingualism between two closely related languages. In such circumstances the investigator may not be able to discern whether a number of shared agreements between two languages should be explained through the sub-group or dialect hypothesis, nor would the attempt to do so necessarily lead to elucidation of the actual relationship between the languages. Even so, the distinction between the notional sub-group and dialect situation is worth preserving as a touchstone for language relationships; more complex models of relationship can be constructed for cases where the facts are not adequately explained by either the sub-group or dialect models.

1.2.4 The common innovation hypothesis

The hypothesis that the presence of shared innovations is the only reliable indicator of a close genetic relationship between two languages has been held by the majority of historical linguists since the nineteenth century. If it can be shown that a number of innovations were made in common by two languages this can only indicate a close relationship.

The same innovation may of course occur independently in different languages for a variety of reasons, and such independent innovations are of no significance for the genetic relationship of the two languages. Whether an innovation was made separately or in common by two different languages is therefore of the utmost importance for the investigation of the genetic relationship between two languages. A number of factors can be used to enable the linguist to assess whether a development common to different languages represents a shared innovation or not. The most important factors are the likelihood of the innovation arising through a separate process, and the chronology of the development relative to other innovations of the language. These factors will be discussed in more detail below.

The term 'innovation' can be used to describe a number of different processes: a common choice of an item from a set of competing forms already present in the parent language; the common creation of a new lexeme or inflectional/derivational category or marker; the common merger of two categories or the common deletion of a lexeme or inflectional/derivational category or marker. Some innovations represent major restructuring of the language system, for example, the merger of the Proto-Indo-European 'voiced aspirate' and 'voiced' obstruent series $*D^h$ and $*D$ in Iranian, Baltic and Slavonic, while other changes are structurally insignificant, such as the change of $*-ln-$ to $-ll-$ in Greek and perhaps other languages (see further **2.4.3**). In this environment (after $*l$) there was no contrast between the phonemes $*l$ and $*n$, since previously the sequence $*ll$ did not occur.[33] Some innovations represent changes which have occurred in many different languages, such as the voicing of intervocalic voiceless consonants, and are therefore quite likely to have taken place independently, while other changes, such as the innovation of a thematic genitive singular case marker $*-\bar{i}$, are less likely to represent separate developments.

It is therefore desirable to have some method of weighting different innovations. The evaluation of the relative importance of different innovations would clearly be a bonus for the assessment of language relationships. For example, if language A shares 6 common innovations with language B but 7 with language C, we cannot say with certainty whether language A is closer to B or C. But if it can be shown that the innovations between language A and C belong to a class of innovations which are likely to arise through situations other than genetic relationship, and which may have been made independently, but that the innovations between language A and B can be shown to have taken place early in the history of languages A and B, and represent developments which rarely arise through any means other than earlier genetic unity, then clearly the relationship between language A and B is closer than between A and C.

We have already discussed how the identification of an innovation relies upon the reconstruction of the parent language. This naturally affects the significance of certain innovations as well. If there is doubt over whether an innovation is in fact a genuine innovation, and not an archaism of the parent language, the significance of the 'innovation' diminishes.

In order to be able to weight innovations we must first decide which shared innovations are most likely to derive from earlier genetic unity, and which innovations may arise through other causes. We need to demonstrate which agreements between languages can be most securely shown to reflect shared innovations from the parent language, and consequently which features of the reconstruction of the parent language are most secure. Furthermore it will be helpful to know how innovations of different types can be related to a relative chronology of other developments of languages.

The best way to proceed in the investigation of the relative weight of different innovations seems to be along the traditional division of language into phonology, morphology, syntax, and lexicon.

1.2.5 Phonology

Sound changes are usually regular. The regularity of sound change allows the comparative method to be used for the reconstruction of the phonology of the parent language. The phonological system of the parent language can be reconstructed with reasonable confidence for a number of language families, including Indo-European, although the phonetic realisations of the phonemes may be uncertain.

For languages which have a number of lexemes with cognates in sister languages it is usually possible to describe the innovations in the phonological system, such as phoneme splits or mergers, which have taken place in the period after the parent language. Since the phonetic realisation of the phonemes of the parent language is not so securely reconstructed, it may not always be possible to identify whether a language has preserved the original phonetic character of the parent language or not. Recent proposals for a reinterpretation of the phonetic values of the Proto-Indo-European obstruent system with ejective consonants in the place of the traditionally reconstructed voiced consonants offer an example. If the 'new look' of Indo-European consonants is correct the Armenian reflexes will represent a preservation of the original form of the consonants rather than an innovatory 'consonant shift'.[34]

It is often possible to order the occurrence of sound changes and sometimes to put a *terminus post* or *ante quem* for changes. For example, in the history of Greek one can be certain that the change of *s to h (with eventual loss intervocalically) did not take place after the assibilation of *$\tau\iota$ to $\sigma\iota$ in East Greek, since otherwise the form -$\sigma\iota$ would also be affected. Loan-words may also help to fix the chronology.

Hence phonology seems a ripe area for detecting common innovations. However, the range of probable sound changes is fairly small, and the possibility of the same sound changes operating independently in two daughter languages is high.[35]

Contact between languages often affects their phonetics and phonology, and this adds a further difficulty to the use of sound change for determining earlier genetic associations between languages. Hoenigswald (1966:11) has noted that an unusual sound change shared by two languages cannot be accounted significant for sub-grouping when contact may have been the cause; this is especially true for sister languages which may have been spoken in contiguous areas at some point in their prehistory.

Therefore common phonological innovations, although easy to detect, can be due to a number of different causes, and are not the most secure indicators for establishing genetic relationships.

1.2.6 Morphology

Morphological change usually proceeds by the irregular process of analogy. The irregular nature of morphological change can be demonstrated from one particular form of analogy usually termed 'paradigm levelling'. Levelling occurs after phonological change has obscured the synchronic relationship between two inflected forms of the same paradigm; the divergent forms are 'levelled' out in order to make the synchronic relationship clear. For example, in Attic Greek the first person plural of the verb 'to be' is ἐσμέν, although the regular phonetic outcome of earlier *esmen should be *εἰμέν. The form ἐσμέν shows the influence of the third person singular ἐστί and the second person plural ἐστέ; the uneven operation of levelling is shown by the fact that in the same paradigm the synchronically irregular form εἰμί 'I am' is retained. Other processes of analogy can lead to the creation of new paradigms and inflectional or derivational categories or to extensions of previous paradigms and categories.

The irregular operation of morphological change is both an advantage and disadvantage for its use in assessing language relationships; an advantage, because it means that the chance of exactly the same change operating independently is small; but a disadvantage, because it means that the reconstruction of the morphology of the parent language is more difficult than phonological reconstruction.

However, if inflectional and derivational markers have not been replaced in the daughter languages through analogical change, they can be reconstructed for the parent language through phonological reconstruction.[36] In many cases this enables the reconstruction of a paradigm for the parent language. Where the reconstructed paradigm itself shows aberrancies, the process of internal reconstruction[37] can be used to reconstruct an earlier stage of the parent paradigm. The reconstruction of the morphology of the parent language entails more than the simple reconstruction of morphological markers. Comparison of the inflectional and derivational categories of the daughter languages sometimes allows their reconstruction for the parent language even where processes of analogy, levelling and extension have made reconstruction of the markers of these categories impossible.

It is more difficult to set up a chronology for morphological change than for phonological change. If the daughter languages show disagreement over the form of the marker of a particular category, it is not always possible to distinguish which of the variants is the older, or whether they may have co-existed at one time. The different formations for the Indo-European thematic genitive singular, discussed above, furnish an example of the difficulties which may be encountered. 'Drift' may be a rough guide in charting a chronology of morphological change.[38] For example, there is a general trend in Indo-European languages away from the athematic declension and conjugation towards the thematic declension and conjugation (this is part of the trend towards less synthetic and more agglutinative morphology).[39] If two languages share a morphological innovation which leads to an extension of, for example, the class of athematic root nouns, then it is likely that this is not a recent innovation in the two languages. The productivity of a morphological form can also be a rough guide to its age. In general more recent formations show a greater productivity; again, the thematic verbal and nominal forms provide an example.[40]

Morphology is the area least affected by language contact. Inflectional categories or morphological patterning may be borrowed. For example, Lithuanian has developed allative and perlative case forms in the nominal declension under the influence of neighbouring Finno-Ugric languages; Modern Armenian has developed a singular and plural noun form to which the case markers are added, which may reflect influence from agglutinative Turkic and Caucasian languages. However, in general, the morphological markers themselves are formed from material within the language. Thus the -er plural marker of modern Armenian has its origin in Classical collective markers (Karst 1901:177f.). The resistance of inflectional, and to a lesser extent derivational, morphs to influence from contact is clearly of importance when one is trying to establish how a shared innovation between two languages may have arisen.

However, it is possible that the same innovations may have taken place through a common 'drift' coupled with the same analogical pressure for change. For example, Meillet (1925a:49) showed that the spread of the marker *-m(i) for the first person singular of the thematic present tense occurred separately in the Indo-Iranian languages, some Slavonic languages and Armenian. In Indo-Iranian, the only indication that the change has occurred after the end of the period of 'Proto-Indo-Iranian' is the survival of some forms with final -ā in Gathic Avestan where in later Avestan -āmi occurs. In Serbo-Croat and Czech the change can be documented to have occurred in the Middle Ages. The change in Indo-Iranian is perhaps motivated by the fact that after the merger of the non-high vowels as *a and *ā the distinction between the thematic form *-ā (from *-ō) and athematic *-āmi (from *-āmi, *-ēmi and *-ōmi) was reduced. Similarly, in the Slavonic languages and Armenian, phonetic changes have led to the erosion of the distinction between thematic and athematic verbs. It is interesting to note that the same change has also come about in Meglenite Rumanian, where the first person singular of the present tense is also marked by -m, under the influence of the Bulgarian language, and this provides one of the few certain cases where an inflectional morph is borrowed.[41]

1.2.7 Syntax

Syntax is the most elusive part of the language system to trace historically. There is a lack of effective models of syntactic change, which is due to the lack of a domain of possible changes or tendencies to change. Attempts have been made to create such a potential domain for word order, and to model the direction of change through word-order typologies. These have largely proved unsuccessful, particularly when applied to highly inflected languages such as Proto-Indo-European and the earliest attested daughter languages. In these languages word order is likely to have had a pragmatic rather than syntactic role.[42]

Syntax of course covers more than word order, and some syntactic rules of case usage, concord, etc. can be reconstructed for the parent language. But in these areas survival of the rule in some of the daughter languages is the only clue to its reconstruction in the parent; for example, the rule of concord by which a neuter plural noun in the subject agrees with a verb in the singular can only be reconstructed from its survival in Greek and Avestan. In this respect syntactic reconstruction is akin to morphological reconstruction which is also reliant on the survival of features from the parent language. However, morphological reconstruction is aided by the understanding of patterns of analogy which enable the researcher to detect which of the morphs in the daughter languages are innovations, whereas the motivation for syntactic change are still only imperfectly understood, and in consequence the researcher is often unable to tell which of two competing rules is the innovation.

For example, to denote the agent of a passive verb different cases are used in the Indo-European languages: genitive, dative, ablative and instrumental. It is not possible to discern whether any one of these usages is original, or whether the parent language allowed a variety of constructions or even whether the parent language could express the agent of a passive verb at all.

Moreover, where the same usage is found in two different languages, it is not certain whether this reflects a common innovation, a parallel development under the influence of each other or other languages, or universal or 'iconic' pressures. For example, Schwyzer (1943:19), aware of the hypothesis of a 'special relationship' between the two languages, notes that the agent of a passive verb is sometimes expressed by the Greek preposition ἐκ 'from' followed by the genitive, which he compares to the Armenian use of the preposition *i* 'from' (which may be etymologically connected to ἐκ) with the ablative. It may be the case that this agreement represents a common syntactic innovation, but the use of similar means of expressing the agent in other languages (note in particular Latin $a(b)$ 'from' with the ablative) makes it impossible to verify.

This example shows some of the difficulties connected with the use of syntax for researchers into language relationships, and in the absence of any criteria for assessing the age of a syntactic construction or for constructing a relative chronology of syntactic change, it seems unlikely that these difficulties can be overcome. I have therefore omitted considerations of possible common innovations in syntax from this work.[43]

1.2.8 Lexicon

Lexical changes are very easy to observe in all languages. However, reconstruction of the lexicon of the parent language is difficult. There is little consistency in lexical change, and it may be impossible to determine whether two languages have made a lexical innovation or share a lexical archaism. The lexicon is also very susceptible to the effects of contact. There are many well documented cases of extensive vocabulary borrowing, although the 'basic vocabulary', that is, the body of words which denote objects or sensations common to all human experience, is more resistant to replacement by borrowed terms.

It is also difficult to fix a chronology to lexical change. One may get a very rough idea of whether one item was replaced before or after another by the degree of integration the new item has in the phonological and morphological systems of the language. If the item is associated with an identifiably archaic phonology or morphology then it is more likely to be an archaism.

The significance of a shared lexical innovation depends upon the nature of the innovation. Lexical innovation in the Indo-European languages can roughly be classed into four different basic categories: innovation of root; innovation of form and meaning; innovation of form only, and innovation of meaning only. I shall use the words ἐχθρός, *filius*, καρδία and θυμός to provide illustrations of these different types of lexical innovation; other explanations of these words than those given below are of course possible.

The Greek word ἐχθρός 'hostile' is one of many derivatives of the root ἐχθ- in Greek (note also ἐχθαίρω 'I hate', ἔχθος 'hatred', etc.). These Greek words have no clear cognates in the other Indo-European languages.[44] The extension of the base ἐχθ- effectively represents the creation of a new root. Creation of 'new' roots of this type may occur in a number of different ways: they may, like perhaps ἐχθ- in Greek, be the result of a particular formal and semantic extension of an existing root, or even generalisation or extension of an aberrant or anomalous form of an existing root; or they may be borrowed from a neighbouring language; or perhaps they represent an onomatopoeic or iconic creation.

Lexical innovations may represent a particular semantic change and morphological extension of a recognised inherited root. An example of this may be Latin *filius* 'son', which has been derived from the root *$d^h\bar{e}y$-* 'give suck' with a suffix *-li-o-*, and which has replaced the inherited term for 'son'. The semantic change from the root meaning to the innovatory meaning may come about through influence from a neighbouring language or culture; however the association of a particular morphological form with that innovatory meaning is more likely to be a creation within the language.

The Greek word καρδία 'heart' represents another type of innovation, more limited in scope. Here the Greek word shares the same root as terms for 'heart' in other Indo-European languages, but the word shows a *-yā-* suffix which is not found in other languages. The meaning of the term has not changed essentially. As we have already seen, morphological change is in general resistant to borrowing, and so lexical innovations of this type are unlikely to arise through contact within another language.

Greek θυμός 'soul' shows a contrasting innovation to the previous type. The Greek word is formally identical with Sanskrit *dhūmáḥ* 'smoke', and Latin *fūmus* 'smoke', but the meaning does not coincide. Semantic changes may come about through influence from other languages or cultures.

The significance of these four different types of lexical innovation can be sketched out briefly. Where two languages share a root not found in other languages (innovations of the ἐχθρός type), there are a number of possible explanations for the similarity. The root can be an archaism which has survived in only these languages, or an innovation, and if the latter it may result from independent borrowing or onomatopoeic creation. If, however, it can be shown that two languages have made the same formal and semantic extension of an existing root, then this is a clear indication of a close genetic relationship between the languages.

If two languages have made the same semantic and morphological innovation from a recognised Indo-European root (a *filius* type innovation), this also is a strong argument for their close genetic relationship. The possibility that the two languages agree only in an archaism is made less likely if it can be shown that derivational formation of the word in question is unknown to other Indo-European languages, and that the meaning represents a later development from the root meaning. It is always possible that the two languages could have arrived at the same form and meaning through independent developments, but this possibility is very small in cases where there have been less straightforward morphological and semantic changes.

A shared change in the formation of a lexeme, with no corresponding semantic change, carries less significance for the close relationship between the two languages concerned, particularly in cases where the derivational process concerned is widespread in the language family. For example, the shared innovation of a new verbal present stem with the *-ye/o-* suffix may occur independently in a number of different Indo-European languages.

It is difficult to prove that what appears to be the same semantic extension made by two languages in a family does reflect the same innovation; for it could also be a parallel development, or the result of contact with a third language, or not in fact an extension of meaning at all, but rather a preservation of a meaning lost elsewhere. The shared agreement of a specific meaning for a lexeme (an innovation of the θυμός type) is consequently the least significant of all the lexical agreements.

I have sketched out the simplest processes of lexical change, and it should be remembered that in practice the situation may be more complex. Two languages, for example, may show the same innovatory change of meaning for a derivative from an inherited root, but use completely different derivational formations to express that meaning. In this case, and indeed in all cases of lexical agreement, the nature of the relationship between the items in the two languages can only be elucidated through examination of the history of the words in question, in order to find, if possible, a chronology for the semantic and morphological changes.

The above discussion has presented some preliminary considerations for assessing how likely it is that a lexical agreement between two languages results from a shared innovation. A small number of lexical agreements of any sort is not significant for the grouping of languages. It is possible that a third language also underwent the same innovations but later replaced the lexical items concerned, or that comparable forms occurred in other Indo-European languages which are now lost, or even that they await discovery in attested Indo-European languages. Furthermore, there is always a chance that the etymology could be incorrect, particularly if the languages concerned have undergone radical changes from the parent language, or that the forms arose independently or were borrowed from another language. The significance of lexical agreements, therefore, increases with an increase in their number.

1.2.9 Weighting of agreements

The preceding discussion provides us with a framework for the weighting of shared innovations. Shared innovations of new inflectional markers are the least likely to come about independently in two languages; such innovations do not normally diffuse across languages in contact, and the possibility of chance innovation of the same form is small. Such innovations are therefore the most significant for assessing the relationship between two languages. The chance of the same innovation occurring independently is even less if the new formation is a new creation of the languages, and not simply an extension of the range of an existing morph. If it can be shown that the innovation occurred at an early stage in the two languages, and cannot be the result of a later independent development, then again the innovation gains in significance. Innovations in derivational morphology are more susceptible to borrowing, and consequently they must occupy the second place in the scale.

Lexical innovations and phonological innovations are also of significance. Their importance increases in proportion to the number and nature of the correspondences, as I have already suggested.

If we accept that some innovations carry more weight in the assessment of the genetic relationship between languages than others, we must abandon some of the methods used to find the relationship between the Indo-European languages. We have already mentioned some attempts to group the Indo-European languages through statistical analysis of the spread of a range of phonological, morphological and lexical features through the Indo-European languages, giving the same weight to all three kinds of agreements.[45] Such methods cannot analyse whether an agreement is an innovation or archaism; its place in the system of a language; or what caused it to arise. They therefore produce a measurement of relationship without showing the nature of the relationship.

The large scale analysis of material in a restricted area is perhaps more defensible. The clear example of such an area is the lexicon, and in particular the basic vocabulary, where there is a large number of comparable discrete items.[46] A comparison of the basic vocabularies of the Indo-European languages might be helpful for the investigation of the interrelationships between them. The strength and weakness of this approach stems from the fact that such a procedure does not require the reconstruction of the parent language. This means that the problems of reconstruction which we have discussed above are avoided, but at the cost of sacrificing the principle of separating shared innovations from shared inheritances. It may happen that in the comparison of a number of different languages, the cases where shared inheritances retained in two different languages are counted as significant balance themselves out, and the correct picture of the interrelationships between the languages emerges. But it is also possible that shared inheritances distort the picture.

For example, one can imagine a case of the comparison of 100 lexical items in three different languages, A, B and C. In their early history languages B and C formed a sub-group, and underwent a series of shared innovations whereby they replaced 10 of the inherited items with new terms. At this stage in the history of the three languages the number of the 100 vocabulary terms shared by the languages is as follows:

Number of items shared by   A and B = 90
B and C = 100
A and C = 90.

In their later history, the three languages replaced the vocabulary items at different rates. Language A was very conservative, and retained all the original vocabulary items of the parent language. Language B was more innovative and replaced 20% of its inherited vocabulary items. In other words, it retained 72 of the 90 terms it had inherited from the parent language, and 8 of the 10 terms which it had innovated in common with C, and replaced the remaining 20 vocabulary items. Language C was extremely innovatory and replaced 80% of its inherited vocabulary; it retained only 18 of the 90 words inherited from the parent, and 2 of the words innovated during the period of sub-group with B. The number of terms now in common to the languages is as follows:

Number of terms shared by A and B = 72
B and C = 16
A and C = 18.

The figures for the terms shared by A and B, and A and C are straight-forward. The figure of 16 items shared between B and C represents the fact that the languages B and C have replaced their vocabulary along independent lines after the end of their sub-group. Of the 20 vocabulary items which C has retained from the 100 items shared between them, 20% of the cognate terms in B will be lost, which means that only 16 items will be common to both languages.

In this example, the immediate conclusion of a statistical examination of the lexical affinities between the two languages would be that the relationship between language A and B is much closer than language B and C. But this conclusion is wrong, and language B and C in fact have been in a closer relationship. The extreme discrepancy between the innovatory language C and the conservative nature of the other languages has distorted the picture. If, on the other hand, the shared lexical innovations of the languages A, B and C had been examined, it might have given a clearer picture, since one or two of the ten innovations made in common by language B and C may still survive in both languages. This example may appear to present an extreme case, but among the Indo-European family, some of the daughter languages are attested three thousand years before other daughter languages (for example Hittite and Albanian), and over such a long period of time similar dis-crepancies are likely to arise.

The use of large-scale statistical comparisons of the lexicon cannot therefore be used to construct hypotheses of language relationship. However, such a comparison, used with an awareness of its limitations, may offer additional support for groupings of languages which have emerged from analysis of the shared innovations, or give cause to treat other results in a more critical light. The question will be discussed more fully in Chapter 5.

1.3 The relationship between Greek and Armenian

The specific aim of this work is to ascertain the nature of the relationship between the Greek and Armenian languages. Hübschmann, in his seminal article which first recognised Armenian as a separate branch of Indo-European, assigned it a place between Iranian and 'Slavo-lettisch' (1875:39, reprinted in 1976:35). Meillet (*MSL* IX (1896) p. 155, reprinted in 1977:30) also noted the links with Greek, and Pedersen (1900) connected Albanian, but neither scholar then saw a particularly close relationship with any single language. Pedersen later noted (1924:225) that the number of Greek-Armenian lexical agreements (some shared with Albanian) was greater than the number of lexical agreements between Armenian and any other Indo-European language. Meillet further investigated the Greek-Armenian relationship in articles on a morphological agreement (*BSL* 26 (1925) pp. 1–6, reprinted in 1977:215–220), and a phonetic agreement (*BSL* 27 (1927) pp. 129–135, reprinted in 1977:233–239) linking the two languages. For Meillet these agreements were evidence that the dialects ancestral to Greek and Armenian had been contiguous in the parent language (*BSL* 26 (1925) p. 1, reprinted in 1977:215). Meillet added more shared features in the second edition of the *Esquisse* (1936:142f.), and since then the Greek-Armenian hypothesis has gathered momentum.[47]

This work will therefore examine whether the Greek and Armenian languages form a sub-group of the Indo-European language family, and, if they did not form a sub-group, how the dialects ancestral to them were related in the parent language.

1.4 The Armenian language

In the following analyses of the phonological, morphological and lexical agreements between Armenian and Greek many points concerning the development of Armenian will be discussed. Owing to the limited importance of Armenian for the reconstruction of Proto-Indo-European a number of scholars are understandably unfamiliar with the intricate developments which this language has undergone. I shall therefore attempt to give a brief sketch of the phonology and morphology of Armenian and the changes which it has undergone from the parent language at the beginning of Chapters 2 and 3. The reader who wishes to find further examples and discussion of some of the points which are not treated fully here is advised to turn to one of the comparative grammars of Armenian.[48]

2

PHONOLOGICAL AGREEMENTS BETWEEN GREEK AND ARMENIAN

2.0 Orthography and phonology of Classical Armenian

St. Mesrop's alphabet, created for the Classical Armenian Bible translation in the fifth century, has thirty-six signs which mostly correspond one-to-one with Armenian phonemes. The phoneme inventory of Armenian can be classed as follows (the symbols used correspond to the Hübschmann-Meillet-Benveniste-Schmitt (see Schmitt 1972b) transliteration system, not to the *IPA* system):

	labial	dental	alveolar	palatal	velar	glottal
stops	plosive	plosive	affricate	affricate	plosive	
voiceless	*p*	*t*	*c*	*č*	*k*	
voiced	*b*	*d*	*j*	*ǰ*	*g*	
aspirate	*p'*	*t'*	*c'*	*č'*	*k'*	
nasals	*m*	*n*				
fricatives						
voiceless			*s*	*š*	*x*	*h*
voiced	*v* (?)		*z*	*ž*		
liquids	*r, r̄, l, ł*					
glides	*y, w*					

Classical Armenian, like modern Armenian, has two phonemically distinct varieties of 'r': *r̄* is a rolled alveolar trill, and *r* is an unrolled approximant. The difference between *r̄* and *r* is neutralised before immediately following *n*, where only *r̄* can appear. The signs *l* and *ł* represent the palatalized and velarized dental/alveolar laterals respectively; in Modern Armenian *ł* has developed into a voiced velar fricative [ɣ].

There are seven vowel phonemes represented in the alphabet by the signs *a, e, ê, i, o, ow* and *ə*. Probable phonetic values for these vowels are [a] [ɛ] [e] [i] [o] [u] and [ə]. The vowel [u] is represented as a digraph *ow* on the model of

Greek ου. This has led to some problems of transliteration; in most older works the digraph is transliterated by *u*. However, this can lead to confusion, particularly where the digraph occurs pre-vocalically.[1] I have preferred to follow Schmitt (1972b) in transcribing the digraph by a digraph *ow*.

A major difficulty for the phonetic interpretation of the orthography concerns the use of the letters *w*, *v*, and the digraph *ow*. These signs appear to occur in complementary distribution; *v* appears word- or stem-initially and after the vowel *o*; *w* is never found word-initially but only after the vowels *a*, *e* and *i* in word-final, preconsonantal and prevocalic position; *ow* only occurs as a vowel or after a consonant and before a vowel. It is therefore tempting to assume that Mesrop assigned these different symbols to allophones of the same phoneme. However, the complementary distribution is not perfect, since *w* is also used post-consonantally in some oblique cases of one declension class: hence *tełwoy* genitive singular of *tełi* 'place', (compare *t'owoy* genitive singular of *t'iw* 'number'). The precise phonetic interpretation of these signs is therefore not yet settled.[2]

Other problems in the interpretation of the orthography concern the diphthongs *ea*, *aw*, *iw*, *ew* and *oy*. Much of the debate centres upon the modern pronunciation of these graphs. Thus in modern Armenian the graph *ea* is pronounced [ja], and some scholars have accorded the same pronunciation to the ancient language.[3]

A peculiarity of the Armenian sound system not yet noted is the phenomenon of vocalic alternation. This results from a process whereby vowels which do not stand under the Armenian accent undergo various changes (analogous to the processes of vowel weakening posited for pre-historic stages of Latin). In prehistoric Armenian the moveable accent of the parent language was replaced by a fixed stress accent originally on the penultimate syllable of each word. The original final syllable was lost, leaving the Armenian accent fixed on the last syllable of the word.[4]

The synchronic rules for vowel alternation are as follows; the vowels *i* and [u] (written *ow*) when not under the accent are reduced to schwa (which, in general, is only represented orthographically in certain cases when it occurs initially), thus *hin* 'old' and *hown* 'ford' have genitive singulars *hnoy* [hənoj] and *hni* [həni] respectively; the vowel *ê* (which stems from earlier **ey*) and the diphthongs *oy* and *ea* can only stand under the accent, when not accented they are reduced to *i*, [u] and *e* respectively, thus

zên 'weapon' has genitive singular *zinow*,
yoys 'hope' has genitive singular *yowsoy*,
seneak 'room' has genitive singular *seneki*.

Other vowels (*a*, *e*, *o* and the diphthong *aw*) are unchanged when not under the accent.

2.0.1 Historical phonology of Armenian

The sound changes which have operated between Proto-Indo-European and Armenian are only imperfectly known, owing to the comparatively small number of Armenian words directly inherited from the parent language and the complexity of the changes. I shall only sketch out here the principal developments which have taken place in Armenian. Many of the specific developments which are not mentioned here, or the environments governing the operation of some of the partial changes, will be discussed in greater detail elsewhere.

Armenian has preserved the distinction between the three separate consonantal series of the parent language. In manner of articulation the Armenian reflexes are closest to those of Germanic; thus Armenian *tasn* 'ten' shows an initial voiceless stop in agreement with the Gothic *taihun* as against Greek δέκα, Latin *decem* and Sanskrit *dáśa*, etc. Similarly the correspondent to Germanic voiced stop/fricative is also voiced, thus -*b*- in *ełbayr* 'brother' corresponds to *b*- in Gothic *broþar* (cf. also Latin *frater*, Greek φράτηρ and Sanskrit *bhrā́tar*-, etc.).[5] However the Armenian data does not exactly match the Germanic: the series represented by voiceless fricatives in Germanic has varied reflexes in Armenian; sometimes they are continued by aspirated stops, sometimes by semi-vowels (as in the word for 'brother' cited above, where the medial -*y*- of the Armenian form derives from **t*) or by /h/. The conditions which have led to this split are not fully known.

Armenian is a *satəm* language: it has lost the labial element of the original labio-velar consonants and the original palatal stops have developed to affricates or sibilants. The word for 'ten' cited above, *tasn*, provides an example of Armenian -*s*- corresponding to Greek -κ-, Latin -*c*-, Gothic -*h*- and Sanskrit -*ś*-.

The resonants **r* and **l* and the nasal consonants **m* and **n* of the parent language are, in general, preserved in Armenian. But the sibilant **s* was lost between vowels and before vowels at the beginning of the word. The semivowel **y* was also lost intervocalically. The semivowel **w* develops to *g*- at the beginning of words.

The most radical changes which mark out the consonant system of Armenian from the reconstructed parent language and its sister languages consist in the simplification of consonant clusters. At some stage in the prehistory of the language a number of clusters, particularly those with **w*, **y* as second member or **s* as first member, developed into single phonemes. For example, the cluster **sw*- develops to *k'*-, as in the word *k'oyr* 'sister' (compare Sanskrit *svásar*-, Latin *soror*, etc.). Clusters with **r* or **l* as second member underwent a metathesis; we have seen above that the Armenian term for 'brother' shows an initial consonant sequence *ełb*- in contrast to the *br*- of Gothic, *fr*- of Latin, etc. This initial sequence is normally explained through the stages *br- > *rb-, with a dissimilation (also found in other words of this phonological shape) from *rb-r to *lb-r.

The development of the vowel system of Armenian is far more straightforward. In general, Armenian has preserved the distinction between the short vowels *i, *e, *a (< *ə), *o, *u,[6] although in some cases (the word *tasn* cited above being one) *e and *o have developed to a. The vowels *e and *o have also been raised to i and u when they occur before a nasal consonant; for example, in the word for 'five' *hing*, the *e vowel, preserved in the Greek cognate πέντε, has been raised to i. We have already seen how the vowels i and u fall together as ə when not under the accent. The distinction between long and short vowels has been lost, and the original long vowels *ē and *ō have merged with *i and *u. The diphthongs of the parent language have also been simplified; the diphthongs *ei and *oi, for example, have merged as the vowel ê. Armenian has replaced the syllabic resonants and nasal with a combination of -a- and resonant or nasal.

2.1 Possible shared phonological innovations made by Armenian and Greek

In the previous chapter I gave a brief summary of the advantages and drawbacks of using phonological agreements for the investigation of language relationships. Phonological changes are normally easily identifiable, but the chances of independent development are fairly high. I shall therefore first consider a number of changes which may have occurred in Armenian and Greek but in only a small number of other Indo-European languages. These involve the development of the reconstructed 'laryngeals' in the two languages, and discussion of some aspects of the development of laryngeal consonants in Armenian and Greek is also intended to preclude detailed discussion in later chapters.

Since the development of laryngeals in Greek has received far more attention than the Armenian treatment of these consonants, I have redressed the balance by considering the Armenian evidence in more detail and referring to the current consensus on the development of laryngeals in Greek.

Throughout this work, I shall broadly follow Mayrhofer's reconstruction of Proto-Indo-European phonology (1986) for the notation of reconstructed forms and the phoneme inventory of the parent language. Hence, where appropriate, three laryngeals (denoted as $*h_1$, the non-colouring, $*h_2$, the a-colouring, and $*h_3$, the o-colouring laryngeal respectively) and three series of gutturals are reconstructed. In most cases where the reconstruction of a laryngeal is open to considerable doubt, I have offered two (or more) alternative reconstructions. As will be seen, the behaviour of the laryngeals in Armenian is by no means as orderly as it is in Greek, and, since the doctrine of the 'three laryngeals' is in large part reliant on the evidence of Greek, this may give some cause to consider that this doctrine is unduly Hellenocentric. But it is beyond the scope of this work to reformulate the laryngeal theory, and such action would not affect the conclusions to the work.

2.2 'Prothetic' vowels

Armenian is perhaps best known to scholars of Indo-European languages and Classicists as the principal Indo-European language other than Greek to show 'prothetic vowels'. The term 'prothetic vowel' is used with respect to these two languages to refer to vowels which occur at the beginning of words in Armenian and Greek but not in cognates in other Indo-European languages; many scholars have considered it possible that some of these vowels are the reflexes of earlier laryngeal consonants. The question of prothetic vowels in the two languages has received a large amount of scholarly attention,[7] and a full treatment of the topic is beyond the scope of this work. However, I shall attempt to show that the appearance of a 'prothetic' vowel in Greek and Armenian does not mean that there has been a common act of innovation,[8] and that in fact the processes may have occurred independently.

The following pairs of words show an initial vowel in Greek and Armenian, but not in other Indo-European languages (excluding, for the moment, the cognate forms in Hittite).

GREEK		ARMENIAN	
ἀστήρ	'star'	astł	'star'
ὀδούς	'tooth'	atamn	'tooth'
ἀνήρ	'man'	ayr	'man'
ἀλώπηξ	'fox'	atowês	'fox'
ἔρεβος	'darkness'	erek	'evening'
ἐρεύγομαι	'belch'	orcam	'belch'
ὄνειδος	'reproach'	anêck'	'curse'
ἐννέα	'nine'	inn	'nine'

The correspondence between ἐννέα and inn will be discussed further at **4.25**, where it is decided that the ablaut difference between the two forms argues against a direct comparison. The correspondence pairs of ἔρεβος and erek, and ἐρεύγομαι and orcam, both show a prothetic vowel arising before initial *r- which is also found in ancient languages of Anatolia and could reflect an areal tendency to avoid initial r-.[9]

There are also a few other forms which some scholars have taken to show an initial 'prothetic vowel', but for which the evidence is uncertain. Greek ὀφέλλω 'sweep' and Armenian awel 'broom' may both stem from a root *h_3b^hel- (see further **4.45**) but there is no cognate to this root in other Indo-European languages. The equation of ὄνομα 'name' and Armenian anown 'name', and the reconstruction of the original form of this word is a familiar crux of comparative philology. Some scholars reconstruct forms with an original 'laryngeal',[10] but this is by no means certain. The Hittite word for 'name', *lāman-*, which may be a dissimilation from **nāman-*, shows no initial laryngeal.[11] Other languages also show an initial vowel, or the reflex of a syllabic **n̥-* at the beginning of this word (Old Irish *ainm*, Old Prussian *emnes*, Russian *imja*, etc.). The Armenian form could be explained by the paradigm **nomn̥*, **n̥mens*, envisaged by Cowgill (1965:156, and supported by Lindeman 1982:64, Bammesberger 1984:140f.); this would develop in Armenian to a paradigm with nominative **nown*, genitive **anman*, which could easily have been levelled to the actual *anown*, *anowan* (*ow* is orthographic for -*w*-).[12]

The theory that the initial vowel in the oblique cases of the words for 'I' in Greek and Armenian (Greek ἐμέ etc., Armenian accusative *is*, dative *inj*, etc.) stems from 'vocalised' $*h_1$ (advanced most recently by Beekes 1987:8–12) is also difficult to substantiate. Hittite *ammuk* 'me' points to a form with initial vowel as perhaps does Albanian *im* 'my'. Several scholars have also put forward non-laryngeal explanations of these forms, for example: Szemerényi (1990:229) considers **em-* to be the archaic form of the oblique cases of the pronoun; G. Schmidt (1978:48f.) also sees the form as old and explains it through the analogical extension of the **e-* from the nominative **eg-* to the oblique cases. Moreover, Schmidt finds a possible trace of **em-* forms in the Sanskrit pronoun *ama-* 'this' (once in the AV *ámo 'ham asmi* 'this am I').

An even less compelling case is presented by the equation of Greek ὄνυξ 'nail' and Armenian *ełowngn* 'nail' from the root $*h_3nog^{wh}$-. The direct comparison of the forms relies upon the supposition of a number of dissimilations in the Armenian word,[13] and it is possible that the initial element was influenced by the word for 'horn' *ełjewr* (Osthoff 1901:280). The nature of the initial of this word is further complicated by the existence of forms in other languages with vocalic initials, such as Latin *unguis* 'nail'. Some scholars derive the Latin word from $*h_3ng^{wh}$-, but one cannot be sure that the form with an initial vowel was not inherited directly from the parent language. In the same way, Latin *umbō* 'boss of a shield' means that the rather doubtful equation between Greek ὀμφαλός 'navel' and Armenian *aniw* 'wheel' (where the meaning has shifted from 'hub', see Ritter 1983) is of little use for the investigation of the relationship between Greek and Armenian prothetic vowels.

We are left therefore with six cases of prothetic vowels shared by Greek and Armenian: ἀστήρ 'star' and *astł* 'star'; ὀδούς 'tooth' and *atamn* 'tooth'; ἀνήρ 'man' and *ayr* 'man'; ἀλώπηξ 'fox' and *ałowês* 'fox'; ὄνειδος 'reproach' and *anêck'* 'curse'; and ὀφέλλω 'sweep' and *awel* 'broom'.

A plausible theory of the origin of these vowels is that they are the reflexes of original laryngeal consonants which have arisen through 'vocalisation' of the laryngeal or through the generalisation of a *Hilfsvokal* originally only standing when the previous word ended in a consonant.[14] Support for this theory is found in the Hittite word for 'star' *ḫašter-* where the initial laryngeal is preserved,[15] and perhaps in the Hittite word *ḫwelpi* 'young animal' (from *ḫwelpi-* 'young, tender, fresh') if Greek ἀλώπηξ, Armenian *aɫowês* and Sanskrit *lopāśá-* (see further **4.3**) represent the reflexes of a metathesised form of this word (compare Latin *volpēs* 'fox'). The Indo-Iranian cognate to ἀνήρ and *ayr*, **nar-*, offers support of a different nature for the reconstruction of an initial laryngeal. In compounds, both in Vedic and Avestan, which have *nar-* as the second member, there are examples of lengthening of the vowel preceding *-nar-*.[16] Although such comparative evidence for ὀδούς, ὄνειδος and ὀφέλλω is lacking, it does not seem unlikely that here too the initial vowel is the reflex of an original laryngeal.[17]

From the above evidence it appears that where an Armenian initial vowel corresponds to a reconstructed initial pre-consonantal laryngeal, the vowel is always *a*.[18] However, Greek seems to have a 'triple reflex' of initial pre-consonantal laryngeals with **h₁-* reflected by *e-*, **h₂-* by *a-* and **h₃-* by *o-*.[19] This would appear, therefore, to suggest that the Greek and Armenian developments of 'prothetic' vowels were independent.

It is possible, however, that the Armenian reflex of *a-* represents a later change of **e-* or **o-*: unaccented initial **o-* in an open syllable becomes *a-* in Armenian (unless it is followed by *o* in the next syllable),[20] so the examples of the development of a laryngeal to *a-* in Armenian alongside *o-* in Greek are not conclusive. A development of **e* to *a* is also found in some words in Armenian, but these can mostly be explained by vocalic assimilation or lowering before **u* in the following syllable.[21] Hence an unambiguous example of the development of initial pre-consonantal **h₁* in Armenian should decide whether the development of prothetic vowels is a shared innovation with Greek or not.

Unfortunately such a clear example is not forthcoming. The Aeolic word ἔδοντες 'teeth' has been taken to show that the original form of this word is **h₁dont-*, and that Aeolic has escaped an assimilation to ὀδ- which took place in the rest of Greek.[22] Armenian *atamn* would thus show **h₁ > a-*. However, it may be that Aeolic has changed the original ὀδούς by analogy to ἔδω 'I eat' (Beekes 1969:55). The exact development of the forms ὄνομα and *anown* is also uncertain, as we have seen above, and the question of which initial laryngeal should be reconstructed, if any, is not settled. Thus the evidence is not yet sufficient to decide the question finally.[23]

A development of all pre-consonantal initial laryngeals to *a-* in Armenian is likely on theoretical grounds. One can envisage the development through the generalisation of the *sandhi* variant when the preceding word ended in a consonant (see above). Elsewhere in Armenian where a laryngeal between consonants gives a vocalic reflex it is always *-a-*. In Greek, on the other hand, there is evidence for a 'triple reflex' of laryngeals in this environment as well.[24] These observations suggest that the development, like the other developments of the laryngeals in the two languages,[25] took place independently. Support for the theory of an independent development of 'prothetic vowels' from laryngeals is given by the equation of Armenian *goy* 'he is' with Hittite *ḫwiš-* 'live' (see also **4.11**). This equation shows that Armenian did not, unlike Greek,[26] develop a vocalic reflex of a laryngeal which preceded **w-*.

Therefore, although the nature of the evidence does not allow for proof, one can say that it seems unlikely that the development of the 'prothetic vowels' in Armenian is a shared innovation with Greek. The reflexes in the two languages appear to be separate developments. Initial laryngeals might also have left vocalic reflexes in Phrygian and in the Anatolian languages,[27] so the Greek and Armenian development of 'prothetic' vowels may represent an areal feature.

2.3   Other laryngeal developments in Armenian and Greek

As we have already seen, the question of 'prothetic vowels' and the reflex of initial laryngeals in Armenian and Greek has attracted a large amount of scholarly interest. There has been less attention paid to the reflexes of laryngeals in other positions, particularly in Armenian. Some scholars have seen in Armenian similar developments of laryngeals following a syllabic element to those proposed for Greek, and it is possible that the development of these sequences represents a common innovation of the two languages. The two developments under consideration can be summarised as follows:[28]

(1) $*RHT > aRaT$ (mirroring the Greek development of $*RH_i > E_iRE_i$ in some environments).

(2) $*UHT > UaT$ (mirroring the posited Greek development of $*UH_i$ either $> UE_i$ or $> U\grave{E}_i$).

The discussion of these developments ultimately rests on the discussion of the forms which have been cited as evidence for them together with any other material which might lead to a different conclusion. Some of the material which is used as evidence for and against is also discussed in detail in Chapter 4, and in the following account I have used some of the conclusions which are made in that chapter in order to save unnecessary reduplication of material.

2.3.1   The Armenian treatment of the Proto-Indo-European 'long sonants'

Meillet (1936:42 and 44) gave only two examples of Armenian reflexes of a Proto-Indo-European sonant followed by laryngeal: *dr-and* 'door-post' which he compared to Vedic *átā-* 'frame of a door', and Latin *antae* 'square pilasters';[29] and *armowkn* 'elbow' which he compared to Vedic *īrmá-* 'arm'.[30] These comparisons suggest that the Armenian reflex of the long sonants merged with the reflex of the normal vocalic sonants. Peters has argued that this development is limited to cases where the long sonant stands word initially (1986:366 n. 7). However, another example of the change might be found word-internally in *kałin* 'acorn' (see **4.30**).

Other scholars have seen different reflexes of the 'long sonants' in Armenian. Normier, who discusses only the reflexes of $*rH$ (= $*\bar{r}$), argues that $*rh_1$ gives Armenian *ar*, but $*rh_2$ or $*rh_3$ gives *ra* (1981:27 n. 40).

The Armenian word for 'forty', *k'aṙasown*, has led other scholars to argue for a development of $*\bar{r}$ to *aṙa*. Winter (1965:104f.) and Klingenschmitt (1970:80 and 1982:68 n. 11) put forward a development of $*nH$ to *ana* and $*lH$ to *ała* in *čanač'em* 'I know' < $*g'nh_3$- and *ałač'em* 'I beseech' respectively, and Klingenschmitt sees a similar development for $*-mH-$. Both scholars also see developments of these sequences to *-anaw-* and *-aław-* in *canawt'* 'known' < $*g'nh_3ti$- and *aławt'k'* 'prayer' < $*plh_3$-*ti* (Winter) or $*slh_2ti$- (Klingenschmitt 1970:80; at 1970:86 n. 10 he also adds the examples *amawt'* 'shame' and *arawt* 'pasture' from $*-mH-$ and $*-rH-$ respectively). Winter considers the possibility that the sequence of syllabic sonant followed by $*h_1$ may have developed differently from combinations with $*h_2$ and $*h_3$ and consequently derives *armowkn* and *drand* from forms with $*h_1$.

With so man conflicting theories, it seems sensible to present all the different Armenian words which may derive from zero grade forms of 'disyllabic' roots. I shall include a brief synopsis of different explanations of the Armenian word where relevant. I have given the more acceptable etymologies first in each case.

(a) Forms which may reflect a development of $*RHT$ to *aRT*:
   dr-and 'door-post' (see above).
   armowkn 'elbow' (see above).
   kałin 'acorn' (see above). Greek βάλανος suggests that the laryngeal here is $*h_2$.
   cicałim 'I laugh' may derive from $*gel-g'lh_2$- (Klingenschmitt 1982:147); for a detailed discussion of the root see **4.26**. Klingenschmitt sees the vocalism of this verb and the verbs with present suffix *-ane-* < $*-nH-$ as the result of *Thematisierung*, i.e. a transfer to the thematic conjugation. However, if one posits a development of the 'long sonant' to *-aRa-*, as does Klingenschmitt, one might expect the verb to be assigned to the *a*-conjugation; an original (middle) third person singular $*gel-g'lh_2$-*to* should develop to $**cicała$-. The thematic form can, of course, be explained from a starting point of the third plural $*gel-g'lh_2$-*enti*. The same argument could be applied to *karem* 'I am able', derived by de Lamberterie (1982a:26 f. and *passim*) from an earlier perfect formation of the root $*g^wrh_2$- (the same root as Greek βαρύς 'heavy', etc.), although this case is less secure evidence, since an original perfect third person

singular form $*g^w rh_2 -e$ would give 'Proto-Armenian' $*kar$, with loss of the laryngeal between vowels.

gaŕn 'lamb': this word is derived by Schmitt (1981:53) from the root in zero grade $*wṛn$-. It has been argued that the word originally contained a laryngeal, on the basis of the Greek compound πολύρρηνες < $*-wṛh_1 n$- (see Mayrhofer 1986:128 and Meier-Brügger 1990a:26f.). If both of these analyses are correct, we shall be provided with another example of $*-ṛH-$ > $-aŕ$-. However, Schmitt's reconstruction of the root in zero grade, presumably motivated in order to produce the sequence $*-rn-$ from which the Armenian $ŕ$ could be explained, need not be correct. The paradigm can be explained from an earlier declension

Nom. $*wṛ(H)-ēn$ (cf. Greek ἀρήν) > *gaŕn*
Gen.-Dat. $*wṛ(H)-en-$ > *gaŕin* (with $ŕ$ analogical from the
               nominative).

The change of $*r$ to $ŕ$ in the nominative may seem surprising in the light of the preservation of r before n in cases where there was earlier a vocalic element between the two sounds, as in, for example *kornč'im* 'I perish' < $*korVnč'im$. However, the loss of the vowel in the final syllable had a different outcome to the 'loss' of unaccented $*i$ and $*u$ in medial syllables: in final syllables the vowel was lost absolutely, but in medial syllables *schwa* was pronounced which prevented the normal rule that r > $ŕ$ before n from applying.[31]

karkowt 'hail', cognate with Latin *grando* etc., could possibly derive from $*gṛH-groHd-$; compare Rasmussen's reconstruction $*gṛ-groHd-$ (1984, only known to me through the summary at *Indogermanische Chronik* 31a p. 83, *Sprache* 31.1, 1985).

barti 'Populus nigra' is derived by Normier (1981:27) from $*b^h ṛh_1 g$-.

t'ał 'district (of a city)' is connected by Hamp (1986b), following Pokorny *IEW* 1061, with the root $*telh_2$- of Latin *tellus*, etc. If this is correct, the word could represent a zero grade $*tḷh_2 -ni$-.

(b) Forms which may reflect a development of $*RHT$ to *aRaT*:

k'aŕasown 'forty' < $*(k^w)twŕ-k'omt$- (Hamp 1982d: 188, Klingenschmitt 1982:68 n. 11 and Winter 1992b:351). Szemerényi (1960c:23) sees the second $-a-$ as the composition vowel $-a-$, following Brugmann (1911:33).

ewt'anasown 'seventy' < $*septṃ-k'omt$- (Hamp 1983c:102, rejected by Szemerényi 1960c:11 and Winter 1992b:352f.).

čanač'em 'I know' < $*g'ṇh_3$- (see above).

ałač'em 'I beseech' < $*pḷh_3$- or $*sḷh_2$- (see further **4.60**).

amač'em 'I am ashamed' < $*(s)ṃh_3$- (Klingenschmitt 1970:86 n. 10 and 1982:68 n. 11).

aracem 'I pasture' < $*(s)ṛHdye$- (Klingenschmitt 1970:86 n. 10, but he gives a completely different explanation of the word at 1982:153f.).

Other scholars connect *aracem* to Greek τρώγω 'I gnaw', following Lidén (1906:33–36), and this may derive from a form with 'long sonant'.

aławni 'dove' < *$pįh_2$-b^h-ni-* (Klingenschmitt 1982:68 n. 11, see also Olsen 1985:7).

aṙaj 'first' has been derived from the root *prH-* (Greek πρῶτος, etc.) by Hamp (1972:471f., who there sees a development of *rH to *ar*), and Winter (1992b:354).

ałand 'heresy' is connected by Klingenschmitt with Greek ἀλάομαι 'I wander' from *$h_įh_2$-* (the suggestion is recorded by Olsen 1989b:19 n. 29 citing a personal communication from H. Eichner).

t'ałar is derived by Hamp (1986b) from *$tįH_a$-*, the same root as in Latin *tellus*, etc. Hamp glosses the word, which is only attested in the modern language, as 'earthen', following Pokorny *IEW* 1061 who glosses 'irden, irdenes Gefäss'; in fact the word only means 'vase' not 'earthen'. Hübschmann (1895:251) explained the word as a Persian loan.

xałał 'peacefully', if related to Greek χαλάω (see further **4.37**), could derive from *$k^hįh_2$-*.

haraw 'south' has been connected to Sanskrit *pūrva-* 'first' from a root *prH-* (Ĵahowkyan 1982: 38).

k'ałak' 'city' is derived by Winter (1955a:8 and 1965a:105) from *$pwįH$-s*, and by Hamp (1985b:52) from *$tpįH_e$-*, although the word seems more likely to be an Iranian loan.

(c) Forms which may reflect a development of *RHT* to *RaT*:

erastank' 'arse' is derived from *$prh_3k'to$-* by Normier (1981:27 n. 40). For a full discussion of this word and other theories of its development see **4.54**.

erkan 'mill' is derived from *$g^wrh_{2/3}nuh_2$-* (via *$krana$-*) by Normier (1981:27 n. 40); other explanations of *erkan* are given by Meillet (1925b:8), Eichner (1978:152 n. 35) and Hamp (1975b).

yawray 'stepfather' < *ph_1trh_3y-* (Normier 1981:27 n. 40).

lar 'string' < *$wįh_1r$-* (?), compare Greek εὔληρα < *$-eh_1r$-* and Latin *lōrum* < *$-oh_1r$-*.[32]

The forms *aracem* 'I pasture' and *aṙaj* 'first' could also belong here if their initial vowel results from the widespread prosthesis before *r-*.

(d) Forms which may reflect a development of *RHT* to *RawT*:

(*a*)*nawt'i* 'fasting' (the forms with initial *a-* seem to arise through analogy with other forms with the privative prefix) may derive from *$ṇ-h_1dt$-* (Klingenschmitt 1982:167), see **4.43** for a full discussion of the word.

cnawt 'jaw' may reflect *$g'ṇh_2d^h$-* (Winter 1965a:110); however the reconstruction of the Proto-Indo-European form for this word is notoriously difficult, see further Winter *loc. cit.* and Beekes (1969:190).

cnawł 'parent' is derived from $*g'n h_1 - l -$ by Winter (1965a:110). De Lamberterie (1982a:41 following Meillet 1936:32) derives this form from $*g'enh_1 tl -$.

(e) Forms which may reflect a development of **RHT* to *aRawT*:

canawt' 'known' < $*g'n h_3 ti -$ (see above). Other scholars give different accounts of this puzzling form; for example Kortlandt (1991) explains the form through a secondary **-ti-* suffix added to 'Proto-Armenian' **canaw* from original $*g'n h_3 to -$. Godel (1975:80) considered the possibility that the medial *-w-* derived from an earlier guttural suffix.

aławt'k' 'prayer' < $*p[h_3 - ti$ (Winter 1965a:103) or $*s[h_2 ti -$ (Klingenschmitt 1970:80); see *alač'em* 'I beseech' and **4.60**.

amawt' 'shame' is derived from $*(s)m h_3 - ti -$ by Klingenschmitt; see *amač'em* above.

arawt 'pasture' is derived from **(s)rHdi-* by Klingenschmitt (1970:86 n. 10) but later he abandons this explanation; see *aracem* above.

In total, therefore, there is evidence for five different outcomes in Armenian of the inherited sequence syllabic sonant and laryngeal. There is no easy way of explaining all these different developments; they are not determined by laryngeal quality or by word position.

The fluctuation between the supposed development to *-aRa-* and *-aRaw-* in several roots (e.g. *čanač'em* and *canawt'*, etc.) is especially puzzling, since there is no straightforward phonetic explanation of why the sonant and laryngeal should have developed in two different ways in the same root. If one considers the pair of forms *čanač'em* and *canawt'* in isolation from material in other Indo-European languages, and applies the methods of internal reconstruction, one might arrive at the conclusion that they show a stem *cana-* (assimilated to *čana-* in *čanač'em*) followed by an unknown element **Z* in contact with different suffixes, i.e.

$$*-Z- + *-y- > -\check{c}' -$$
$$*-Z- + *-t- > -wt' -.$$

The identity of **-Z-* is not certain. Winter (1965a:104 and 114–115) thinks that a laryngeal could fulfil these conditions, but it is not clear how a laryngeal could be responsible both for the stem *cana-* (which must derive from $*g'n H -$) and at the same time for a consonantal reflex. Godel (1975:80) reconstructs **-Z-* as a guttural suffix **-k-* (which, in his terminology can represent a velar or labio-velar) following Pedersen (1906:348). It might also be possible to posit **-sk'-* for **-Z-*, following Meillet's derivation of *-č-* from **-sk'y-* (1936:109). The development of the sequence **-sk't-* to *-wt'-* at first sight seems impossible, yet the cluster **-sk'-* seems to have developed to a unitary phoneme at an early date in 'Proto-Armenian'. The development of the ('Proto-Armenian') sequence **-ct-* to *-wt-* would mirror the change of **-pt-*, **-tt-* and **-kt-* to *-wt-*.[33]

If the above explanation for the forms showing a development to - (*a*)*Raw-* is correct, we have only to account for the three divergent developments of *ṚH* to -*aR-*, -*aRa-* and -*Ra-*. The examples adduced for the development to -*Ra-* are uncertain. Normier's reconstructions for *erkan* and *yawray* are entirely personal, and the words can probably be better explained in different ways.[34] It is not so easy to dismiss either the posited development to -*aR-* or to -*aRa-*. A case could be made for either development to the exclusion of the other: the development to -*aR-* in *armowkn* and *drand* could be explained by deriving these words from forms with the full grade, that is, *$^*h_2anHt$-* and *$^*h_2arHm$-* rather than forms with zero-grades, *kaḷin* could be taken to be a 'non-Indo-European' word (following Beekes 1969:195) and the other forms could be dismissed as uncertain. On the other hand *k'aṛasown* and *ewt'anasown* could be explained through the secondary insertion of a medial -*a-* (perhaps on the pattern of original *$^*tria$-$k'omt$-* reanalysed as *$^*tri$-$ak'omt$-*, see further below) and *čanač'em* and the other verbal forms derived from forms with an **-ak-* or **-ak^w-* suffix, and the other etymologies discounted. To subscribe to either view would show more dogma than balance, and it seems best to assume that the development of the 'long sonants' in Armenian was either -*aR-* or -*aRa-* under unknown phonetic conditions.

However, the double development of the long sonants cannot be directly equated with the well-known supposed double development in Greek of *$^*ṚH_i$ > E_iRE_i* and *$^*ṚH_i$ > $R\bar{E}_i$* (as, for example, in γένεσις 'creation' and κασίγνητος 'brother' from the root *$^*g'ṇh_1$-*, see Rix 1976:72f. and Mayrhofer 1986:128f.), because the Armenian reflexes do not show the variation in vowel quality found in the Greek forms, and the development to -*aR-* cannot be seen as parallel to the Greek development to -*Rv̄-*. Moreover the only two clear correspondence pairs *k'aṛasown* and (West Greek) τετρώκοντα and *čanač'em* and γιγνώσκω do not agree; the Greek forms show a development to -*Rv̄-* but the Armenian to -*aRa-*.

2.3.2 The Greek and Armenian treatment of **-iH-/*-uH-*

The suggestion that the outcomes of the sequences **-iH-* and **-uH-* in Greek might be something other than *v̄* and *ī* was first made by Francis in his PhD thesis (1970) on Greek disyllabic roots, written under the supervision of Warren Cowgill, which was unfortunately never published (a detailed summary of the thesis is given by Hettrich (1973), but this barely mentions Francis's theories on the development of **-iH-* and **-uH-* in Greek). Francis, in his attempt to explain strong aorist formations of the type of ἐβίων 'I lived' without recourse to a *Schwebeablaut* form of the root (i.e. a form *CReC-* alongside *CeRC-*), postulated that they could be satisfactorily explained if one assumed a regular phonetic development of **-Cih_3-* (**-CyO-* in Francis's notation, *C* here representing any non-syllabic element) to pre-Greek $*$-$y\bar{o}$-. He supported this phonetic law, which met with Cowgill's approval, by the etymologies of ζωός 'alive' from $*g^{w}ih_3$-$w\acute{o}$-[35] (Vedic jīvá-) and πρόσωπον 'face' < $*proti$-$h_3k^{w}o$- (Vedic prátīka-) (1970:276f.). He also investigated the development of $*i$ and $*u$ in contact with the other laryngeals. For the sequence $*$-Cuh_2- ($*$-CwA- in Francis's notation) he cited the correspondence between Greek δηρός 'long-lasting' and Vedic dūrá- to argue for a development to $*$-$w\bar{a}$- (1970:280, see further **4.15** for full discussion of this form). Francis also discussed the outcome of the combination $*$-Cyh_2- (1970:282) which he thought might be $*$-ya-, in order to explain the feminines in -ια; the combination $*$-Cih_1- for which he could not decide between $*$-$\bar{\imath}$- (as in ἰθύς 'straight') and $*$-ye- (as in ἵεμαι 'desire') (1970:283); and finally the combination $*$-Cuh_3- for which, again, he could not decide between $*$-$\bar{u}$- and $*$-$w\bar{o}$- (1970:283).

Francis's thesis suggestions were repeated and exemplified by Normier (1977:182 n. 26) who summarised the findings as follows: $*i/uh_2$ developed to $*y/w\bar{a}$, $*i/uh_3$ to $*y/w\bar{o}$, and $*i/uh_1$ to $*\bar{\imath}/\bar{u}$.[36] Normier provides some fresh material to support these sound changes: δίζημαι 'I seek' < $didih_2$-; Arcadian ζατός 'sought' (Attic ζητέω 'I seek') < $*dih_2t\acute{o}$-; ἠνορέη 'manliness' < $*su$-h_2nor- (Vedic sūnára- 'youthful'); Πάν 'Pan' < $*p(w)\bar{a}hon$- < $*puh_2son$- (Vedic Pūṣán-); ζωρός 'unmixed' (of wine) < $*g^{w}ih_3r\acute{o}$- (Vedic jīrá- 'quick'); μωρός 'foolish' < $*muh_3r\acute{o}$- (Vedic mūrá- 'stupid'). The words ἄριστον 'breakfast', εἴκοσι 'twenty', (Doric ϝίκατι), εἶμεν 'may we be' (optative first person plural of εἰμί 'I am'), ἴς 'force', πίων 'ripe' and ὗς 'pig' provide examples of combinations with $*h_1$. Supposedly similar developments in Tocharian were noted independently by Winter (1965b:191f.) and some scholars have accepted the phonetic changes for both Greek and Tocharian.[37]

If Francis's derivation of δηρός 'long-lasting' < $*duh_2r\acute{o}$- (Vedic dūrá-) is correct, it also holds significance for the Armenian word erkar 'long-lasting' which Meillet had connected directly with δηρός, deriving both forms from a full-grade $*dw\bar{a}ro$- (REArm 4 (1924) 1–2, reprinted in 1977:209f.). Francis knew of the existence of the word erkar (1970:281), but did not make the assumption that it, like δηρός, might derive directly from $*duh_2r\acute{o}$- which was left to Olsen (1989b:7 n. 7). This correspondence led Olsen to postulate a change of $*$-uh_2- to $*$-$w\bar{a}$- in Armenian, parallel to the supposed Greek and Tocharian developments.[37A]

However, the Francis hypothesis has not met with general acceptance. Bammesberger (1984:46) and Beekes (1988:73 n. 4) argue against the change but without giving any counter-examples. The supposed development of $*ih_3$ is denied by Rix (1976:71, following Beekes 1969:129) who derives $*\acute{o}\pi\acute{\iota}\pi\eta$ (the base of the verb ὀπιπεύω 'stare at') from $*opi$-h_3k^{w}-eh_2 and Lindeman who cites Greek πῖθι 'drink!' (imperative) (1989:273). Other counter-examples are given by de Lamberterie (1990:490f.): γλωχίς 'point' < $*$-ih_2 and ἔφῡ 'he/she became' < $*$-uH; Ruijgh (1988:446): πολύ-ρῑτος 'worthy of high honour' < *-$k^w ih_2$-tó-; and Peters (1988:376): ἐχῖνος 'hedgehog', βρίθω 'I weigh down', θῦμός 'soul', κινέω 'I move', πίνω 'I drink' and the Mycenaean man's name qi-wo (if this is correctly interpreted as the cognate with Latin vīvus). If Laroche is right to see a connection of θῦμός 'soul' with Hittite tuḫḫima- 'panting, gasp' (1956:80, a suggestion ignored by Frisk GEW and Chantraine DELG s.v., but defended by Roider 1981 and Meier-Brügger 1989), this word may derive from *$d^h uh_2 mó$- and provide a clear example of *-uh_2- > Greek -ῡ-.

Francis had already anticipated these objections to some extent; at (1970:284) he states that ἔφῡ and θῦμός do not necessarily contradict his findings, and that he would show 'elsewhere' that the forms βρίθω and κινέω did not continue disyllabic roots, a promise which was sadly never fulfilled. The verb πίνω 'I drink' does not make a convincing counter-example to Francis's theory, since the alternation between forms with πω- and πι- has not yet been satisfactorily explained by the laryngeal theory, and γλωχίς and ὀπῖπεύω are without clear correspondences outside Greek (Klein 1988:264 and n. 9).

It is curious that some of the same scholars who have opposed Francis's hypothesis for the development of *-CUH- in Greek have themselves been in favour of similar developments for the same sequence at the end of the word. For example, Peters (1980:127f.) thinks that a sound change of *-iH and *-uH to *-yV and *-wV is likely on the basis of the feminine nouns in -ια < *-ih_2 (although he readily agrees that these could be analogical in origin) and the dual ὄσσε 'eyes', taken from *-ih_1 by Forssman (1969:46).[38] Rix (1976:75) uses the example of the neuter plurals of the type of τρία and δοῦρα < *-ih_2 and *-uh_2, and de Lamberterie and Peters (following Eichner) think that a similar development may have occurred in the early history of Armenian.[39]

I can add little to these previous discussions of the Greek outcome of *i and *u followed by laryngeal, and I shall rather examine the Armenian material which has been brought forward to support the claim that the same developments took place in that language. Firstly, evidence for the development of *-iH- and *-uH- in medial position.

Olsen only gives two other examples of the supposed development of *-uH- to 'proto-Armenian' *-wā- as well as erkar 'long-lasting' < *$duh_2 rō$-: stowar 'thick' < *$stuh_2$-ro- (Vedic sthūra- 'thick'[40]) and k'aw 'expiation' < *puH-to-.[41] Both of these examples are highly uncertain: stowar may alternatively derive from the same form as Vedic sthāvará- 'compact'; it may continue a form *stipar- (Godel 1975:76; de Lamberterie 1990:521 compares Greek στιβαρός 'compact', στιφρός 'firm' and Lithuanian stiprùs 'strong'); or it may be a borrowing from Iranian, cf. Pahlavi stavar 'thick' (Ačaryan HAB IV² 279). The sound change of *pw- to k'-, on which the etymology of k'aw depends, is, as Olsen herself admits, very uncertain. An alternative etymology of k'aw which has met with widespread acceptance, and which will be discussed more fully at **4.63**, was proposed by Godel (1984:291–293) who connected Greek σῶς (< *σαϝος) 'safe'. It seems likely that the Greek word derives from a root *tuh_2- (de Lamberterie 1990:171–178), and if the Armenian word were also connected it would provide another example of *-uh_2- > Armenian -*wa*-.[42] Another example of the supposed change was given by Hamp (1975:104), who connected *lowanam* 'I wash' directly with Greek πλύνω with the sequence -*owa*- derived from *-*uH*-, which gave ū in Greek.[43] Other scholars have also sought to connect this word to the root *$lewh_3$- 'wash', compare Greek λούω, Latin *lavo* (so Hübschmann, tentatively, 1897:454, Barton 1965:14 n. 21 and Klingen-schmitt 1982:115 f.).

It is clear that the four examples *erkar* < *duh_2ro-, *stowar* < *$stuh_2ro$-, *k'aw* < *tuh_2- and *lowanam* < *pluH*- cannot all represent the same development of *-uh_2-, since for *erkar* and *k'aw* the development must proceed via stages *dwar*- and *twa*-, whereas *stowar* and *lowanam* must be derived from *stuwar*- and *luwa*-; the difference could result from a desire to avoid complex clusters in pre-historic Armenian, yet since the sequence *-stw*- was admissible, for example, *oskr* 'bone' < *ostw-er* (Meillet 1936:51), this seems unlikely.

The words *erkar* and *stowar* both share the ending -*ar*, which is also found in several other adjectives, for example, *ardar* 'just', *dalar* 'green', and it is possible that this reflects a suffix which had limited productivity in the prehistoric period of Armenian. The existence of a doublet form *erkayn* beside *erkar* in the Classical period, with a suffix -*ayn* commonly used for adjectives (e.g. *miayn* 'only', *ownayn* 'empty') shows that in the Classical period the final *-*ar* was certainly understood to be a suffix by the native speakers, although of course this may be the result of a later re-analysis.

Evidence for an Armenian change of *-*iH*- and *-*uH*- to *-*ī*- and *-*ū*- is also scarce: Schmitt (1981:51) gives three examples of the change of Proto-Indo-European *-*ū*- to Armenian -*ow*-:

> *mowkn* 'mouse' < *mūs*,
> *jowkn* 'fish' alongside Greek ἰχθῦς. (Mayrhofer 1986:118 reconstructs *d^hg^huH-),
> *srownk'* 'leg' < *$k'rūs$-ni- (following Hübschmann 1897:493 f.), compare Latin *crūres*.

Unfortunately, none of these forms is conclusive. The words for 'mouse' and 'fish' both show an unexplained -*k*- which Winter (1965a:105) derived directly from a laryngeal.[44] One could therefore imagine a double develop-ment of *-*uH*- to -*owk*- in monosyllabic words but *-*wa*- elsewhere. The word for 'leg', although at first sight a sure cognate of the Latin word, has caused much discussion as it seems to be the only example of a cluster *Cr*- which has not been metathesised.[45] Moreover, despite Winter's theory, it seems likely that the three forms do not derive from an original cluster *-*uH*-, but that the long vowel represents the *Dehnstufe* of the nominative singular. Thus the nominative **mūs* may have arisen through simplification of original **mus-s* with compensatory lengthening (Szemerényi 1990:122, see also Mayrhofer 1986:171).

A better example of the development of **-uH-* > *-ow-* (i.e. [u]), may be provided by the Armenian word for 'empty', *ownayn*, which has long been connected with Vedic *ūná-* 'deficient' and Latin *vānus* derived from **uh₂no-* and **weh₂no-* respectively. The unaccented *ow-* is not reduced since it is in initial position. There is consequently no need to follow Hübschmann in an **o-*grade reconstruction **ow(h₂)n-* (1897:484). There are a few other examples which might also be added here, although they are all somewhat dubious:

t'owk' 'saliva' < **-uH-* (Winter 1965a:104),
xowł 'hut' < **kʰūlo-* (Solta 1960:339 and Pokorny *IEW* 951, both following Patrubány),
cowr̄ 'bent' < **g'ūro-*, compare Greek γυρός 'round' (see further **4.27**),
kow 'dung' < **gūto-*, compare Sanskrit *gūtha-* (Hübschmann 1897:461),
[how 'purulent blood' < **pū-* (Hübschmann 1897:468, Solta 1960:174, Pokorny *IEW* 849); the word is a borrowing from Persian (Hübschmann *IF Anz.* 10 (1899) p. 45, reprinted in 1976:329),]
howr 'fire' < **puh₂r* (Winter 1965a:106; the original etymon of this word is probably **peHur* (nom.) **pHunos* (gen.)),
mown 'fly' < **musno-* (Hübschmann 1897:476) or **mūsno-* (cf. Pokorny *IEW* 752),
mownǰ 'dumb' < **mundyo-* (Hübschmann 1897:476) or perhaps **mūndyo-* (cf. Pokorny *IEW* 751),
šowk' 'shade' < **sk'uH-* (Winter 1965a:104),
p'owk'k' 'bellows' < **pʰuH-* (Winter 1965a:104).

Olsen provides no examples of a change from **-iH-* to **-ya-* in medial position (see below for discussion of *metasan* 'eleven' and *eresown* 'thirty'),[45A] and the Armenian reflex of **-ī-* and **-iH-* appears to be *-i-* from the following examples:

ǰil 'sinew, cord' < **g'ʰīslo-* (Schmitt 1981:51 and J̌ahowkyan 1982:34),
siwn 'pillar' < **k'īwōn* (Schmitt 1981:51, see further **4.35** on this etymology; in my view the word represents a very early borrowing into Armenian and therefore is not diagnostic for the treatment of original **-iH-*),
c'in 'hawk' < **tkiH-* compare Greek ἰκτίν (Schmitt 1981:51, see **4.36** for full discussion of the reconstruction of this word); it is not certain what the original suffix of the word was: Schindler (1977:32) argued that the Armenian and Greek terms could both be derived from **tkih₂-ino-* in

which case the laryngeal would have been lost between two vowels, and this example would have to be given up,

tik' 'years, age' < *$dī$- (Jahowkyan 1982:34),

and finally perhaps also *k'san* 'twenty' if this derives from *$(d)wī$-k'*mti via *$gisan$* (Hübschmann 1897:504, see also the full discussion of theories concerning this word given by Schmitt 1980).

As so often in the study of the early development of Armenian, we are left with a very small number of seemingly contradictory examples. The most secure example of an Armenian reflex of *-iH- or *-uH- is *ownayn* < *uh_2n- which appears to indicate a development of *uH- > *ow-* presumably by way of *$ū$-. However the Greek cognate to this word, $εὖνις$ 'deficient', does not show a development to *-wā- and adherents of the Francis hypothesis may seek to explain the form differently. The most secure example of a change of *-uH- to *-wV̄- is provided by the pair *erkar* and $δηρός$ < *duh_2ro-; however, these forms could derive from the root in full grade (perhaps taken over, as J. H. W. Penney suggests to me (personal communication), from a root noun *$dweh_2$- 'distance' which survives in Greek $δήν$ 'for a long time' and Hittite *tuwa* 'far') and therefore do not present conclusive evidence for a common phonetic change in the two languages. The significance of the correspondence will be discussed further at **4.15**.

Some scholars have sought to find evidence for an Armenian development of the cluster of *-i- or *-u- followed by laryngeal in final position parallel to that proposed for Greek. The evidence brought forward for this is as follows:

(1) some irregular plural formations, which are taken to reflect earlier duals with the formant *-ih_1 (for which see Forssman 1969:46). The plural marker -*k'* is a later addition to characterise the words as plural. The relevant forms are:

ač'k' 'eyes' < *$h_3k^wyh_1$ (Eichner 1978:146 n. 17, Klingenschmitt 1982:148, de Lamberterie 1990:I.269),

akanjk' 'ears' < *$h_2awsnyh_1$ (Eichner *loc.cit.*, following Klingenschmitt 1970:86 n. 9),

cowngk' 'knees' < *$g'onwyh_1$ (Eichner *loc.cit.*),

lanjk' 'breast' < *$lng^{wh}yh_1$ (Klingenschmitt 1982:149, de Lamberterie 1990:I.186).

(2) words taken as reflexes of *-ih_2:

mi 'one' from *$smih_2$ with a development via *$smyh_2$ to *$smiya$ (Peters 1980:132 n. 80); Winter (1992b:348) proposes that the form *$miya$- has survived in the forms *mekin* 'single' and *metasan* 'eleven' < *mea- < *$miya$-,

sterj 'sterile' < *$sterih_2$, beside Greek $στεῖρα$ (Peters *loc.cit.*),

eresown 'thirty' is derived by Winter (1992b:351) from *$erea$-sun where the form *$erea$- reflects the neuter plural of *$treyes$ 'three' which Winter writes as *$triyA$ but could be written as *$trih_2$ (cf. Vedic *trī*).

Of the first set of examples *ač'k'* proves nothing as it is possible that *k^w* develops to *č'* before *i* as well as *y*, although the only other examples of this change are *inč'* 'something' (where the *č'* is taken to reflect *$k^w i(d)$*) and possibly *oč'* 'not'.[46] The same explanation can be offered for *lanjk'*, which may derive from *lng^{wh}-ī*. Eichner's derivation of *cowngk'* introduces the question of the fate of *wy-* in Armenian, which is by no means certain,[47] but surely a syllabification *$g'onwih_1$* (as proposed by Meillet 1936:84) would give *cowng-(k')*. The history of *akanjk'* is notoriously vexed, and Klingen-schmitt's derivation is by no means secure.[48]

Peters's explanation of *mi* meets with the objection that the word is declined as an *o*-stem. The Armenian *o*-declension normally continues the Proto-Indo-European *o*-stem declension, or adjectives with *o-* and *$ā$*-declension.[49] Armenian *mi* must therefore be derived from an earlier paradigm with masculine *$smiyo$-* and feminine *$smī$* or *$smiya$* in order to explain the *o*-stem declension. A paradigm with masculine *$smiyo$-* and feminine *$smī$*, or *$smiya$*, could reflect analogical reshaping of an original paradigm of masculine *sem-* and feminine *$smī$*.[50]

Winter's derivation of *metasan* and *mekin* offers an attractive piece of support for the hypothesis that *ih_2* > *ya*. These words do not, however, make a conclusive case, since it is possible that the form *$miya$-* was reshaped after *$miyo$-*, itself refashioned from *mi*. Moreover, the original *a-* suggested by these forms may be of an entirely different origin; it is difficult to see why the *dvanda* compound for 'eleven' and the word for 'single' should be formed from the feminine stem of the numeral.

The numeral *eresown* 'thirty' can be used to justify development of *iH-* either to *i-* or to *ya-*: it could derive from *$ereasun$* < *$eria$-sun*, as Winter suggests, or it could come from earlier *$erisun$*, with lowering of *i* to *e* due to the *u* in the following syllable.[51] However, Winter's explanation is perhaps preferable since it helps to explain the puzzling numerals *k'aṙasown* 'forty' and *ewt'anasown* 'seventy' which shows a medial *-a-* of uncertain origin. If the form for 'thirty' was originally *$ereasun$* the final element of the two other numerals could be explained as extensions from this form (compare the spread of *-ā-* in the Latin decads *sexāgintā, septuāgintā*, etc.). The form *$ereasun$* might stem from *tri-H-$k'omt$-* or it might, as Winter suggests, derive from composition with the neuter form of the numeral. If it stems from a neuter form, there is a possible means of explanation which does not entail the sound change *iH-* > *ya-*: the neuter may have been remodelled from the thematic neuters in *$ā$* (< *eh_2*) (and possibly the athematics in *a* (< *h_2*)) to give prehistoric *$erea$* < *tri-a*, compare the Latin numeral *tria*. The theory that *a* was extended throughout the neuter plurals finds support elsewhere. The Armenian word for 'tears' *artasowk'*, which seems to reflect an old neuter plural *$drak'uh_2$*, must derive from an original trisyllabic form with final *ua*.[52]

The word for 'barren', *sterj*, first occurs in the Armenian translation of

Ephraim (with a variant reading *sterd*[53]); the derived verb *sterjanam* (or *sterjim*, the text is uncertain) is used at *Gen.* 31:38 to translate ἀτεκνόω 'be barren'.[54] The *NBHL* list the declension class of *sterj* as either *o*-stem or *i*-stem, but give no examples of the word in an oblique case. The Armenian word need not be explained by a phonetic change of $*-ih_2$ to $*-ya$; an original declension pattern

Nom.	*sterī
Gen., Dat., etc.	*steryā-

might well have been replaced by a declension

Nom.	*sterya
Gen., Dat., etc.	*sterya-.

This explanation seems more likely since there may be other examples of words in this declension class developing to Armenian *i*-stems, for example *gort* 'frog' < $*wordih_1$ (cf. Latvian *vařde*) and perhaps *ayc* 'goat' < $*aig'ih_2$ (see Meillet 1936:76 and **4.1** for further discussion of *ayc*). This suggests that the different declension patterns arose from paradigm levelling which proceeded different directions: for *ayc* and *gort* the nominative form was generalised, for *sterj* the oblique form.

None of the examples brought forward in support of the theory that $*-iH$ and $*-uH$ develop to $*ya$ and $*wa$ in the prehistory of Armenian have proved resistant to all other explanations. The original neuter plurals *artasowk'* and *mawrowk'* and the original $*-iH$ stems *ayc* and *gort*, if the above explanations of them are correct, appear to require a sound change $*-iH > *-i$ and $*-uH > *-u$. The hypothesis of a parallel Armenian sound change to Greek cannot be accepted or rejected on the above evidence alone, and in the absence of fresh data the question must remain unsettled.

De Lamberterie (1990:490) holds the view that while the clusters $*-uH-$ and $*-iH-$ developed phonetically to $*-ī-$ and $*-ū-$ in Greek and Armenian, both languages underwent a common morphological change.[55] He argues that ablaut patterns of the type

FULL GRADE	ZERO GRADE
$*-yā- < *-yeh_2-$	$*-ī- < *-ih_2-$
$*-wā- < *-weh_2-$	$*-ū- < *-uh_2-$

were replaced by ablaut

$*-yā-$	$*-ya-$
$*-wā-$	$*-wa-$

by analogy to the ablaut pattern

$$*-ā- < *-eh_2- \qquad *-a- < *-h_2-.$$

This allows him to explain the relation between Greek ταΰς and Armenian *k'aw* (see above) and the word-final developments mentioned above. For

Greek the explanation seems a good one, yet with such a paucity of certain information about the Armenian changes, the theory of a common innovation cannot be confirmed. It is possible that the morphological innovation posited by de Lamberterie has also taken place to a limited extent in other Indo-European languages. For example, the Gothic word for 'empty' *wans* shows an unexpected *-a-* in comparison with Latin *vānus* and Vedic *ūná-* < *$u(e)h_2n$-, and a short vowel is also found in the Latin words *vaco* and *vastus* which may be derived from the same root.[56] The Vedic verb *svádati* 'be pleased with' shows a similar reformation of the root *$sweh_2d$-, although here the ablaut *svad-* is synchronically a full grade, not a zero grade. The Vedic form does, however, show the same process of analogous reformation of an anomalous ablaut pattern. Therefore, even if one were to find conclusive evidence that a similar reformation of the ablaut pattern had taken place in Armenian, it need not reflect a common innovation with the supposed change in Greek, but might have occurred independently.

In conclusion, the evidence for a peculiar phonetic development of the sequences *-iH-* and *-uH-* in Greek and Armenian is not conclusive for either language.

2.4 Bonfante's Greek–Armenian isoglosses

Bonfante (1937) compiled a list of twenty-four phonetic agreements which linked Greek and Armenian, in order to support the theory of a close genetic relationship between the two languages. These can be presented briefly as follows:

1. Armenian and Greek retain distinct *o and *a, *$ō$ and *$ā$.
2. Armenian and Greek conserve *e.
3. *$ə$ > *a*.
4. *schwa secundum* followed by a resonant > *a*.
5. Vocalic *$r̥$, *$l̥$ develop to *ar* and *al*.
6. Prothesis before *r-.
7. Intervocalic *-y-* lost.
8. Intervocalic *-wy-* retained.
9. *-ln-* > -ll-.
10. 'Épenthèse' of *-ny-* and *-ry-* to -yn/r-.
11. Non-final *s > *h*.
12. *sl-* > *l*-, *-sl-* > -*l(l)-*.
13. *sr-* > *r*-.
14. *sm-* > *m*-, *-sm-* > -*m*-.
15. *sn-* > *n*-, *-sn-* > -*n(n)-*.
16. 'Voiced stops' and 'voiced aspirates' kept distinct.
17. 'Voiceless aspirates' retained.
18. Armenian more resistant to '*satəm*isation' than some other *satəm* languages.

19. $*-k^w->*-wk^w->-wk'-$ (in some words).
20. Armenian reflex of $*g^w$ resistant to palatalisation, as in Greek; in Armenian $*k^wi$ palatalised, but not $*k^we$.
22. Of the original pre-consonantal and pre-vocalic variants of the nominative singular resonant stems, $*\bar{e}/*\bar{o}$ and $*\bar{e}R/*\bar{o}R$, Greek and Armenian have uniquely retained $*\bar{e}R/*\bar{o}R$.
23. Word-final $*-m\#>-n$.
24. Word-final $*-t\#/-d\#->\emptyset$.

This list is composed of a number of features of a different status. It does not distinguish agreements which are unique to Greek and Armenian from those which are also found in other Indo-European languages; it makes no attempt to differentiate between innovations and inheritances; it does not assess whether a change affects the phonological structure of the language or merely represents a merger of two features which occur in a previously neutralised environment;[57] and there is no attempt to fit the changes to any relative chronology for the two languages. Moreover some of the isoglosses make false assumptions about the development of Armenian and Greek phonology.

The isoglosses which represent shared retentions of features which also survive in other Indo-European languages (numbers 1, 2, 8, (which is of doubtful status),[58] 16 and 17[59]), will not be discussed. They are not without significance in the assessment of genetic relationship, but they can only be used as secondary support for an affinity which has been established through a number of common innovations. Bonfante's agreements numbered 3 and 6 have already been discussed above; number 19 is examined more fully in the discussion of the correspondence between Greek αὐχήν 'neck' and Armenian awjik' 'necklace' (**4.12**), and number 4 rests on false reconstructions.[60]

The other isoglosses all require some brief discussion. I shall attempt to fix a chronology for the developments to see if they could have occurred at the same time in Greek and Armenian. Some of the agreements represent developments which have not taken place in all Greek dialects. This does not necessarily preclude a connection with Armenian developments if the change can be shown to have taken place at an early enough date. Greek, like every language, must have had dialectal divisions throughout its prehistory. If Armenian consistently shows agreement with one dialectal group this may be significant;[61] but if Armenian shows developments which agree with a diverse range of Greek dialects then the agreements are more likely to have arisen by chance. For example, if one Armenian phonetic development matches a phenomenon found in Cypriot alone, another in Aeolic alone, and a third in all the dialects except Aeolic, then it is less likely that the agreements represent a shared development with a pre-historic Greek dialect.

2.4.1 The development of the syllabic liquids

The development of *r̥* and *l̥* to *ar* and *al* (number 5 of Bonfante's list) cannot be regarded as a common development of Greek and Armenian. The developments in Greek varies between αρ, αλ and ρα, λα, with developments to ορ, ρο, etc. in Aeolic. Indeed in Greek the normal interconsonantal reflex of a syllabic resonant is ρα or ρο not αρ or ορ.[62] Thus Aeolic Greek βροτός 'mortal' shows a different phonetic development from the exact Armenian cognate *mard* 'man'; the change cannot be viewed as a common innovation.[63] Furthermore, the Greek development may be late. The syllabic sonants may still have been maintained in some positions in Mycenaean Greek. Evidence to support this was presented by Heubeck (1972), who noted that the variation between, for example, *ma-to-ro-pu-ro* and *ma-to-pu-ro* for *Matr̥pulos* might bear testimony of scribal uncertainty in the face of a sound for which there was no sign in the script, but there is still no consensus in support of this view.[64] Perhaps more convincing is the argument that syllabic sonants were still preserved in earlier stages of the Greek epics, most famously preserved in the formulaic line-ending λιποῦσ᾽ ἀνδροτῆτα καὶ ἥβην (*Iliad* 16.857 and 22.363) where the short first syllable of ἀνδροτῆτα may continue the original scansion of a sequence *anr̥-.*[65]

2.4.2 Proto-Indo-European *-y-

The loss of intervocalic *-y- occurred not only in Greek and Armenian but also in Irish, Latin, Oscan-Umbrian and Albanian.[66] It is difficult to place this development in the relative chronologies of the languages. In Greek inherited *-y- is already lost intervocalically by the time of Linear B (Ventris and Chadwick 1973:78) and in Armenian the change has taken place before the passage of *-t- to -y- before front vowels, and before the loss of final syllables (Meillet 1936:52). The Latin change may also be old; inherited *-y- is also lost in Oscan and Umbrian and this may have been a common Italic development.

Kortlandt (1980:101) thinks that the Armenian loss of *-y- occurred after the development of inherited *ē > i, on the grounds that the result of the contraction of two inherited short *e vowels after the loss of *-y- does not merge with the inherited *ē. Thus *treyes 'three' develops to *erek'* 'three' not **erik'*. Unfortunately, this is not conclusive, as *ee may have contracted to a long vowel which differed from inherited *ē in quality, and later merged with inherited *e.[67] The Greek contraction of *-ee- after the loss of the medial *-y- in *treyes took place independently in the dialects: note the surviving uncontracted form τρέες at Gortyn.

It is possible that a weak intervocalic pronunciation of *-y- was a dialectal feature of the parent language and led to the later independent loss of the sound in Latin, Greek, Armenian, etc. But the inherent weakness of the glide

[j] in intervocalic position, and the loss of the sound in a number of different languages, mean that the coincidence of the change in Greek and Armenian has very little significance.

The question of 'epenthesis' (Bonfante's isogloss number 10) is best discussed here. The term *epenthesis* is (mis)used to describe the process in Armenian where an original sequence of resonant followed by *y develops to a sequence of resonant preceded by y.[68] The Armenian development may have been limited in occurrence to cases where the preceding vowel was *a. A similar development is also found in Greek but it appears to have taken place after the loss of syllabic sonants[69] and the combination of *-ly- develops to *-ll- outside Cypriot so it is difficult to see the Greek and Armenian process as a shared development. The development of a cluster of resonant and yod to palatalised resonant, and anticipation of the palatalisation in the preceding vowel is not uncommon.[70]

Finally, another development of *y- which has been used to link Greek and Armenian is the double treatment of initial *y-. Greek cognates of words which show initial *y- in other Indo-European languages either begin with ζ- (as ζυγόν, Latin *iugum*, English *yoke*) or *h*- (ὅς 'who' alongside Sanskrit *yaḥ*); this aberrant behaviour has been explained in many different ways, and several scholars have held laryngeals responsible.[71] Pisani (1950a:180f.) saw a similar double treatment of *y- in Armenian to give *j* and ∅.[72] However, the lack of evidence in the form of two series of secure correspondences, one with in initial ζ- in Greek, *j*- in Armenian and *y*- elsewhere, and one with an aspirate in Greek, loss in Armenian and *y*- elsewhere, does not allow a verdict on this matter. Indeed, words with initial *y*- in other Indo-European languages appear to have Armenian cognates with initial *ǰ*, *j*, *l* and ∅. For example:[73]

> *ǰowr* 'water', Lithuanian *jūrès* 'sea'
> *jer* 'your (plural)', Sanskrit *yūyám* 'you (plural)'
> *leard* 'liver', Sanskrit *yákr̥t* 'liver'
> *lowc* 'yoke', Sanskrit *yugá*- 'yoke'
> *or* 'who', Sanskrit *yá*- 'who'.

2.4.3 The development of *-ln- to *-ll-

This sound change, which is dialectal in Greek,[74] may not have taken place at all in Armenian. The reflex of *-ln- is *ł* (the velar *l*)[75] which is the normal reflex of *l before a consonant. As the sequence *-ll- was unknown in the parent language and did not arise independently in the prehistory of Armenian it cannot be ascertained whether *-ln- passed through a stage *-ll- in its development to Armenian *ł*. Moreover, as *-ll- and *-ln- did not contrast in the parent language or earlier stages of Greek and Armenian, this change, which also took place in other languages,[76] is structurally insignificant.

2.4.4 The development of *s > h

This sound change has taken place in Armenian, Greek, Iranian, Phrygian and Lycian (and also in Brythonic Celtic). In both Greek and Armenian the development appears to have taken place early in the history of the languages. In Greek the shift of *s to h had already taken place by the time of Mycenaean where h is probably still retained between vowels (Ventris and Chadwick 1973:398). In Armenian inherited *s has disappeared inter-vocalically before the loss of final syllables; thus in the nominative of the word for 'sister' k'oyr, the medial -oy- stems from a contraction of -esō- (Meillet 1936:39).[77] The product of the contraction of *-oo- (after the loss of *s) merged with inherited *o, not with inherited *ō, in the word bok 'barefoot' < *bʰoso- (cf. English bare); but this cannot be taken to show that the complete loss of *s took place after the merger of inherited *u and *ō (see the remarks on contracted *ee at 2.4.2 above).

Thus there is nothing in the relative chronology of the two languages to show that the development of *s to h could not have taken place when the two languages were in a period of common unity. But this theory is made less likely by the changes to inherited clusters containing *s. The development of *s in clusters may be part of the same change as the aspiration of initial and intervocalic *s. The different Greek dialectal developments of, for example, *-sm-, (Aeolic ἐμμί, Ionic εἰμί, etc.), can be explained by seeing a change of *-sm- to *-hm- in 'Common Greek', which may have taken place at the same time as the change of intervocalic and initial *s to h.[78] A change of *-sn- to *-hn- has also taken place in the prehistory of Armenian (e.g. zgenowm, see 2.64). However, in Greek *s is also aspirated and eventually lost in clusters of nasal followed by *s (for example, in ἔμεινα originally a sigmatic aorist of μένω 'I remain', and ὦμος 'shoulder' < *omso- or *ōmso-[79]), while in Armenian *s is not aspirated in such clusters (for example mis 'flesh' alongside Vedic māṃsá- 'flesh').[80] It seems likely that the aspiration of *-s- after a nasal took place at the same time as the change before a nasal in Greek, and the fact that this change was not made in Armenian suggests that change of *s > *h took place separately in the two languages. This line of reasoning is unfortunately not conclusive, since the clusters of nasal plus *s and *s plus nasal may have changed at different times in the prehistory of Greek; compare the change of *s to *h in interconsonantal position, which seems to have occurred later than the aspiration of *s in other positions in Greek, to judge from the equation of Mycenaean a₃-ka-sa-ma with αἰχμή.

The parallel change of *s to h in Iranian and Phrygian suggests that the change may have been due to contact.[81] Szemerényi (1966:191f., 1968, 1985), on the basis of a reading Huža in Old Persian which he equated with Susa, assigned a date to the Iranian change which placed it later than the Linear B tablets, and thus a separate development to the Greek.[82] However, there are hazards in this method of 'absolute chronology'; the Iranians may have known the name of *Susa* before coming into contact with it, or they may have changed *Susa* to *Huža* when borrowed at a later date, by a process Hock has termed 'etymological nativization'.[83] Thus there is no reason to dismiss the theory that the common change is an areal phenomenon, although given that the sound change is not uncommon, independent innovation is not unlikely. The tendency to pronounce a strongly aspirated **s* is found in historical times in both Greece and Armenia, where aspiration may have been a concomitant feature of the /s/ phoneme.[84] This may be evidence of a continuation of the process which earlier led to the replacement of **s* by *h*.[85]

In Armenian **rs* develops both to *r̄* and *rš*; the standard example of this is the pair *t'aršamim* and *t'ar̄amim* 'I wither' (from the root **ters-*). This two-fold development has attracted the attention of many scholars; the arguments are summarised by Bolognesi (1960:28 ff.), who comes to the conclusion that the difference reflects an early Armenian dialectal divergence. Pisani (1951:65 f.) had earlier compared the double development of **-rs-* to -ρρ- and -ρσ- in Greek. The assimilation of -ρσ- to -ρρ- occurs chiefly in Attic and adjoining areas (North-west Greek and west Ionic), and the development of δέρρις 'a leathern covering' (Thucydides) < δέρσις < **δερτις* shows that the change is after the assibilation of **ti* (cf. Miller 1976:164 and Allen 1987:44 f.). Morani (1981b:15) also compared the 'double development' in Armenian to the Greek treatment of the cluster, but saw the diversity between -ρσ- and -ρ- with lengthening of the preceding vowel as the relevant Greek developments. But there is no certain evidence in Greek for the second process outside the sigmatic aorist, where it may be analogical to the roots with final nasal.[86]

2.4.5 The *centum/satəm* division

The *centum/satəm* division is a matter of embarrassment to those who have tried to see a close genetic relationship between Armenian and Greek. Armenian belongs to the *satəm* group of languages which show palatalisation of the 'palatal series' and absence of a labial element in their reflexes of 'labiovelars', but Greek is a *centum* language.[87] However several features of the development of Armenian suggest that at an earlier stage in its pre-history it did have a 'labio-velar' series: the merger of palatals and labio-velars after **u*, which can best be explained as a loss of the labial element of labio-velars after **u* (Meillet 1936:37), rather than by a palatalising effect of **u* (as Solta 1963:97);[88] the development of **Kʷ* to **wK'* in certain words, as *awj* 'snake' alongside Latin *anguis*;[89] and the palatalisation of words which appear to have been loaned after the end of the period of common unity, such as *siser̄n* 'chick-pea' beside Latin *cicer*.[90]

Bonfante's isogloss number 20, reiterated by Solta (1965–6:282), concerns the palatalisation of labio-velars in Armenian and Greek, and is thus relevant to the *centum/satəm* issue. Unfortunately the nature of the evidence means that the details of the Armenian palatalisation are not fully known.[91] However Bonfante's comparison cannot be upheld. In Greek *g^w*- is palatalised before *e* but not before *i*,[92] whereas in Armenian it appears not to be palatalised in any circumstance: compare *g^w* unpalatalised in Greek βίος 'life' and Armenian *keam* 'I live', *eker* 'he ate'; but palatalised in Greek δελφύς 'womb'.[93] The process appears therefore to be independent in the two languages, as the divergences across the Greek dialects suggest.

2.4.6 Word-final developments

Bonfante's last three isoglosses deal with developments of word-final consonants. In the parent language many of the phonological oppositions were neutralised word-finally (Meillet 1937:137 f.) and so loss or merger of word-final consonants is often of little consequence structurally, and has taken place independently in many Indo-European languages. In Armenian the loss of the final syllable of polysyllables has meant that the behaviour of word-final consonants is difficult to elucidate.

Bonfante's assertion that the choice between *-$\bar{e}$/ *-$\bar{o}$ and *-$\bar{e}R$/ *-$\bar{o}R$ ($R =$ any resonant) as the nominative singular of resonant stems was dependent on the initial of the following word is unsubstantiated. It is possible that there was a complete loss of a word-final resonant in the parent language, but that it has been analogically restored in some of the daughter languages.[94] In Armenian the nominative and accusative singular have fallen together in all paradigms, so the final resonant of, for example, *šown* 'dog' (Greek κυών, Vedic *śvā*) may reflect the original accusative and not the nominative.

The treatment of final Armenian *-*m* is another vexed question of Armenian philology. In polysyllables final *-*Vm* was lost, but *-*m* became *-*n* in monosyllables (e.g. *k'an* 'than' alongside Latin *quam*, which suggests a development of *-*m* to -*n*). However the chronology of the change is uncertain. Pisani tries to show (1951:47 ff.) that although final *-*Vm* is lost with the final syllables (thus the loss of the accusative in *o*-stems, etc.), final *-*n* is not lost. However, in this case the change of *-*m* to -*n* would have occurred after the loss of final syllables and so should have affected the first singular present verbal marker -*m* < *-*mi*.[95] Thus, it is not possible to determine whether the change of final *-*m* to -*n* was made in a period of Greek-Armenian unity or not. The change also took place in all other Indo-European languages except Italic and Indo-Iranian.[96]

Bonfante's theory that final *-*t* and *-*d* were lost in Armenian cannot be verified. Armenian appears to have preserved the final *-*t* added to the nominative singular of *-*r/n* stems in the words *leard* 'liver' and *neard* 'sinew' (cf. Sanskrit *yákr̥t* 'liver' and *snávan-* 'sinew'), and later remodelled the paradigms as *i*-stems.[97] But it is possible that these forms derive from forms with final *-*ti*; compare the correspondence of *sirt* 'heart' with Vedic nominative singular *hárdi* 'heart' (Hübschmann 1897:490, Eichner 1978:154 n. 44, following Klingenschmitt).

The only other possible cases which might demonstrate whether a final *-t* was lost or not are the nominative-accusative singular neuter of the pronouns and the third person singular of a monosyllabic aorist. The only surviving neuter pronoun is *zi* 'what' (formed by the addition of the preposition *z-* to a pronoun **i* which also survives in *č'ik'* 'there is none'). The prehistoric Armenian pronoun **i* could either stem from a form **(kʷ)-im* (Sanskrit *kim*), with the same loss of final nasal as in the preposition *i* 'in' < **en*, or **(kʷ)-id*. The first option is favoured by the existence of the pronoun *inč'* 'something' which Meillet took as an exact correspondent to Sanskrit *kiṃcit*.[98]

Since all originally monosyllabic forms of the aorist took the augment, their endings were lost with the loss of final syllables and they are not diagnostic for our problem: thus *et* 'he gave', *ed* 'he put', *ekn* 'he came'. The final example, *ekn* (< **egʷem-t*, compare Sanskrit *agan* 'he came') shows a case where final **-nt* (< **-mt*) has developed to *-n*. It is worth considering this development in a little more detail since Olsen has recently suggested that Armenian and Greek shared a double development of **-nt-* dependent on the position of the original accent (Olsen 1989a). The sequence **-nt(V)* develops in Armenian to both *-n* (for example *beren* 'they carry' < **bʰerenti*) and *-nd* (for example in *dr-and* 'door post' besides Latin *antae*), and Olsen argued that the sequence **-ṇt-* in Greek developed to *-aδ-* in Greek when under the accent, and to *-aτ-* elsewhere. Olsen's account of the double development in Armenian is *a priori* unlikely since there are no other examples of Armenian phonetic developments which must be explained by the original position of the accent. A more simple explanation for this discrepancy could be that word-finally (after the loss of final syllables) **-nt* became *-n* but word internally it developed to *-nd-*. For a case such as *beren*, the word-final development was preserved, but the regular form **dr-an* < **-nt-* was replaced by *drand* by the influence of other forms in the paradigm, such as the genitive *drandi*, etc.[99] In other paradigms, such as *hown* 'ford' (cf. Sanskrit *pánthāḥ* 'path', Latin *pons* 'bridge') the nominative form has been generalised.

2.5 Conclusions

This brief survey of possible phonological isoglosses between Armenian and Greek has shown that there is no isogloss which must represent an exclusive shared innovation by the two languages. Furthermore there are few isoglosses which tell us about the relationship of the two languages as dialects of a parent language. The earliest stages of both languages may have shared a pronunciation of a *Hilfsvokal* between initial laryngeal and a following consonant; a weakly articulated intervocalic *-y-; an aspirated pronunciation of *s; and a tendency to replace final *-m by *-n. But each of these developments is shared with other languages, and each one could have been made independently. The loss of intervocalic *-y- and the changes of *s to *h and of final *-m to *-n are found in several other languages, and their occurrence in both Greek and Armenian is of little significance. Each of the two languages has also undergone major independent changes; Armenian has lost the labial element of inherited labio-velars and undergone a consonant shift; Greek, alone of the Indo-European languages, shows a voiceless aspirate series of consonants for the inherited 'voiced aspirates'.[100] These changes do not mean that the languages cannot have been close at a dialectal level of the parent language as they may have taken place at a later stage of the development of the languages.[101] Armenian also seems to have undergone a palatalisation of *s after *r and *k', a change which is found in other *satəm* languages.[102]

None of the arguments considered are conclusive either for or against the theory of a special Greek-Armenian relationship. They leave the burden of proof on those who subscribe to it, and, in doing so, illustrate the problems arising from using phonological evidence to investigate the genetic kinship of languages.

3

POSSIBLE MORPHOLOGICAL INNOVATIONS SHARED BY GREEK AND ARMENIAN

3.0 The morphology and syntax of Classical Armenian

Armenian has seven cases in the nominal and pronominal declensions: nominative, accusative, locative, genitive, dative, ablative and instrumental. There is no separate form for the vocative case, which is syncretic with the nominative.[1] However partial syncretism of many cases has reduced the array of separate case markers found in other languages. Thus the dative case only has a distinct case form in the pronominal declensions; elsewhere it is syncretic with the genitive. The locative only has a distinct case marker in the singular of one declension; elsewhere it is syncretic with the genitive-dative or the nominative in the singular, and with the accusative in the plural. The nominative and accusative of all nominal declensions are syncretic in the singular.

There are two numbers, singular and plural. The language uses a large number of *plurale tantum* nouns (for example, *mahičk'* 'bed') and nouns which can take equally the singular or plural number (for example *mit(k')* 'mind').[2]

The language has four separate 'quasi-thematic' nominal declensions with characteristic thematic vowels *-a-*, *-i-*, *-o-*, and *-ow-* [-u-]; thus they show an instrumental singular in *-aw*, *-iw*, *-ov* and *-ow* [-u], and genitive plural in *-ac'*, *-ic'*, *-oc'* and *-owc'* respectively. There are further 'quasi-athematic' declensions based around resonant-stems in *-r*, *-n* and *-ł*, with characteristic instrumental singulars in *-rb*, *-mb* and *-łb* respectively; the *-n* declension in particular has a number of sub-classes with different vocalisms of the element preceding the resonant. There are also other minor, synchronically irregular, declension classes.[3]

The Classical Armenian verbal system is based around the opposition between present and aorist stems. From the present stem are derived a present and imperfect indicative, a subjunctive/future and an imperative (always used with a negative to function as a prohibitive). Within the aorist system there is likewise an aorist indicative, a subjunctive/future and an imperative. The difference between the two systems is one of aspect, corresponding roughly to the aspectual distinction between the present and aorist systems of Greek.

There is no regularly formed present participle; different verbal adjectives are used where necessary (see further **3.4**). There is, however, a past participle in -*eal* which is usually formed from the aorist stem although for a number of verbs it is formed from the present stem. A periphrasis of the past participle with the verb 'to be' or a synonym is used as a perfect.[4] A present infinitive is formed with -*l*, which declines as an -*o*- stem noun and fulfils many of the roles of a verbal noun. There is no aorist infinitive.

There are four different verb conjugations in the present system, with characteristic vowels -*a*-, -*e*-, -*i*- and -*ow*- [-u-]. Verbs in the -*i*- declensions either serve as passives to those in the -*e*- declension or are deponent; thus *berem* 'I carry' has a passive *berim* 'I am carried' while *nstim* means 'I sit', and there is no form **nstem. In the imperfect and the infinitive the -*i*-conjugation agrees with the -*e*- conjugation. For the -*a*- and -*ow*- conjugations there is no diathesis in the present. In the aorist there is a diathesis between active and passive/deponent conjugations.

For some verbs the root functions as the aorist stem in opposition to a present stem characterised either by a nasal suffix (for example present *lk'anem* 'I leave', aorist *lk'i* 'I left') or the suffix -*č'*- (for example present *t'ak'č'im* 'I hide', aorist *t'ak'eay* 'I hid'); some show the root functioning as the present stem, with the aorist marked with the suffix -*c'*- (for example present *gorcem* 'I work', aorist *gorcec'i* 'I worked'); some verbs show both a characterised aorist and a characterised present stem (for example present *stanam* 'I acquire', aorist *stac'ay* 'I acquired'); and for a few the root functions as both the present and the aorist stem (for example present *berem* 'I carry', aorist *beri* 'I carried').

Armenian shows a more fluid syntactic structure than the classical languages. Word order is mostly free. Gender has been lost as a grammatical category, and even the pronouns are unmarked for natural gender reference. Adjectives may decline with the noun, but they often remain undeclined;[5] sometimes, the noun stands in the plural but the adjective in the singular. Similarly, a plural noun, especially a *plurale tantum* noun, is sometimes followed by a singular verb form.

The accusative (in the singular undifferentiated from the nominative in all nominal declensions), is preceded by the preposition *z*- when it denotes a definite object. This rule applies even to the pronouns. The usage of the oblique cases corresponds roughly with their counterparts in other Indo-European languages. There are six prepositions: *ənd*, *əst*, *z*-, *i* (*y*- before vowels), *c'*- and *aṙ*. The meaning of the prepositions varies greatly with the cases with which they are used; thus *i* used with the accusative means 'into', with the locative 'in', but with the ablative 'from, out of'.

Armenian has not one, but three definite articles. These take the form of indeclinable postposed clitics -*s*, -*d* and -*n* with deixis corresponding to speaker, addressee and subject respectively.

The aorist and present subjunctive are used in wishes and a variety of subordinate sentences; they are also used to express the future (hence my designation of them as subjunctive/future above). Armenian makes wide use of subordinate clauses, introduced most usually by *et'e* or *zi*, to express nominal, adjectival and adverbial clauses.

An unexplained syntactic peculiarity of Armenian concerns the past participle, which regularly expresses its logical subject by the genitive.

3.1 Possible morphological innovations made by Greek and Armenian: introduction

As stated above inflectional morphs are rarely borrowed from one language to another. Common morphological innovations are therefore among the most certain signs of close linguistic kinship. In this chapter I shall examine some of the morphological developments made by Greek and Armenian which have been taken to represent common innovations.[6] In each case I shall attempt to establish the meaning and usage of the relevant morphs in the synchronies of the two languages and then elucidate the most likely courses of development. The reconstructed development may then be compared to the development of cognate or parallel forms in other Indo-European languages. It should then be possible to assess whether the agreement is a genuine innovation shared by the two languages alone; whether it is a chance result of independent innovation of the same feature; or whether the form represents an archaism which has been lost by chance from other languages, or retained by the two languages in preference to an innovatory feature found elsewhere.

3.2 Greek and Armenian locatives: introduction

Meillet (1936:73) compared the Armenian locative singular marker -*oǰ* with the Homeric Greek locative formations in -*οθι*.[7] The direct comparison of the two forms is only possible if one reconstructs a form *-*od^hi*,[8] with the corollary that Armenian extended the form with a particle which was subsequently lost with the final syllables. By this theory, Armenian *ǰ* derives from a pre-vocalic alternant *-*od^hy*-; this development is comparable to the derivation of *mêǰ* 'middle' from **med^hyo*-.[9] A locative marker *-*od^hi* may be related to forms in other Indo-European languages which are used as adverbial markers of place or time and are derived from morphs with the element *-*d^h*-: for example, the Old Church Slavonic interrogative adverb *kŭde* (Russian *gde*) 'where?'.[10] It will here be argued that the locative forms in -*oǰ* are more easily seen as a recent extension of a morph -*ǰ*, which itself does not derive from a *-*d^h*- locative marker.

3.2.1 -oǰ in Armenian

The morph -oǰ occupies an anomalous place in the Classical Armenian nominal and pronominal declensions. In the nominal system it is used as the locative singular of one relatively small declension class, the nouns with nominative singular in -i; as the genitive-dative-locative singular of one irregular noun, *kin* 'woman' (see **4.31** for further discussion of this word); and as the genitive-dative-locative of one irregular pronoun and pronominal adjective *mi* 'one'. There are also sporadic instances of the form used to mark locatives of adjectives and o-stem nouns.[11]

3.2.1.1 Nouns with nominative singular in -i

The Armenian nouns with nominative singular in -i follow two distinct declensions; some have an instrumental singular in -eaw (termed by Jensen 1959:52 the ea-class), and others have an instrumental singular -wov (the wo-class). The modern standard grammars of Classical Armenian[12] make a distinction between the occurrence of -oǰ in the two classes, giving the following paradigm types:[13]

	wo-	ea-
SINGULAR		
Nom., Acc.	hogi	tełi
Loc.	hogi	tełwoǰ
Gen., Dat.	hogwoy	tełwoy
Abl.	hogwoy	tełwoy/tełwoǰê
Instr.	hogwov	tełeaw
PLURAL		
Nom.	hogik'	tełik'
Acc., Loc.	hogis	tełis
Gen., Dat., Abl.	hogwoc'	tełeac'
Instr.	hogwovk'	tełeawk'

The paradigm of *hogi* indeed matches the usage in the Bible translation, but it is not representative of all nouns in the wo-declension:[14] *jori* 'mule' clearly belongs to the wo-class (*jorwovk'* 1 *Chron.* 12:40, *Ezek.* 27:14; *jorwoc'* 4 *Kings* 5:17, *Zech.* 14:15), yet the loc. sing. form *jorwoǰ* is found four times in the Bible (*i jorwoǰ* 2 *Kings* 13:29, 3 *Kings* 1:33, 38, 44 translating Greek ἐπὶ τὴν ἡμίονον); *ordi* 'son' is also of the wo-class yet the phrase *y-ordwoǰ* 'in the son' occurs in the fifth century author Eznik (4.1, section 358 of Mariès and Mercier's edition 1959:515). Therefore Meillet's theory that the forms in -woǰ are limited to the ea-class seems not to be right; the locative in -woǰ is found for both classes.

The reason why there are not more examples of -woǰ forms for the wo-class is not difficult to find. The Armenian locative is always used after prepositions, most frequently after *i*.[15] The preposition *i* means either 'into' or 'in' or 'from', depending on whether it is construed with the accusative, locative or ablative respectively. A distinct locative form is therefore most necessary for nouns denoting a position in space or time (the same semantic restriction affects the masculine nouns which take the special locative marker -*ú* in Russian (Dumbreck and Forbes 1964:64)). The *wo*-declension class is very small; the most frequently occurring nouns of this type are *hogi* (also *ogi*) 'spirit, soul', *ordi* 'son', *jori* 'mule', and the adjectives and nouns which end in -*ac'i* derived from place names, such as *Kołbac'i* 'from/of Kołb'. For these nouns a distinct locative form is rarely necessary. This stands in contrast to the most frequently used nouns of the *ea*-class: *tełi* 'place', *ekełec'i* 'church', *aygi* 'vineyard', and *kłzi* 'island', for which a distinction between locative and accusative is clearly desirable.

In support of this theory it may be noted that some nouns of the *ea*-declension never use the -*oj* form. The word for 'enemy' *t'šnami* (genitive plural *t'šnameac'* etc.) is listed over four hundred times in the Armenian Bible concordance (Astowacatowrean 1895) but the locative form *t'šnamwoj* and the ablative *t'šnamwojê* never occur.[16] A further indication that the -*oj* marker may have earlier been an optional reinforcement of the locative meaning is provided by a passage in Eznik (2.6, Mariès and Mercier 1959:468, section 176):

k'anzi barin ew č'ar i miowm tełi ankanel oč' mart'ein.

The meaning of this sentence, which occurs in a passage which attempts to refute the Zurvanite heresy that the evil god and the good god could have been conceived in the same womb, should be something along the lines of 'for the Good and the Bad are not able to fall [or 'coincide'] in one place.' However the Armenian phrase *i miowm tełi* has caused problems for translators, because *i miowm* is in the locative, and *tełi* is normally interpreted to be nominative or accusative.[17] The text is normally therefore read as *i miowm tełwoj ankanel* (with *tełwoj* in the locative), or *tełi* is omitted altogether. However, our previous discussion points a way out of the textual difficulty; it is possible that the phrase *i miowm tełi* was already sufficiently strongly marked as locative to dispense with the optional additional locative marker -*oj*. The phrase *i miowm tełi* 'in a single place' in this passage would therefore be a unique archaism, which has not survived elsewhere due to the pervasive influence of the normal locative *i tełwoj*.

An interesting Armenian parallel to the use of -*oj* in these nominal classes is found in the use of the morphs -*i*, -*ean* and -*owm* in nouns and adjectives of the *o*-declension. The paradigm of the singular of the *o*-declension noun *mard* 'man' is as follows:

Nom.-Acc.-Loc.	*mard*
Gen.-Dat.-Abl.	*mardoy*
Instr.	*mardov*

The declension is distinguished from all other declension classes by the unique case syncretism in the singular. All other classes show a different case syncretism in the singular, which is exemplified by the declension of the *a*-stem *azg* 'people':

Nom.-Acc.	*azg*
Gen.-Dat.-Loc.	*azgi*
Abl.	*azgê*
Instr.	*azgaw*

In this declension pattern the three cases which have local significance when in combination with the preposition *i*, namely the ablative, locative and accusative, are kept distinct, whereas in the singular of the *o*-declension accusative and locative are syncretised.

For a number of *o*-stem nouns a distinct locative form is found, marked by the morph -*i*. Thus *gišer* 'evening' has a genitive *gišeroy* (e.g. *Mark* 6:48 etc.), but a locative *gišeri* is very frequently used (e.g. *Mark* 13:35 etc.).[18] This marker is not fully incorporated into the *o*-stem declension, but only used for those nouns which have meanings, or are used in contexts, that require a distinct form for the locative. The position is thus analogous to the use of the marker -*oǰ*. The morph -*i* which marks the locative seems to have been transferred from the *i*- and *a*-declensions where it is used as a marker of the genitive, dative and locative (cf. the declension of *azg* above).

For one *o*-stem noun, *amis* 'month', a distinct locative *amsean* is regularly found in the Bible translation.[19] The -*ean* morph serves as a marker of genitive-dative-locative singular in some other declensions; for example, *ankiwn* 'corner' gen.-dat.-loc. *ankean*; *hangowst* 'rest' gen.-dat.-loc. *hangstean* etc. (see further Jensen 1959:57f. and 59f.).

For adjectives of the *o*-stem declension a locative singular -*owm* is used (with corresponding ablative -*mê*). The history of this morph is interesting: -*owm* is originally a dative-locative singular marker in the declension of pronouns,[20] and derives from Proto-Indo-European dative and locative forms incorporating the element *-(o)-sm-*.[21] By the classical period -*owm* has spread to the class of *o*-stem adjectives, but its usage has been restricted from a dative-locative marker to a locative marker only.[22] In post-fifth-century literature the morph spread to mark substantives, and in Modern Eastern Armenian it is the regular locative formant.[23]

Thus we have seen three separate instances of the same process. A desire to create distinct ablative, accusative and locative forms in the singular of the *o*-stem declension, the only declension lacking such a distinction, has led to the borrowing from other declensions of morphs which mark the locative along with other case functions. These borrowed morphs have been restricted in use to markers of the locative alone. It seems very likely that the morph -*oǰ* has a similar history and has spread to nouns with a nominative in -*i* from the genitive-dative-locative forms *knoǰ* (from *kin* 'woman') and *mioǰ* (from *mi* 'one'),[24] with a corresponding restriction to the locative. This would explain the skewed distribution of the marker over the nouns in this class. If *-oǰ* were original to the declension then it would be found with all members of the class. But, as it is, the limitation of its use to some nouns exactly parallels the spread of the borrowed marker *-i* in the *o*-declension. The marker *-i* was probably avoided as a locative marker in the *ea*- and *wo*-classes in order to avoid the sequence **-*ii* (Godel 1975:30).

The origin of the marker *-oǰ* in *knoǰ* and *mioǰ* is uncertain, but it may be connected with the marker *-ǰ* which is found in the genitive-dative(-locative) *gełǰ* from the anomalous noun *gewł* 'village'. The declension of *mi* 'one' shows a number of competing case endings, and it is perhaps worth devoting some space to the distinction between the endings, since they have recently received a new explanation.

3.2.1.2 *mioǰ*

The Armenian cardinal number and pronoun *mi* 'one', which is also used as an indefinite article 'a' (see **4.61** for its etymology) is found with the following declined forms:

mi	nominative, accusative
mioy	genitive, dative, ablative
miowm	dative, locative
mioǰ	genitive, dative, locative
mioǰē	ablative
miov	instrumental

For the oblique cases there are therefore two sets of forms. Kortlandt (1984:100) has proposed that the two sets of endings represented a masculine and feminine declension,[25] and this theory has received support from Weitenberg (1984 and 1989:68f.). Classical Armenian has no gender distinctions, but these scholars have seen the declension of *mi* as preserving traces of an earlier distinction. Weitenberg examined the occurrences of *mioy/miowm* and *mioǰ* in Classical texts, working principally with the *Patmowt'iwn Hayoc'* of Agat'angełos. Starting from the hypothesis that a noun had earlier been feminine if it co-occurred with the form *mioǰ*, he deduced, from the usage in Agat'angełos, that *a*-, *i*- and *n*-stems and the noun *ayr* 'man' had been of feminine gender in an earlier stage of Armenian.[26] The fact that this method finds *ayr* 'man' to have earlier been feminine does not worry Weitenberg, who sets up a system of rules to account for the changes in nominal gender from Proto-Indo-European to Proto-Armenian (1984:210–214).

However, the hypothesis that gender distinctions, although lost everywhere else in Classical Armenian, are still reflected in the oblique cases of a single pronoun, and further that the co-occurrence of nouns with that pronoun matches their earlier gender, is extremely unlikely. Moreover, Weitenberg notes earlier in his article the fact that 'the masculine forms of *mi* [i.e. *mioy* and *miowm*] precede the noun, feminine forms [i.e. *mioj*] follow it' (1984:199). He denies however that this is anything other than an interesting point of historical syntax: 'no relation can be found between the meaning "one" or "a" and the distribution or place of the masculine and feminine forms' (1984:200).

This last statement is based primarily on the usage of Agat'angełos, but the meaning of passages in this author often cannot be precisely verified and the number of examples of usage in the text is small.[27] The Bible translation provides more material for which the meaning can be more precisely ascertained. From the usage in the Bible, chiefly the Gospels, I have formulated the following rules relating the position and meaning of *mi*:[28]

1. *mi* when preceding the noun with which it agrees means 'one', and translates Greek εἷς and μόνος, whether the Greek word precedes or follows its noun. Thus:

Luke 15:7   *vasn mioy meławori*
            ἐπὶ ἑνὶ ἁμαρτωλῷ
            'over one sinner',

Luke 17:34 *ełic'in erkow i mi mahičs*
            ἔσονται δύο ἐπὶ κλίνης μιᾶς
            'there shall be two in one bed',

John 5:44   *i mioyn Astowacoy*
            παρὰ τοῦ μόνου θεοῦ
            'from God alone'.

2. *mi* when following the noun is used when introducing someone or something not previously mentioned (and can be translated in English by 'a' or 'a certain'); it is often used when there is no Greek equivalent.[29] Thus, for example,

Mark 14:3   *ekn kin mi*
            ἦλθεν γυνή
            'there came a woman'.

This is the most common usage of postposed *mi* in the Gospels. Sometimes *mi* following the noun translates Greek εἷς following a noun, when εἷς is itself used as an indefinite article (following Semitic usage);[30]

Matt. 21:19 *ew teseal t'zeni mi*
             καὶ ἰδὼν συκῆν μίαν
             'and when he saw a fig tree'.

3. In the following cases *mi* follows the noun and can be translated as 'one':

(a) Where the word order directly follows the Greek:

Matt. 19:5   *ew ełic'in erkok'ean i marmin mi*
καὶ ἔσονται οἱ δύο εἰς σάρκα μίαν
'and the two shall be one flesh'.

The phrase is a quotation from *Genesis* 2:24 where the Greek word order exactly follows the Hebrew word order.

(b)   Where quantities of money or measurement are referred to, whether εἰς appears in the Greek text or not:

Luke 15:8   *et'e korowsanic'ê dram mi*
ἐὰν ἀπολέσῃ δραχμὴν μίαν
'if she lose one drachma',

Mark 12:15   *berêk' inj dahekan mi*
φέρετέ μοι δηνάριον
'bring me a denarius',

Prov. 17:4   *ew oč' dang mi*
οὐδὲ ὀβολός (17:6 in the Greek text)
'not an obol'.

This appears to be an Armenian idiom.

(c)   In one case in the Gospels *mi* does not follow the expected order and cannot be explained by corollaries (a) and (b).

Mark 14:37   *oč' karac'er žam mi art'own kal*
οὐκ ἴσχυσας μίαν ὥραν γρηγορῆσαι;
'couldest not thou watch one hour?'

However, at *Matthew* 26:40 the same phrase is translated *mi žam* in Armenian.

Therefore the distinction between preceding and following *mi* can be explained in terms of the above rules. There is no need to follow the Kortlandt-Weitenberg hypothesis of a prehistoric difference between masculine and feminine. In the Bible translation and Eznik *mioj* always follows the noun and is never found preceding it.[31] The forms *mioy* and *miowm* are mostly found preceding the noun although there are examples of them following the noun; for example:

ar̄n mioy 'a man' 2 *Kings* 17:18, *Acts* 4:9, P‘awstos Bowzand 4.14, Koriwn
    1.15;
nkanaki mioy 'a piece of bread' 1 *Kings* 2:36, P‘awstos Bowzand 5.24;
ap'oy mioy 'a handful' *Ezek.* 13:19;
awowr mioy 'a day' *Luke* 2:44;
k'ałak'i mioy 'a city' *Luke* 9:10;
ar̄n miowm 'a man' *Job* 32:14, 2 *Cor.* 11:2.

In the majority of these cases *mi* is used as an indefinite article (but the passage at 2 *Cor.* 11:2 translates Greek ἑνὶ ἀνδρί). These forms may represent later scribal 'corrections' of earlier *mioj* forms made after the distinction between preceding and following forms had been lost.[32]

The form *mioj* is also found when the word is used pronominally and not modifying a noun, e.g. *mi ar̄ mioj* 'one by one' at 1 *Macc.* 5:34 (no equivalent in the Greek text), and *i mioj-n* 'in the one' in Eznik (4.1, section 358 of Mariès & Mercier's edition 1959:514).

The distinction between pre- and post-posed *mi* was already being eroded in the Bible translation. As we have seen, in some circumstances the translators seem to have violated native usage in order to follow the word order of the original.

3.2.2 Greek forms in -οθι

In Homeric Greek the locative marker -οθι exists alongside a number of Greek quasi-adverbial formants (as -θεν and -θα).[33] It is found attached to both nouns and adjectives. The thematic form -οθι has become productive (hence κηρόθι; athematic forms are also found as θύρηθι,[34] ἐκεῖθι etc.). The forms in -οθι seem to have been favoured as metrically convenient alternatives to locative forms in -ου or -οι.[35]

The majority of the examples of -οθι in Homer are used as true locatives. However the formula Ἰλιόθι πρό (four times in Homer) and the phrase οὐρανόθι πρό (at *Iliad* 2.3) are the only cases where -θι appears not to mark a locative but a genitive-ablative. For the phrase Ἰλιόθι πρό refers not to events which have taken place 'within Troy towards the front' (πρό) but to what happens on the plain 'in front of Troy'. However this usage is not original, but represents a later false archaism replacing an earlier locution of the type *Ἰλιόο πρό.[36] Thus there is no evidence in Greek for an original usage of -οθι for any case other than a locative.

3.2.3 Greek and Armenian locatives: conclusion

The preceding discussion has shown how the direct comparison of the Armenian locative form *tełwoj* with the Greek locative formations in -οθι is unlikely to be correct, and there is no need to see a common innovation made by the two languages. The Armenian locative marker -*oj* has arisen from a late extension of a morph -*oj* and a restriction in its function from genitive-dative-locative to locative only. The Greek morph had an original restriction to a locative function. The equation of the function of the two morphs is thus not correct. The formal correspondence is of itself not strong enough to support an equation because the Armenian form has to be taken from an extended form *-$d^h y$- for which there is no comparative evidence.

Alternative theories for the origins of the Armenian morph -*oj*, along the lines of those suggested by Pisani and Kortlandt,[37] or Meillet in his earlier work,[38] seem preferable to a connection directly with the Greek -οθι forms.

These theories explain the irregular forms *mioj̑*, *knoj̑* and *geƚj̑* as archaisms, rather than as unmotivated extensions of the locative case marker of a small declension class to the genitive-dative-locative.[39]

3.3 Instrumental singular and plural: introduction

A commonly cited morphological agreement shared by Greek and Armenian alone is the use of the reflexes of a morph **-bʰi* as the marker of the athematic instrumental singular.[40] Greek and Armenian also show the reflex of a **-bʰ-* morph in the thematic declension (as Greek ζυγόφι(ν) which stands for the genitive or dative singular or plural of ζυγόν 'yoke' in Homer, Armenian *mardov* instrumental singular of *mard* 'human'); this is an innovation, but it has also taken place in the ancestor of Old Irish.[41] Morphs formed with the reflex of **-bʰ-* are used to mark the instrumental and dative-ablative case in the plural and dual in Indo-Iranian, Latin and Osco-Umbrian, and Celtic (see Meillet 1937:298f., and K. H. Schmidt 1963). Particularly relevant to our discussion is the instrumental plural marker **-bʰis* in Indo-Iranian, and the Old Irish dative plural morph -(*i*)*b* which could derive from **-bʰi* or **-bʰis*.[42] Baltic, Slavonic and Germanic forms are found corresponding to these **-bʰ-* morphs, but with **-m-* in place of **-bʰ-*. In Baltic and Slavic the instrumental singular is also marked by **-mi*, and some scholars have related this to a Greek-Armenian use of **-bʰi* in the singular.[43]

3.3.1 -φι in Greek

The ending φι(ν) is found almost exclusively in Mycenaean and Homeric Greek.[44] The usage of the ending is sharply differentiated in these two sources, and scholars have disputed which of them preserves a more archaic usage. In Homer -φι is a 'metrically convenient poetic suffix for the instrumental, ablative and locative (and occasionally dative and genitive) singular and plural' (Risch 1974:361). But in Mycenaean the meaning appears to be restricted to instrumental and locative (or perhaps ablative) plural function.[45] The two areas of usage which are relevant to the relationship with the Armenian instrumental are the use of -φι in the singular and in the thematic declension.

In Mycenaean Greek the ending -*pi* is very frequent; Lejeune (1956b:190) counted 173 examples of the form in the Mycenaean corpus.[46] Despite this wealth of material the interpretation of the meaning and spread of the formation is still not certain.

The nature of the Mycenaean documents means that it is not always possible to tell whether a given form is singular or plural. Lejeune noticed (1956b:206) that in the *Ta* series of tablets there is an alternation between forms with -*pi* and forms with -*e* (e.g. *a-di-ri-ja-te/a-di-ri-ja-pi, e-ka-ma-te/ e-ka-ma-pi, po-ni-ke/po-ni-ki-pi*) and he suggested that this might represent an alternation between singular and plural. These words stand in parallel contexts in texts describing decorated furniture, and it is difficult to interpret the alternation between -*e* and -*pi* as representing anything other than a difference between singular and plural. But in a few contexts forms in -*pi* can be translated by a singular noun: Lejeune interpreted *e-ru-ta-ra-pi* (at KN *Ld* 573 etc.) to mean 'with red', and the Mycenaean man's name *wi-pi-no-o* (KN *V* 958) appears to contain an earlier form of Homeric ἶφι 'with strength'. However, some scholars have argued that these forms do not necessarily represent singulars: *e-ru-ta-ra-pi* could mean 'with red (spots, patterns)' (Ventris and Chadwick 1973:546), and the use of the plural ἶφι to mean 'strength' can be paralleled by the use of the Latin cognate *vis* 'power, force' which in the plural form *vires* denotes bodily or mental strength.[47] The inscriptional use of -φι likewise offers no form which must be read as singular. Boeotian ἐπιπατρόφιον 'patronymic' could just as well be derived from a form meaning 'with his fathers' as 'with his father' (Morpurgo Davies 1970:51).

The Homeric usage of -φι has been the subject of a number of studies, the most recent of which was made by Nieto Hernández (1987). Nieto Hernández lists all the occurrences of forms with -φι in Homer (1987:283–285), and shows that in the *Iliad* the ending is more frequent than in the *Odyssey*, and that its use shows more flexibility. These findings suggest that the use of -φι in the *Iliad* may continue archaic features, one of which may be its use as singular or plural. And indeed Shipp (1961:29–39) has argued that the predominant use of the ending in Mycenaean with reference to the plural is an innovation whereas Homeric Greek preserves an archaic use 'where the question of number is irrelevant', and he is followed by other scholars.[48] This theory is certainly plausible; the integration of quasi-adverbial suffixes into the declension system as plural case markers is documented in other languages,[49] and the interpretation of *e-ru-ta-ra-pi, wi-pi-* and ἐπιπατρόφιον as continuing singular formations is more straightforward than the interpretation of them as plural.

However, it is also possible to account for the Homeric use of -φι as a later development than the Mycenaean. The extension to the singular may have been motivated by the confusion of *plurale tantum* and singular nouns; if Chadwick and Ruijgh are right to see ἶφι as an original plural form, this would provide a clear route for the transfer of the ending to forms such as βίηφι 'with force' (singular) from βίη 'force' on the analogy of ἶφι 'with strength' (plural, but with apparently singular meaning) to nominative ἴς 'force' (singular).[50]

Therefore a case can be made for the original Greek use of -φι to be either indifferent to number or to be restricted to the plural. The evidence does not allow a decisive conclusion for either theory.

The extension of -φι to thematic stems is also poorly attested in Mycenaean. The only examples of -οφι come from Knossos: *e-re-pa-te-jo-pi* occurs twice on one tablet (KN *Se* 891) and may also be found in the reading *e-]re-pa-te-jo-pi* on a fragment (KN *X* 7814).[51] These tablets stand against widespread evidence from Pylos showing a writing -*o* (?/-*ois*/) for the thematic instrumental plural.[52] The form *e-re-pa-te-jo-pi* may represent a development peculiar to Knossos or the desire to mark out the form graphically as instrumental.[53]

This suggests that by the time of the destruction of the Mycenaean palaces Greek had not yet fully made the innovatory extension of the morph -φι to the thematic declension. The Homeric evidence also suggests that the ending -οφι is a late creation in Greek. The ending -φι is, as we saw above, less frequent in the *Odyssey* than the *Iliad*, and where its usage is not modelled on the *Iliad*, the form -οφι is used (for example κοτυληδονόφιν 'with suckers' < κοτυληδών at *Odyssey* 5.433). Nieto Hernández (1987:290) therefore proposes that -οφι does not represent an extension of the morph to the thematic declension which has come about in -*o* and *ā*-stem adjectives, as Mycenaean *e-re-pa-te-jo-pi* would seem to suggest, but rather that the form derives from a 'liaison vowel' -*o*- inserted between stem and ending (compare the extended Homeric adjectival suffix -οεις beside inherited -εις < *-*ents*). Nieto Hernández thinks that the insertion of the 'liaison vowel' also arose in the spoken language, and is not merely the artificial extension of a moribund form by the oral tradition, but in view of the scanty epigraphical evidence this seems uncertain.[54]

In conclusion, while the Greek evidence for the original number reference of the ending *-bʰi* is unclear, it seems safe to say that the transfer of the ending to the thematic declension took place recently in the history of the language.

3.3.2 The Armenian instrumental

The Armenian instrumental marker presents a textbook example of 'morphophonemic alternation'. The morphs in the different paradigms are as follows:

a-stems	-*aw*
i-stems	-*iw*
u-stems	-*ow*
o-stems	-*ov*
n-, *r*-, *l*-stems	-*b*.

For all of these declensions the plural morph is regularly the same as the singular with the addition of final -*k'*, which also serves to mark the nominative plural of all nouns. Thus -*awk'* is the instrumental plural of the *a*-stems, -*iwk'* is the instrumental plural of *i*-stems, etc.

The Armenian instrumental case is clearly derived from a Proto-Indo-European $*-b^h-$ morph. The reconstruction of the earliest form of the Armenian instrumental as $*-b^hi$ rests on a single piece of evidence, the instrumental of the inanimate indefinite pronoun: *iwik'*. In this word the vowel following $*-b^h-$ has been preserved because it was followed by $*-k^we$ at the time of the loss of final syllables.

The use of a morph deriving from a $*-b^h-$ form to mark the instrumental singular may reflect an original situation where $*-b^h-$ was used for both the singular and plural instrumental case, or it could possibly be an independent development within Armenian. There are two pieces of evidence which suggest that an earlier stage of the language the case-forms which in Classical Armenian denote the instrumental singular (-*b*, etc.) were used for the instrumental plural.

Firstly, when nouns in the instrumental plural are found with declined modifying adjectives the adjective sometimes takes the instrumental singular form, not the instrumental plural. Thus at *Mark* 5:42 the Armenian translation has *zarmac'an mecaw zarmanaleawk'* 'they were astonished with great astonishment' using the singular *mecaw* of the adjective rather than the plural *mecawk'*.[55]

Secondly, Meillet noted (*MSL* 11 (1900) p. 381, reprinted in 1962:51 n. 1) a passage of the Bible translation (2 *Cor.* 10:12) where a noun takes the instrumental singular form rather than the expected instrumental plural when the plurality is clear from the context: *ayl anjamb yanjins zanjins č'ap'en ew i kšřel anjamb yanjins oč' ařnown i mit* 'but they measuring themselves by themselves among themselves, and comparing themselves among themselves, are not wise' (Greek ἀλλὰ αὐτοὶ ἐν ἑαυτοῖς ἑαυτοὺς μετροῦντες καὶ συγκρίνοντες ἑαυτοὺς ἑαυτοῖς οὐ συνιᾶσιν).

If -*b* and its allomorphs did in fact earlier serve to mark the instrumental plural, as is suggested by this evidence, the Classical Armenian system of -*b* etc. to mark the instrumental singular, and -*bk'* etc. to mark the instrumental plural can be explained in two ways. By one possible theory the marker $*-b^h-$ originally served to mark both the singular and the plural, and the plural later received secondary marking with -*k'*. By this theory the form *mardov*, instrumental singular of *mard* 'man', originally served to mark both instrumental plural and singular, but the instrumental plural *mardovk'* represents a later distinction. An alternative explanation is that $*-b^h-$ was originally limited to denoting the instrumental plural, but with the loss of a (hypothetical) separate instrumental singular marker the old instrumental plural form was re-used as instrumental singular, and the plural form was re-marked. By this theory the form *mardov*, instrumental singular of *mard* 'man', may originally have been restricted to the instrumental plural; it is remarked as plural by the addition of -*k'* and the earlier form is then free to be used as an instrumental singular.

Pedersen (1905:211) presented an argument in support of the theory of a late transfer of the morph from the instrumental plural to the singular. He maintained that in nouns which show a different singular and plural stem the instrumental singular is coincident in form with the plural stem, rather than the singular stem. However, this is not borne out by the facts. For example, the instrumental singular *kanamb* of *kin* 'woman', which Pedersen cited in support of his theory, does not occur in the Bible translation, which shows *knaw* as the instrumental singular and *kanambk'* as the instrumental plural.[56]

The use of the marker -*k'* in the instrumental plural should be viewed in conjunction with other developments of the nominal paradigm. With the loss of final syllables many of the inherited case-marking morphs have disappeared. In Classical Armenian the nominative plural in several declensions differs only from the nominative singular by the addition of final -*k'* (see above). Thus *mard* 'man' has a plural form *mardk'*;[57] in this declension the difference between plural and singular must have been marked secondarily, because it is impossible to derive both *mard* from *$mr̥tos$ and *mardk'* from *$mr̥tōs$. Therefore the morph -*k'*, whatever its origin,[58] has acquired the status of an agglutinative particle marking plurality.

The history of the nominative singular and plural might help explain the history of the instrumental singular and plural. In the nominative the difference between plural and singular forms, which might have fallen together phonetically, has been re-marked with -*k'*, and it is tempting to assume that similarly in the instrumental a form which originally served for both plural and singular has been marked as plural with -*k'*.

Thus the Armenian morphs -*w*/-*v*/-*b* seem likely to reflect an inherited formation used for both singular and plural. The Armenian forms probably derive from an original formation *-b^hi or possibly *-b^his.

3.3.3 The instrumental case: conclusion

The origin and spread of the instrumental cases in *-b^hi- in Greek and Armenian can be explained in three different ways. By the first theory the two languages have made independent extensions of an original instrumental plural marker to the singular: this theory would interpret the small number of forms marked with -*pi* in Mycenaean Greek which appear to be singular as plurals, or possibly as the first stages of the spread of the suffix to the singular; the Homeric use of -*φι* would thereby have arisen from artificial extension and misunderstanding of the ending. The comparative evidence in support of this theory rests on the plural usage of other *-b^hi- and *-b^h- forms in Indo-Iranian, Celtic and Italic nominal declensions.

The second possible explanation conversely interprets the Homeric usage to be the oldest. The case-forms originate, by this theory, from a quasi-adverbial usage, which was later incorporated into the case-system, originally used without reference to number; later developments led to the creation of new markers for the oblique cases of the singular, and a tendency to restrict the $*-b^h$- to plural usage. The few examples of -pi with singular reference in Mycenaean are explained by this theory as archaisms. The scarcity of Mycenaean examples with singular reference may be explained either by the fact that -pi has been restricted to the plural in Mycenaean or by the nature of the content of the Mycenaean tablets: furniture or chariots in general are ornamented or fitted with more than *one* decoration or piece of equipment. Comparative evidence in support of this theory comes from the Baltic and Slavonic use of the $*-mi$- case forms (which may be related to the $*-b^hi$-forms phonetically, and are certainly functionally parallel) in both the singular and plural. By this theory the Greek and Armenian usage of the case marker in the singular represents an archaism considered against, for example, Indo-Iranian, which has restricted the form to the plural. Armenian shares with Indo-Iranian the restriction of function to exclusively instrumental usage, whereas Greek retains the wider spread of instrumental, locative and dative functions.

The third possible theory interprets the Greek and Armenian material as evidence that the two languages jointly extended an original instrumental plural case marker $*-b^hi(s)$ (preserved in Indo-Iranian) to the singular; and thus interprets the forms as evidence of a common innovation. This theory is not falsifiable from the available evidence, but to me it seems a less attractive explanation than either of the other two theories. The problem with it arises from the fact that it is difficult to see why the extension should have taken place. The theory of independent extensions of the case marker to the singular in Homeric Greek and Armenian sketched out above is explainable in terms of the developments of each language: in Homer the bards extended an existing form to singular use for metrical convenience and by false analysis of earlier moribund forms; in Armenian phonetic change led to the erosion of an earlier distinct instrumental case in the singular and a plural form was employed to retain the distinct case usage. But neither of these explanations will suffice for the pre-historical stage of the two languages, before large scale phonetic change had taken place and while the original functions of the case were still understood, and while, presumably, there were already distinct singular instrumental forms.

The innovation of a morph $*-ob^hi$- is also unlikely to represent a shared development of two languages. The innovation had not yet taken place in Mycenaean texts from Pylos and consequently should probably not be reconstructed for 'common' Greek. The extension of the $*-b^hi$ case marker to the thematic declension has also taken place separately in Celtic and Indo-Iranian.

The two languages may agree on having inherited a form $*-b^hi$ rather than $*-b^his$, but the treatment of final $*-s$ in Armenian is not known with certainty[59] and the Armenian forms could equally as well have derived from $*-b^his$ as from $*-b^hi$. It is also possible that the form $*-b^hi$ was inherited into Celtic (see **3.3**), and so Greek and Armenian, if they did in fact both inherit a form *-$b^h i$, may have only made the same choice from a set of options. The agreement between the two languages is not established with enough certainty to make this isogloss significant.

3.4 The suffix *-olā-

Meillet (1936:129) and Schwyzer (1946) saw a close link between formations of the type seen in Greek μαινόλης 'raving' and the Armenian quasi-participles in -oł. The Greek and Armenian forms have received full treatments by Schwyzer (1946:49–57) and de Lamberterie (1982a:37–45) respectively, so I shall do no more than present a summary of their findings here.[60]

In Greek the suffix -όλης is not common. It is only found attached to seven verbal stems; three of these forms occur only in Hesychius and one is only attested as a proper name.[61] The adjective μαινόλης 'raving' sets the pattern for all forms of this type: the suffix is added directly to the present thematic stem. In all but one of the examples (οἰφόλης, Hesychius) the present stem is characterised by the *-yo- suffix. There are no examples of the attachment of -όλης to athematic forms.[62] The suffix appears to be used to signify a characteristic tendency or inclination to perform the action denoted by the related verb.

In Armenian the suffix -oł declines as an a-stem. It is not productive in the Classical period, but in later Armenian it becomes a regular present participle formant. The suffix is found attached to present and aorist stems in the Bible translation.[63] The use of the suffix with aorist stems may be a secondary development following a tendency to make the aorist the base of all derived forms in Armenian (Meillet JA (1903) II p. 502 f., reprinted in 1977:316 f., and de Lamberterie 1982a:40 n. 57). The meaning of the form in the Armenian Gospels is 'un adjectif qui désigne les aptitudes d'une personne ou ses mauvais penchants' (de Lamberterie 1982a:40).

The two forms are clearly comparable with each other, yet do they represent an archaism or an innovation? Suffixes comprising a reflex of *-l- are widespread Indo-European formants of participles and quasi-participles.[64] Particularly relevant here is the addition of a suffix which may derive from *-olo/ā- or *-elo/ā- to present tense formations in Latin to form verbal adjectives denoting a habitual performance of the verbal action, such as bibulus, -a, -um, 'fond of drinking'; credulus, -a, um 'prone to believe'.[65] Similar formations are also found in Tocharian, such as akalşälle (Toch. B) 'student, pupil',[66] and Germanic.[67]

The Greek and Armenian formations only differ from other Indo-European forms by their declension as *ā-stems. This may be a secondary development within the two languages.[68] The Greek forms occur beside suffixes in -oλις (which function as feminines to the -όλης forms). In

Armenian it is possible that the *a*-stem declension has arisen from a generalisation of feminine forms from an original adjective paradigm with **o*-stem masculine and **ā*-stem feminine declension. Armenian adjectives which derive from Proto-Indo-European **-o-/-ā-* adjectives generally decline as *o*-stems (Godel 1975:93), but a close parallel to the *a*-stem inflection of an adjective of this type is given by the declension of the verbal suffix *-ič'*, which forms agent nouns and is also used in the Armenian Bible translation to render Greek present participles.[69] It also declines as an *a*-stem although it derives from an Indo-European suffix **-ik-yo-/-yā-*.[70] Another influence which may be relevant here is the agent nouns which may derive from formations in **-t(e)l-*, such as *cnawł* 'parent', which is declined as an *a*-stem in Classical Armenian.[71]

In conclusion this isogloss seems to reflect the survival of an Indo-European verbal adjective suffix in the two languages; the agreement in the declension class of the forms in the two languages may be the result of separate innovation.[72]

3.5 Ionic iteratives and the Armenian aorists in -*c'*-: introduction

The reflexes of the Proto-Indo-European verbal suffix **-sk'*- have different functions in the daughter languages. In Latin, Greek, Indo-Iranian and Tocharian the reflex of **-sk'*- is used to characterise the present stem of some verbs.[73] In several languages it is also found with other usages. In Latin it is also used to mark inchoatives; in Hittite it forms duratives in both present and preterite; and in Tocharian it forms causatives.[74] A number of scholars have explained these forms from an original iterative or durative function.[75]

The morphological behaviour of the suffix in the parent language can be demonstrated by the form **pr̥k'-sk'é/ó-* which is reconstructed from the correspondence of Latin *posco*, Sanskrit *pr̥cchāti*, Armenian *harc'anem*, etc. (cf. Pokorny *IEW* 821). The pattern of zero grade of the root and thematic inflection of the suffix shown by **pr̥k'-sk'é/ó-* can be assumed to be general for **-sk'*- formations in the parent language.[76]

The 'Ionic iterative' formations found in Homer and Herodotus show the Greek reflex of **-sk'*-, (or an extended form **-esk'*-, see further below), used with iterative force, but restricted in reference to past time. The Armenian aorist formants -*c'*-, -*ac'*- and -*ec'*- have been derived from **-sk'*-. Some scholars consider that the Greek and Armenian usages of the suffix reflect an innovation made jointly by the two languages.[77]

3.5.1 Ionic iteratives

The Ionic iteratives have been the object of a number of studies.[78] These forms are found in Homer and his imitators, and in Ionic writers, notably

Herodotus.[79] In Homer the formations are used with an iterative or intensive meaning,[80] always restricted to reference to past time. Iteratives in Homer are very rarely found with the augment, and when the augment is used its absence would in general not affect the metre; thus, for example at *Odyssey* 14.521 παρεκέσκετ᾽ could be a later 'correction' for original παρακέσκετ᾽.[81] The iteratives are built on athematic and thematic stems of both present and aorist. Thus the following types of formation are found:

(1) Formed from the present stem:

  (a) Attached to thematic present stems of all types (see below for contract verbs). For example:

ἔχεσκε	from	ἔχω 'I have' (*Il*. 3.219, 5.126 etc.);
ἐποπτεύεσκε	from	ἐποπτεύω 'I look over' (*Od*. 16.140);
ἵζεσκον	from	ἵζω 'I sit' (*Il*. 24.472);
βοσκέσκετο	from	βόσκομαι 'I feed' (*Od*. 12.355);
θαυμάζεσκον	from	θαυμάζω 'I am amazed' (*Od*. 19.229);
θαρσύνεσκε	from	θαρσύνω 'I encourage' (*Il*. 4.233);
κτείνεσκε	from	κτείνω 'I kill' (*Il*. 24.393).

This formation occurs over eighty times in Homer with -εσκ- attached to over fifty different stems. The form -εσκ- is always used.

  (b) Attached to *-mi* verbs. There are only six examples of this formation, all except one occurring only once:

ἵστασκε	from	ἵστημι 'I set' (*Od*. 19.574);
ζωννύσκετο	from	ζώννυμι 'I gird' (*Il*. 5.857);
πέρνασκε	from	πέρνημι 'I export for sale' (*Il*. 24.752);
ῥήγνυσκε	from	ῥήγνυμι 'I break' (*Il*. 7.141);
ῥύσκευ	from	*ῥῦμαι 'I defend' (*Il*. 24.730);
κέσκετο	from	κεῖμαι 'I lie' (*Od*. 21.41, *Od*. 14.521 (παρε-)).

  (c) Attached to *-έω* verbs. There are two alternative forms -εεσκ- and -εσκ-. Kimball (1980) noticed that the alternation depends on whether the syllable preceding the suffix is heavy or light. The form -εεσκ- is used when the preceding syllable is light, giving forms such as φιλέεσκε etc.; -εσκ- is used when the preceding syllable is heavy, for example πώλεσκε (-εεσκ- would, of course, be metrically impossible in this environment). The only contradiction to this rule is καλέσκετο (*Il*. 15.338) which occurs alongside the expected καλέεσκε (*Il*. 6.402, 9.562); the form καλέσκετο may be a derivative from athematic κάλημι and thus belong to class (b) above. Iteratives of this type are formed on fourteen present stems, occurring 30 times in all.

  (d) Verbs in *-άω* show a variation between -ασκ- and -αασκ- in the same conditions as the *-έω* verbs (class (c)). The form -αασκ- probably masks earlier *-αεσκ- which has contracted to -ā- in the spoken language but is kept as -αα- for the epic metre (i.e. 'diektasis', see Chantraine 1973.75 ff.). Iterative forms from -άω verbs occur twenty-four times built on eleven roots; but only three forms, ἔασκε (also εἴασκε), ναιετάασκον and περάασκε, occur more than once.

(e) Irregular formations, showing the spread of -ασκ-, probably by analogy to the forms from -άω verbs and to forms taken from the sigmatic aorist (see below):

κρύπτασκε	from	κρύπτω 'I hide' (*Il.* 8.272);
ἰσάσκετο	from	ἰσάζω 'I make equal' (*Il.* 24.607);
ῥιπτάσκε	from	ῥίπτω 'I throw' (*Il.* 15.23, 23.827, *Od.* 8.374, 11.592).

The last iterative could be derived from a present stem ῥιπτάζω which occurs at *Hymn to Mercury* 279.

(2) Formed from aorist stems:

(a) Formed from thematic root aorists:

προβάλεσκε	from	ἔβαλον 'I threw' (*Od.* 5.331);
γενέσκετο	from	ἐγενόμην 'I was' (*Od.* 11.208);
ἴδεσκε	from	εἶδον 'I saw' (*Il.* 3.217, *Od.* 23.94 (ἐσ)-);
εἴπεσκε	from	εἶπον 'I said' (*Il.* 2.271, etc. frequent in the formula ὧδε δέ τις εἴπεσκε);
ἔλεσκε	from	εἷλον 'I took' (*Il.* 24.752, *Od.* 8.88, 14.220);
ἀπολέσκετο	from	ἀπωλόμην 'I am undone' (*Od.* 11.586);
φύγεσκε	from	ἔφυγον 'I fled' (*Od.* 17.316).

A very small number of verbs of this type are also found in Herodotus, who has κατελίπεσκε (from κατέλιπον 'I left', 4.78), λάβεσκε (from ἔλαβον 'I took', 4.78, ἐλάβεσκον 4.130) and perhaps βαλέσκετο, unless this should be read βαλλέσκετο, at 9.74 (Rosén 1962:126).

(b) Formed from athematic root aorists:

στάσκε	from	ἔστην 'I stood' (*Il.* 3.217, 18.160);
δόσκε	from	first person plural ἔδομεν 'we gave' (*Il.* 9.331, 14.382, 18.546, *Od.* 17.420, 19.76);
παρέβασκε	from	παρέβην 'I stood beside' (*Il.* 11.104);
δύσκεν	from	ἔδυν 'I sank' (*Il.* 8.271).

(c) Formed from the sigmatic aorist, such as αὐδήσασχ' (*Il.* 5.786). This formation occurs 26 times built on 16 verbs in Homer (only five formations of this sort in the *Odyssey*). However, all but six of the occurrences of this type occur in conjunction with other iteratives (see below).

(d) One form φάνεσκε(-το) (Il. 11.64, Od. 11.587, 12.241, 12.242, 13.194) is based on an aorist in -ην, ἐφάνην 'I appeared'.

Slightly less than half of all the occurrences of iterative formations are found in close proximity (i.e. within three lines of verse) to other iterative formations. The grouping of iterative forms is noticeably more prevalent in the acknowledgedly later books.[82] However, iterative formations are marginally more frequent in the Iliad than the Odyssey. On a rough count I found 141 iteratives in the 15695 lines of the Iliad and 104 in the 12112 lines of the Odyssey (not counting ἔσκε and φάσκε); this works out as an average of 9.0 iteratives for every thousand lines of the Iliad, but 8.6 iteratives for every thousand lines of the Odyssey.

Chantraine (1973:325) thought that the Ionic iteratives were a recent development of the language of Homer, but the high number of iterative formations in the Iliad does not support this hypothesis. Although some of the iterative formations do show late features, such as the loss of initial digamma,[83] this does not necessarily prove that the process of formation is in itself recent. From linguistic evidence alone it is not possible to determine decisively whether they are a recent creation or not. The matter is further confused by the fact that as a specifically Ionic feature they may not have been known in the dialect in which the epic tradition was first developed. The almost total absence of the augment with the iterative formation suggests that it is a creation of a time when the use of the augment was not obligatory.

Several scholars have attempted to find the origins of the Ionic iteratives within the development of the Greek language. Brugmann (1903) derived them from a periphrasis of participle and *σκω, an augmentless form of ἔσκε. This theory is highly unlikely; *σκω is not found elsewhere in Greek, and the posited phonetic changes are uncertain.[84]

Chantraine (1973:321) isolated the verbal forms ἔσκε and (ἔ)φασκε as the source of the formation. The form ἔσκε occurs 49 times in Homer, ἔφασκε 13 times and φάσκε 4 times. However, these forms do not seem to provide an adequate origin for the iteratives for two reasons. Firstly, they are not always used with an iterative force but may be used as imperfects;[85] secondly, the augmentless φάσκε occurs only four times, all in the Odyssey. The paradigms of εἰμί and φημί are unique in that they do not have an aorist, and this deficiency may explain the usage of the -σκ- forms of these verbs. The forms ἔσκε and (ἔ)φασκε appear to function as marked imperfect formations whereas the old imperfects take on the meaning of an aorist; in the case of ἔφην the transfer is complete.[86]

The origins of the Ionic iteratives may stem from the parent language. In meaning they accord well with the function of the reconstructed *-sk'- suffix (see 3.5) and some forms show the expected morphological pattern of root in the zero grade. Thus δόσκε, synchronically interpreted as a formation from the aorist (first person plural ἔδομεν 'we gave'), may derive directly from

dh_3-sk'e-, an -*sk'*- formation of the parent language forming an alternative imperfective stem to *di-deh_3-* (which gives the Greek present δίδωμι 'I give'). Similarly στάσκε, δύσκε and παρέβασκε could be imperfective formations of the parent language, preserving the original iterative nuance.

The spread of the -εσκ- and -ασκ- forms remains to be explained; it is possible that these formations have arisen through Greek treatments of inherited disyllabic roots. For example, καλέσκετο could reflect *$k'lh_1$-sk'-*; βάλεσκε could reflect *$g^w lh_1$-sk'-*; ἔασκε could reflect *$sewh_2$-sk'-*; and γενέσκετο could reflect *$g'nh_1$-sk'-*.[87] However these forms show different developments or ablaut grades to the expected reflexes. Thus *$k'lh_1$-sk'-* should develop to *κλησκ-* (compare κικλήσκω *Il.* 10.300 etc.), and *βλήσκε, *γνήσκε are the expected reflexes of the other two forms;[88] *$sewh_2$-sk'-* shows the full grade rather than the expected zero grade. An explanation for this could be that the forms are analogous to the present or aorist stem, thus καλέσκετο agrees in vocalism with καλέω and καλίζομαι. These forms do not however explain the most common formation in Homer, the addition of -εσκ- to thematic verbs, such as ἔχεσκε (type (**1a**) above). The model of καλέω:καλέσκετο cannot lead to a creation of ἔχω:ἔχεσκε.

It is probable therefore that there are other motivations for the creation and extension of -εσκ-. A desire to preserve the distinctive form of root and suffix may have been an important factor. A Proto-Indo-European *-*sk'*-* formation added to a root with final consonant would contain a cluster of three consonants, for example a *-*sk'*-* formation on the root *leip-* would be of the form *lip-sk'-*. This consonant cluster would be susceptible to simplification which in turn leads to the erosion of the identifiability of root and suffix. This process has indeed taken place in many of the *-*sk'*-* formations: πάσχω 'I suffer' in Greek cannot be recognised in the synchrony of the language either as a form with the suffix -σκ- or as containing the root πενθ-. The -σκ- present formation is not opposed to other present formations with a difference of meaning by the time of Classical Greek, so the erosion of the distinctive form of the root and suffix of πάσχω is not disruptive to the verbal paradigm.

In two areas of Indo-European, Tocharian and Hittite (where the suffix was still a productive formant creating causatives and duratives respectively), a vowel is also inserted between the root and suffix. Thus in Hittite a vowel of *e*-quality is regularly inserted between the final consonant and *-*sk'*-* suffix (Oettinger 1979:318); in Tocharian a '*Bindevokal*' is inserted between root and *-*sk'*-* suffix.[89] These phenomena offer some support for a Proto-Indo-European variant *-*esk'*-* alongside *-*sk'*-*,[90] but it is also possible, and perhaps more likely, that the three languages have made independent innovations motivated by the same desire to keep the root and suffix distinct when the suffix is used with a definite function.

In conclusion, the Ionic iteratives appear to be based on Proto-Indo-European formations with *-*sk'*-* used to lend an iterative, durative or intensive nuance to the verbal action. Analogy with the imperfective stem led to the erosion of the original ablaut pattern (perhaps also influenced by the form ἔσκε which appears to show the same vocalism as ἐστι) and -σκ- was attached to the present stem. Meanwhile forms such as δόσκε were synchronically re-interpreted as a formation from the aorist stem, which led to the analogous creation of iteratives from aorists as well. The difference between -εεσκ- and -εσκ-, and between -αασκ- and -ασκ-, arises from the addition of the suffix to verbs in *-εyω and *-āyω and originally athematic verbs in *-ημι and *-āμι; the later coalescence of the two types as *-έω and *-άω verbs enabled the two formations to be used for metrical convenience.

3.5.2 The Armenian aorist morph -c'-

In Armenian the morph -c'- is widely used in the verbal system. It functions as the marker of the present and aorist subjunctive, and for the majority of verbs it is also used to mark the aorist stem. The following classes of Armenian verbs form their aorists with -c'-:

(1) Verbs with present tense -nowm. Only six verbs of this class have an aorist in -c'-:

> lnowm 'I fill', aorist lc'i, third singular elic';
> zgenowm 'I get dressed', aorist zgec'ay;
> ənkenowm 'I throw', aorist ənkec'i, third singular ənkêc';[91]
> xnowm 'I stop up, plug', aorist xc'i, third singular exic';
> ənt'eřnowm 'I read', aorist ənt'erc'ay;
> yenowm 'I lean upon', aorist yec'ay.

Two of these verbs have secure Indo-European etymologies: lnowm derives from *pleh₁-, the root of Greek πίμπλημι, Latin pleo, etc., and zgenowm derives from *wes- (see further 4.64). The etymology of ənkenowm is disputed; the two most probable theories are: (a) a derivation from a compound of ənd and *kenowm < *g'es- the root of Latin gero, etc. (Frisk 1944:21f., and Klingenschmitt 1982:249); or (b) from *songʷ-eye/o- a causative of the root *sengʷ-, which is inherited into Armenian as ankanim 'I fall' (Godel 1969:256).[92]

(2) Verbs with present tense in -am. The aorist morph -ac'- is regular for this class. For example, kam 'I stand', aorist kac'i; keam 'I live', aorist kec'i (with internal e by regular vocalic reduction of -ea- when not under the accent); mnam 'I remain', aorist mnac'i. The majority of verbs of this type which have cognates in Indo-European are formed by the addition of a suffix *-āye- to the root which has taken place independently; thus mnam derives from *men-āye- etc. (cf. Meillet 1936:110f.). A few verbs of this type may stem from athematic verbs of the parent language; such as kam 'I stand', gam

'I go' and *tam* 'I give'[93] (note that *gam* and *tam* have irregular aorists *eki* and *etow*).

(3) Verbs with present tense -*anam*, aorist stem -*ac'i*, as *banam* 'I open', aorist *bac'i*. Only a few verbs of this class, which has become very productive in Armenian, continue Indo-European verbal roots. The origins of the class seem to be in roots with final laryngeal. Thus *stanam* 'I acquire', aorist *stac'i*, is the reflex of an *n-infixed form of the root *$steh_2$- 'stand' with causative meaning (compare Latin *destinare* 'establish' etc.).[94]

(4) Verbs with present tense -*em*. This class is divided into two groups:

(a) There are four verbs which have a present tense -*em* and aorist -*ac'i*:

asem 'I say', aorist *asac'i*,
gitem 'I know', aorist *gitac'i*,
karem 'I can', aorist *karac'i*,
mart'em 'I can', aorist *mart'ac'i*.

It seems likely that these verbs derive from earlier perfect formations. This is most apparent in the relationship between *gitem* and *$woid$-(Greek οἶδα, Vedic *veda*, etc.). The verb *asem* is usually set alongside Greek ἦ 'he said', and Latin *aio* 'I say', and is derived from *ag'- showing the same irregular change of *g' to s found in the first person pronoun *es* 'I' < *eg'-.[95] Klingenschmitt (1982:138f.) and de Lamberterie (1982a:26f. and *passim*) have independently come to the conclusion that *asem* and *karem* could also be derived from earlier perfect formations (both deriving *karem* from the root *g^wer- familiar in the *u*-stem adjective Greek βαρύς 'heavy', Vedic *gurú-*, etc.).

(b) The majority of other verbs with present tense -*em* have aorists -*ec'i*, third singular -*eac'*. For example *grem* 'I write, *grec'i* 'I wrote', *greac'* 'he wrote'.

Godel made a direct comparison between the verbs of the last class (**4b**, type *grem*) and the Greek iteratives in -εσκ- (1969:256f.). He thought that the third singular form -*eac'* gave no evidence that the whole paradigm had earlier shown -*eac'*- (thus *$greac'i$* etc.), which reduced to -*ec'*- where in non-final syllables in accordance with Armenian phonological rules; but rather that -*eac'* was a secondary development from original -*ec'* by analogy to cases where -*e*- in a non-final syllable alternated with -*ea*- in the final syllable. He found support for his theory from the third singular *ankêc'* 'he threw' of the aorist *ankec'i* (see above), which he took to derive directly from *-esk'-.

Godel's theory is untenable for a number of reasons. Firstly, although -*ea*- in the final syllable does alternate with non-final -*e*- in many cases, there are a number of instances where there is no alternation; particularly relevant here are the root aorists with medial *-e-*, such as *beri* 'I carried', *eber* 'he carried'. Secondly, the verbal form *ənkêc'* cannot be used to support the theory because it shows the vowel *ê*, not *e*; the two vowels were not confused in the earliest manuscripts.[96] Finally the four verbs of the pattern *gitem*, *gitac'i* show that a morph *-ac'i* was productive at some stage in the prehistory of the language.

We saw above that three of the four verbs of the *gitem* class might derive from ancient perfects. If this is so then it explains why they have aorist forms in *-ac'i*; at the time of the spread of the *-ac'i* morph they would not have been incorporated into the *-em* class. Thus, the productive aorist marker *-ac'i* would have been added directly to **gêt*, the regular phonetic derivative of **woid-*, to give *gitac'i*. For the majority of verbs of the *-em* class, the morph *-ac'i* is added to the stem *-e-*, as *gre-* from *grem* 'write', to give **greac'i >* *grec'i*.[97]

Hence the innovatory aorist morph of Armenian is *-ac'i* which may derive from **-āsk'-* or **-ask'-*.[98] Armenian shows nothing which corresponds to the characteristic **-esk'-* of the Ionic iteratives. The distribution of the morphs *-ac'i* and *-c'i* over the different classes of Armenian verbs shown above suggests that the morph has spread from verbs of the *-nowm*, *-am* and *-anam* classes.

The Armenian aorist marker *-c'-* could be the reflex of an **-sk'-* formant, which, like the Ionic iteratives, has been restricted in usage to reference to the past time only. Thus *kac'i* 'I stood' might derive from an iterative formation **g^{w}h$_2$-sk'-* which has been limited to use as a preterite, and is later used as an aorist, on the creation of a new imperfect.[99]

However, the Armenian aorists in *-c'-* differ from the **-sk'-* formations of the parent language because they show the full grade of the root. Thus *elic'* 'he filled' must derive from **e-pleh$_1$-sk'-* not **e-pļh$_1$-sk'-*. This is in contrast to Greek iteratives from roots of this type which never show a long vowel before the **-sk-* suffix. The one Armenian form considered to be a reflex of an **-sk'-* formation which must show a zero-grade in the root is *tac'* which corresponds exactly to Greek δόσκον iterative of δίδωμι; but *tac'* is the aorist subjunctive, not an aorist of *tam* 'I give'. This suggests that the reflex of **-sk'-* with zero grade had a different function from the suffix attached to the full grade at an earlier stage of Armenian.

This difference in formation weakens the link between the Armenian and the Greek forms. A number of scholars would deny the connection altogether and explain the Armenian aorists by a different process. Armenian has lost intervocalic **-s-* and consequently has no direct reflex of the sigmatic aorists.[100] Pisani, in a number of studies,[101] proposed the theory that the Armenian aorists in *-c'-* represent morphological replacements of the **-s-* aorists. This theory has received support from Watkins, who has shown that the suffixes **-s-* and **-sk'-* have a parallel distribution throughout Indo-European.[102] An advantage to this theory is that the vocalism of *elic'* is easily explained in parallel to the vocalism of Vedic *aprās* 'he filled'. A somewhat similar suggestion is made by Adrados (1963:438), who also derives the Armenian *-c'-* aorists from an earlier sigmatic aorist, yet explains the outcome as the result of a phonetic change of **-s-* to **-c'-* following a laryngeal consonant. Another explanation for the *-c'-* aorists comes from Klingenschmitt (1982:287) who tentatively suggests that *-c'-* is the regular development of **-ss-*; this is a consequence of his theory that *č'*, not *c'*, is the regular reflex of **-sk'-* in medial position (see **4.60**). The lack of examples of the change **-ss-* > *-c'-*, and the apparent counterexample of *es* 'you are' < **essi* make the theory improbable.[103]

3.5.3 Ionic iteratives and Armenian aorists: conclusion

We have seen that the productive morph for the Armenian aorist is *-ac'-*, which can derive from **-āsk'-* or **-ask'-*, and that the productive formant of the Ionic iteratives is **-esk'-*. It has also been shown that the vocalism of the Armenian forms which show the most archaic structure does not accord with that of the Greek forms. The Armenian formations are found with the augment, which again separates them from the Ionic iteratives. The only shared feature of the two languages is a use of the **-sk'-* suffix restricted to past time. This may have been a common innovation or may reflect independent development; the second option seems preferable given that the Ionic iterative formation is limited to a single Greek dialect, and that there were pressures within the early history of the Armenian language to substitute **-sk'-* for **-s-*.[104]

3.6 Verbs with a nasal affix in Greek and Armenian: introduction

Classical Armenian and Greek use nasal affixes to form the present stem of a number of verbs. The affixes derive from nasal infixes and suffixes in the parent language which were used to mark the imperfective stem.[105] Hamp (1975a) sees several parallels in the development of the inherited forms in Greek and Armenian. I shall only discuss the developments which might reflect common innovations made by the two languages at a stage in prehistory.[106]

3.6.1 The affix **-n(e)u-* in Greek and Armenian

The productivity of the affix **-n(e)u-*[107] in the early history of the two languages will be further discussed with reference to the one root which shows the reflex of a suffix **-nu-* to form its imperfective stem in Greek and Armenian (see on **wes-* at **4.64**). In both languages the reflex of the **-n(e)u-* affix is used as a productive marker to form the present stems of other verbal roots. However, the processes of extension of the affix in the two languages appear to be separate.

An innovation which has taken place in Greek is the attachment of the affix -νῡ-/-νυ- to the full grade of the root to form present stems; for example: ζεύγνυμι 'I yoke', δείκνυμι 'I show', etc.[108] Three of the verbs of this type which are already attested in Homer have cognates in other languages which form their present tense with a nasal infix. Thus ζεύγνυμι is cognate with Latin *iungo* and Sanskrit *yunákti*; ὀρέγνυμι 'I stretch out' is cognate with Sanskrit *ṛñjáti* 'stretch', and πήγνυμι 'I fasten' is cognate with Latin *pango* 'I fasten'.[109] It is therefore possible that the affix -νῡ-/-νυ- was used by Greek as one means of replacing the inherited nasal-infix formation.[110] Several of the new Greek present-stem formations in -νῡμι are first attested after Homer and are used to replace older present-tense formations; for example, μείγνυμι 'I mix' replaces Homeric μίσγω. It is interesting to note that the majority of forms of this type are formed on roots with a final guttural.

In Armenian no verbs of the -*nowm* class replace earlier infixed forms of the *yunákti* type. The only two -*nowm* verbs which may replace earlier nasal affixed forms are *lnowm* 'I fill' < **plēnumi* which may replace earlier **pl̥nāmi* (cf. Vedic *pṛnáti*),[111] and *t'oɫowm* 'I let, leave' which, according to Klingenschmitt (1982:243f.), replaces a present of the form **tl̥nāmi*.[112] In general the Armenian -*nowm* class either continues Proto-Indo-European imperfective formations with nasal infix and root-final **-u-* or is added to roots without a secure Indo-European etymology.[113]

Thus the two languages agree on forming new present stems with the reflex of an affix **-n(e)u-*, but they seem to have utilised the affix in different ways. The productivity of the affix **-n(e)u-* is not an exclusive isogloss of the two languages, as will be shown at **4.64**.

3.6.2 The affix **-n̥-* in Greek and Armenian

The Sanskrit present system formations of the seventh class show an infixed nasal before a final consonant; thus *yunákti* from the root *yuj-* 'join'. This formation is also found in Hittite and must be reconstructed for the parent language. However in the majority of Indo-European languages the inflectional pattern has been modified. Barton (1965:32) and Hamp (1975a:106) independently proposed that Greek and Armenian had taken the same steps in refashioning present-stem formations of this type. They see the process of reformation along the following lines, exemplified by the development of the nasal infixed present of the root **leikʷ-* (Latin *linquo* 'I leave', Vedic *riṇákti*):

Stage 1: Proto-Indo-European **linekʷ-/*linkʷ-*
Stage 2: Greek-Armenian **linkʷ-n̥-*

which develops regularly to Greek λιμπάνω 'I leave' (first attested in the compound forms κατα- and ἀπυ-λιμπάνω in Sappho frag. 94 (Lobel and

Page)).[114] In Armenian the infixed -*n*- is lost giving *lik^w-n̥- which develops regularly to the Classical Armenian *lk'anem* 'I leave'.[115] Hamp justifies this theory by the fact that Armenian -*anem* must derive from *-n̥- rather than *-*n*-. He sees the *-n̥- as a Sievers variant of *-*n*- after a preceding heavy syllable. The reconstruction *$link^w$n̥- provides the right environment for this syllabification, but *lik^wn- does not. However this argument is not strong enough as it is not certain whether Sievers patterns of syllabification were still operative at this stage in Armenian prehistory. Moreover a nasal suffix -*in*- is used to form causatives in Lithuanian, for example *bùdinu* 'I awake' (from the root *b^heud^h-, see Pokorny *IEW* 150f.); this suggests that a suffix *-n̥- (or *-ⁿn-) has an Indo-European pedigree.[116]

Kuiper (1937:117), who saw a similar origin for the Armenian -*anem* class to that suggested by Hamp, gave stronger support for the theory that Armenian had at some stage in its prehistory converted a formation of the type *$link^w$-n̥- to *lik^wn-. He noted that in one Armenian verb *awcanem* 'I anoint', cognate to Sanskrit *anakti* 'I anoint', Latin *unguo*, the *w* could be derived from *-*n*- before a labio-velar,[117] which suggested that the nasal infix had been retained at the time of the change of *-*n*- to -*w*- in this environment. Furthermore, Kuiper thought that the verb *bekanem* 'I break' derived from a root *b^heng- with -*n*- as part of the root, and that this -*n*- had been wrongly abstracted from the root in the prehistory of Armenian because it was synchronically interpreted as a nasal-infix. Thus when *li-*n*-k^w-n̥- (with infixed *n) was remodelled to *lik^w-n̥-, *b^heng-n̥- (with *n as part of the root) was reshaped to *$b^hegn̥$-.

However, Kuiper's theory rests on the reconstruction of roots *e/og^w- 'anoint' and *b^heng- 'break', whereas it is equally, if not more, likely that *e/ong^w- and *b^heg- are the roots ancestral to the Armenian verbs.[118] Moreover the existence of Armenian verbal forms such as *ankanim* < *$seng^w$- where the root nasal is retained argues against Kuiper's theory.

In conclusion one can only say that the evidence is not sufficient to support the theory that Armenian passed through a stage of combined nasal suffix and infix in the remodelling of nasal infix verbs. It is possible that Armenian replaced inherited formations of the type *li-*n*-k^w- directly by *lik^w-n̥-, showing no intermediate stage.

3.7 Other Greek-Armenian morphological isoglosses

The preceding discussions have dealt with five areas of the nominal and verbal systems of Greek and Armenian which have been taken by some scholars as evidence of earlier Greek-Armenian linguistic unity. I have not dealt with every morphological isogloss between the two languages which has been posited, but only those which are most frequently cited, or which were most likely to stem from common innovations. I shall, however, briefly set forth morphological isoglosses which I have not discussed and give my reasons for omitting them.[119]

Meillet (*BSL* 26 (1925) pp. 1–6, reprinted in 1977:215–220) found Armenian parallels to the Greek present-stem-forming guttural suffixes -κ-, -γ-, -χ-, seen most clearly in the formation ἐρύκω 'I hold back' alongside ἐρύω 'I guard', etc.[120] The only Armenian verbs with secure etymologies which show this suffix are *lsem* (aor. *loway*) 'I hear' and *bowsanim* (aor. *bowsay*) 'I grow', and only *lsem* has *-k̒- as a present forming suffix. As the formation of *lsem* can be explained by other means,[121] the isogloss is based on very insecure grounds.

Meillet also saw parallels between the Armenian and Greek present tense formations which are based upon total reduplication of the root (1936:113). Meillet compares formations of the type of Armenian *azazem* 'I dry', *hototim* 'I smell', with Greek verbs of the type of παμφαίνω 'I shine brightly', etc. However, the Greek verbs appear to be survivals of the Proto-Indo-European 'intensive' formation, whereby a present stem was created through total reduplication of the root, and which was still productive in Vedic (cf. Schwyzer 1939:647 for the Greek verbs and Rasmussen 1987:56f. on the type in Proto-Indo-European). It is possible that the Armenian verbs have also arisen from the intensive formation, but the original ablaut pattern has been lost, and the continued productivity of the process may reflect influence from South Caucasian languages which also form verbal stems through total reduplication (Deeters 1927:52f.). A peculiarity of verbs of this type which is shared by Greek and Armenian is the dissimilation of liquids, for example, Greek δαιδάλλω 'embellish' < *dal-dal-ye/o-, Armenian *cicaɫim* 'laugh' < *cei-cal- < *gel-gl̥-, but this is more likely to represent an independent development of the two languages; note that the Greek forms appear to have arisen after the replacement of the original vocalic sonants by a combination of vowel and sonant, and that in Armenian dissimilation of this kind also affects reduplicated forms with consonants, as well as sonants, for example *t̒awt̒ap̒em* 'I shake', beside *t̒ap̒em* 'I overturn'; *p̒op̒oxem* 'I change' beside *p̒oxem* 'I change' etc. and is also found in nominal forms such as *t̒it̒eṙn* 'butterfly' from *t̒er* 'wing' (Klingenschmitt 1982:147f.). The use of total reduplication of the root as a marker of the aorist in Armenian and Greek will be discussed in detail under the lexical correspondence of Greek ἤραρον 'I fitted' and Armenian *arari* 'I made' (**4.7**).

Bonfante (1981:64) considered the extension of the verbal suffix *-u- in Greek and Armenian to be a unique development of the two languages. But this seems to be a retained archaism rather than an innovation, since a verbal suffix *-u- must be reconstructed for Proto-Indo-European on the basis of comparisons such as Latin *volvo* 'turn' with Sanskrit *valati* 'turn'.[122]

Klingenschmitt (1982:60 n. 1) compares Greek formations of the type of ὀδάξ 'with the teeth' with a suffix -(a)c̒i found attached to a few Armenian words such as *maglc̒i* 'with the claws' (*magil* 'claw') and *bṙnc̒i* 'with the fist' (*bowīn* 'fist'). Klingenschmitt sees the origin of these formations in $*h_1dnk's$ (giving Greek ὀδάξ), which represents a common simplification of $*h_1dnt\text{-}dnk'\text{-}s$ 'biting with the teeth' in the two languages. There is no form **atanc'i* (< $*h_1dnk's\text{-}iyo\text{-}$) in Armenian, so this must remain speculation. The Greek and Armenian suffixes may not be related; Armenian -*c'i* could derive from an $*\text{-}sk'\text{-}$ suffix, and there are other explanations for ὀδάξ (see most recently Szemerényi 1990:176).

Cowgill (1960:349) saw a structural parallel in the two languages in 'the development of the rather loose PIE aspect system in the direction of a rigid organisation around the opposition of present and aorist stems'. It is not exactly clear whether Cowgill refers here to the semantic opposition between the aorist and imperfect system of Greek and Armenian or the formal means employed to mark a root as a present or aorist stem. It is worth recalling the fact that the imperfect and aorist appear to have merged at an early stage of Armenian into a single preterite.[123] The Armenian tense system most closely parallels the Old Georgian; the two languages both show a present, imperfect and imperfective subjunctive/future (Marr and Brière's (1931) 'imparfait second' in Georgian) formed from a present stem, and an aorist and perfective subjunctive/future formed from the aorist stem. Therefore the opposition of present and aorist stems in Armenian may be due to later influence from a Caucasian substrate.[124] The development of a more rigid formal organisation of the verbal paradigm, with a single present stem opposed to a single aorist stem, seems to have been a late development of Greek after the composition of the Homeric epics.[125]

3.8 Greek and Armenian morphological isoglosses: conclusion

In conclusion, we have found no morphological agreement between Greek and Armenian which must reflect a common innovation. There are several morphological features of the two languages which might be taken as the result of shared innovations made by Greek and Armenian – the extension of the morph $*\text{-}b^hi\text{-}$ to the singular, the restriction of verbal formations in $*\text{-}sk'\text{-}$ to reference to past time, the spread of a verbal suffix $*\text{-}n\text{-}$ to form present stems, etc., – but I have presented arguments which suggest that these morphological developments have arisen independently or reflect processes from within the parent language itself. The two languages share several important features of inflectional morphology with the Indo-Iranian family but with only a few other Indo-European languages: for example, the augment (shared also by Phrygian), the marker $*\text{-}b^hi(s)$ for the instrumental case (perhaps also found in Celtic), and the thematic genitive singular marker $*\text{-}osyo$ (found also in Italic). The paucity of morphological isoglosses which can be conclusively shown to represent exclusive shared innovations makes it extremely unlikely that there was a separate Greek-Armenian sub-group of Indo-European.

UNIQUE ARMENIAN-GREEK LEXICAL CORRESPONDENCES

4.0 Introduction

Since Pedersen first highlighted the existence of a number of exclusive lexical agreements between Greek and Armenian (1924:225f.), several scholars have investigated, or merely listed, the vocabulary items which are shared by these two languages alone.[1] Further investigation into this field would therefore seem otiose were it not for the fact that the lists of shared vocabulary do not always agree, and that, in general, scholars have been content to list the cognates without attempting to assess the precise nature and status of the connections. This can only be be done through explaining the exact phonetic, morphological and semantic developments responsible for the final form and meaning of the cognates. It can then be decided whether the isoglosses reflect a preserved archaism, a common innovation through contact or chance, or a borrowing from another language.

At the end of this Chapter I have given a list of further Greek-Armenian correspondences which, although seen as significant by one or two scholars, are not widely accepted and are mostly uncertain for a number of reasons.

The following list of cognate pairs is arranged in alphabetical order of their posited reconstructions following Pokorny *IEW* and Jahowkyan (1987:111–157) ('laryngeals' are discounted in the alphabetical order).

4.1 *aig'- (*h₂eig'-) 'goat'

The comparison of Armenian *ayc* 'goat' and Greek αἴξ (accented αῖξ in Attic according to Herodian) appears in most lists of the vocabulary exclusive to the two languages.[2] Phonetically the correspondence is perfect; the two words can both be derived from a reconstructed *aig'-* or *h₂eig'-*.[3] Semantically the agreement is also very close. In the Armenian Bible *ayc* usually translates Greek αἴξ where the Greek word refers to female animals; thus at *Genesis* 30:35 the opposition between τράγος 'buck' and αἴξ 'nanny-goat' is rendered by Armenian *k'ał* and *ayc*. However *ayc* is also, like Greek αἴξ, used for the generic term. For example *maz ayceac'* (*Exodus* 25:4 etc.) translates τρίχας αἰγείας 'goats' hair', and *ayc* is used as the term for 'goat' at *Matthew* 25:32f. in the simile of the Day of Judgement to a shepherd's separation of the sheep from the goats.[4]

Greek αἴξ (genitive αἰγός) is a consonant stem, but Armenian *ayc* is an *i*-stem (genitive plural *aycic'*).[5] Meillet (1936:75f.) explained the *i*-stem declension of the Armenian word by deriving it from a feminine form of the parent language, **aigī-*.

Forms from a plural *aycik'* occur in the Bible translation (for example *ayceac'* and *z-aycis* at *Matthew* 25:32, 33), and this may appear to give support for Meillet's theory.[6] Proto-Indo-European feminine forms with a nominative singular in **-ī* or **-īs* formed their oblique cases on a stem **-yā-* which, after a heavy syllable, had a Sievers variant **-iyā-*.[7] The forms *aycik'*, etc., could therefore be explained as derivatives from earlier forms in **-iyā-*; the nominative *ayc* would be the normal Armenian reflex of the nominative singular **aig ī*. The singular *ayci* 'goat' appears first in post-Biblical texts. The form *aycik'* may have been preserved by analogy to other terms for animals such as *awdi* 'sheep', *mak'i* 'ewe', *andik'* '(herd of) cattle', etc. Further evidence to support a pre-apocope stem **ayci-* comes from the word for 'gazelle' *ayceamn* (which translates Greek δορκάς in the Bible), which seems to derive from **ayci-* with a suffix -(*a*)*mn*, used in other animal names such as *jaylamn* 'ostrich'.[8]

Armenian has eliminated the inherited consonant-stem declension class. Several words which have cognates declined as consonant stems are *i*-stems in Armenian; for example, *sirt* 'heart', *ał* 'salt' and *otn* 'foot' which is declined as an *n*-stem in the singular but has genitive-dative-ablative plural *otic'*. The replacement of an earlier consonant-stem declension by an *i*-stem declension could thus have been a regular process in the development of Armenian.[9] The noun *ayc* could thus equally well derive from an earlier consonant stem or an original *ī*-stem.

The assumption of an original **ī*-stem (= **ih₂*-stem) receives support from the correction of the Hesychius gloss δίζα · αἶζα, Λάκωνες to αἶζα made by Perpillou (1972:116–117). For, if Perpillou's interpretation is correct, the Laconian word may represent a 'pre-Dorian' derivative from **aig'-yə* < **aig'-ih₂* and offer a perfect parallel to Meillet's reconstruction for the Armenian form.[10]

Greek also shows a number of derivatives of the root where a compositional form αἰγι- is used, for example Mycenaean *a₃-ki-pa-ta* 'goatherd' (KN *Fh* 346 etc.), Ἀιγιπᾶν 'goat-Pan' (for possible interpretations of this compound see Bader 1989:41f.), αἰγιπόδης 'goat-footed' and others.[11]

The function of the compositional -ι- in these compounds is not clear, but it is possible that it derives from an archaic morphological process of Proto-Indo-European.[12] The use of **-i-* as a composition vowel is reminiscent of the 'Caland forms' of adjectives in **-ro-* which form compounds with a link-vowel **-i-* (for example, Greek κυδιάνειρα 'bringing men glory' beside the adjective κυδρός 'glorious').

Therefore a consonant stem **aig'-* and possibly also a feminine/collective form *aig'-ih₂- can be reconstructed from the Greek and Armenian terms, and both languages agree in showing the relics of a compositional form *aig'i-. The morphological behaviour of this reconstructed item suggests that the word was inherited, not borrowed, into the two languages.[13] We have no way of knowing whether or not goats were known to the speakers of Proto-Indo-European, and the difficulty in reconstructing a common Indo-European term for 'goat' may be due to individual replacements of the inherited term in the daughter languages.[14]

Terms related to the Greek and Armenian words may occur in the Indo-Iranian language group. The term most commonly connected is Avestan *izaēna-* (or *izaēna*) 'leather (adj.)', which might be taken to reflect a zero grade of the root *ig'- (i.e. *h₂ig'-) with the suffix -aēna-.[15] Bailey (1979:484) derives the Avestan word from a root *iza- 'hide, skin' found elsewhere in Iranian, but this may be a later semantic development from an original meaning 'goat' or 'of a goat'. Other Indo-European words which may be connected are Sanskrit *eḍaka-* 'sheep, wild goat'[16] and Albanian *edh* 'kid, goat' (Huld 1984:61).[17] Note also that the reconstructed root *aig'- may be connected with the root *ag'- 'goat' (Sanskrit *ajá-* etc. cf. Pokorny IEW 6–7) with irregular fluctuation of the root vocalism.[18]

If the Avestan term is related, its vocalism would show that the original term underwent the Proto-Indo-European process of ablaut with full-grade *h₂eig'- and zero-grade *h₂ig'-. The reconstruction of an original consonant stem noun with different ablaut grades, if correct, would be further evidence that the lexeme was well integrated in the proto-language. The class of ablauting consonant stem root-nouns was all but eliminated in the daughter languages and the type seems to have had only a very limited productivity.[19]

In conclusion the evidence suggests that the term for 'goat' common to Greek and Armenian reflects an archaism rather than an innovation made by the two languages, and the existence of possible cognates in Albanian and Indo-Iranian suggests that the terms have an Indo-European pedigree. Greek and Armenian may therefore agree only in retaining an inherited term.

4.2 *al(h₁)- (*h₂el(h₁)-) 'mill, grind'

This root has reflexes in Indo-Iranian,[20] Armenian and Greek. It is attested in a number of different words in both Armenian and Greek. Three pairs of Armenian and Greek derivatives from this root have been taken to show agreements in form and meaning not found in cognates in other languages:

(a) Armenian *ałam* 'I grind', Greek ἀλέω 'I grind'.

(b) Armenian *aławri* 'mill', Greek ἀλέτριος 'mill' (Meillet 1936:142).

(c) Armenian *aliwr* or *alewr* (genitive *aler*) 'flour', Greek ἄλευρον 'flour' (Meillet 1936:142).

(a) The correspondence between ἀλέω and *ałam* is uncertain. Eichner (1978:153 n. 37) derived both verbs from *h_2alh_1mi;[21] by this theory the Greek verb has been transferred to the thematic conjugation in the prehistoric period. Eichner cites the reconstruction of a present *$wemh_1mi$ from the comparison of Greek ἐμέω 'I vomit' and Vedic *vámiti* as a parallel to the formation *h_2alh_1mi.

Normier (1980:20) reconstructs an original thematic verb *h_2lh_1-ye/o-. He explains that *a*-conjugation of the Armenian verb as the result of a prehistoric contraction of *-ae- (from *-aye-) to -a-. This sound change is doubted by Klingenschmitt (1982:91) since there is no certain parallel outside the *a*-conjugation.[22]

At first sight Normier's explanation of the Greek form also seems odd. One would perhaps expect *ἀλη- as the reflex of *h_2lh_1- as does Beekes (1969:234). However, the treatment of *HRH- in Greek is a vexed matter, and, to my knowledge, there are no examples which can prove or refute Normier's hypothesis with certainty: thus ὀνοτός (Pindar) 'blamed' < *h_3nh_3-(?) points one way, but ὄνητο 'he profited' < *h_3nh_2-to (Beekes 1969:95) another.[23] Peters (1980:26) even suggests that the expected outcome of *HRH- is Rῡ- as in νῆσσα 'duck' < *Hnh_2tih_2.[24] It is striking that for the majority of roots which can be derived from *HRH- forms comparable to ὄνητο (i.e. with structure *v*Rῡ*C*- from *HRHC-) are not quotable. There is no form *ἐλη- or *ἐλᾱ- (or even *λᾱ-) from the root *h_1lh_2- continued in ἐλαύνω 'I drive'; no *ἀρω- from *h_2rh_3- (ἀρόω 'I plough'); no *ἀρη- from *h_2rh_1- (ἀρέσκω 'I please'); no *ὀμω- from *h_3mh_3- (ὄμνυμι 'I swear'); no *ὀνω- from *h_3nh_3- (ὄνομαι 'I blame'); no *ὀλη- from *h_3lh_1- (ὄλλυμι 'I destroy').[25] The only forms besides ὄνητο which might point to a development *HRHC- to *v*Rῡ*C*- are:

ἄμητος 'harvest', ἀμητήρ 'harvester' (*Iliad*) from ἀμάω 'I mow' (all forms with long ā-). It is probable that these forms reflect *h_2meh_2-to-, especially given the connections with Old High German *mād* 'mowing', but the length of the initial vowel has not yet received a satisfactory explanation;

ἐρῆμος 'lonely, deserted', if from *h_1rh_1-mo-, although the connection with Latin *rārus* etc., given at Pokorny *IEW* 332f., is highly doubtful (thus Frisk *GEW* I 557, Chantraine *DELG* 370);

the Hesychius gloss τέρρητον · τριήρης if this is correctly interpreted as the outcome of original *τρι-ερητον (Schwyzer 1939:274). All other forms of this root (*h_1rh_1-), such as ἐρετμόν 'oar', show ἐρε-, although this may be because they reflect *h_1erh_1-;

the forms ἀλήθω 'I grind' (first in Hippocrates), ἄλημα 'fine flour' (only at Sophocles *Ajax* 381 and 389 where used metaphorically to mean 'knave'), ἀλήσιον 'meal' (Hesychius, and [ἀ]λέhιον in a fifth century inscription in Sparta), and a few other later forms in ἀλη- from the root under discussion. It is possible that all these forms continue a formation *h_2leh_1-, if they are not secondary.[26]

Therefore it does not appear that there is sufficient evidence to reject Normier's reconstruction for the Greek verb. There is no comparable material in Armenian to support or oppose the phonetic development *h_2lh_1-*ye*/*o*- to *alaye*-.

The Armenian verb may, however, have a different history; Klingen-schmitt (1982:93f.), while leaving open the possibility that *ałam* continues an athematic root present, shows that it could derive from a nasal infixed present *h_2l-*n*(*e*)h_1-,[27] for which there are Iranian parallels; for example Khotanese *ārr*- 'grind'. Another possibility is that the present was recharacterised by the addition of *-*na*-, abstracted from nasal infix verbs of the type of the Sanskrit ninth class (Proto-Indo-European *-*neH*-/*-*nH*-).[28]

If the Greek and Armenian verbs do both derive from an athematic present, then this probably does not reflect a common innovation. The athematic conjugation generally implies a more archaic formation. The replacement of athematic by thematic forms seems already to have been taking place during the last stages of Proto-Indo-European, and it is unlikely that a new formation would have followed the athematic conjugation.[29] But, if Normier's analysis is correct, the common form is more likely to be an innovation. Given the uncertainty over the Greek and Armenian phonetic developments, this seems less likely.

(b) This comparison rests on incorrect evidence. The Greek term ἀλέτριος 'mill', cited by Meillet, is a ghost-word.[30] Nor does *aławri* mean 'mill' in the earliest texts. The word *aławri* is used to translate the Greek present participle ἀλήθουσα at *Ecclesiastes* 12:3 and 12:4 and so should mean 'female grinder (of corn)'. At *Jeremiah* 52:11 *town aławreac'* translates Greek οἰκία μύλωνος 'the mill house', but this does not prove that *aławri* means 'mill' as the Armenian phrase could denote the house by its occupants.[31] In the Bible translation the word *erkan* is normally used for '(hand-)mill' and the plural *erkank'* for the larger installation (illustrations of the Biblical usage are given by Meillet 1925b:6).

The Armenian term *aławri* 'female who grinds corn' appears to match Greek ἀλετρίς 'female slave who grinds corn' perfectly.[32] However this does not fit with other developments of agent nouns in Armenian. Armenian seems to have differentiated agent and instrument nouns early in its history, generalising the reflex of *-*tl*- for agent nouns, for example, *cnawł* 'parent' (derived from *$g'enh_1$-*tl*-) and the reflex of *-*tr*- for nouns of instrument, for example, *arawr* 'plough' (derived from *arh_3-*tr*-).[33] Therefore *aławri* appears to derive from an instrument noun rather than an agent noun. The suffix -*i* is widely used in Armenian to derive secondary adjectives and nouns from adjectives, nouns and verbs.[34] *Aławri* could be a secondary derivative of an unattested instrument noun *aławr* 'mill'. The original meaning would therefore be 'connected with a mill' and hence 'one who grinds'; for the use of the -*i* suffix compare *ayr-i* 'widow' (with meaning developed from 'woman connected with a husband') from *ayr* 'man, husband',[35] *gorci* 'tool, thing connected with work' from *gorc* 'work', *matani* 'ring, thing connected with the finger' from *matn* 'finger', etc.

The Greek and Armenian forms may therefore be separate developments. Furthermore Bailey (1979:22) derives several words in Iranian languages which mean 'mill' from this root with a *-tr- suffix; for example Modern Persian *ās* 'mill'. The morphological agreement between Greek and Armenian may not therefore be unique.

(c) There remains the comparison of Armenian *alewr* 'flour' and Greek ἄλευρον 'flour'. The noun *alewr* has genitive-dative-locative singular *aler* in the earliest Armenian texts (for example *Matthew* 13:33, *Luke* 13:21).[36] It belongs to a very small declension class comprising only *alewr* and three other nouns: *ełjewr* 'horn', *ałbewr* 'spring', *ałtewr* or *ełtewr* 'marsh'.[37] For all of these words there is variation in later texts between the orthography -*ew*- and -*iw*-. However, in the oldest manuscripts the two diphthongs are distinct (as shown by Meillet *JA* (1903) II pp. 493–497, reprinted in 1977:307–311), and the above words are written with -*ew*-. The graph *ew* in these words most likely denotes a high front-back diphthong [eu].[38]

Of the other words in this class only *ałbewr* has a secure etymology (for which see **4.13** below) and derives from **bʰrewr̥*; compare Greek φρέαρ with quantitative metathesis from **φρηϝαρ*, from a form with lengthened grade **bʰrēwr̥*. The original declension was of the **-r/n* type.[39]

The Homeric form ἀλείατα 'flour' (*Od.* 20:108) suggests that the Greek words may derive from an earlier declension with nominative **ἄληϝαρ*, and genitive **ἀληϝατος*; ἀλείατα would stand in the same relation to *alewr* as Homeric φρείατα stands to *ałbewr* (Meillet *REArm* 4 (1924) p. 6, reprinted in 1977:214). In later Greek the thematic form ἄλευρον replaces the earlier noun. However, Frisk (*GEW* I 70) reconstructs an original Greek form **ἄλεϝαρ* not **ἄληϝαρ* on the basis of ἀλέατα found in a sixth-century B.C. inscription on Miletus, and interprets the Homeric form as the result of metrical lengthening. Unfortunately, the inscriptional evidence may not be decisive, since it is likely that the form has undergone the Ionic quantitative metathesis, and thus stands for ἀλέᾱτα.[40] Francis, in his unpublished doctoral dissertation on the Greek disyllabic roots, argued that the form **ἄλεϝαρ* was the original, not **ἄληϝαρ*, on the basis that the other forms of this root with initial **ἀλη*- were late or secondary creations and that the original vocalism of the root must have been **h₂elh₁*- not **h₂leh₁*-.[41] This objection need not, of course, be sufficient to dismiss the derivation if one accepts *Schwebeablaut* for the Proto-Indo-European root.[42]

The derivation of the Armenian nouns *alewr* and *ałbewr* still needs to be explained. Original **h₂(e)leh₁wr̥* and **bhrēwr̥* (as reconstructed by Eichner

1978:152, see also Hamp 1970:228) would develop regularly to *aliwr* and *ałbiwr* with final *-iwr*. Hübschmann (1897:415) derived *ałbewr* from **bhrewṛ* with a short **e*. This analysis is not possible for *alewr*, which seems to derive from a root with final laryngeal (Eichner 1978:153 n. 37). There is no evidence to suggest that the Armenian reflex of **h₁* in internal position could be *-e-*; the normal outcome would be *-a-* or *-∅-*. Eichner (1978:154 n. 43) therefore derives the words in question from **-ēwṛ* which gives **-iwr*, which in turn develops to *-ewr* by analogy to the genitive (*-er*). The later forms in *-iwr* result from sound change or dialect differences.

Eichner (1978:153) derives the genitive forms of the type *ałber* from **bʰrewros*, etc., which replaced original **bʰrewnos* in an early form of Armenian. This is entirely *ad hoc*. The Proto-Indo-European paradigm of **bʰrewṛ* must have had forms based on **bʰrun-* in the oblique cases in order to give the prototype for Gothic *brunna*, etc. (Schindler 1975a:8). Eichner (*op. cit.* n. 41) dismisses Godel's (1972:57, 1975:97) suggestion that the paradigm was modelled on other Armenian *r*-stems (for example *oskr* 'bone' genitive singular *osker*, etc.). However Godel's theory seems preferable. An anomalous paradigm of the following type:

nominative	**ałbewr*
genitive	**ałbown* (< **bʰrun-*)

is very likely to have been replaced and *r*-stems of the type of *oskr* would have provided the model. Thus the new paradigm was:

nominative	**ałbewr*
genitive	**ałbewer*.

The genitive **ałbewer* developed to *ałber* by regular loss of intervocalic **-w-* before **-r* (this derivation is given by Meillet *MSL* 15 (1909) p. 355, reprinted in 1977:134, Jahowkyan 1982:31 and Godel 1982:12). This explanation of the paradigm is considerably simpler than that put forward by Eichner, and, incidentally, gives support for the interpretation that the diphthong *-ew-* is the original form. It means that we must follow Hübschmann's derivation of *ałbewr* < **bʰrewṛ* (with short **e*) and seek a different explanation of *alewr*.

It is possible that *alewr* is a borrowing from Greek ἄλευρον. Hübschmann (1883:17, reprinted in 1976:172) denied that the word was a loan on the grounds that the Armenian word has *-l-* not *-ł-* which is the normal phoneme used for Greek *-l-* in loanwords. Hübschmann admits that the rule is not without exception, and there are several counter-examples among the Armenian words loaned from Greek listed in his *Armenische Grammatik* including the following:[43] *balistr* 'catapult', *delpʿin* 'dolphin', *zmelin* (Greek σμιλίον) 'penknife', and *halowē* 'aloe' (although this last may not come directly from the Greek; cf. Greppin 1988). The first three of these words agree in having *-l-* for Greek *-l-* when in the environment of a front vowel, which is where one would expect the Greek -*l*- to be pronounced more as a palatal *l* and thus be replaced by the palatal Armenian -*l*-. The -*l*- of ἄλευρον is also in the environment of a front vowel and could have been rendered by Armenian -*l*-. The presence of -*l*- rather than -*ł*- in *alewr* is therefore not a valid argument against the view that the word is a loan.[44]

Hence connection (c) is also not significant, as either *alewr* is a loan, or it stems from a different prototype from that ancestral to the Greek forms. Furthermore, if the two nouns do both continue the same formation with the meaning 'flour', it seems unlikely that this is an innovation. The Greek noun shows that the original declension class of the word was of the *-*r/n* type which was an archaic declension class of the parent language, eliminated in Armenian.

Therefore the Greek and Armenian derivatives from the root *al*- do not appear to represent common innovations but common survivals or parallel derivations. The correspondences *ałam* 'I grind' and ἀλέω 'I grind' and *aławri* and ἀλετρίς both meaning 'female slave who grinds corn' may possiby reflect the same original formations, but arguments have been presented to suggest that the terms reflect independent innovations. The scattered derivatives of this root in Indo-Iranian languages suggest that a number of formations from the root *al*- were at one time shared by the dialects ancestral to Greek, Armenian and Indo-Iranian but were subsequently lost in most Indo-Iranian languages.

4.3 *alōwpek'- (*h₂lōwpek'-) 'fox'

Solta (1960:119) takes Greek ἀλώπηξ 'fox' (genitive ἀλώπεκος) and Armenian *ałowês* (genitive *ałowesow*)[45] 'fox' to the stem from the same prototype *alōwpek'-. However, the intitial *a*- in both languages may stem from a common phonetic change, the vocalisation of an original 'laryngeal' consonant, and this has been dealt with at **2.2**.[46]

The -*ê*- of the Armenian nominative singular does not show the regular vocalic reduction to -*i*- in non-final syllables in the oblique cases; thus the genitive is *ałowesow*, not the expected *ałowisow*, compare *sêr* 'love' genitive *siroy*. There are two possible explanations for this.

The first explanation rests on the Armenian tendency to lower vowels when the next syllable contains the vowel [u], hence *têr* 'lord' has a denominative verb *tirem* 'I rule' with the expected reduction of -*ê*- to -*i*-, but there also exists a derivative *terowt'iwn* (often written *têrowt'iwn*) 'sovereignty' with -*e*- not -*i*- before [u].[47] By this theory the alternation between *ałowês* and *ałowesow* is explained.

The second option is to see the writing *ałowês* as a late scribal replacement for original *ałowes* after the difference between the two vowels was lost in speech.[48] This view receives some support from the fact that the nominative plural form *ałowesk'*, rather than *ałowêsk'*, occurs at *Neh.* 4:3 and *Ezek.* 13:4 in the Zōhrab Bible edition, but without the evidence of the earliest manuscripts this must remain uncertain. The Armenian word follows the *u*-declension which has become the standard declension for nouns denoting animals.[49]

The Vedic word for 'fox' or 'jackal', *lopāśá-*, shows a similar construction to the Greek word except for the absence of the initial vowel and the difference between the vocalisms: Vedic *-o-* derives from **-e/ou-* whereas Greek shows *-ω-*.[50] There is no way of knowing what the original medial syllable of the Armenian word was; it may have been **ō, *ōw, *ow* or even **u*. The ablaut between *-η-* in the Greek nominative and *-ε-* in the oblique cases may reflect the original ablaut pattern of the parent language,[51] and it is possible that the Vedic and Armenian words have generalised the long and short ablaut grades respectively. Therefore, apart from the shared development of the initial 'prothetic vowel' with Greek, the Armenian word can be linked no more closely to the Greek form than to the Vedic.[52] The isogloss is not therefore significant for the question of the Greek-Armenian relationship.

4.4 **ām-r/n* 'day'

Homeric Greek ἦμαρ, (genitive ἦματος) 'day' and Armenian *awr* (genitive *awowr*) 'day' (as opposed to 'month' etc.) have been taken as the only reflexes of this root since first connected by Meillet. The aspiration of the Attic form ἡμέρα must be secondary (*pace* Hainsworth 1988:26 f.) since unaspirated forms are found in non-psilotic dialects (ἄματα in Arcadian and ἀμέρα in Doric (Locrian)).

The phonetic and morphological development of the Armenian noun is not entirely clear. The nominative singular may derive from **āmōr* (Meillet *IF* 5 (1895) p. 331, reprinted in 1977:23). The development of **-m- > -w-* in this position (before following **-u-* from Proto-Indo-European **-ō-*) may have been a regular Armenian sound change, but there is a lack of conclusive examples to make this change certain.[53]

It is easier to see the development of **-m- > -w-* in this word proceeding via '*u*-epenthesis', as most scholars term the development of a *u*-glide before a consonant originally followed by **-u-*, a process which took place in a stage of Armenian before the loss of final syllables but after the development of **ō* to **u*.[54] Olsen (1985:6 n. 6) accounts for most of the accepted cases of both *u-* and *i-* 'epenthesis' by a rule that limits its occurrence to words which were disyllabic at a stage before the loss of final syllables, and had **a-* in the first syllable and unaccented **i* or **u*, **y* or **w* in the second.[55] By this theory **āmōr* would develop via **amur > *aʷmur > *awowr*, with loss of **m*; compare the loss of **n* in *ayr* 'man' < **aʸnir < *anēr*.

The declensional paradigm of *awr* is unique in Armenian, although it only differs from the normal -*r* declension type in having -*owr*- not -*er*- as the stem form of the cases outside the nominative-accusative singular. Most old *-*r*/*n* stems in Armenian have been remodelled on the basis of the nominative singular: for example, *ałbewr* (cf. **4.2** above and **4.13** below); *neard, nerdi* 'fibre' from *(s)nēwṛ-t(i)* with the final -*d* from *-t(i)* of the Proto-Indo-European nominative generalised throughout the paradigm;[56] and *howr* (*o*-stem) 'fire' (Godel 1975:97). The genitive *awowr* therefore probably derives from earlier *amuros*, formed on the nominative singular *aʷmur* (the *m* to *w* change in the oblique cases is by analogy to the nominative).[57]

Thus Armenian *awr* derives from a paradigm with nominative singular *āmōr* whereas Greek ἦμαρ must derive from *āmṛ. The fluctuation between *-ōr* and *-ṛ for the nominative singular of *-*r*/*n* stems dates back to the parent language and is found within Greek itself in the pair τέκμαρ and τέκμωρ 'goal'; the forms in *-ōr may derive ultimately from a collective formation.[58] Peters (1980:243 n. 195a), on the basis of the interpretation of Mycenaean *a-mo-ra-ma* as an iterative formation /āmōr āmṛ/ thinks that in early Greek a similar pair *āmōr and *āmər co-existed as free variants. He supports his theory with the observation that in Homeric compounds such as ἐννῆμαρ 'for nine days' ἦμαρ functions as a collective, a use which should be associated with *ῆμωρ (note also νύκτας τε καὶ ἦμαρ at *Il.* 5:490 etc., where ἦμαρ is used with plural reference).[59] However, this interpretation of the Mycenaean forms is open to considerable doubt; even if *a-mo-ra-ma* is connected with ἦμαρ, it is not sufficient evidence for a form *āmōr, since there is evidence for a Mycenaean vocalism of *ṛ as /-or-/, compare *to-pe-za* 'table' for τράπεζα. The Homeric compounds of the type ἐννῆμαρ may continue an ancient process of formation of numeral compounds with the second element standing in the singular (compare τρίετες 'for three years') and they may have given rise to the plural usage of ἦμαρ (Leumann 1950:100f.).

The ancestor of the Greek and Armenian forms must be reconstructed as a member of the archaic *-*r*/*n* stem declension.[60] There are no certain connections of the root with terms in other Indo-European languages; but it is possible that the Old Irish word *amm* 'time, season' preserves a relic of the oblique forms of the *-*r*/*n* stem (i.e. *$h_2$mn, beside a full grade *eh_2m-, preserved in Greek and Armenian).[61] The archaic nature of the reconstructed form, and the fact that Greek and Armenian show the reflexes of alternative nominative singular forms, imply that the term is either an archaism, or, if an innovation, an innovation which occurred dialectally within the parent language.

4.5 *antro- 'cave'

The comparison of Greek ἄντρον 'cave' and Armenian *ayr* 'cave' (an *i*-stem: instrumental *ayriw* at *Genesis* 23:17) is not included in Solta's (1960) list of inherited Armenian vocabulary, although the words had long been connected.[62] The Latin word *antrum* 'cave' is probably a loanword from Greek, and so this connection could be another exclusive isogloss. Pisani (1944:161f.) was the first to give a possible phonetic basis for the evolution of the Armenian form, and this etymology is accepted by Frisk and Chantraine. The most comprehensive treatment of the supposed phonetic development of the Armenian form is given by de Lamberterie (1978:243f.) who reconstructs *antēr* for Armenian, which stands in the same relation to Greek ἄντρον as ἀστήρ 'star' does to ἄστρον within Greek. De Lamberterie accounts for the phonological development of the Armenian word as follows: *antēr* > *ántēr* > *ántir* > *ánthir* > *ándhir* > *áyndhir* > *ayr*. He sees this development as analogous to the development of *ayr* 'man' from *anēr*.

This derivation is highly questionable. There are no other examples of '*i*-epenthesis' (for which see **4.4** above) which takes place over a boundary greater than a single consonant. Moreover the stage *ayndhir* > *ayr* in de Lamberterie's derivation is without a certain parallel.[63]

The Armenian and Greek words cannot therefore be grouped together with certainty. The origin of the words and their link with other Indo-European forms is also uncertain. Schwyzer (1939:532) derived the Greek word from the root *an(ə)-* 'breathe', and reconstructed the original meaning of ἄντρον as 'where it emits vapour'. But Greek shows a disyllabic reflex of this root in the word ἄνεμος 'wind' (Frisk *GEW* I 105), and the evidence for a reflex *an-* in Greek is meagre (see Frisk *GEW* I s.v. ἄνται 'winds' and ἄσθμα 'panting'). The Armenian word may be connected to Hittite *ḫariš* 'valley' (Čop 1957:136f.).

4.6 *aps-(*h₂eps-)* 'limb(?)'

Pedersen (1906:428) was the first to connect Greek ἄψος (genitive ἄψεος) with Armenian *ap'* (*o*-stem). In Homer ἄψος is used only in the formula λύθεν δέ οἱ ἄψεα πάντα (*Od.* 4:794 and 18:189) conventionally translated 'she (in both passages referring to Penelope) loosed her joints (in sleep)'; the meaning 'joint' is expressedly given in some ancient scholia and lexica.[64] But Hellenistic authors use ἄψεα to mean 'limbs' and the translation of the Homeric passages 'loosed the limbs (in sleep)', recommended by some ancient authorities, is supported by the epithet λυσιμελής 'relaxer of limbs' which is applied to ὕπνος at *Od.* 20:58 and 23:344.[65] Clearly the ancient scholars' accounts of the word are based on a presumed etymological connection with ἅπτω. It is possible that the meaning 'joints' which some of them give for ἄψος has arisen out of the desire for a clear etymological relation and that the original meaning is 'limbs' or some other body-part.

The Armenian word *ap'* translates Greek δράξ at *Isaiah* 40:12 (with meaning '(palm of the) hand') and *Ezekiel* 13:19 (meaning 'handful'), and at *Luke* 6:1 the disciples are described τοὺς στάχυας ψώχοντες ταῖς χερσίν 'rubbing the ears of corn in their hands' which is translated in Armenian as *šp'ein ənd ap'*.[66] In the *Epic Histories* ascribed to Pʻawstos Bowzand the phrase *ap's harkanelov* is used in the description of dances after the death of Nersēs (5:41, p. 233 of the Venice (1933) edition), which seems to mean 'slapping their hands'. The meaning of the Armenian term is thus clearly 'palm of the hand'.

This etymology raises a number of questions which need to be discussed in full:

(a) Is the phonetic and morphological development of Armenian *ap'* from **apsos-* plausible?

(b) What is the relationship between Greek ἄψος and the verb ἅπτω 'I touch'?

(c) Could the Armenian word be connected with Greek ἁφή 'touch' and derive from a root with an original 'voiceless aspirate'?

(d) Are there any related terms in other Indo-European languages?

(a) The fate of original **-ps-* in Armenian needs to be clarified in order to account for the development of **apsos-*. Pedersen gave his etymology of *ap'* in a discussion of the fate of **ps*, **bs*, **bhs*, and **phs* in Armenian, in which he attempted to prove that all etymologically isolated cases of this combination develop to Armenian *p'*. However, his argument contains many doubtful etymologies. For example, he takes the verb *p'ṙnč'em* 'I sneeze' from a form with initial **ps-* which he posits was a pre-Armenian simplification of the cluster **pst-*. But, as Strunk has shown (1985:228f.), this does not correspond with the development of the cluster **pst-* to Armenian *st-* in the word for 'breast' *stin* < **pstēn-* (Avestan *fštāna-*). The initial aspirate of *p'ṙnč'em* seems to have arisen through onomatopoeia.[67] Pedersen's rule for the development of **ps-* in Armenian is countered by *sowt* 'false' (see **4.55**) which gives a clear example of **ps-* developing to *s-*.[68]

The apparently divergent treatment of **ps* in Armenian, which is seen in the cognate pairs *sowt*, ψεῦδος and *ep'em*, ἕψω, has recently been discussed by Witczak (1989:29 n. 3 and 1991:70–71). He accounts for the different reflexes of the original cluster by a rule that if the cluster occurred after the original accent it developed to *p'*, if before, to *s*. However, he only gives two examples for the second development; *sowt* and *eres* 'face' which he derives from **prep-só-* which stands next to **prep-* (Armenian *erewim* and Greek πρέπω 'I seem'). This etymology for *eres*, which was first proposed by Osthoff (1901:234), is semantically unsatisfying; a preferable explanation of the word is given by Normier (cited by K. T. Schmidt 1987:296) who derives it from a plural *trens-ə which would be comparable to the dual *trens-iə which survives in Avestan θraŋhi 'the two corners of the mouth'.[69]

When *eres* is removed from Witczak's list of examples for the development of *ps, the double development of this cluster can be formulated simply (following Strunk 1985:229): when in initial position *ps- developed to Armenian s-, whereas medial *-ps- gave -pʿ-. The difference may be due to a different syllable division: *.ps- when initial but *-p.s- when medial; for *.ps- the *-s- would be retained in a cluster and *p- subsequently lost; but for the cluster *-p.s-, *-s- was aspirated at an earlier date than *-p- and gave *-pʰ-. Phonetically, therefore, the connection of ἄψος and *ap'* is unobjectionable, and one might reconstruct *saps- or *aps-, the latter form if the Greek initial aspirate is unetymological.

Morphologically the two forms are also in agreement. The o-stem declension of the Armenian word stands beside an s-stem declension in Greek. The replacement of the *s-stem by the o-stem declension seems to have been regular in the pre-history of Armenian. Another example is provided by the o-stem noun *erek* 'evening' beside Greek ἔρεβος 'darkness'.[70] Pedersen (1906:428, followed by Pokorny *IEW* 51) takes the locative form *y-ap'i* as evidence that *ap'* can be declined as an *i*-stem. Witczak (1989:24) sees this locative form as the relic of an *s-stem, deriving *yap'i* from *ápsesi*, which is phonetically impossible. However, the locative in -*i* does not necessarily indicate the existence of an *i*-declension, but has been transferred from the *i*- and *a*-declension to provide a distinct locative form for o-stem nouns in the singular (Meillet 1913:49f.). It is significant that in the earliest text in which the word occurs (St Luke's Gospel) the locative form *ap'* is used.

(b) The relationship of ἄψος to the Greek words ἅπτω 'I touch' and ἁφή '(sense of) touch' has long been debated. Chantraine (*DELG* 99f.) and Frisk (*GEW* I 126f.) both accept that the terms are related. If this is so ἄψος must show the addition of a *-se/os- suffix. Schwyzer (1939:513) gives several other examples of this suffix, yet none of these is fully secure.[71] Chantraine (or possibly Taillardat) *DELG* 1179 s.v. φάρσος noted that in the synchrony of the language the pairs φάρσος 'piece, part' and aorist φάρσαι (glossed as σχίσαι 'split' in the *Etymologicum Magnum*) and ἄψος and aorist ἄψαι appear to point to a suffix -*sos*-, but the comparative data rather indicate that φάρσος is an Indo-European *s-enlargement of the root *bher- 'split'. If the original meaning of ἄψος was 'limb' not 'joint' (as suggested above), the connection with ἅπτω is semantically, as well as morphologically, uncertain.

(c) Meillet (1977:258 reprinted from *MSL* 23 (1929) p. 276, and 1977:275 reprinted from *BSL* 36 (1935) p. 110) did not mention the connection of ἄψος with *ap'*, but credits Pedersen with connecting the verb ἅπτω and noun ἁφή (*sic*) 'sense of touch' with the Armenian term. He took these Greek and

Armenian forms from a root with an original 'voiceless aspirate'. Meillet does not reconstruct a root, but a form such as *sapʰ- would explain the initial aspiration of the Greek forms. However, the Greek evidence for a 'voiceless aspirate' rests solely on the φ of ἀφή, and this word could be explained as a derivative of ἅπτω by analogy with ῥαφή from ῥάπτω, etc.[72] The initial aspirate of ἀφή points to its creation after the operation of Grassmann's law, and therefore recently in the history of Greek; compare the loss of aspiration in ἔχω from *segʰ-. Meillet's connection should therefore be abandoned.

(d) Witczak (1989) separated ἄψος from ἅπτω and related ἄψος and ap' to Tocharian A āpsā (pl.) 'limbs',[73] Sanskrit ápsas- 'breast, forepart of body, forehead',[74] and Hittite ḫappeššar- 'limb, part of the body'.[75] He is correct to say that semantically and derivationally the relationship between ἄψος and ἅπτω is suspect, and may be right to see a popular connection of the verb and noun resulting in the initial aspiration of ἄψος. Formally, also the connection between ἄψος and ápsas- is attractive. Witczak's reconstruction of the original meaning 'limb, part of the body' is satisfactory for the Tocharian, Hittite and Greek forms, but less so for the Armenian and Sanskrit meanings. The reconstruction of a Proto-Indo-European form *apsos- (or *h₂epsos-) also raises some doubts, since the root shape *aps- appears to be aberrant.[76]

If the Armenian word is connected to any Greek forms, then it would appear to be closest to ἄψος. However, the meaning 'limb' and 'palm of the hand' are difficult to reconcile. It is very likely that the words belong to a wider family of terms in the Indo-European languages. The connection between Greek ἄψος, Tocharian A āpsā and Hittite ḫappeššar- seems the closest in semantic terms, while Greek, Armenian and Sanskrit appear to share the same inherited formation which describes a part of the body.

4.7 *ar- (*h₂er-) 'fit'

The Greek aorist ἤραρον 'I fitted, equipped, etc.', frequently found in Homer, is an exact match to the irregular Armenian aorist arari 'I made'.[77] The unreduplicated root exists in both languages: in Armenian it is found in the present stem aṙnem 'I make' which has been transferred to the -nem conjugation (Klingenschmitt 1982:162); and in Greek it survives in a number of forms, such as the participle ἄρμενος and aorist ἄρσε in Homer. The Greek present stem ἀραρίσκω, which only occurs once in Homer at Od. 13:23, is a new creation modelled on the aorist (Chantraine 1973:317); elsewhere the perfect is used with present sense (cf. LSJ s.v.).

The reduplication of the initial vowel and following consonant to form the aorist is not without parallel in Greek (compare ἤγαγον from ἄγω 'I lead', ἤπαφον from ἀπαφίσκω 'I cheat', ἤκαχον from ἀχεύω 'I vex', ἄλαλκον 'keep off', ἤνεγκον 'carry' and ὤρορον from ὄρνυμι 'I rise')[78] but is confined to this root in Armenian. Ruijgh (1972:229) considers that the process was retained and expanded in early Greek because the development of initial laryngeals to vowels obscured the ablaut relation of the present and aorist of roots with initial laryngeals. Thus, for example, from the root *h_2er- 'fit', the root present with e-grade vocalism *h_2er- would have merged with the root aorist *h_2r- with zero grade vocalism, as ἀρ-. Since prothetic vowels from pre-consonantal laryngeals only arose in Greek and Armenian, Ruijgh's theory could explain the phenomenon in the two languages.

This process for the formation of aorists is also found in Indo-Iranian; for example, Vedic has an aorist *āmamat* from the root *am-* 'injure' (other examples are given by Brugmann 1913:144f.). It is possible that these aorist formations are connected to the 'intensives' which are formed with total reduplication of the root in Vedic, for example *alarti* (for *ararti*) 'go with speed' from the root *r-*, and for which there may be parallels in Anatolian languages.[79] The existence of isolated aorists formed with this type of reduplication in Greek, Vedic and Armenian suggests that the process is of Indo-European origin.

This root in extended form appears to be widely spread in Indo-European languages.[80] The unextended root probably also underlies the forms of *rnóti* with the meaning 'fasten' found in the Rg-Veda, although formally it has become confused with the derivatives of *$or-$ (*h_3er-) 'move, rise' and *$ar-$ (*h_2er-) 'grant, provide'.[81]

The connection of ἀραρίσκω and *aȓnem* is unobjectionable on semantic and phonetic grounds and their agreement on the abnormal aorist form is significant.[82] However, the wide spread of derivatives from this root in Indo-European suggests that the root is ancient, and the peculiar aorist formation might belong to an earlier stratum of Indo-European morphology. The agreement could therefore represent an archaism.

4.8 *$ar-$ (*h_2er-) 'deny'

Greek ἀρνέομαι 'I deny, disown' and Armenian *owranam* 'I deny, disown', which is used to translate ἀρνέομαι in the Bible (e.g. *Matthew* 10:33), appear to be a perfect semantic match. They were included by Meillet in his list of significant Greek-Armenian lexical isoglosses (1936:142). The etymological connection is doubtful on phonetic and morphological grounds. The chief obstacle in the comparison is the ablaut difference between *$r-$ which underlies the first syllable of the Greek verb and *$ōr-$ from which Armenian *owr-* could derive. Klingenschmitt (1982:127) sees only one way to derive these two forms from a single root: *owranam* is a denominative verb from a (lost) root noun *owr which derives from *$h_2ōr-$ and ἀρνέομαι is a denominative verb from *ἀρνός < *$h_2(e)rno-$ (cf. ἔξαρνος 'denying'). This solution is unlikely. The Greek word may derive from a root *h_2res- which can be reconstructed from Avestan *rah-* 'be unfaithful' (Mayrhofer 1953:74–77).[83] The Avestan word stands closer to the original meaning of ἀρνέομαι, which in Homeric Greek seems to describe a state 'be reluctant, reserved' rather than an act of repudiation (cf. *LfrgE* I 1525f.).

The connection is therefore too uncertain to carry any weight for the question of Greek-Armenian relationships.

4.9 **ard-* 'dirt'

The connection of the rare Greek word ἄρδα 'dirt' with Armenian *ałt* 'grease, dirt' (*o*-stem) is seen as a significant isogloss by Arutjunjan (1983:262f., following Ačaṝyan *HAB* I² 136). In this word Armenian shows *ł* in place of *r*, which is the regular reflex of Proto-Indo-European **r*. Arutjunjan and Ačaṝyan see a parallel to this development in the word *neł* 'narrow' which they connect to Old English *nearu*.[84] However other explanations are possible for both the Armenian and the Greek word: *ałt* may derive from a root **e/ol-* 'be dirty' (as given by Solta 1960:279f.); and ἄρδα may be connected with ἄρδω 'I water' and derive from a root **ward-* or **h₂werd-* (Chantraine *DELG* 105, Peters 1980:23 n. 18).

Therefore this etymology, which rests on an irregular sound change, cannot be taken as certain.

4.10 **arti* (**h₂erti*) 'just now'

Greek ἄρτι 'just now' and Armenian *ard* '(just) now' agree on form and meaning, and are seen as an exclusive lexical isogloss by Meillet (1936:142). Both forms probably preserve an ancient locative formation from the root **(h₂)ar-*.[85] The root meaning appears to have been 'fit together, join' (cf. ἀραρίσκω).

The use of ἄρτι to mean 'recently' is not found in Homer.[86] The simple form of the adverb does not occur in the Homeric poems, but it may be used as the stem of the adjective ἄρτιος 'suitable' and the first member of the three compound adjectives ἀρτίπος 'swift', ἀρτίφρων 'sensible' and ἀρτιεπής 'glib' (Frisk *GEW* I 155) where it seems to retain the original meaning 'fittingly'.[87] In post-Homeric Greek a large number of new compound forms of the type ἀρτιγενής 'new-born' are created where the first part ἀρτι- has the meaning 'recently', and some of the Homeric forms undergo a corresponding shift in their meaning, for example, ἄρτιος from 'suitable' to 'ready' in Herodotus and Sophocles (cf. *LSJ* s.v.), and ἀρτίπος/ἀρτίπους from 'swift' to 'coming just in time' (Sophocles *Tr.* 58). These facts indicate that the adverb ἄρτι with the meaning 'recently' was unknown to Homeric Greek. This is still the case even if the Homeric forms with first part ἀρτι- were not originally connected with the adverb ἄρτι, but derive from a compositional form of the verbal root *αρ- (Bader 1970:134, Calame 1977:212); the meaning of the adverb has clearly influenced the whole family of words, and the fact that the Homeric forms are untouched by this influence argues that ἄρτι did not then have a temporal meaning.[88]

The original meaning of the adverb may have been 'fittingly' which could have developed a moral connotation, 'suitable', or a local one 'at hand'. In either case the semantic shift to 'recently' is plausible and not uncommon in the history of other languages. For the first Chantraine (*DELG* 117) compares the change of meaning from French *juste* to *justement*, and one can also add the use of the English adverb *just* in phrases of the type 'I have just arrived' etc. For the second there are many parallels, for example English 'at hand', etc. In fact, while the semantic change from spatial to temporal proximity seems fairly common, there are few examples of the opposite change. The Homeric data lead one to think that the semantic shift to 'recently' took place independently in Greek and Armenian.

The reconstructed adverb *art(-i) is not exclusive to Armenian and Greek. The Lithuanian cognate *arti* 'near' clearly continues the same, or a closely related form, and refers to proximity of space rather than time.[89] There are therefore no grounds to suggest that Greek ἄρτι and Armenian *ard* bear a special relationship to one another.

4.11 *au- (*h₂ew-) 'spend the night'

The connection of the Greek verb ἰαύω 'spend the night', and nominal forms such as αὖλις 'place for passing the night', ἰαυθμός 'sleeping place', with the Armenian verb *aganim* (aor. *agay*) 'spend the night' and noun *awt'* 'sleeping place, pernoctation' has been seen by some scholars as an exclusive isogloss on the grounds that only these two languages continue a verbal root *au- (*h₂ew-).[90]

A number of forms in Indo-European languages can be derived from a root *h₂wes- with the meaning 'spend the night, dwell, live': for example, Hittite ḫwiš- 'live', Vedic *vásati* 'stay, dwell, spend the night', English *was*, etc. (see further Pokorny *IEW* 1170f.).[91] Derivatives from the root *h₂ew- 'spend the night' are not found elsewhere. It is possible that the Greek and Armenian forms derive from a root *h₂ews-.

The Greek present tense form ἰαύω can be derived from a root *h₂ew- or *h₂ews-. If it is from the root *h₂ew-, it must continue an athematic present *h₂i-h₂ew-mi which has been transferred to the thematic conjugation; if from *h₂wes-, then the Greek present could be derived from *h₂i-h₂(a)ws-ye/o-.[92] There is little to choose between these two derivations. The reconstruction of the root as *h₂ews- is made the more likely option by the existence of the aorist form ἄεσα (with either long or short initial ά-), which, in Homer, functions as the aorist to ἰαύω.[93] The aorist ἄεσα can be derived from a sigmatic form *(e)h₂wes-s-; the double *-ss- may be preserved in the alternative reading ἀέσσαμεν for νύκτ' ἄσαμεν at Odyssey 16:367.[94]

If these reconstructions are correct the Greek present ἰαύω derives from the root in Benveniste's 'thème I' *h₂ews- and the aorist ἄεσα from the root in 'thème II' *h₂wes-. This Schwebeablaut within a single paradigm is exactly comparable to Schindler's reconstruction (1970:152) of the Proto-Indo-European root aorist *gʷyeh₃- 'live' beside the present *gʷeyh₃-; and root aorist *Hnek- (Vedic ānaṭ) beside present *Henk- (Hittite ḫenkzi).[95] There is therefore no need to reconstruct a simple root *au- (*h₂ew-) to account for the Greek verbal forms (the nominal forms will be discussed below).

Hovdhaugen (1968:123 f.) had already proposed a similar Schwebeablaut to account for the Armenian verbal forms, deriving the anomalous verb gom 'I am, exist' from *h₂wes- and aganim from *h₂ews-.[96] Hovdhaugen's theory is attractive because it provides a way of explaining why aganim has initial a- whereas gom does not; namely that 'prothetic' vowels arising from pre-consonantal laryngeals do not develop before *w-. However he does not explain in detail how the paradigm of aganim arose from a root *h₂ews-. The most likely development is that the aorist agay derives from *h₂ews- or *h₂ewse/o-, and continues an earlier aorist or, more likely, an imperfect form; the present stem is most probably formed from the new aorist (compare harc'anem 'I ask' < harc'i 'I asked' < *pṛk-sk-e/o-, an ancient imperfect which functions as an aorist in Armenian). This derivation involves the sound change of *-ws- to Armenian -g-, which is phonetically plausible if one assumes that *-s- was lost in this position before the development of *-w- to -g-.[97] However there is no secure parallel for this change.[98]

An alternative solution is given by Peters (1980:40 f.) who posits an aorist or imperfect third singular *h₂west which develops to *aw (> ag-) on which the whole Armenian paradigm was remodelled, as well as derived forms such as awt' (i-stem) 'pernoctation, lodging'. But he comes into difficulties when explaining why in this form *h₂- should develop to a- while it does not in other words deriving from initial *Hw-. His explanation, that the development of *Hw- differs for monosyllables and polysyllables, is neither convincing nor necessary; a third singular aorist or imperfect form almost certainly would have had the augment from the earliest stages of Armenian, and *e-h₂west must develop to *aw.

Barton (1988) explained the Greek and Armenian forms differently, deriving ἄεσα and the Armenian aorist agay 'I spent the night' from a root aorist *h₂ewh₁-. There are possible parallels for Barton's proposed etymology of the Armenian verb; compare the aorist keray 'I ate' < *gʷerh₃- and de Lamberterie's direct connection of the Armenian aorist cnaw 'he was born' with Greek γένετο < *g'enh₁to (1982a:41). The development from root to sigmatic aorist in Greek may also be paralleled (cf. the co-existence of root and sigmatic aorists ὠλόμην 'I am undone' and ὤλεσα 'I destroyed' in Homer). However, Barton's reconstruction of a root with final laryngeal is not supported by any other evidence besides the direct equation of Greek *αϝε- with Armenian aga-.

It seems preferable to connect the Greek and Armenian verbal forms with the same root *$h_2$wes- which is found in other Indo-European languages. In support of this it should be noted that the Greek and Armenian verbs share close phrasal similarities with the Vedic and Gothic and Old Irish cognates. In Homeric Greek the aorist ἄεσα is always found with νύκτα(ς) 'night(s)'. Similarly in the Armenian Bible translation aganim is joined with z-gišer(s) 'night(s)' (accusative); for example at Ruth 3:13 agir ast zgišers zays for Greek αὐλίσθητι τὴν νύκτα 'tarry this night'. This does not seem to be a calque of the Greek usage, since aganim is also used to translate other Greek verbs conjoined with durative time phrases. For example, Greek μένω 'I stay' is most frequently rendered in the Bible translation by its Armenian cognate mnam, e.g. Mark 14:34: mnac῾ēk῾ ast ew art῾own kac῾ēk῾ μείνατε ὧδε καὶ γρηγορεῖτε 'tarry ye here, and watch.' But when conjoined with an expression of time aganim is used, thus John 1:39: aṙ nma agan ayn awr παρ᾽ αὐτῷ ἔμειναν τὴν ἡμέραν ἐκείνην 'they remained with him that day'. Similarly ὑπομένω 'I stay' and καταλύω 'I lodge' are translated by aganim zgišer when used with τὴν νύκτα 'night' (Numbers 22:8 and 22:19) but by mnam and hangč῾im elsewhere (e.g. Acts 17:14 and Luke 9:12). In Gothic the cognate wisan also translates μένω when followed by a time phrase, for example at Luke 19:5: himma daga auk in garda þeinamma skal ik wisan σήμερον γὰρ ἐν τῷ οἴκῳ σου δεῖ με μεῖναι 'for today I must abide at thy house' (Armenian: aysawr i tan k῾owm aržan ê inj aganel). But wisan also translates μένω when there is no conjoined time phrase, so the usage may be modelled on the Greek. However, evidence that this Gothic usage is native to the language is presented by the Gothic translation of Greek παραχειμάσω 'I shall winter' by wintru wisan at I Corinthians 16:6. In Vedic vásati is frequently conjoined with rātrim and rātrīs 'night(s)', and similarly Old Irish foaid is frequently used with aidchi accusative of adaig 'night' (cf. Barton 1988:55 n. 31 and the citations for foaid in the RIA Dict. s.v.). Thus the collocation of this verbal root with a word for 'night(s)' or another expression of time in the accusative appears to stem from the parent language.

The majority of the Greek nominal derivatives can also come from a root *$h_2$ews-; thus αὖλις may reflect *$h_2$ewli- or *$h_2$ewsli-. The exception to this is ἰανθμός which cannot derive from *$h_2$ews-. Solta cited ἰανθμός as a close parallel to Armenian awt῾, and took both words to contain the reflex of a *-t^h- suffix. This follows the work of Frisk (1936:30f.) who had argued that awt῾ must derive from a *-t^h- suffix because *awt- would develop to awd in Armenian.[99] This sound change is not certain. There is other evidence which suggests that *-t- developed to Armenian -t῾- after *-w-; for example, the nominal suffixes -oyt῾ and -owt῾iwn, which are more likely to continue the

*-ti- suffix than a *-tʰ- suffix.[100] The suffix *-ti- seems, however, to have remained productive until a late stage of the development of Armenian, and it is possible that the form *aw-ti- was first created after the change of *h₂ews- to *aw-.[101] The word awt' is therefore not incontrovertible evidence for a root *au-.

Greek ιαυθμός is only attested in Lycophron, Hesychius and Callimachus (ἐνιαυθμός) and the retention of the reduplicating vowel i- in the noun shows it to be a late creation. The suffix -θμός had a limited productivity in late Greek poetry: for example, γευθμός 'tasting' in Nicander (Alex. 399) is formed from the verb γεύω, and not from the original root *geus- which would have given *γευσθμός (Schwyzer 1939:492f.). Greek ιαυθμός cannot therefore be used to support a reconstruction *au-.

Hence, the Greek and Armenian material can be referred back to a root *h₂wes- which is well attested in other Indo-European languages, and is found with equivalent meaning in Vedic. In keeping with the principle that entities should not be multiplied, the reconstructed simple root *au- should be abandoned as it is an unnecessary creation. Greek and Armenian do appear to share the reflex of the root in 'thème I' *h₂ews- which is not found in other languages. The process of *Schwebeablaut* within a verbal paradigm, as reconstructed by Schindler, must, if correct, be interpreted as an archaism, not an innovation, since remnants of it are scattered throughout the Indo-European languages and it does not seem to have been productive in early Greek or Armenian.

4.12 *augʰ- (? *angʷʰ-/ *angʰw-) 'neck'

The Armenian word awjik' 'collar, hem' (plurale tantum, genitive awjeac'; the word is used to translate περιστόμιον 'collar' at Exodus 28:32, 39:21) was first connected to the Greek word αὐχήν 'neck' by Adontz (1937:10). The comparison of the two words is complicated by the (literary) Aeolic word for 'neck' ἄμφην which occurs in one of the Aeolic poems of Theocritus (30.28).[102]

The analysis of the Greek and Armenian forms rests on whether one takes ἄμφην to be related or not. If not, then both words will derive from a root *augʰ-, with different Greek and Armenian suffixes. The derivation of the Armenian word from this reconstruction is not without problems. Intervocalic *gʰ regularly develops to -z- in Armenian (as ozni 'hedgehog' < *ogʰīn-). Pedersen thought that the change of *gʰ to z did not take place after *w (1905:201). This is open to doubt; the only other example of the combination is awj 'snake' of which the aw- sequence is not original (see further below). The reconstruction of a velar *-gʰ- does not make the Armenian derivation any easier, as the velars and labio-velars merged with the palatals after *-w- very early in the pre-history of Armenian (Meillet 1936:37, Pisani 1950a:191 f.).[103]

If Greek ἄμφην is related to αὐχήν and awjik', then all the words must stem from a root *ang'ʰw- or *angʷʰ-. This suggests the possibility of a shared phonetic innovation in Greek and Armenian: the change of *n to w under the influence of a following *w or labio-velar, with subsequent merger of the following guttural with the palatal series. Bonfante (1937:25) posited a similar development in the prehistory of Armenian to explain the two words awcanem 'I anoint' (Latin unguo) and awj 'snake' (Latin anguis).

However, the exact process of this development in Armenian is uncertain; the change has not taken place in exactly similar phonetic conditions, such as ankanim 'I fall' < *sengʷ-, hing 'five' < *penkʷe and perhaps anjowk 'narrow', if this derives from *angʷʰu- as Lehmann (1986:60) and de Lamberterie (1990:I.267) suggest. Morani (1981b:7) may be right to see the change as sporadic and irregular; de Lamberterie (1990:I.267f.) even proposes that Greek ἀγχύ- 'narrow' and αὐχήν 'neck' and Armenian awjik' 'collar' and anjowk 'narrow' all derive from the same root. As often in the study of the phonetic history of Armenian we are hampered by the lack of etymologically certain material. It is interesting to note that there may be other possible examples of a sporadic change of *n to w where a following labio-velar is not involved, such as giwt 'discovery' next to Vedic vindáti 'he finds' (Meillet 1936:44).[104]

In Greek there is even less certain evidence for such a change; of the material given by Brugmann (1897:596), Schwyzer (1939:296) and Morani (1981b:8) there is no other example of the change of *-nKʷ- to -wK- (K = any guttural). Judging from θαλυκρός 'hot' (next to θάλπος 'heat') < *dʰalkʷro- one would expect *ang'ʰw- (or *angʷʰ-) to develop to *ἀνυχ-. Hence αὐχήν must be derived from a form with vocalic *-n̥-. But the only other examples of the change of *Kʷ to wK immediately after a vowel are highly suspect; Thessalian δαύχνη 'laurel' may not be of the same origin as δάφνη 'laurel' and the word is almost certainly borrowed from a non-Indo-European language; the derivation of οὐκ from *okʷi rests only on the comparison of Armenian oč' (see 4.46).[105]

The evidence for a common Greek-Armenian sound change is therefore uncertain. The two languages also show different suffixes. An alternative explanation of the Armenian word as a derivation of awj 'snake' with the -i suffix is also possible.[106] By this theory the meaning has changed from 'object pertaining to a snake' to 'snake-shaped object' to 'collar, hem'; a possible parallel for this change is the late Greek use of δράκων 'snake' to describe a bracelet or necklace cited by LSJ, but the one passage in which this use occurs ((Pseudo-)Lucian Am. 41) implies that the ornaments referred to are made in the form of snakes. In the absence of any more reliable parallels, this theory must remain uncertain.

Hence the connection of awjik' and αὐχήν, whether from *aug'ʰ-, *augʰ-, *ang^{wh}- or *ang^{h}w-, is doubtful. It is possible to account for *awjik'* in specifically Armenian terms, and ἄμφην may be connected to words in Germanic for 'neck'.[107] Alternatively the two Greek words may be borrowings from a lost source.

4.13 *b^{h}rēw- 'source, spring'

The Greek word φρέαρ 'well' and Armenian *ałbewr* 'spring' are among Pedersen's and Meillet's lists of unique Greek-Armenian isoglosses. But the word is also well represented in Germanic: Gothic *brunna*, German *Brunnen* 'well, spring' (see further Pokorny *IEW* 144). All these forms can be derived from an ancient *-r/n stem; Armenian has generalised a form deriving from the original nominative-accusative in *-r (as in the case of other *-r/n stems, see **4.2**), and Germanic one deriving from the *-n- stem of the oblique cases. Hence there is no need to posit a special Greek-Armenian connection.

4.14 *drepan- 'sickle'

De Lamberterie (1983:21f.) has recently suggested a new etymology for the Armenian term for 'eyelids': *artewanownk'* (genitive plural *artewananc'* or *artewanac'*), connecting Greek δρεπάνη 'sickle' with a semantic development from a 'sickle' to 'brow' to 'eyelid' in the prehistory of Armenian.

The use of the term for 'sickle' to denote the eyebrow may seem an unlikely semantic change. It must have arisen through the comparison of the curve of the brow to the curve of the sickle blade, just as one might refer to an 'arched brow' in English. There are some other Armenian words for body-parts which might have arisen through equally vivid semantic extensions; for example, the word for 'fist' *bowṙn* (also 'violence') is connected by de Lamberterie with the root *b^{h}er- with an original meaning 'ce qui emporte' (Létoublon and de Lamberterie 1980:315). However, I know of no parallel for the shift from 'sickle' to 'eyelid' via 'eyebrow', and the semantic connection of the Greek and Armenian words remains doubtful.

Phonetically the connection meets with no objection; for the change of *dr- to Armenian *art-* there is the parallel of *artawsr* 'tear' < *drak'u- (German *Träne*), and for the development of medial *-p- to -w- there are many examples such as *ew* 'and' from *epi.

De Lamberterie supports his theory by citing the Armenian translation of ἔως ὀφρύος τοῦ ὄρους at *Luke* 4:29, *minč'ewyartewann lerin*, which he thinks points to an earlier Armenian meaning of 'brow' for *artewan*. The Greek word ὀφρῦς does not occur elsewhere in the New Testament, but the Armenian version of *Leviticus* 14:9 has *yawns* for Greek τὰς ὀφρύας.

Armenian *yawns* is the accusative of *yawnk'* the standard Armenian term for 'eyebrow'. In the Armenian Old Testament *artewanownk'* is the standard translation for βλέφαρον 'eyelid'.

As the Gospels are likely to have been the first books of the Bible translated by the Armenians it is possible that an original form *artewan* 'eyebrow' (probably originally an *a*-stem to explain the irregular genitive plural form *artewanac'* which occurs at *Psalms* 131:4, *Proverbs* 6:4) was later extended to *artewanownk'* with a change in meaning to 'eyelids'. The transfer from *a*-stem to *n*-stem declension class may have arisen by analogy to the large number of Armenian terms for body-parts with *n*-stem declension.

The semantic development from 'eyebrow' to 'eyelid' is paralleled by Greek uses of ὀφρῦς with a probable meaning 'eyelid' (not listed in *LSJ* but gathered by Gow 1944:38f.) and similar interchanges in other Indo-European languages (cf. Buck 1949:219).

The Greek word δρεπάνη is derived from δρέπω in all the standard etymological works. This derivation rests on a meaning 'reap, cut' for δρέπω, alongside the usual 'pluck', which is attested in Hesychius and the *Etymologicum Magnum*. The comparison of δρεπάνη and *artewan* appears to show the two languages sharing the same process of derivation for a noun of instrument: addition of **-an-* (**-ṇn-*) to the verbal root in **e*-grade. The suffix -*an* is also found in other Armenian words which have been exclusively connected to Greek (see **4.19** and **4.54**). It is therefore worth devoting some space to the history of the suffix in Armenian.

I shall first give a brief survey of the main usages and origins of the -*an* suffix in Armenian, and then discuss the arguments for and against a possible Greek-Armenian morphological innovation. There are a number of words with final -*an* in Armenian, for example: *aman* 'pot', *geran* 'beam', *hawran* 'herd', *keunk'* 'life' (and the many other *pluralia tantum* abstract nouns in -*ank'*), *erastank'* 'arse'. The suffix is also found extended by **-iy-* which develops to -*ani* in *kendani* 'living, animal' next to *ankendan* 'lifeless' (see further on -*ani* below), or by **-y-*, giving -*ayn* as perhaps *erkayn* 'long' next to *erkar* 'long'.[108]

Not all examples of the -*an* suffix have the same origin. The chief productive use of the suffix in Classical Armenian arose from a conflation of the Iranian participle formant -*ana-* or -*āna-* with the Iranian nominal suffix -*ana-*.[109] Pairs loaned from Iranian such as *držem* 'fail, infringe', *držank'* 'infringement', and *niš* 'sign', *nšan* 'sign' have led to a spread of the suffix within Armenian. The lack of any distinction of vowel length in Armenian has brought about the merger of the separate Iranian suffixes with the result that a form such as *patsparan* (from the Iranian loan-word *patsparem* 'I protect', Hübschmann 1895:226) is both an agent noun 'refuge, shelter' and an action noun 'protection'. In general, however, the action nouns are *pluralia tantum*.

For many words one cannot tell with certainty whether the suffix reflects an earlier Armenian suffix or the later addition of the -*an* suffix borrowed from Iranian. For example, Olsen derived the -*an* suffix of the abstract noun *keank'* 'life', from an Indo-European participle form in **-nt-* (1989a:225 f.).[110] But *keank'* could alternatively reflect the addition of the Iranian -*an* suffix to the root of *keam* 'I live'. Since *keank'*, like the majority of Iranian loans,[111] declines as an *a*-stem, the latter explanation is preferable.

Other words with an -*an* suffix may continue Indo-European **n*-suffixed forms, for example: *geran* 'beam' which has been connected to Middle Irish *fern* 'alder, mast'; *beran* (*o*-stem) 'mouth' alongside Lithuanian *burnà* 'mouth', Middle Irish *bern* 'slit'. Only very few words ending in -*an* can be explained in this way. Other Armenian words show different treatments of original **n*-suffixed forms, for example: *k'own* 'sleep' < **swop-no-* (possibly with original **o* vocalism); *gin* 'price' (either from **wes-no-* or **wēs-no-*); and *kaɫin* 'acorn', *lowsin* 'moon', *getin* 'earth' and *beṙn* 'burden' (for which see further **4.30**).

A third class of words (noticed by Arutjunjan 1983:280) appears to show the suffix with limited productivity as a marker of body parts: *erastank'* 'anus', *srban* 'anus', *mkan* 'loins', *nerban* 'sole of the foot', *erank'* 'groin', *caṙan* 'penis', *beran* 'mouth' and perhaps also *artewan*. All of these words for which a declension class is known are *a*-stems, except for *beran*, which is an *o*-stem.

The suffix -*ani* is productive in the Classical Language, for example *bokani* 'barefooted' next to *bok* 'barefooted', *lezowani* 'having a tongue' (*lezow* 'tongue'). The -*ani* suffix in these words probably does not reflect the survival of an Indo-European **-n̥n-* suffix, but is rather transferred from *n*-stem nouns with the *i*-suffix; for example, *akani* 'having eyes' (Olsen 1989a:225). In *akani* the *i*-suffix is attached to the genetive form *akan* of *akn* 'eye', compare *aṙni* 'masculine' from *aṙn*, genitive of *ayr* (see Gjandschezian 1903:58 for further examples).

Greek derivatives in -ανο-/-ανᾱ- of the type found in στέφανον 'crown' next to στέφω, etc. are fairly numerous (see Chantraine 1933:198f. and Schwyzer 1939:489f.). The suffix seems to have been extended from two sources: the use of the Indo-European **-no/ā-* suffix after 'disyllabic' roots; and a Sievers variant **-n̥n-* after a preceding heavy syllable (evidence for which is given by the comparison of the Hesychian gloss θέππανος 'burning' with Lithuanian *dègtinas*).

The -ᾱνᾱ- suffix in Greek is used to derive nouns of instrument from verbal roots, for example, σκαπάνη 'spade' from σκάπτω 'dig', θηγάνη 'whetstone' from θήγω 'sharpen', στεφάνη 'brim' from στέφω 'encircle'. As these examples show, the suffix does not cause a change in ablaut of the root and therefore may be an innovation of recent date. The Mycenaean term for 'ewer' *qe-ra-na* (PY *Ta* 711) may show the same type of derivation although in this case the verbal root is not certain.

If Armenian were to show the same type of derivation as this, it would clearly be a strong argument for a Greek-Armenian morphological innovation. Indeed, there are a number of Armenian instrument nouns which show a similar formation, for example: *top'an* (*a*-stem) 'beetle for beating clothes' next to *top'em* 'beat with a beetle'; *xt'an* 'goad' (*a*-stem, used to translate κέντρον at *Acts* 26:14) next to *xt'em* 'I goad', etc. As we have seen, the Armenian words with the *-an* suffix could have other explanations. Bolognesi (1962:105f.) believes that the words contain a reflex of the Iranian participle suffix *-ana-/-āna-*, and notes that a parallel relation between noun of instrument and participle is found in the use of the instrument noun suffix *-ič'* to translate Greek present participles in the Armenian Gospels. However Bolognesi is unable to present a recognised Iranian loan used in the same way (*patsparan* 'refuge' and *xap'an* 'impediment' are not exactly comparable). Some of the words involved may have Indo-European roots,[112] but most are of uncertain origin. It may be therefore that these words and the suffix have been loaned from a language now lost. The question cannot be decisively resolved.

If δρεπάνη and *artewan* do both derive from the same prototype, it will provide strong evidence to support a common morphological development shared by the two languages. However, as we have seen it is also possible that the final *-an* of *artewan* derives from an Armenian suffix used to mark body parts, in which case the connection with the Greek word will no longer be tenable.

Another possibility is that the Armenian term is the reflex of a loan-word which was borrowed before the Armenian sound shift. The sickle is an item of culture which may have been passed from one community to another and therefore the term for it is also susceptible to transfer. Indeed, the Greek word δρεπάνη was borrowed into the ancestor of Albanian giving Modern Albanian *drapër* 'sickle' (cf. Huld 1984:54). Other Armenian words which may reflect loans made before the sound shift will be discussed at **4.35**.

This correspondence is also open to doubt because of the peculiar semantic shift from 'sickle' to 'eyebrow'. If the connection between δρεπάνη and *artewan* is correct, it may show a Greek-Armenian innovation, or it may be an example of a very early Armenian loan from Greek.

4.15   **dwāro-* (**dweh₂ro-*) 'long'

Meillet lists Greek δᾱρός (Pindar, Choral Lyric and dialectal, δηρός in Homer), 'long (of time)' and Armenian *erkar* 'long' among his special Armenian-Greek isoglosses (1936:142). The semantic agreement between the two terms is close; in Homer δηρός is conjoined with χρόνος 'time' in all its four occurrences as an adjective, and the adverb δηρόν 'for a long time' occurs forty-four times (cf. *LfrgE* II 281), and *erkar* is used twice in the Armenian Bible translation with reference to length of time.[113]

Greek and Armenian appear to share a peculiar ablaut form $*dweh_2\text{-}ro\text{-}$, which contrasts with $*duh_2\text{-}ro\text{-}$ (with the root in zero grade) which is the ancestor to Vedic *dūrá* 'distant' and possibly also to Latin *dūrus* 'hard'.[114] Benveniste saw a similar ablaut form to that underlying the Greek and Armenian words in Hittite *tuwala*- 'distant' (1932:143). However, the word seems more likely to be a Hittite derivative from *tuwa* 'distant', so this cannot be reckoned to be an exact parallel. The ablaut grade of the Greek and Armenian forms will be further discussed below.

First, however, the phonetic development of the Armenian word should be discussed. This comparision shares with the correspondences discussed at **4.16** (Armenian *erknč'im*) and **4.23** (Armenian *erkn*) the necessity of positing a sound change from $*dw$- to *erk*- to explain the Armenian forms. Indeed the connections of this and the other two Armenian words to forms in Greek comprise, together with the derivation of *erkow* '2' < $*dwō$, the most secure examples of the change.

The sound change has received a large amount of discussion since first put forward by Meillet (*MSL* 11 (1900) p. 394, reprinted in 1977:61). De Lamberterie (1988:221–228) and Kortlandt (1989) have recently given very full surveys of the scholarly literature and discussions of the phonetic difficulties with the posited sound change, and I do not think that it is necessary to repeat these discussions here. In view of the denial of the sound change by such scholars as Pedersen, Pisani, Winter, Szemerényi and Kortlandt,[115] it cannot be taken as secure. However, in the absence of entirely safe counter-examples to the change, and as the phonetic arguments against the change are not conclusive, it cannot be dismissed. The correctness of Meillet's posited sound change must be decided on the etymologies involved. If the words can be satisfactorily explained in other ways, then it is probably best to dispense with the posited change. If, however, to deny the sound change means to dismiss otherwise unobjectionable connections in form and sense, in favour of correspondences which are not so close, then one should accept the changes as valid.

The alternative etymology for *erkar* given by Kortlandt (following Meillet *MSL* 9 (1896) p. 150, reprinted in 1977:25) connects it with Lithuanian *eȓdvas* 'spacious'. The Lithuanian word shows an independent development of meaning from a root $*erd$- or $*erd^h$- which is ascribed a meaning 'loose' by Pokorny *IEW* 333. Armenian *erkar* must derive in Kortlandt's analysis from $*erdw$- not $*erd^h\text{-}w$, but the Vedic word *árdha*- 'side, part, place', which is closer than the Armenian terms to the Lithuanian root in form and meaning, favours a reconstruction $*erd^h$-. Consequently this etymology of *erkar* is open to doubt. Kortlandt also mentions (1989:49) Pisani's connection of *erkar* and *erkayn* with Latin *grandis* 'big' which has little to recommend it. Neither of these etymologies is therefore sufficient to argue against a connection of *erkar* and δηρός.

Greek δηρός < $*dwāro$- < $*dweh_2\text{-}ro$- appears to show the *thème* II ablaut of the root rather than the zero grade (*$d\bar{u}$- < *duh_2-) which is continued by the Latin and Sanskrit forms. Greek also shows similar ablaut grades in other adjectives derived from disyllabic bases. For example, ζωός 'alive' from $g^wy\bar{o}w\acute{o}s$ (from *g^wyeh_3-wo-) as against *$g^w\bar{\imath}wos$ < *g^wih_3-wo- in Vedic $j\bar{\imath}v\acute{a}$-'alive', etc.;[116] a number of forms which derive ultimately from participles in *-$t\acute{o}$-, such as κασίγνητος 'brother' with -γνητος possibly from *$g'neh_1$-to-, which stands beside Vedic $j\bar{a}t\acute{a}$- 'born' from the zero grade *$g'n\!h_1$-to-; and perhaps μωρός 'stupid' < *$mw\bar{o}r\acute{o}s$ next to Vedic $m\bar{u}r\acute{a}$- 'stupid' (Normier 1977:182 n. 26).

Some scholars (following Francis 1970:280) have suggested that the original Greek form *$dw\bar{a}$-ro- is the regular phonetic outcome of *duh_2-ro-. This question has been dealt with in more detail at **2.3.2**, where the possibility that Armenian may have undergone a similar sound change was discussed and rejected on the grounds that in other words (in particular *ownayn* 'empty') the development of Armenian -*ow*- < *-uh_2- is found. It is preferable to view Greek δηρός as a derivative of an original form *$dweh_2$-ro-. It is difficult to say whether the Greek ablaut in words of this type is an archaism or an innovation. Forms also showing a *thème* II ablaut rather than a zero grade are found in Vedic: for example, $pr\bar{a}t\acute{a}$- 'full' < *$pl\bar{e}t\acute{o}$- (< *$pleh_1$-to-) beside $p\bar{u}rt\acute{a}$- from *$p\!lt\acute{o}$- (< *$p\!lh_1$-to-), and in Latin: for example $pl\bar{e}nus$ 'full'. It is therefore not impossible that the Greek development represents an archaism, although it is perhaps more likely that the Greek vocalism is an innovation.

It is not certain that the Armenian word *erkar* directly continues a protoform *$dw\bar{a}ro$-/-$\bar{a}$-. The *NBHL* lists the word as an *a*-stem, but gives no citations which support this view, nor do the Biblical occurrences reveal the declension class. The declension class may well be a post-classical transfer from the original *o*-stem declension. The suffix -*ar* (normally *o*-stem, sometimes *a*-stem) shows some productivity in the preliterate stage of Armenian (see further **4.18** below). The existence of the word *erkayn* 'long, wide', which cannot be separated from *erkar* (Meillet *REArm* 4 (1924) pp. 3–4, reprinted in 1977:211–212), indicates also that -*ar* may be a suffix. The -*ayn* of *erkayn* is found as a suffix in other adjectives, for example, *miayn* 'only', *ownayn* 'empty' (Lidén 1906:23; note also the semantically close *layn* 'wide'). The adjective *erkar* could therefore represent a base *erk*- with a suffix. The Armenian base *erk(a)*- may in fact be equivalent to the base δη- of Greek δη-ρός and could derive from the root noun *$dweh_2$- 'distance in space and time' reconstructed by Schindler (1972:37) from Greek δήν 'for a long time' and Hittite *tuwa* 'far'. The root noun may also have influenced the full grade vocalism of Greek δηρός, as suggested at **2.3.2**.

In conclusion, *erkar* and δηρός show a formal and semantic agreement which may be the result of a common innovation, and this correspondence is one of the closest lexical agreements between the two languages. However, the Armenian word *erkayn* suggests that the language also inherited a meaning of spatial distance, not present in the Greek forms, and suggests that the -*ar* of *erkar* may be a later addition.

4.16 **dwei-* 'fear'

Greek δεδίσσομαι 'I frighten' (Epic δειδίσσομαι) and Armenian *erknč'im* 'I fear' (aor. *erkeay*) are seen by Meillet (1936:109) as parallel formations from a prototype **dwi-sk'-yo-*, 'sauf redoublement que l'arménien n'a pas, et la nasale qui ne se trouve pas en grec.'

The verbal root *dwi-* 'fear' is found elsewhere in Indo-European, in Vedic *dvéṣṭi* 'hate', Tocharian A and B *wi-* 'fear' (for phonetic development see Schindler 1966–7:236 f.), and perhaps also Luvian *kwaya-* 'fear' (Szemerényi 1985:793 f.). I shall concentrate on Meillet's posited morphological agreement of the Greek and Armenian verbs.

Meillet's explanation of the Greek form is made difficult by the fact that the verb shows reduplication with -ε- not -ι-. Although other Indo-European languages show reduplication for present stems with **-e-* (for example Sanskrit *dadāti* 'he gives'), in Greek all other inherited reduplicating present stems have -ι- as the reduplication vowel; verbs with reduplication in -ε- in the present are of secondary origin. This suggests that there may be an alternative explanation for the forms δεδίσσομαι and δειδίσσομαι, and it is tempting to see them as originating from the addition of -σσ- to the stem found in δείδω 'I fear', which is re-interpreted as a present tense although actually derived from an ancient perfect **δεδϝογα 'I fear'. The stem vowel -ι- of δεδίσσομαι and δειδίσσομαι would arise from forms with the weak grade, such as δείδιμεν (*Iliad* 9.230 etc.), δείδιθι (*Iliad* 5.827 etc.) and others (see the list of Homeric forms at *LfrgE* II 228). A less likely explanation of the formation of δειδίσσομαι is that it stems from the reduced grade of the perfect δείδοικα, δειδικ-,[117] with added **-ye/o-* suffix. The form δειδίσκομαι which would appear to support Meillet's theory in fact only occurs once in Greek at Aristophanes *Lysistrata* 564 (ἐδεδίσκετο) and should perhaps be corrected to ἐδεδίττετο (with Attic -ττ- for -σσ-).

The morphological development of *erknč'im* is extremely difficult to explain. There are only three Armenian verbs with presents formed with a suffix -*nč'im*. The other two verbs are *martnč'im* 'I fight' and *kornč'im* 'I perish'. The -*nč'im* ending may have arisen through a conflation of -*č'im* and -*nowm*. All verbs of the -*č'im* class and the majority of verbs of the -*nowm* class are distinguished by their aorists in -*eay*, which marks no other Armenian verb class. Some verbs conjugate their present stem in both classes: for example, *p'axč'im* 'I flee' (aorist *p'axeay*) has an alternate form *p'axnowm*, and both forms occur in the Bible translation.

Armenian *erknč'im* has several alternative etymologies. Pedersen (1906:399) connected it with Gothic *faurhtjan* from a root **perg/g^w-*,[118] and

Ačaṝyan (*HAB* II² 64f.) connected the nouns *erk* 'work', and *erkn* '(labour) pains'. Benveniste (1954:254f., reprinted in 1971:253) noted the semantic connection between 'two', 'doubt' and 'fear', and saw the Indo-European roots **dwei-* 'fear' and **dwei-* 'two' as originally identical. This raises the possibility that the Armenian verb might be a later derivative from the numeral *erkow*, or, at least, reformed by comparison with the numeral (Pisani 1951:55). The other two verbs with present suffix -*nč'im* may also be denominative formations from the nouns *mart* 'fight' (so Klingenschmitt 1982:81) and *kor* 'ruin' (preserved in the phrase *i kor* 'into ruin'; elsewhere it has the meaning 'bent').

Therefore the connection of the Armenian and Greek forms is not fully certain. Even if the correspondence is accepted, the two languages show no special morphological agreement against related terms in other languages.

4.17 $*d^h\bar{a}g$- ($*d^heh_2g$-) 'cut'

Lidén (1906:55) was the first to connect Greek θήγω 'sharpen' (*Iliad* 2.382 etc.) with the Armenian word *dakow* (gen. plur. *dakowac'*) 'adze, axe'. Lidén saw the Armenian word, which does not occur in the Bible translation,[119] as developing from an adjective $*d^h\bar{a}gu$- 'sharp'. In Greek the original $*-\bar{a}$- is preserved in dialectal forms (θάγοντες at Aristophanes *Lys.* 1256 etc.)[120] and the Hesychius gloss τέθωκται 'be drunk, excited' (with a change in meaning from 'sharpened' to 'excited', compare English *eager*, which derives from Latin *acer* 'sharp') may preserve the original perfect form of θήγω with ō deriving from $*oh_2$.

The correspondence of the Armenian and the Greek words points to a root with an original 'velar' $*g$ (as opposed to a palatal or labio-velar). In Armenian original palatals, velars and labio-velars all merge after $*u$ to give the same reflexes as the palatals, a change which may stem from within the parent language (Meillet 1936:37). In Greek the merger also occurs before $*u$, and *a priori* one would expect this in Armenian as well. Pedersen (1906:381f.) and Winter (1962:257) have given examples of a merger before $*u$: *sowzanem* 'cover' next to κεύθω (Pedersen *loc. cit.*; this connection is uncertain); *t'anjr* (genitive *t'anjow*) 'thick, heavy' next to Lithuanian *tingùs* 'lazy, sluggish' (Pedersen 1906:140) or *tánkus* 'thick' (Winter *loc. cit.*, following Hübschmann 1897:448);[121] and Winter cites the Armenian pair *cowṝ* and *kor* both 'bent' next to Greek γῡρός (see further **4.27**). Another example may be *šowrǰ* 'around' if from $*kury->*k'wury-$ (Meillet *BSL* 37 (1936) p. 35, reprinted in 1977:293).

Lidén (1906:121f.) argues against the change, but he does not mention the equation of *t'anjr* to Lithuanian *tánkus* which presents a correspondence of form and meaning far closer than any of the etymologies he gives to support his objection. Armenian *kow* 'dung' (Sanskrit *gūtha-* 'dung') is cited by Meillet (1889:59n.) as an example of a labio-velar before *$*u$, but the word probably retains its velar by analogy to the full grade *$*geu-$ which survives in the Armenian word *koy* 'dung' (see further Pedersen 1906:383).

Thus, the merger of velars and palatals before *$*u$, although not proven beyond doubt, seems a likely Armenian sound change, and argues against the direct derivation of *dakow* from *$*dʰāgu-$. Furthermore, other Proto-Indo-European *u*-stem 'antonymic stative' adjectives inherited into Armenian show an irregular declension (as *t'anjr* mentioned above), with *-r* in the nominative singular and the plural inflected as an *n*-stem. Substantives derived from these adjectives show the ending *-owk*; for example, adjective *manr* 'small', genitive singular *manow* (cf. Greek (Hesychius) μάνυ from *$*mṇnú$) and substantive *manowk* 'child'.[122] One therefore expects either *$*dakr$ or *$*dakowk$ as the Armenian continuation of *$*dʰāgu-$. The form *dakowr* cited by the *NBHL* as a parallel to *dakow* might be relevant here; one could imagine that it results from a contamination of *$*dakr$ and another form. Unfortunately the form *dakowr* is cited with no reference or date; it appears to survive in the dialect of Akn according to Ačaṙyan *HAB* I² 614. Lidén (1906:55) thought that the form *dakowr* had arisen by analogy to *sakowr* (also *sakr*) 'battle-axe', and this seems more likely than the contamination theory.

The direct continuation of an otherwise unattested Proto-Indo-European adjective *$*dʰāgu-$ in Armenian is therefore unlikely. However it is possible that the Armenian word shows the later addition of the Armenian suffix *-ow* to a root *$*dak-$ as suggested by Solta (1960:413) and Ĵahowkyan (1987:241). The Armenian suffix *-ow* was discussed by Gjandschezian (1903:59f.) but has since received little attention. The suffix is found in the classical period attached to a small number of verbal roots to form agent nouns which are especially prevalent as the second member of compounds; for example, the verb *acem* 'I bring' forms the compound *k'nacow* used by Eznik to mean 'narcotic, that which brings sleep'. The uncompounded form *acow* means 'bed of a garden' (translates πρασία at *Sirach* 24:31[123]) and seems to have developed in sense from 'producer' (compare the Armenian word *ac* 'shoot (of a plant)').[124] The difficulty with this explanation of *dakow* is that the word should mean 'sharpener' *vel sim.* instead of 'axe'.

There are also a few other Armenian words which appear to show an *-ow* suffix which is unrelated to the agent-noun forming suffix. Some of these, such as *aṙow* 'canal' and *mawrow* 'mother-in-law' can be explained diachronically (from *$*sru-ti-$ and *$*mātru(w)ya-$ respectively) but are synchronically opaque. Other forms, such as *mełow* 'bee' (beside *mełr* 'honey') and *ełjerow* 'stag' (beside *ełjewr* 'horn'), cannot be explained synchronically or diachronically.

It is thus possible that *dakow* has been formed by the addition of a suffix which was productive at an earlier stage of the language, but whose function is now irrecoverable. The connection of the Armenian word with the 'Wanderwort' *dagger* (Late Latin *daga*, etc.) offers an alternative explanation of the word which is semantically more satisfying. The borrowing of vocabulary items for terms of weaponry is very common while, conversely, none of the words for 'axe' listed by Buck (1949:561) is derived from a root meaning 'sharpen'.[125]

In conclusion, while it is possible that the Armenian and Greek words are derived from a common root, it is by no means certain. The two languages show no agreement on the suffixation of that root.

4.18 $*d^hal(e)$- ($*d^h(e)h_2l(h_1)$-) 'sprout, be fresh, green'

The root $*d^hal$- is found in a number of Greek words, for example, the verb θάλλω 'bloom, thrive', the nouns θαλία 'abundance' and θαλλός 'shoot', the adjectives *θαλύς (only the feminine θάλεια 'rich, plentiful' is found, as an epithet of δαίς 'feast' or a substantive in Homer; see *LfrgE* II 962f.) and θαλερός 'blooming, fresh, abundant' (applied in Homer to (young) humans, tears, voice, hair, thighs, fat, weeping and marriage; see *LfrgE* II 963f.). The same root may also be found in the Armenian word for 'green, fresh' *dalar* (translates χλωρός at *Mark* 6:39 and ὑγρός at *Luke* 23:31) and other Armenian forms (see further below), and perhaps also in Albanian *dal* 'sprout, enter, come' (aorist *dolla*) and possibly Hittite *talleš*- 'be favourable', *talli*- 'favourable', with *-ll-* < *$*lH$- (Bader 1990:13) and Tocharian (B) *šäktālye* 'sowing' (Arutjunjan 1983:280).

A number of scholars since Solta (1960:350) have seen the agreement of root and suffix in Greek θαλερός 'blooming, fresh' and Armenian *dalar* (*o*-stem) 'green' as significant, but the exact formal correspondence between the Greek suffix -ερο- and Armenian -*ar* is difficult to assess. Klingenschmitt (1970:86 n. 9, followed by Mayrhofer 1986:126 n. 118) posited *$*d^halh_1ro$- as the ancestor of the two words, yet this entails either the reconstruction of an otherwise unknown suffix *$*-h_1ro$- or a root with final laryngeal, for which there is no other evidence.

Hamp (1984:159), Godel (1984:289f.) and de Lamberterie (1990:II.654) explain the formal difficulties through different grades of the suffix in the two languages, *$*-ero$- for Greek but *$*-ro$- for Armenian. However, the suffixes of both words could be equally well explained as individual developments within the two languages. There are other examples of an -*ar* suffix in Armenian, such as in *ardar* 'just' from *$*r̥t$- (Hübschmann 1897:424 and 438),[126] and the suffix seems to have been productive at an earlier stage of the language (Godel 1975:65, see also **4.15**).

In Greek there are a number of examples of the productivity of a suffix -ερος, particularly formed from υ-stem adjectives. The adjective θαλερός may have been built from *θαλύς in the same way as γλυκερός is formed from γλυκύς, κρατερός from κρατύς, etc. (Chantraine *DELG* 420, de Lamberterie 1990:II.646).

The agreement between the two forms is further complicated by other forms in Armenian. The Armenian words *deł* 'herb, medicine' and *dełin* 'yellow' led Ačaṝyan (*HAB* I² 649) to posit a root *d^hel- (which developed to *deł*-) with ablaut *$d^h\c{l}$- (which developed to *dal*-). This root could also explain scattered words in Celtic and Germanic (for instance Welsh *dalen* 'leaf').[127]

The connection of the Armenian adjective *dalar* with Greek θαλερός therefore offers a methodological problem for the historical linguist. The semantic agreement between the two terms is close, and the formal difficulties of the connection rest solely on the disagreement between a suffix *-ero-* and *-ṛ(r)o-*. One could, therefore, accord more weight to the semantic agreement, and seek a way to account for the formal disagreement. It is possible, for example, that the original Greek form of the suffix has been remodelled by analogy to the other *-ερο-* forms (de Lamberterie 1990:II.654 n. 1), or that an original form *θαλαρός was dissimilated to θαλερός (P. Considine, personal communication), or that the two languages generalised different ablaut forms of the suffix.

Alternatively, one could take the other extreme and attribute the semantic agreements and the morphological similarity to chance; by this hypothesis the Armenian word either derives from the same root as θαλερός and has developed along the same lines independently, or it stems from a separate root *del*- which lies behind other Armenian forms.

The problem is even more confused by the Armenian word for 'jaundice' *dalowkn* (translating ἴκτερος 'jaundice' in the Bible), which de Lamberterie (1990:II.655) has derived from a noun *$d^h alū$-, comparing other Armenian nouns and adjectives with a suffix *-owk(n)* derived from earlier *$ū$-stem nouns and *u-stem adjectives, such as *mowkn* 'mouse' < *$mūs$-, *jowkn* 'fish' beside Greek ἰχθύς, *anjowk* 'narrow' < *$ng^{'h}u$- and *manowk* 'child' < *$mṇnu$-.[128] De Lamberterie proposes that some *$ū$-stem nouns may be derived from feminine *u-stem adjectives, formed with a suffix *-h_2-: compare Greek ἰθύς 'direction' beside ἰθύς 'straight'. This theory allows the connection between *dalowkn* and the Greek adjective *θαλύς. De Lamberterie's etymology thus provides a more satisfying formal connection between Greek and Armenian derivatives of a root *d^hal-. However, the semantic equation suffers in the process, since the meaning 'jaundice' is far removed from the probable meaning 'rich, abundant' of the adjective *θαλύς.

Indeed, the meaning of *dalowkn* might support the view that the base meaning of the Armenian root is 'green' rather than 'fresh', and that the use of *dalar* with reference to 'green' as opposed to 'seasoned' wood (*Luke* 23:31) represents a secondary development. However, as de Lamberterie (1990:II.654) notes, the word *kanač'* is the normal Armenian word for 'green' and *dalar* is in general restricted to use with vegetation. This suggests that the meaning of *dalowkn* is secondarily built upon *dalar*, and enables 'fresh' to be kept as the primary meaning of the Armenian root.

The word *dalowkn* does not consequently shed any fresh light on the question of whether the semantic agreement between the Greek and Armenian words is significant. Hamp (1984) has seen the meanings of the two adjectives as evidence for a shared development made by the two languages, which have, in his view, innovated a meaning 'emerge with moisture' (later to develop to 'fresh' in Armenian) from the original meaning 'spring forth' which developed to 'go out' in Albanian. Hamp follows Lowenstam's investigation of the semantics of the Greek forms (1979) who sees the principal sense as 'spring forth or emerge with or from moisture'. However, de Lamberterie (1990:II.646 n. 2) has rejected the hypothesis that 'moist' is a necessary factor in the meaning of *θαλύς* and *θαλερός* (and the Homeric usage supports this view) and he notes that the earliest attested meaning of *θαλύς*, 'abundant', has to be explained as a secondary development by Lowenstam's theory. By de Lamberterie's reckoning 'abundance/fertility' is the base meaning of the Greek terms. The semantic development of *dalar* and *θαλερός* may therefore be independent. The original meaning of the root might be something like 'sprout, come into fruit' from which Greek has generalised the notion of abundance, Armenian has generalised the notion of freshness, and Albanian has extended the meaning to refer to motion.

The foregoing discussion has set forth alternative explanations of this correspondence between Greek and Armenian, and the interpretation of the data ultimately depends on the respective weight given to semantic and morphological agreements. Since there are some grounds for rejecting the connection between the Greek and Armenian forms altogether, this correspondence cannot stand in the front line of lexical agreements.

4.19   *$d^h(e)mb^h$- 'bury'

The Greek words *θάπτω* 'bury', *τάφος* 'grave, tomb' (but never with this meaning in Homer, always 'funeral rites', etc.), *τάφρος* 'ditch, trench' and Armenian *damban*, *dambaran* 'tomb, grave' may share the same root. The phonetic grounds for linking the forms are straightforward enough; for the development of *$*-mb^h$- see **4.28** below.

Neither of the Armenian terms, nor their derivatives, is found in the oldest literature; *dambaran* first occurs in the work of Johannes Katʻołikos in the tenth century, and *damban* in the earlier, but post-classical, work of Grigor Narekecʻi;[129] no examples of the declension class of either form are cited in the *NBHL*. Lidén (1906:42, followed by Benveniste 1935:12) takes the two forms in -*an* and -*aran* as evidence that the word was once declined as an *$*-r/n$ stem. However the Armenian form in -*aran* is more likely to show the suffix -*aran* borrowed from Iranian (de Lamberterie 1984:238 n. 49). The suffix of *damban* may also be an Iranian loan (for -*an* see **4.14**).

The absence of *damban* or a derivative from the earliest Armenian literature suggests that the word may not be native to the language, particularly since the same concept is represented by different words in the earliest texts. In the Armenian Bible translation the terms *gerezman* 'tomb, grave, sepulchre' translates μνῆμα 'sepulchre' (e.g. *Mark* 5:3), μνημεῖον 'sepulchre' (e.g. *Mark* 5:2), τάφος 'tomb' (e.g. *Matt.* 23:27) and ταφή 'burial' (e.g. *Matt.* 27:7), and *širim* 'tomb, sepulchre' translates μνῆμα (2 *Chron.* 34:28), μνημεῖον (e.g. *Gen.* 23:6), τάφος (e.g. *Matt.* 23:29) and σπήλαιον 'cave, grave' (*Judith* 16:23). These two terms are found frequently, but the forms in *damb*- do not occur. It is not clear whether there is any semantic difference between the terms *gerezman* and *damban* and *dambaran* (the Biblical passages suggest that *širim* might refer in particular to a rock-cut or built sepulchre). The passage from Johannes Kat'ołikos cited in the *NHBL* uses the phrase *i dambarani t'ałec'an* 'they were buried in a *dambaran*', which seems equivalent to the Biblical expression *t'ałec'aw i gerezmani* 'he was buried in a grave' (e.g. *Judges* 8:32).

Even if the term *damban* is an inherited word, it is not certain that it is in fact a unique isogloss to Greek τάφος etc. The Greek words have long been connected with Old Prussian *dambo* 'ground', which is phonetically unobjectionable, although dismissed by e.g. Pokorny *IEW* 248f. Further connections have been made with Gothic *faur-dammjan* 'dam up' (< *d^hemb^h-n*-, Benveniste 1935:12), Rumanian *dîmb* 'bank' (taken as a survival from 'Dacian', Băltăceanu 1980:21) and Avestan *daxma*- 'grave' (dissimilated from *$dafma$*- < *$d^hm̥b^h$-mo*-, Hoffmann 1965). The Greek word τύμβος 'sepulchre' could also be related if it reflects some pre-Greek Indo-European dialect which presumably underwent a change analogous to Grassman's law and then a *Lautverschiebung*; compare πύργος 'tower' < *$b^hr̥g^h$*- for exactly parallel phonology.

Hence Greek and Armenian agree only on a root, which may have survived elsewhere. The late and scanty attestation of the Armenian words casts doubt upon the comparison.

4.20 *$d^hr̥b^hu$*- 'thick'

De Lamberterie (1990:II.680–682) has recently connected the Greek adjective ταρφύς 'thick, close' (applied in Homer to e.g. a shower of arrows (*Il.* 11.387) and to snowflakes (*Il.* 12.158)) with the Armenian adjective/ substantive *derbowk* or *darbowk* 'rough (place), stony (place)'.

If one assumes that the original Armenian form was *darbowk* the formal connection between the two words is indeed close. There are parallel Armenian forms in -*owk* which may derive from earlier *u*-stems, for example, *anjowk* 'narrow' < **angᵈʰu-*, *manowk* 'child' < **mṇnu-*, and consequently both forms can be derived from a form **dʰrbʰu-*. The root **dʰerbʰ-* is also found in Baltic (Lithuanian *drẽbti* 'bespatter, daub') and perhaps also in other Indo-European languages, but, by de Lamberterie's analysis, the **u*-stem adjective is limited to Greek and Armenian.

The connection between ταρφύς and *darbowk*, though formally satisfying, is open to considerable doubt on semantic grounds. De Lamberterie defends the semantic connection by comparing the use of the Greek derived form τραφερός to mean 'solid (earth)' in the Homeric formula ἐπὶ τραφερήν τε καὶ ὑγρήν (*Il.* 14.308 etc.) 'on land and sea'; this meaning, he claims, is not far removed from the uses of the adjective τραχύς 'rocky, harsh', normally applied to the earth when used in a physical sense. This offers a possible path for the semantic development, but in the absence of secure parallels it remains an uncertain and difficult one. The connection of the Greek adjective with the Lithuanian verb *drẽbti* and other Indo-European forms made by de Lamberterie suggests that the root meaning was 'coagulate' or similar, and none of the other correspondences show a development similar to that supposed for Armenian.

While this etymology of the Armenian term has some allure, the semantic difficulties involved do not allow any weight to be put on the presumed correspondence with Greek.

4.21   **dʰregʰ-/*dʰregʰ-* 'turn'

Létoublon and de Lamberterie (1980) have recently discussed the development of this verbal root in Greek and Armenian. In Greek the meaning has evolved from 'turn' to 'run', although in passages of Homer τρέχω can still be interpreted as 'turn'; for example, the verb is used of τροχός 'a wheel' at *Iliad* 23.520. The Armenian verb *daṙnam* (aorist *darjay*) has retained the original meaning 'turn'. De Lamberterie connects the Armenian aorist *darjay*, which he thinks continues an ancient imperfect, directly with the Doric present τράχω both of which derive, in his analysis, from a Proto-Indo-European present formation of the type of Vedic *tudáti*.

This would therefore appear to be an important addition to our list of Greek-Armenian isoglosses. However, Klingenschmitt, in his discussion of the Armenian verb (1982:110f.) does not mention the Greek connection but concentrates on the Albanian verb *dreth* (aorist *drodha*) 'twist, spin' which he takes from the same root as the Greek and Armenian words, together with Albanian *derth* 'pour out'. Létoublon and de Lamberterie (*op. cit.* p. 319) claim that the semantic development of the Albanian word separates it from the Greek and Armenian terms, but one cannot tell at what stage this development took place; if we only had Modern Greek τρέχω 'run, hasten', Modern Albanian *dreth* 'spin', and Modern Armenian *daṙnam* 'turn', then we would probably see the connection between Albanian and Armenian as closest.

Hence the verbal formation is not limited to Armenian and Greek, and the verbs τρέχω and daŕnam are best interpreted as separate formations from an inherited root.

4.22 *d^hrew- 'cry aloud'

Frisk (1944:8f.) first connected Greek θρέομαι 'cry aloud' with Armenian erdnowm 'swear' (irregular aorist erdoway). Phonetically and morphologically the connection is unobjectionable; both forms can be derived from a root *d^hru-. However, although a semantic shift from 'cry aloud' to 'swear' is possible, it is not directly paralleled by any of the words for 'swear' listed by Buck (1949:1437).[130] The connection of the Armenian word with the root *d^hru-, which survives in Sanskrit dhruvá- 'fixed', made by Pedersen (1906:355) and Klingenschmitt (1982:247), seems as plausible as Frisk's explanation. A cognate to the Greek verb may also be found in Iranian (Manichaean Parthian dr'w- 'cry aloud'; Klingenschmitt 1982:246f.).

In conclusion, the connection of the Greek and Armenian words is not secure, and if they are connected, then it is possible that the root survives also in Iranian.

4.23 *edun-/*edwe/on- 'pain'

Greek ὀδύνη 'pain' and Armenian erkn (n-stem) 'pain, labour pains'[131] were first compared by Frisk (1944:11). Solta (1960:419) took the pair as another significant Greek-Armenian lexical isogloss. If the Armenian term is connected to the Greek (on the difficulties of the sound change *dw- > erk- see 4.15), then the isogloss is probably not exclusive as the Old Irish word idu 'pain' ('labour pains' in the plural idain) may also have the same origin. Schindler has discussed the three forms with his usual display of learning and insight (Schindler 1975b), and I shall do no more than summarise his findings here.

Schindler derives erkn from a *n-stem noun *$h_1$edwon-, where the prevocalic form of the stem *$h_1$edw- has been generalised throughout the paradigm at the expense of the variant *$h_1$edun- (p. 55). The Greek word, conversely, represents the generalisation of this second form *$h_1$edun- (or possibly *$h_1$dun-) and its later 'thematisation' is into the predominantly feminine ā-class because of its feminine gender. For this 'thematisation' Schindler compares the transfer of the feminine athematic noun *d^hwor-/ *d^hur- to the Greek first declension noun θύρά (p. 56). The initial vowel of ὀδύνη is explained by Schindler as the result of an assimilation of initial *e- to *o-* when an $*o$ or $*u$ follows in the next syllable which took place in some dialects; the unassimilated form survives in 'Aeolic' ἐδύνᾱ (cited by Gregory of Corinth). Irish *idu* (accusative singular *idain*, nominative plural *idain*, genitive plural *idan* etc.) is explained as the result of paradigm levelling from a paradigm (pp. 59–60):

nominative singular $*iud < *h_1edw\bar{o}$,
accusative singular $idain < *h_1edun-$.[132]

From these reconstructions Schindler builds an original Proto-Indo-European paradigm as follows (p. 61):

nom. sing. $*h_1\acute{e}dw\bar{o}$
acc. sing. $*h_1\acute{e}dwon-m$
gen. sing. $*h_1dun-\acute{e}s$, etc.

The feminine Old Irish and Greek derivatives suggest that the noun was originally feminine. Schindler suggests (p. 62) that the word may be a derivative from the root $*h_1ed-$ 'eat', if the original meaning was 'bite' (cf. $*h_1dont-$ 'tooth') with subsequent semantic development to 'eat' and 'cause pain'.

If Schindler's conclusions are correct, and there is no good reason to suspect that they might not be, the three languages have made different developments from a commonly inherited lexical item, and there is no reason to suppose that Greek and Armenian have made a common innovation or even made the same selections from a set of options.

4.24 $*e/og^{wh}\bar{\imath}n-$ 'hedgehog'

The Armenian word *ozni* translates Greek ἐχῖνος 'hedgehog' in all five of its Biblical occurrences. The root is also found in other Indo-European languages (cf. Modern German *Igel*, Russian *ëž*), but Solta (1960:195f.) thought it significant that only the Greek and Armenian words show an $*n$-suffix. However, the $*l$-suffix of Germanic may have replaced an earlier $*n$-suffix (cf. Frisk *GEW* I 601). The different vocalisms of Greek and Armenian argue against a shared innovation.

4.25 $*enewn / *h_1newn$ 'nine'

The Greek and Armenian words for 'nine' stand apart from the other Indo-European words for this numeral since they both have an initial vowel, *e-* in Greek ἐννέα and *i-* in Armenian *inn*, which could derive from earlier $*e-$ which was raised before the following nasal. This correspondence is taken as a significant isogloss, or as the result of a Greek-Armenian innovation, by

Meillet (1936:143), Pisani (1951:49), Solta (1960:112), Arutjunjan (1983:287) and others. The origin of the initial vowel is uncertain; it may stem from an original initial 'laryngeal', $*h_1$-. However, this causes problems for the Armenian form, since, as was shown at **2.2**, when an Armenian 'prothetic vowel' reflects an earlier 'laryngeal', the vowel seems always to be *a*-. The hypothesis that the initial vowel of *inn* represents a vocalised 'laryngeal' is therefore uncertain. Moreover apparent cognates in Anatolian languages (Lycian *nuñtāta*, a numeral of unknown meaning, use of the sign for '9' with phonetic value *nu* in Luvian; see further Eichner 1992:87) point to a root without initial laryngeal. The frequently repeated connection of the word for 'nine' with the word for 'new' would support a reconstruction without laryngeal for the numeral, but in my view this brand of etymological speculation is of little worth.

The Greek and Armenian words, despite their surface similarity, cannot derive from the same original form. The double *n* of ἐννέα has never been satisfactorily explained, but the final element of the word clearly continues *-ewn* (or *-ewn̥*), which also lies behind Latin *novem*, Vedic *náva*, etc. Accordingly, Szemerényi (1964:113) and Winter (1965a:101 and 1992b:350) propose the following development for the Armenian numeral:

$$*newn̥ \text{ or } *h_1 newn̥ > *enewan > *inowan > *inown,$$

the form **inown* is then reduced to *inn* by analogy with *tasn* 'ten'. This explanation relies on uncertain sound changes (it is by no means evident that the sequence *-ewn̥* would have developed in this way), and a less than convincing analogical change. If the form **inown* was remodelled to *inn* by analogy to *tasn* as is suggested, why does *inn* not follow the same declension pattern as *tasn*? Winter himself shows that the declension of *inn* is anomalous, in that it forms a genitive-dative-ablative plural *inownc'* unlike the regularly formed genitive-dative-ablative of *tasn*, *tasanc'*. An alternative theory to this is clearly preferable.

Some scholars have tried to link the Armenian numeral with the form **ἐνϝα*- which is found as the first member of some Homeric compounds, for example εἰνάετες 'for nine years', and derived *inn* from **(h₁)enwn̥* (Hübschmann 1897:451, Pisani 1951:49).[133] But this explanation also requires very uncertain phonetic developments; the normal Armenian treatment of **-nw-* seems to be **-ng-* (compare *cowngk'* 'knees' < **gonwī*[134]).

The reconstruction which would account for the Armenian form the best would be **(h₁)enun* and this has been proposed by a number of scholars (Eichner 1978:152 n. 35, Godel 1982:13, de Lamberterie 1982c:83, Olsen 1985:15). Eichner provides a satisfactory account for the origin of the Armenian form, and for its differing syllabification to Greek **ἐνϝα*-; he thinks that both forms have arisen from old ordinal formations, and that the original ordinal which influenced the creation of the Armenian form was **enun-o-*, while **enwn̥t-o-* lies behind the Greek form. Another theory is advanced by

Olsen (following Pisani 1951:49), who considers that both forms reflect a metathesis of *newṇ.[134A]

The significance of the correspondence between ἐννέα and *inn* is difficult to assess. The agreement between the two languages is limited to the presence of an initial vowel, and if the two forms continue *$h_1$newṇ and *$h_1$enun respectively, then the Greek form agrees with the forms in the other Indo-European languages, and the Armenian shows an individual peculiarity of that language. The correspondence between them therefore merely reflects the fact that Greek shows a vowel as the continuation of a pre-consonantal laryngeal which is lost elsewhere. If, however, the Luvian and Lycian forms are taken as evidence that the root was originally lacking a laryngeal (and this is by no means certain), Armenian and Greek then must share a very peculiar ablaut form of the word, which is very likely to reflect a common innovation or metathesis.

4.26   *$g'el(h_2)$- 'laugh'

Both Armenian and Greek show a variety of words which may be derived from this root. The agreement is closest between Armenian *caŧr* (*u*-stem, gen. sing. *caŧow*) 'laugh' and Greek γέλως. The history of the two forms and their relation to other derived terms in the two languages requires a rather long exposition. I shall start by examining the relevant forms in Armenian and Greek. The Armenian word for 'laugh', *caŧr* (translating γέλως in the Bible, e.g. *James* 4:9), has genitive *caŧow* (twice in the Bible, *Ecclesiastes* 2:2, and *Job* 8:21) and thus belongs to a small group of Armenian *u*-stem nouns which have -*r* in the nominative. The only other nouns in this class are *asr* 'fleece' (gen. *asow*) and *meŧr* 'honey' (gen. *meŧow*) and probably the singulars *cownr* 'knee' (irregular plural *cowngk'*, *cngac'*, no declension in singular) and *artawsr* 'tear' (plural *artasowk'*, no declension in singular). There is also a small number of adjectives which have this declension in the singular, but decline as *n*-stems in the plural such as *tanjr* 'thick' etc. (see above under *dakow* **4.17**).

The other nouns in this class can all be derived from Proto-Indo-European *u-stem neuters. This is clearest seen for *cownr* next to Greek γόνυ, and *artawsr* next to Greek δάκρυ; *asr* seems to continue the type of Latin *pecū* 'cattle', Sanskrit *paśu*-, rather than Greek πόκος 'fleece' (see **4.49**) and the declension of *meŧr* has been explained since Meillet (*MSL* 11 (1900) p. 401, reprinted in 1977:68) as the result of a conflation of *meli- and *medʰu-.

In view of the origin of the other Armenian nouns of this type, *caŧr* can be derived straightforwardly from *$g'elu$. The *a* vocalism of *caŧr* matches that of *asr* < *pek'u*. De Lamberterie (1978:271) explains the irregular vocalism as the result of the action of the following *u* in the genitive form. A *u* regularly lowers $*i$ to e in the preceding syllable and there is other evidence for a similar lowering effect on e; for example in *vat'sown* 'sixty' beside *vec'* 'six'.[135]

The Armenian declension *caṙr caḷow* may therefore represent the reshaping of an earlier paradigm *$*ceṙr$ *$*caḷow$, with the velar *ṙ* generalised from the nominative and the *a* vocalism generalised from the oblique cases. For *meṙr* 'honey' the vocalism of the nominative has been retained throughout the paradigm. However, Klingenschmitt (1982:147) derived the Armenian word from a different source: a Proto-Indo-European non-neuter *s*-stem with the following paradigm:

nominative $*g'elh_2\text{-}\bar{o}s$
genitive $*g'l̥h_2\text{-}s\text{-}e/os.$

By this theory the *ow*-stem declension of *caṙr* has arisen from the nominative after the Armenian sound change of $*\bar{o}$ to *ow*; and the *a*-vocalism of the root represents the generalisation of the zero grade throughout the paradigm. Other scholars had earlier proposed to link the *u*-stem declension of the Armenian noun with the -ω- of the Greek word (for example Frisk *GEW* I 295). However, if the form $*gelh_2\bar{o}s$ had been inherited into Armenian then one would expect the pre-apocope reflex *$*celuh$ which would have been assimilated, one assumes, into the normal *u*-declension, not the -*r*/-*ow*-declension (i.e. the *asr* type) since the *r*/*u*-type comprises only original neuters, and therefore would have had a pre-apocope ending $*\text{-}u(r)$ not $*\text{-}uh$.

Moreover, other forms which may have been inherited into Armenian with final $*\text{-}\bar{o}$ in the nominative have not been assimilated into the -*r*/-*ow* declension; compare Eichner's tentative reconstruction of *arew* 'sun' < *$*aréwu$ < $*h_2réw\bar{o}$ (1978:146) and the independent derivation by Klingenschmitt (1982:154) and Rasmussen (1987:31f.) of the word for 'village' *gewḷ* (genitive *geḷj*) from a paradigm with nominative $*\text{-}l\bar{o}(i)$, genitive $*\text{-}lye/os$. Furthermore, most of the Indo-European neuter *$*s$-stems have been transferred to the *o*-stem declension of Classical Armenian; for example *erek* (*o*-stem) 'evening' which comes from the same prototype as Greek ἔρεβος 'darkness' (Brugmann 1906:520, Meillet 1936:74), and there is no certain example of the Armenian treatment of a Proto-Indo-European non-neuter *$*s$-stem with lengthened grade in the nominative singular (i.e. the type of Greek ἔως 'dawn', Sanskrit *uṣā́s* 'dawn').[136] The derivation of the Armenian noun from a neuter *$*u$-stem is therefore preferable to Klingenschmitt's theory.

Other Armenian derivatives from this root offer little insight into the reconstruction of the original form. The verb *cicaḷim* 'I laugh' (translates γελάω in the Bible, e.g. *Luke* 6:21) may continue an original 'intensive' $*g'el\text{-}g'l(h_2)\text{-}$ which has undergone a dissimilation to *$*cei\text{-}cal\text{-}$ (Meillet *MSL* 13 (1905) p. 375, reprinted in 1977:125, Schwyzer 1939:647). But it is also possible that the verb *cicaḷim* was created within the individual history of Armenian, during which many new forms were created through reduplication; Klingenschmitt (1982:147f.) compares *cicaṙn* 'swallow', *t'it'eṙn* 'butterfly'. It is possible that the Armenian word for 'flower' *całik* is also connected to this root. Petersson (1916:289) accounted for the semantic development necessary for this etymology by comparing the Hesychius gloss γέλειν · λάμπειν, ἄνθειν 'shine, bloom'.

Greek offers a much larger array of forms which may be derived from the root *$g'el$- and the relationship between the forms is much more complex. I shall first consider the noun γέλως 'laugh'. The following case forms are attested in Homer (cf. *LfrgE* II 126):

nominative: γέλως, once in the *Iliad*, thrice in the *Odyssey*;
accusative: γέλον or γέλων or γέλω; at *Od*. 18.350 and 20.8 the accusative (whatever its form) is scanned as an iamb before a following consonant, but at *Od*. 20.346 γέλω is scanned as a pyrrhic before a following vowel; the other readings here are γέλον, γέλων and γέλωτ', the last two unmetrical;
dative: γέλῳ, only in the phrase γέλῳ ἔκθανον 'died with laughing', *Od*. 18.100, again scanned as a pyrrhic.

The Greek nouns with -ως in the nominative form a heterogeneous class and have different origins. The following types occur:

(a) forms arising from 'quantitative metathesis' or contraction of second declension nouns and adjectives such as λεώς 'people' (earlier λᾱός), ζώς 'alive' (beside ζωός).

(b) forms which can be derived from earlier non-neuter *s-stems; for example ἔως 'dawn' (Homeric ἠώς, Argolic ἀϝώς) < *$(h_2)ewsōs$, compare Latin *aurora* and Vedic *uṣā́s*. The original declension of nouns of this type has been disrupted by the loss of intervocalic *-s-, but uncontracted forms are sometimes still metrically possible in Homer (passages are given by Chantraine 1973:47). In later Greek masculine nouns of this type are transferred to a declension in -ως, -ωτος, while feminine nouns retain the original declension (in Attic some nouns follow the 'contract' declension).

(c) some forms may continue original animate *u-stems; the example usually cited in this connection is ἥρως 'hero' (cf. Schwyzer 1939:479, Rix 1976:148, etc.). As Rix admits, the interpretation of the Mycenaean divine name *ti-ri-se-ro-e* as /$Tris(h)ēro(h)ei$/ argues against this, although this interpretation of the name is open to doubt.[137] Other members of this class are ἅλως 'threshing floor', μήτρως and πάτρως 'mother-/father-in-law', and δμώς 'slave' (Schwyzer 1939:479, Schindler 1976:352).

(d) some forms may derive from earlier root-nouns. For example δώς 'giving' (*hapax* at Hesiod *Works and Days* 356), *βρώς and *γνώς (and others) in compounds such as ὠμοβρώς 'eating raw flesh' and ἀγνώς 'unknown, ignorant'. The latter forms are declined with genitive in -ωτος. The noun γέλως is not of this type.

(e) Perfect participles with masculine -ως (acc. -οτα in post Mycenaean Greek, but -wo-a in Mycenaean). The noun γέλως is not of this type.

The noun γέλως probably belongs to class **(b)** or **(c)**. It is generally understood to belong to the class of animate *s-stems (type **(b)**). This theory is not supported by the Homeric declension of the forms (which is distinct from the declension of the *s-stems such as ἠώς; Chantraine 1973:211), but by the existence of a form *γελασ- which is supposed to underlie other forms, such as the verb γελάω < *γελασ-ω or *γελασ-yω with sigmatic aorist *γελασ-σ-, as γέλασσε at *Iliad* 15.101 and 19.362, and the adjective γελαστά 'laughable' (only at *Odyssey* 8.307 in Homer) and γελᾱνής 'cheerful' (only Pindar *O*. 5.2 and *P*. 4.181) < *γελασ-νης.[138] The alternation between γέλως and *γέλας was seen as parallel to the alternation found in the pair τέκμαρ and τέκμωρ both 'goal, end' by Benveniste (1935:124f.).[139] However, there is no evidence to support the existence of a neuter noun *γέλας; nor is there any motivation for such a noun to disappear in favour of γέλως.

A more attractive explanation for the form *γέλας was proposed by Francis in his unpublished PhD thesis (1970:181), who reconstructed an original paradigm of the type:

Nom.   *g'elh₂ōs
Gen.   *g'elh₂s-os.

(Compare the reconstruction of the paradigm made by Klingenschmitt given above.) This original nominative form would explain Greek nominative γέλως from which the rest of the paradigm appears to have been built. The Greek forms with *γελασ- would result from the abstraction of the stem of the oblique cases.

It may also be possible to derive γέλως from an original animate *u*-stem noun (type **(c)** above) with a paradigm:

Nom.   *g'el(h₂)ōw-(s)
Acc.   *g'el(h₂)owm̥.

This paradigm might fit the Homeric forms better; the pyrrhic accusative γέλω (*Od*. 20.346), mentioned above, would stand for *γέλοϝ' elided from *γέλοϝα, and similarly γέλω at *Od*. 18.100 may be for *γέλοϝι (with *-o- analogical from the strong cases). The weak cases of *g'elh₂ōws would have been of the form *g'l̥h₂u- and this may have given rise to related words such as γλαυκός 'gleaming' (on this connection see de Lamberterie 1978:273f. and below). The later declension of γέλως in Greek may have arisen by analogy to ἔρως.

It is not possible to account for the element *γελασ- (see above), which supposedly underlies the Greek verbal forms, by this theory. However, the evidence for *γελασ- is not overwhelming; γελάω may derive from a thematised athematic verb *γέλᾱμι (as suggested by Schwyzer 1939:680). The other *γελασ- forms, such as ἀγέλαστος might arise by analogy. For ἀγέλαστος compare the numerous verbal adjectives in -το- with 'unetymological' -σ-, such as ἄγνωστος, listed by Schwyzer (1939:503). After the creation of (ἀ)γέλαστος and the aorist ἐγέλασσε (the only forms with *γελασ- in Homer) the stem *γελασ- may have been extracted and used to form the later derivatives γελάσιμος, γελασῖνος, etc.

But there is no clear model for the formation of the adjective γελάνής. However, the standard explanation for this formation is hardly satisfactory, since there was no Greek suffix -νης. Manessy-Guitton (1972:93) assumes that the adjective *γελασνο- was transferred to the -ης type by analogy to adjectives of the type of ἀπηνής 'ungentle, rough'. But it is just as likely that the suffix -άνης/-ήνης, which is found in σαφηνής 'clear' (first in Pindar) and perhaps ἀπηνής, πρηνής 'head down' (both already in Homer) and προσηνής 'soft',[140] was added directly to a root γελ-.

In summary, γέλως can be plausibly derived from either an *s-stem noun or a *u-stem. The derivation from an animate *u-stem of the parent language would match the reconstruction of a neuter *u-stem for Armenian caṙ. The interrelationship of the derivatives of this root with Greek (for example the verbs γελάω, γελοίω, γελοιάω and γελώω) is not our concern here, but in order to arrive at the correct reconstruction of the root a few other forms must be considered.

A number of scholars have assumed that the original root was 'disyllabic', or, in other words, had a root-final laryngeal. The verb γελάω, whether taken as a derivative of *γελασ- or as the thematic continuation of an earlier athematic form, supports this conclusion. But Szemerényi argued that the verb may be a derivative of a thematic noun γέλος by a derivative process which may stem from the parent language (1967:78, 82 and 84). He further derives the *γελασ- which underlies other forms from a conflation of γελάω and an element *γελοσ- which underlies the verb γελοίω and the adjective γελοῖος (or γέλοιος).

Szemerényi's hypothesis can be met with objections on two counts. Firstly, the evidence for a thematic γέλος and for the underlying form *γελοσ- is very scanty. The adjective γελοίϊος only occurs once in Homer (Il. 2.215) and may stand for γελοῖος metri gratia, or it may disguise original *γελωιος (Chantraine 1973:168), and the verb γελοίω can be replaced by γελώω in all its occurrences in Homer (e.g. Od. 20.347, 20.390). The adjective γελοῖος seems to be derived from γέλως by analogy to αἰδοῖος next to αἰδώς, etc. and is itself likely to have been the point of departure for the verbal forms which may have been introduced late into the Homeric text.

The 'Aeolic' thematic form γέλος is of even more uncertain pedigree. The evidence for it relies only on the statements of Tzetzes (commentary on

Hesiod's *Works and Days* at 1.412), Gregory of Corinth (in the περὶ διαλέκτων), and the anonymous compilation περὶ διαλέκτων known as the *Grammaticus Meermannianus* (published with the works of Gregory of Corinth by Schaefer in 1811).[141] There is no literary or inscriptional evidence for γέλος and it may have been invented on the analogy of 'Aeolic' ἔρος beside ἔρως and to explain the variant reading γέλον (for *γέλοϝ') in the Homeric passages cited.

The second objection to Szemerényi's theory is that it does not take account of other words which may be derived from this root. The forms which occur in Homer are the *hapax* γλήνεα 'gaudy(?) things', used to describe treasures in Priam's palace at *Il.* 24.192, γλήνη 'eyeball, toy', γαλήνη 'calm' and γλαυκ- in γλαυκῶπις 'with gleaming eyes'. Semantically, these forms seem far removed from γελάω, but they could all be derived from a root meaning 'shine', which might be the root meaning of the verb also. At *Iliad* 19.362–3 γελάω is used in a context which favours the interpretation 'shine' rather than 'laugh': αἴγλη δ᾽ οὐρανὸν ἷκε, γέλασσε δὲ πᾶσα περὶ χθὼν / χαλκοῦ ὑπὸ στεροπῆς 'the radiance reached to heaven, the whole earth beamed under the splendour of the bronze'. Note also the Hesychius gloss cited above γελεῖν · λάμπειν, ἄνθειν 'shine, bloom'.[142]

The semantic connection between 'shine' and 'laugh' has a parallel in the Latin verb *renideō* 'shine, laugh' and in English *beam*. Thus it is possible that all the above forms continue the same root as γελάω. Once the connection of the meanings 'shine' and 'laugh' is acknowledged, the semantic development of the words γλήνεα and γλαυκῶπις is straightforward; the forms γλήνη 'eyeball' and γαλήνη 'calm' require intermediate steps of 'shining (part of the face)' and 'shining (water)' > 'time of no waves, calm' ('calme lumineux' as it is glossed by Manessy-Guitton 1972:94) respectively. The exact morphological derivation of γλήνεα and γλήνη is not certain; they may continue original *glh₂n- (thus Francis 1970:241) or *glh₂-s-n- (Manessy-Guitton 1972:94), but they indicate that the original root did have a final laryngeal.

Therefore we can reconstruct for Armenian *caŕr*, and perhaps also Greek γέλως, an original *u*-stem noun, and the Greek verb can be derived from an athematic present with *ā vocalism. Formally the Latin words *gelū* 'ice' and *gelāre* 'freeze' seem exactly comparable, but semantically the connection is more difficult. However the meaning 'shine' which was reconstructed for the Greek root may point the way to a connection. The use of a root with meaning 'shine' to denote 'ice' is semantically plausible; 'ice' can clearly be referred to as the 'shining thing'.[143]

Greek and Armenian therefore show different morphological formations but a unique agreement on the semantics of the term. The morphological structure of the terms in the two languages appears to continue patterns from within Proto-Indo-European, particularly so, if the above analysis of γέλως is correct which shows an old and unproductive type of noun inflection. The case for an independent innovation made jointly by the two languages is therefore less strong. The two languages may preserve an original connotation of the meaning of the root which has been lost in Latin (and in the cognate terms in other languages listed in Pokorny *IEW* 365f.).

4.27 *g'ūr- 'curved'

Solta (1960:437f.) included the comparison of Greek γυρός 'curved' and Armenian *cowr̄* 'bent' (*o*-stem, genitive *cr̄oy*) among the exclusive Greek-Armenian isoglosses. The Armenian word is not used in its simple form in the Bible translation, where other words are used for 'crooked',[144] but the derived noun *cr̄owt'iwn* and verb *cr̄em* occur at *Proverbs* 8:8 and *Sirach* 27:23 respectively, translating σκολιόν 'crooked' and διαστρέφω 'pervert'.

The final *r̄* of *cowr̄* cannot be explained by regular sound change if the word derives from the same original formation as γυρός. The regular reflex of *g'ūros* would be *cowr*. Meillet (1936:57f.) maintains that final *r* sometimes develops to the trilled *r̄* due to generalisation of the development before initial *n*- in a following word. The phonemes *r* and *r̄* were neutralised before *n* as *r̄*; this can be seen in the paradigm of *ayr* 'man' with genitive *ar̄n* but instrumental *aramb*. Meillet gives no parallels for the sporadic change of *r* to *r̄*, and the development seems unlikely given that there is no corresponding alternation in the earliest texts or in dialectal forms (compare the alternation in manuscripts between final -*l* and -*ł*).[145] The Armenian word is better derived from *gūr-so-* or *gur-so-*.

Lidén (1906:111–122) dismissed this etymology of *cowr̄*, and rather connected Armenian *kor* 'crooked' with Greek γυρός and a number of words in other Indo-European languages coming from a root *geu-* 'bend', with initial velar rather than palatal consonant. It is possible that both *cowr̄* and *kor* are derived from a root *geu-*, if one supposes a merger of the Proto-Indo-European velar consonants with the palatals before *u* in the earliest stages of Armenian (Winter 1962:257; see further **4.17**). By this analysis *cowr̄* would reflect a zero grade *gu-* and *kor* a full grade *gow-* (for the loss of *-w-* before *r* compare *nor* 'new' from the root *ne/ow-*).[146]

The reconstruction of the Indo-European root *geu-* is far from certain. The diverse forms in the Indo-European languages which are listed by Pokorny *IEW* 393–398 (who largely follows the work of Lidén 1906:111–122) cover a wide range of disparate meanings and are mostly first attested late in the individual histories of the relevant languages (for example, Middle Irish *gūaire* 'hair', Norwegian *kūr* 'curdled milk'). The reconstructed root shows irregular alternation between *geu-*, *gēu-*, *gu-* and *gū-*.

However, the fluctuations in the form of the root in the daughter languages may have arisen through the wide use of the root for terms referring to marginal items in the lexicon (such as 'curly hair' etc.) which may also have been subject to 'expressive' forms. Moreover, words denoting the concepts 'curved' and 'crooked' are apt to be applied to moral or religious deviation and may therefore undergo deformation or replacement (compare the English terms 'bent', 'crook' etc.). One should not therefore expect the same rigorous application of sound laws for this root as for more stable items of the lexicon. And indeed, the irregular sound change proposed by Meillet for *cowr* may be explained in this way.

There are a number of other Armenian words which could also derive from the same root, once the more rigorous application of sound changes is dropped. Thus, for example the Armenian word for circle *cir* (which is semantically close to γυρός; note that the derived noun γῦρος 'circle' is translated by *cir* at e.g. *Isaiah* 40:22), may be connected to this root with an 'irregular' change of vowel.

Similarly, there are forms in other Indo-European languages which could be more closely connected to γυρός. The Sanskrit word for 'globe', *gola-*, may, for example, also belong here (cf. Pokorny *IEW* 396).[147] There are also a number of forms which appear to derive from an initial **k* or **k'* such as Latin *curvus* 'rounded', *circus* 'circle', Irish *cor* 'circle', Armenian *šowrj* 'round' and others. In summary, the words γυρός and *cowr* cannot be directly derived from the same prototype by regular sound change because of the final -*r* of the Armenian word. And if the strict requirements of 'sound laws' are temporarily suspended for this comparison, then a much larger family of words in other Indo-European languages can also be connected.

4.28 **g'mbʰel-* 'jaw'

Solta (1960:255) and Arutjunjan (1983:290) see the agreement in suffix of Greek γαμφηλαί 'jaws' (thrice in Homer, cf. *LfrgE* II 120) and Armenian *cameli* 'jaw, cheek, temples (of the head)' as significant.

If the connection is correct, the Armenian word would show a unique example of the development of **-mbʰ-* to -*m*-. A different development of the cluster is seen in *amb* 'cloud' (cognate with Sanskrit *ambhas-* 'water', etc.; see Pokorny *IEW* 316) and the instrumental form of *n*-stems, in -*mb(k')*.[148]

The suffixes of the two words disagree substantially; Greek -η- should correspond to Armenian -*i*- (which would fall when not under the accent). The Armenian word belongs to the *ea*-declension which stems from earlier **-iyā-*, and this does not tally with the *ā*- declension of the Greek word. The two words agree only on containing the reflex of an **-l-* suffix, and both forms can be easily explained as developments within the individual languages. An -ηλο-/-ηλᾱ- suffix is productive within Greek, compare θυηλή 'offering' (e.g. *Iliad* 9.220) derived from θύος 'offering', and the suffix is also used to mark another term for a body part, τράχηλος 'neck'.[149] The Armenian word is best seen as an agent noun derived from the verb *camem* 'I chew' by a regular and widely productive process, compare *banam* 'I open', *banali* 'key'.[150]

This isogloss is therefore extremely dubious and should be dropped.

4.29   *$g^web^hury\bar{a}$-* 'bridge'

The comparison of Greek γέφῡρα 'bridge' and Armenian *kamowrj* 'bridge' (genitive plural in *-ac*) has provoked a certain amount of scholarly interest because, like the comparisons of αἴξ and *ayc* (**4.1**) and κίων and *siwn* (**4.35**), the connection appears to offer a common Greek-Armenian term for a cultural item which is not shared with other Indo-European languages.

However, the comparison meets with a number of difficulties on phonetic and semantic grounds. The phonetic development of *kamowrj* from *$g^web^hury\bar{a}$-* supposes a change of medial *$-b^h-$* to *-m-* which is unparalleled. Between vowels *$-b^h-$* generally gives Armenian *-w-*. However, there are no other examples of the treatment of *$-b^h-$* after a vowel and before *u*. Some scholars have argued that there is a special development of *-m-* > *-w-* in this environment (see **4.4** and note 53), to which a change of *$-b^h-$* to *-m-* might be comparable. The change of inherited *e* to *a* seems to be regular before a stressed *u*, and is not therefore an effective objection to the etymology (see **4.3** and **4.26** for this rule).

On the Greek side the difficulty arises from the variant forms of the word, such as Cretan (Gortyn) δεπυρα, Laconian δίφουρα (Hesychius) and βλέφῡρα given as a Boeotian word by the comic poet Strattis and usually corrected to βέφῡρα; note also the Hesychius gloss βουφάρας · γεφύρας. These forms suggest the reconstruction of an initial labio-velar, but, if this is so, then γ- of the standard form is unexplained. It might have arisen by dissimilation of the labial element of the labio-velar from the labial -φ- in the following syllable. However, the same dissimilation has not affected words such as βάπτω 'dip in water' or δελφύς 'womb'.[151]

Solta (1960:424 f.) sees the semantic agreement as close enough to outweigh the phonetic difficulties. However, the meaning 'bridge' may not be original in Greek; at *Iliad* 5.88, 89 the meaning of γέφυρα is 'dyke' (as also in an inscription from Miletus *SEG* 29 (1979) 1139 (p. 283)) or 'dam' (note also the verb γεφυρόω 'dam up' *Iliad* 15.357 and 21.245). Elsewhere in Homer the word is used only in the formula πολέμοιο γέφυραι referring to the ranks, or the space between the ranks, on the battlefield; the precise meaning of this formula is obscure.[152] The earliest attestations for the Armenian word show a meaning of 'bridge'; the word is used to translate γέφυρα at Isaiah 37:25 and διαβάθρα at 2 *Kings* 23:21.[153]

The irregularities of the phonetic changes involved in this correspondence, and the disagreement in meaning between the earliest attested Greek usages and the Armenian word, make the genetic connection of the two terms highly unlikely. To dismiss the phonetic disagreements as the effects of folk-etymology (Meillet 1920:17) or 'tabu' (Solta *loc. cit.*) is a desperate resort. It is preferable to explain the development of the words as individual creations within the languages themselves or as borrowings (perhaps ultimately from the same source).[154]

4.30 $*g^w \bar{l}no$- ($*g^w \bar{l}h_2no$-) 'acorn'

Arutjunjan (1983:293) lists Greek βάλανος 'acorn' and Armenian *kałin* (*o*-stem, gen. *kałnoy*) 'acorn' among the unique Greek-Armenian lexical agreements. The agreement in sense is exact: *kałin* translates βάλανος in the Bible e.g. at *Isaiah* 6.13. The root is found in other Indo-European languages to denote the acorn (cf. Pokorny *IEW* 472f.; Frisk *GEW* I 213 adds Albanian *lende*[155] 'acorn' to the Indo-European cognates, but Huld (1984:87) and Orel (1988:112) give different explanations of the Albanian word). Greek and Armenian share a $*$-no- suffixed form; a root noun can be reconstructed for the ancestor of the forms in the Baltic languages, and the cognates in Slavic (Russian *žolud'* 'acorn'), Latin (*glans*) and perhaps Albanian (see above) show the addition of a suffix $*$-nd- to the root.

It is difficult to reconcile the Armenian suffix -*in* from $*$-*eno*- with Greek -ανο-. A possible explanation is that the Armenian nominative has been extended from $*kałn$, the reflex of $*g^w \bar{l}(h_2)no$-, to *kałin* on the analogy of other *o*-stems with final -*n* such as *hin*, genitive *hnoy* 'old', etc. The change has arisen in order to avoid a final cluster -*łn*, which, although acceptable on phonetic grounds,[156] would have been subject to the synchronic rule that all words ending -*Cn* (*C* = any consonant) are declined as *n*-stems. Hence the nouns which in a prehistoric stage of Armenian were declined:

nominative $*$-*Cn*
genitive $*$-*Cnoy* or $*$-*Cni*,

are declined in the Classical language either as an *o*-stem or *a*-stem with nominative in -*in* as follows:

nominative   -*Cin*
genitive   -*Cnoy* or -*Cni*,

or as an *n*-stem with nominative -*Cn* thus:

nominative   -*Cn*
genitive   -*Cin* or -*Can*.

Other examples of the extension of the nominative from expected $*$-*Cn* to -*Cin* may be *lowsin* 'moon' < $*lowk'(s)$-*no*-/-*nā*- (genitive *lowsni* but instrumental *lowsnov* in the Bible)[157] and *getin* 'earth, ground' < $*wed$-n-,[158] and an example of the transfer to the *n*-stem declension is given by *beṙn* 'burden' (genitive *beṙin*) from $*b^h er$-*no*-/-*nā*- (Greek φερνή 'dowry').[159]

Therefore it is possible that Greek and Armenian show exactly the same formation for this word. The correspondence thus shows a morphological agreement between the two languages which is not shared with other Indo-European languages. The inflection of the two terms as thematic stems makes it likely that the agreement is not a shared archaism. It is noteworthy, however, that the Latin and Slavic terms for 'acorn' also show a form peculiar to those two languages.

4.31 *$g^w nai$- 'woman'

Greek γυνή 'woman' and Armenian *kin* 'woman' both have irregular declensions; Greek uses a stem γυναικ- in all cases except the nominative and vocative singular, and the Armenian declension is as follows:

	SINGULAR	PLURAL
nominative	*kin*	*kanayk'*
accusative	*kin*	*kanays*
locative	*knoǰ*	*kanays*
genitive-dative	*knoǰ*	*kananc'*
ablative	*knoǰê*	*kananc'*
instrumental	*knaw* or *kanamb*	*kanambk'*

The instrumental singular *knaw* is the only form used in the Bible translation (as noted by Hübschmann 1897:460) where it occurs eleven times.

Many scholars have connected the -*ay*- of the Armenian nominative-accusative-locative plural with the -αι- of the Greek case forms which have later been extended by -κ-,[160] and some have even seen the Armenian nominative plural ending -*ayk'* as the direct reflex of *-*aik*-.[161]

However, there are numerous alternative explanations for both words which do not rely on a common development. The plural *kanayk'* has been derived from: the transfer of an earlier collective form in -*ay* to the plural (Pedersen 1906:398); the pre-Armenian nominative plural of *a*-stems, *-*ai*, which survives only in this word (Szemerényi 1960b:22); or an *i*-stem plural form *$g^w nnh_2 eyes$ preserving the intervocalic *-*y*- by analogy to the locative ending *-*ey-si/u* (Rix 1976:149, Klingenschmitt 1982:148 n. 8).[162] Szemerényi (1960b:26f.) takes Greek γυναικ- to contain an -ικο- suffix which has been transferred to the athematic declension.

The Armenian declension of *kin* shows a fluctuation in the grade of the root syllable, with *kin* and perhaps *knoǰ* etc. showing *$*e$ grade and *kanayk'* etc. showing zero grade. This variation in the root syllable is an archaism paralleled in the inflexion of the cognate in Old Irish: nominative *ben* 'woman', genitive *mná*. The *n*-stem declension of the oblique cases of the plural of *kin* is paralleled by the *n*-stem declension of the word in Germanic languages (Gothic *qino* 'wife'). However, a number of the original **-ā* stems have been transferred to the *n*-stem declension in Germanic, and so it is not certain that Armenian and Germanic share an inherited formation.

The declension of the Armenian word *kin* therefore has parallels not only with the declension of the Greek cognate, but also with the Old Irish cognate and possibly with forms in Germanic. Moreover the **-ai-* element shared by Greek and Armenian might possibly also occur in Tocharian; the Tocharian B word for 'woman' *klyiye* (oblique forms *klai*, *klaim̥* and *klaiñ*, see Krause & Thomas 1960:121 for full declension) could be derived from **gʷn̥(n)ai-* (Mayrhofer 1986:109 citing K. T. Schmidt 1980:409f.). However, this etymology of *klyiye* is not certain and *-ai-* (of uncertain origin) also occurs in other Tocharian nouns.[163]

It is difficult to make any firm conclusion about the origin of either the Greek or the Armenian word for 'woman', and it is not clear that direct comparison of the two words helps to explain the development of either word. The disparity between the paradigms of γυνή and *kin* argues against the supposition that the words result from a shared innovation.

4.32 **gʰiyom-* 'snow'

Greek χίων and Armenian *jiwn* (genitive *jean*) alone of Indo-European languages show a meaning 'snow' for the reflex of the root noun **gʰi(e/o)m-*. Other languages show a meaning 'winter' (Latin *hiems*, Avestan *zyå̄*). Benveniste (1956:32), following Meillet (1936:142), saw the limitation of the meaning of the base noun to 'snow' and the development of nouns with a suffix **-r* for 'winter' (Armenian *jmeřn* 'winter', Greek χειμερ-in χειμερινός 'in winter') as an important isogloss.

Greek and Armenian have made no shared innovation in the phonology and morphology of the inherited terms. Both have generalised *-n*, resulting from original final **-m* in the nominative singular, throughout the paradigm.[164] Another root noun with original final **-m*, **de/om-* 'house', has been treated in different ways by Armenian and Greek. Armenian has generalised *-n* throughout the paradigm to give *town* (genitive *tan*), 'house' but the Greek reflexes, δῶ and δῶμα 'house', do not show *-ν*.[165] The separate treatment of the root **de/om-* suggests that the generalisation of *-n* in the reflexes of **gʰi(e/o)m-* took place independently. In the oblique cases Greek has generalised the *o*-grade but Armenian has generalised the zero grade (Meillet 1936:45).[166]

Benveniste's parallel of *jmeřn* and χειμερινός is not a significant isogloss since the same suffixes are found in Latin *hibernus*. As Szemerényi (1960a) has shown, the three words can be explained as arising from separate developments within the individual histories of the languages. The Armenian and Greek terms for 'winter', *jmeřn* and χεῖμα show completely separate formations from the same root.

We are left, therefore, with the shared meaning of 'snow' as the only significant agreement between the two languages. It has been argued that the original meaning was 'snow-time' which was restricted to the sense 'snow' only in Armenian and Greek.[167] But the meaning 'snow' may be original. Benveniste (1956) compared the usage of νιφ- and χίων in early Greek and came to the conclusion that χίων is 'la neige matérielle' but νείφειν is used to describe 'la phénomène atmosphérique'.[168] He connects the Sanskrit root *snih-* 'conglomerate' with the root *sneigʷʰ-* and reconstructs an original meaning 'coagulate, conglomerate' which was used specifically with reference to the atmospheric process which was believed to cause snow. If this is correct, the Greek distinction between χίων and νιφ- could reflect the Proto-Indo-European distinction between the two roots.

The semantic agreement between the Greek and Armenian terms is not unique. The Iranian Pamir language Waxī (Wakhi) shows the same root also with the meaning 'snow' in the word *zəm* 'snow' (Gamkrelidze and Ivanov 1984:II.681), and Vedic *hím* (which only occurs in the instrumental *himá* which could continue the original instrumental to *gʰiōm*) means 'cold, frost, snow'.

Hence the meaning 'snow' of χίων and *jiwn* may reflect an archaism; it is possible that both languages have preserved the base meaning of the word, while other languages have promoted the secondary meaning 'snow-time'. If the meaning 'snow' is an innovation, the presence of the root with the same meaning in Indo-Iranian lessens the significance of the Greek-Armenian correspondence.

4.33 *k'enw-* 'empty'

Greek κενός (Attic) 'empty' and Armenian *sin* (*o*-stem, gen. sing. *snoy*) 'empty, vain' appear to form a perfect semantic match. Some scholars have also seen the phonetic agreement as perfect.[169]

However the Attic form has developed from *κεν-ϝο-*, as can be seen from Ionic κεινός. The Homeric form κενεός and Cypriot *ke-ne-u-wo-ne* can both be derived from a form *κενεϝος*. The alternation between -εϝο- and -ϝο- in the suffix suggests that the forms arise from a transfer of an original *u*-stem to the thematic declension.[170]

Szemerényi, in his discussion of the relation between κενεός and κενός (1964:101–106), agrees that thematised *u*-stems are either formed in -εϝο- or -ϝο-. But he denies that the same word could admit both forms, and derives *κεν-ϝο-*, the father of the Attic and Ionic forms, from *κεν-εϝο-* by syncope. However, the choice between κεινός and κενεός in Homer seems to be metrically conditioned (κεινός occurs at the beginning of the line at *Iliad*

3.376, 11.160 and 15.453, cf. *LfrgE* II 1381), and there is nothing to suggest that one form is later than the other. A parallel pair of derivatives in -εϝο- and -ϝο- from an original *u*-stem might be provided by ἐτεός 'true' (from *ἔτεϝος) and *ἔτϝος, preserved in the Hesychian gloss ἐτά · ἀληθή.[171]

Conversely, the Armenian word must derive from *k'en-o- not *k'enwo-, which would develop to **sing (see the discussion of *cowngk'* 'knees' at **2.3.2**), or *k'enu-, which would develop to **sinr or **snowk.[172]

It is worth remarking that the Armenian adjective is not used in the Bible translation, but that other words translate Greek κενός: for example, *ownayn* at *Luke* 1:53 and *snoti* at *Colossians* 2:8. Indeed the simple adjective is not found in the fifth century literature, and first appears in the post-fifth-century translation of Chrysostom. Moreover, the *NBHL* cites only one example of its declension as an *o*-stem (in the Armenian translation of Ephraim). The Classical language does know the suffixed form *snoti* 'vain', which translates Greek κενός, for example at *Colossians* 2:8, or μάταιος, for example at *Titus* 3:9, and compounds such as *snaparc* 'vain-glorious', which translates Greek κενόδοξοι at *Galatians* 5:26. One cannot therefore be sure that *sin, snoy*, reflects the original form of the adjective.

Hence Greek and Armenian share a root not found in other Indo-European languages,[173] but seem to show disagreement in the suffixation.

4.34 *k'er- 'cord'

Greek καῖρος 'the row of threads connecting the warp-threads to the loom' and Armenian *sarik'* (*plurale tantum*, gen. *sareac'*, inst. *sareawk'*, an *ea*-stem) are taken by Pokorny (*IEW* 577) as the reflexes of a root limited to Armenian and Greek.

The meaning of *sarik'* in its earliest attestations is clearly 'chain', 'fetters' or 'bands'. For example, *erkat'i sareawk'* means 'with iron bands' at [P'awstos Bowzand] *The Epic Histories* 4.16.[174] The word does not occur in the Armenian Bible translation, although a number of different words are used to translate words for ropes and chains.[175]

In Homer καῖρος does not occur, but καιροσέων (feminine genitive plural, an ancient mis-reading of the earlier spelling of trisyllabic καιρουσσέων from unattested *καιρόεις) occurs once as an epithet of ὀθονέων 'fine linen cloths' (*Od.* 7.107) and seems to mean 'well-woven'. The later Greek derivatives of this word (for example καιρωστρίδες or -ωστίδες or -ωτίδες '(female) weavers', καιρόω 'tie the καῖροι onto the loom') could indicate that the root meaning was 'knot' rather than 'thread' and that it is in some way connected with καιρός 'opportunity' (Chantraine *DELG* 480).

The semantic connection between the two words is not strong. The meaning of the Armenian term might make a connection with Sanskrit *śṛnkhala-* 'chain, fetter' more likely.[176] Moreover, the reconstruction of a root *k'er- 'weave' for καῖρος, sarik', Armenian sard 'spider' and Albanian thur 'fence, knit' (Frisk GEW I 756) rests on very slender evidence. It seems more likely that these diverse terms are of separate origins.

4.35 *k'īwon- 'pillar'

The correspondence between Greek κίων 'pillar' and Armenian siwn (gen. sean) 'pillar', which translates κίων in the Armenian Bible (e.g. Judges 16:25), is frequently cited as a significant isogloss.[177] While it was thought that the Greek form derived from *k'īyōn (as Hübschmann 1897:490) or *k'īsōn (Benveniste 1935:153) the comparison was relatively unproblematic. However the decipherment of Linear B reveals that the Greek form derives from *k'īwōn. The writing ki-wo-qe occurs at the end of a list of building materials (PY Vn 46 given in Ventris and Chadwick 1973:503f.) and is clearly to be interpreted as /kīwōn-qe/ 'and a pillar'.[178] If the Armenian word derives from the same prototype then the development of intervocalic *-w- must be clarified.

The treatment of *-w- in Armenian has received a fair amount of scholarly attention, as the sound appears to develop in three distinct ways:

(a) to -g- as loganam 'I wash' < *low-
(b) to -w- as tiw 'day' < *diw-
(c) to -∅- as in nor 'new' < *ne/ow-.

As so often in questions of Armenian developments there are not enough secure etymologies to make the exact phonetic conditions for these changes clear (as realised by Meillet in his discussion of the matter 1936:49f.), although many scholars have tried to isolate the specific environments for the different developments.[179]

Pedersen (1905:196) put forward the theory that original intervocalic *-w- remains as -w if it occurs word-finally in Armenian, but elsewhere (except before sonant *r) develops to -g-. This theory explains the majority of the facts better than any other, and is phonetically plausible (Grammont 1916:225). Most counter-examples can be explained by paradigm levelling; thus a paradigm with nominative arew but genitive aregi develops to both arew, arewow 'sun' and areg, aregi 'sun, eighth month of the year'.[180]

By this theory the expected Armenian reflex of *k'īwōn is **sign (development (a)). In order to give siwn the original *-w- must either have been retained (development (b) above) or lost (development (c)).

Eichner (1978:152f.) argues for the regular retention of *-w- in the diphthong iw, as jiwn 'snow', tiw 'day' and aliwr 'flour'. But, apart from nouns with nominative singular in -ewr (on which see 4.2), all his examples involve either -w in word-final position (as tiw 'day'), or the diphthong -iw- which has developed from *-iō- (as jiwn 'snow', on which see 4.32).

Eichner also argues for the retention of *w before 'urarmenisch' *u,[181] which might be used to support the posited development of siwn, which would have had a nominative *siwun in a pre-apocope stage of Armenian. However, again he produces no examples which do not involve word-final -w. The second possibility is that *-w- in this word was lost early in the history of Armenian, and that the nominative *siwun contracted to siwn via *siun. Godel (1982:12) thinks that *-w- might be lost before -n- in the following syllable, and cites as a parallel erkan 'mill stone' which he compares to Vedic grāvan- 'pressing stone'. But there is no need to posit a *-w- in the ancestor to this Armenian word[182] and in other words *-w- becomes -g- before a following *-n-, for example, loganam 'wash'. Godel's theory is therefore unlikely.

The declension of siwn does not help to explain the word's history. It might have arisen by analogy with other words with nominative singular in -iwn (for example jiwn 'snow' (see **4.32**)) and abstract nouns in -owt'iwn.

The phonetic derivation of siwn is therefore not clear. There are no other examples of the treatment of *-w- in this environment.

The Armenian term for 'door-post', seamk' (o-stem), has received no satisfactory etymological explanation; no etymology is given for the term by Hübschmann or Ačaṙyan. The Armenian word translates a number of Greek terms in the Septuagint, most frequently σταθμός '(door-)post' (six times) and φλία 'doorpost' (four times).[183] The term is only found in the plural in the Bible and in the earliest Armenian literature, and it usually refers to the two sides of a door. In form and meaning the term is clearly very close to siwn and it may be possible to derive both forms from the same original paradigm, if the original term is reconstructed as:

Nom. sing.   *k'iwōm
Nom. plural (or dual?)   *k'iwṃmes (or *k'iwṃm(e)h₁.

The plural, or more likely the dual, will have become isolated in the meaning 'the two pillars of a door, doorposts' and thus developed separately from the general term for 'pillar'. In the latter the final *-m changed to -n which was generalised throughout the paradigm (as also in Greek). The plural/dual form retained its *-m in non-final position (compare am 'year' beside Vedic sámā). However the disappearance of *-w- in the medial syllable of seamk' is difficult to explain.

The isogloss is significant as it concerns a cultural item for which other Indo-European languages do not share a common term. The word can be seen either as a shared innovation of the two languages, which have extended the meaning and morphology of an inherited root, or as a borrowing made by the two languages from a non-Indo-European source.

If the two languages have extended the meaning of an inherited root, traces of the root may be found elsewhere. But there is no discernible cognate to

*kʹīwon- in other Indo-European languages. A reconstructed item *kʹīwon-
is theoretically possible for Proto-Indo-European, compare the reconstructed adjective *pīwon- 'ripe' (cf. Greek πίων and Vedic pívan-) of the
same phonological shape. Morphologically, however, this form would be
difficult to explain. The *-won- suffix in Indo-European seems to have had
the following functions (following Schindler 1975b:62–64):

(a) to form secondary adjectives (and sometimes substantives) from nouns,
with the meaning 'provided with, abounding in' (cf. Vedic maghávan- 'rich in
gifts'); these are usually associated with animate beings, or things considered
as animate;

(b) to form nouns from *u-stem adjectives and nouns; the meaning of the
derivatives is not easy to isolate, but Schindler thinks it possible that the suffix
originally had an 'individualising' function, which accounts for formations
such as *gʷréh₂w-on- 'pressing stone', i.e. 'the heavy thing', from *gʷr̥h₂ú-
'heavy'.

(c) to form one adjective (*pīwon- 'ripe') from a *-wer/n-stem (cf. Greek
πεῖραρ 'end').[184]

This helps little with our attempt to find an Indo-European etymon for
*kʹīwon-; it is possible that it represents a formation from a *u-stem adjective
or *-wer/n-stem noun, but there are no such forms surviving in other Indo-
European languages, and it is difficult to see what the original root and
meaning would have been. One possibility is *(s)kʹiH- 'shade' (Pokorny
IEW 917f.) which could have formed an adjective *skʹiHú- 'shady', and the
pillar could thus be 'that which gives shade'. But I think few people would be
willing to accept this etymology. Another explanation was given by Thieme
(1953:54) who derived κίων and siwn from the root *kei- 'lie, be situated'
(Greek κεῖμαι), but this does not explain the -i- of the Greek form and the
semantic connection is not strong. Even less convincing is Schwyzer's
connection with κίς 'woodworm' (1939:486).

If, as suggested above, Armenian seamkʹ 'doorpost(s)' is connected to siwn
the reconstructed noun must be *kʹīwom- which cannot have been a Proto-
Indo-European derivative formation, since there was no *-we/om- suffix.
The only nouns to decline in *-m- in the parent language seem to have been
the root nouns *dom- 'house', *dʰ(e)gʷʰom- 'earth' and *gʷʰi(e/o)m- 'snow,
winter', and *kʹīwom- cannot be a root noun because of its phonological
shape.

Therefore we should probably look elsewhere for the origin of the word.
Terms for cultural artefacts, such as a column, are the most susceptible to
borrowing, and it is tempting to explain the word as a loan-word. However,
the initial s- of the Armenian term corresponds to Greek κ-, as in words
inherited from the parent language, and this is taken by some scholars as
evidence that the word cannot have been borrowed.[185] But there are other

examples of a correspondence between Armenian *s-* and *k-* in other languages in words which might have been borrowed from a 'Mediterranean' source: for example, *siseṙn* 'chick pea' alongside Latin *cicer*.[186] It is therefore possible that the Armenian 'palatalisation' took place after the introduction of these loan-words into the language.

In conclusion, the agreement between the Greek and Armenian terms for column is too close in form and sense to be dismissed. However, the word is isolated in the two languages and seems not to have been derived from their inherited lexical stock by any recognisable process. It is likely that it represents a borrowing into both languages from a lost source. The phonetic derivation of the Armenian term would be more easy to understand if it was borrowed from a language or dialect where the medial *-w-* of the word had been lost.

4.36 *(i)kᶿīno- (*tkih₂ino-) 'hawk, kite'

Greek ἰκτίν or ἴκτῖνος (accented ἰκτῖνος by Herodian) and Armenian *c'in* (*o*-stem) both refer to large birds of prey. *C'in* translates ἰκτίν at *Leviticus* 11:14 and *Deuteronomy* 14:13.[187] The *o*-stem declension of the term in Greek is probably the older, as the consonant stem declension occurs mostly in later texts (although first attested in Aristophanes). The interchange between consonant and thematic stems occurred in all periods of the history of Greek (Schwyzer 1939:458).

The two words stand in the same phonetic correspondence as Greek ἰχθῦς 'fish', Armenian *jowkn* 'fish'. In both cases the Armenian initial affricate corresponds to the Greek combination of initial *i-* and velar-dental cluster. The correspondence is taken as significant by Solta (1960:432), Klingenschmitt (1982:61 n. 1) and Arutjunjan (1983:305). However, the root may also survive in the Sanskrit word *śyená-* 'falcon' and Avestan *saēna-* (Hübschmann 1897:499, Schwyzer 1939:325). The comparison of Greek (ἐ)χθές 'yesterday' to Sanskrit *hyás* 'yesterday' (< *g'ʰy-*) shows a parallel for the correspondence of a Greek velar-dental cluster to the Sanskrit reflex of an original palatal followed by *-y-*. A reconstruction of *k'y-* for the initial consonant cluster is possible, and Allen has argued that the Greek development can be accounted for in phonetic terms, although he expresses some doubts about the change (1957:129f., 1973:117).

An objection to the reconstruction of an original initial *k'y-* cluster is that, in this comparison, Avestan *s-* corresponds to Sanskrit *śy-*. Elsewhere Avestan *sii-* corresponds to Sanskrit *śy-*: for example, Sanskrit *śyāvá-* 'dark' beside Avestan *siiāuua-* 'black'. This problem is met by the reconstruction of initial *tk'y-*, which was first proposed by Merlingen (1957:53). Sanskrit has simplified the cluster by eliminating initial *t-*; Greek has eliminated *-y-* and then the cluster *tk-* was metathesised;[188] the ancestor of Avestan may also have lost *-y- at an early stage, and then simplified *tk'- to *k'-, which develops regularly to s-. The Armenian development may have been via *tk'- which has developed to *t's- > c'-.

Schindler (1977:32) reconciles the differences of initial consonantism and vocalism of the Greek and Sanskrit terms by reconstructing an original paradigm for the Proto-Indo-European term for 'bird of prey' (presumably a derivative of the root *tek'- 'seize' cf. Pokorny *IEW* 1057 f.) as follows:

nominative   *tek'ih₂
genitive   *tk'yeh₂s
instrumental   *tk'ih₂eh₁.

In Schindler's analysis this paradigm was later replaced (not surprisingly one might think) by forms built by the addition of a suffix *-ino- which was attached to the allomorph *tk'yeh₂- in the ancestor of Indo-Iranian, but to *tk'ih₂- in the ancestors of Greek and Armenian.

The different vocalisms of the Indo-Iranian and the Greek and Armenian forms could alternatively be explained as due to the addition of different suffixes. The suffixes *-eino-, *-ino- and *-īno- are all used in Indo-European for animal names, as Sanskrit *hariná-* 'gazelle', and Lithuanian *žvėrienà*, Old Church Slavonic *zvěrina* 'game'; many of these forms originate from diminutives (Brugmann 1906:271–279). The suffix *-ῑνο-/-ῑνα-* has become productive in Greek for animal and plant names (Schwyzer 1939:491). Armenian -*in* could derive from *-ino-, *-īno-, *-ēno- or *-eno-.

Hence Greek and Armenian may show agreement on the suffixation and on the initial consonant cluster, but this is not certain. As closely related forms are found in Indo-Iranian the isogloss is of minimal significance.

4.37 *kʰl̥- 'loose(?)'

Pisani (1944:167) was the first to make the connection between Greek χαλάω 'slacken', χαλία (glossed by Hesychius as ἡσυχία 'peace') and the Armenian word *xałał* 'peaceful' (translates ἡσυχῇ at *Isaiah* 8:6), and he is followed by Solta (1960:436 f.). Meillet (*BSL* 36 (1935) p. 111, reprinted in 1977:276, and 1936:36) had earlier connected the Armenian word *xał* 'game' to the Greek forms, and saw the initial consonant as a derivative of the Proto-Indo-European 'voiceless aspirate' *kʰ-.

These connections are very uncertain as they rest on the reconstruction of an initial Proto-Indo-European 'voiceless aspirate' velar consonant. Meillet (*BSL* 36 (1935) pp. 109–120, reprinted in 1977:274–285) first put forward the theory that Proto-Indo-European voiceless aspirates *kʰ- or *kʷʰ- developed to x- in Armenian, presenting comparisons such as *sxalem* 'I err, stumble' beside Sanskrit *skhálati*, *mowx* 'smoke' beside Greek σμύχω, etc. However, Meillet's theory of 'voiceless aspirates' has been rejected by a number of scholars, and the reconstruction of roots with such consonants on the evidence of Armenian alone is highly tenuous.[189]

A more cogent objection to Pisani's comparison is that the precise formal equivalence of the Greek and Armenian words is difficult to assess. The Armenian word *xałał* might perhaps be taken as the reflex of an original **-l* participle from a verbal root which was lost before the classical period.[190] This would entail the reconstruction of a 'disyllabic' root ($*k^h\b{l}h_2$- in laryngeal terms) and depend upon an Armenian sound change of a 'long sonant' $*-\b{l}$- ($*-\b{l}h_2$- in laryngeal terms) to -*ała*- (for which see **2.3.1**). The verb *xałam*, which formally could be taken as the continuation of this verbal root, in Classical Armenian functions as a denominative to *xał* 'game' and covers a wide range of meanings from 'play, jump, move' to 'march, invade' (a frequent use in the early historical works).[191]

Some of the diverse Greek forms related to the root χαλ(α)- appear to continue earlier 'disyllabic' formations; for example χαλαρός 'loose' and χλᾱρός (a *hapax* at Pindar *Pythians* 9.38). However, Beekes thought the Lesbian forms (third plural present χόλαισι and ἄχολος) made the reconstruction of a disyllabic root uncertain (1969:192).[192] The form which comes closest to the Armenian word in meaning, the Hesychius gloss χαλία, gives no support for the reconstruction of a disyllabic root.

The semantic connection between the concepts 'loose' and 'peaceful' is not strong, and the Greek gloss χαλία is not connected with the verb χαλάω by all scholars (Frisk, for example, does not include χαλία in the article on χαλάω *GEW* II 1066f.). Chantraine (*DELG* 1242 s.v. χαλία) is tempted to group the word with the family of χαλάω, comparing French *détente* for the semantic development from 'relaxation' to 'peace' (via 'relaxation of a strained situation').

The etymological connection between Greek χαλία and Armenian *xałał* is possible and the two languages may share a common root not found in other Indo-European languages, or they may both have borrowed the terms from the same source.[193] However, the phonetic correspondence between Greek χ- and Armenian *x*- is uncertain and the two words show no agreement on their morphological formation. The significance of the correspondence is therefore slight.

4.38 **mātruwyā-* 'step-mother'

Meillet (1936:142) lists the connection of Greek μητρυιά (Ionic and epic μητρυιή) and Armenian *mawrow* (genitive *mawrowi*, hence *i*- or *a*-stem) among his lexical isoglosses. The Greek word is found in the earliest texts (three times in Homer, *Iliad* 5.389, 13.697 and 15.336). The Armenian term, however, is not found in the earliest literature but first occurs in the later literature translated from Greek (the *NBHL* cites passages from the

Armenian translations of Plato, Aristotle and Philo).[194] These Armenian translations are renowned for their slavish adherence to the original which even led to the creation of a 'feminine' pronoun *nê*, alongside *na* (used elsewhere as masculine and feminine) on the model of Greek (Hübschmann *IF* 12 *Anz*. (1901) p. 52, reprinted in 1976:396). Hence, when one meets with the translation: *vasn zi mawr ew mawrowi anown azgakic' en* 'because the name for a mother and the name for a step-mother are related' for Philo's διότι μητρυιᾶς καὶ μητρὸς ὄνομα συγγενές (*De specialibus legibus* III 20), it is tempting to see the Armenian term as a calque of the Greek. However, this theory is made less likely by the survival of the term in a few modern Armenian dialects,[195] and by the fact that Armenian seems to have a native term for 'step-father' in *yawray*, which does not seem to be a calque of any Greek word.

Greek μητρυιά is peculiar in showing final *-ιά*. Wackernagel (1895:574 n. 1) suggested that the original nominative form was *μάτρυιά* which underwent a change of accent and length of final vowel by analogy with other nouns. If this is so, then one would reconstruct an original nominative in -*ih₂* (in laryngeal terms) which would have given an original syllabification (following the rules of Mayrhofer 1986:163):

nominative	*mātr̥wī* (or *meh₂tr̥wih₂*)
genitive	*mātruyās* (or *meh₂truyeh₂s*),

which seems to have been replaced in Proto-Greek by a paradigm:

nominative	*mātruwyā*
genitive	*mātruwyās*.

The regular Armenian reflex of *mātr̥wī* should be **marw* or **marg*.[196] The form *mawrow* must derive from *mātru-[197] and thus might be taken as evidence of a common Greek-Armenian morphological and semantic innovation.

However, Old English *mōdrige* 'mother's sister' (*n*-stem) must also be derived from a form *mātruwyā-*, and so the peculiar syllabification *-truwyā-* may stem from an Indo-European date. The motivation for this syllabification may be a desire to retain the form of the suffix *-wy-* which may have occurred in other kinship terms (compare Sanskrit *pitr̥vya-* 'father's brother').[198] The Old English word has been transferred from the *ā*- to the *n*-stem declension, but this is common in Germanic and the declension of *mōdrige* may also have been influenced by the *n*-stem *cwene* 'woman'.

Hence all that Greek and Armenian share is the common meaning of 'step-mother' as opposed to 'mother's sister'. The suffix *-wy-* is found in other Indo-European kinship terms, as, for example Sanskrit *pitr̥vya-* 'father's brother'. The meaning of this suffix has been investigated by Delbrück (1889:500f.) and Benveniste (1969a:259f.); Delbrück takes the root meaning of *mātruiā-* as 'eine Art von Mutter' (1889:473) and according to Benveniste's formulations the addition of the suffix *-*wy*- to a term for a parent shows 'une situation de proximité à celui-ci, une relation particulièrement étroite et en quelque sorte homogène au nom de base' (p. 262). Clearly from either of these original situations the extension of the term to 'step-mother' could have been made independently in the two languages, as was already recognised by Delbrück (p. 470f.). Szemerényi (1977a:60f.) takes the words to derive originally from *mātr-awi*- (!) 'aunt on the mother's side' with the meaning 'step-mother' arising from a custom of marriage of the wife's sister after the death of the wife.

The semantic isogloss should also be considered in the light of the Armenian words *yawray* 'step-father' and *owrǰow* 'step-son', which are to be connected to *hayr* 'father' and *ordi* 'son', although an exact morphological analysis is extremely difficult. It seems, therefore, that Armenian has derived a new set of terms for step-relations. This is in contrast to Greek, where μητρυιά stands in isolation as there is no special term for 'step-father': πατρυιός is late and formed by analogy to μητρυιά (Benveniste 1969a:263, Szemerényi 1977a:60); μητρυιός (in Comedy) is clearly comic; κηδεστής (used for 'step-father' in Demosthenes 36.31) merely means 'connection by marriage'; ἐπιπάτωρ is only attested at Pollux 3.27 who recommends this term above πατρωός, which itself is first attested in Cercidas (third century B.C.).

The innovation of a new meaning of 'step-mother' for the reflexes of this term in the two languages may therefore have been made in common or separately. It could also represent the promotion of a secondary meaning of the Proto-Indo-European term which has been lost elsewhere.

4.39 *mēd*- 'measured plans'

A number of scholars have noted the agreement in form and meaning of Greek μήδεα 'plans' and Armenian *mit(k')* 'mind, intelligence'.[199] The Greek word, found in Homer and later poetry, only occurs in the plural and usually refers to the plans of the shrewd (note that it is coupled with the generic term βουλαί 'plans' at *Iliad* 2.340). The Armenian word, which follows the *a*-stem declension (genitive singular *mti*, genitive plural *mtac'*), is found in both the singular and the plural (for example *yamenayn mtac'* 'with all the understanding' for Greek ἐξ ὅλης τῆς συνέσεως at *Mark* 12:33); the singular use is more common in the many set phrases where verbs are construed with the noun, such as *i mit aṙnowm* 'understand' (translates συνίημι at *Mark* 7:14), literally 'take in mind'.[200]

The two words correspond closely in form and meaning. The ablaut form of the root *mēd*- and the use of the root to refer specifically to mental activity mark out the Greek and Armenian terms.

Frisk (*GEW* II 223) thought that the long **ē* of the Greek and Armenian words was the result of a confusion between the roots **med-* 'measure' and **mē-* 'measure', and if this is correct it would be strong evidence for a common innovation made only by the two languages. However, forms with a long medial vowel are also found in other Indo-European languages, such as in the Old Irish preterite *ro-mīd(a)ir* 'he judged', and Old High German *māz* 'measure' and it is possible that the ablaut between **med-* and **mēd-* has originated within a verbal or nominal paradigm. In Greek, verbal forms both with long and with short **e* are found (μήδομαι 'intend' and μέδομαι 'be mindful of') and this might suggest that the alternation originated within a *proterodynamisch* conjugation (reconstructed by Narten 1968 from verbs of the type of Vedic *tā́ṣṭi* 'he fashions'),[201] with **ē* in the strong forms and **e* in the weak, and that the long vowel of the verb was transferred in Greek and Armenian to the noun.

It is also possible to explain the vocalic alternation from within a nominal paradigm. The Greek noun derives from a neuter *s*-stem, which also lies behind Umbrian *mers* 'law, justice' (from **medos*) and some Latin formations (e.g. *modestus* 'restrained') and can hence be reconstructed for the parent language.[202] The ablaut patterns of the neuter *s*-stem declensions in Proto-Indo-European have been investigated in detail by Schindler (1975c), and he notes that several nouns of this class appear to show a variation between **e* and **ē*, or an unexplained **ē*, in the root (1975c:267).[203] Schindler compares the ablaut pattern to that of other declensions which also show an alternation between **e* and **ē*; compare, for example, the neuter noun for 'liver' which has a short **e* in the root syllable in Latin *iecur*, but a long **ē* in Greek ἧπαρ (the '*akrostatisch b*' pattern). If the neuter *s*-stem **medos/*mēdos* originally followed this ablaut pattern, the Greek and Armenian generalisation of the long vowel throughout the paradigm could have arisen separately.[204]

The formal agreement between the Greek and Armenian nouns may therefore reflect a common retention of an ablaut grade which has been lost in the cognate forms in the Italic languages. The semantic agreement between the two forms could similarly represent a preservation of an original connotation of the root rather than a common innnovation. The meanings of this root range over a wide semantic field in the Indo-European languages. In Germanic the root means 'measure' with a secondary meaning 'judge' (cf. German *messen* 'measure', *ermessen* 'judge'); in Celtic and Oscan and Umbrian the root is used to form words relating to the law and justice (Old Irish *midiur* 'I judge', Oscan *meddix* 'magistrate', etc.), and some Latin derivatives (*medicus* 'doctor', etc.) agree with the Avestan use of the root (*vimad-* 'doctor') with a specifically medical significance.[205] Benveniste (1969b:122–132) gives an overview of the various Indo-European derivatives of the root **med-* and attempts to explain their semantic relation and development. He arrives at the conclusion that the original meaning of the root is '"prendre avec autorité les mesures qui sont appropriées à une difficulté actuelle; ramener à la norme – par un moyen consacré – un trouble défini" et le substantif *medes- ou *modo- désignera "la mesure éprouvée qui ramène l'ordre dans une situation troublée"' (1969b:129). From this formulation it is easy to see the relationship between Umbrian mers 'law' and Greek μήδεα; the meaning of the Greek word has emerged from considering the 'proven measures' from the stand-point of an individual, who relies upon his experience to provide him with the means for future action; the Umbrian word developed from the stand-point of society, which has enshrined the 'proven measures' as law. Benveniste emphasises that the process of redressing the order through 'proven measures' relies upon prior reflection and consideration of the situation, and this connotation accounts for the various words for 'judge' or 'contemplate' derived from the root (Irish midiur 'judge', Latin meditor 'contemplate', Greek μέδομαι 'be mindful of'). The Armenian meaning, 'mind, intelligence' may therefore stem from, or be influenced by, this aspect of the original meaning.

In conclusion, therefore, there is no compelling reason to see a common innovation in the development of μήδεα and mit(k'). However, the two words are so similar in form that it would perhaps be unwise to ignore the correspondence altogether. The two languages have made the same choice from a set of ablaut grades and meaning, and this may be significant.

4.40 *meg'ar- (*meg'(h_2)r-) 'great'

Porzig (1954:157) and Solta (1960:70) saw a significant agreement between the parallel verbal derivations formed with an *r- suffix to the root *meg'h_2- 'great' in Greek and Armenian. The form *meg'(h_2)r- has been assumed to underlie the Greek word for 'regard as excessive, grudge', μεγαίρω (Homeric and later Greek, and perhaps also the name of one of the Furies Μέγαιρα) as well as the Armenian word for 'honour' mecarem and its derivatives.[206] The semantic development of the Greek verb may have taken place via the intermediate stages 'regard as great' to 'regard as too great' and finally to 'grudge'.

The process of formation of the two verbs must have taken place independently, since the Greek verb has been formed with a *ye/o- suffix which is not evident in the Armenian word. Of the few other Greek verbs which are formed with a suffix -αίρω, several fall into the same semantic field as μεγαίρω: ἐχθαίρω 'hate', γεραίρω 'honour', epic ἐλεαίρω 'pity' and ἐλεφαίρομαι 'cheat'. The verb ἐχθαίρω may shed some light on the formation of these verbs. The etymology of the adjective ἐχθρός derives it from *ekstro-, the same formation as Latin extrā 'outside'. However, after the development of the cluster *-kst- to *-χθ- the adjective was reanalysed as a *-ro- adjective which then entered into a Caland system of suffixation. Thus an *s-stem noun ἔχθος, a comparative ἐχθίων and superlative ἔχθιστος were created by analogy to other genuine *ro-stem adjectives, such as κυδρός (see, for further discussion of the family of ἐχθός, de Lamberterie 1990:I.22f.). The derivation of verbal forms with a suffix -αίρω from adjectives formed in -ρό- was thus a productive process in prehistoric Greek.

The epic by-form of ἐλέω 'I pity', ἐλεαίρω, suggests that at a later stage of Greek the suffix -αίρω became productive to form verbs from nouns, since there is no other r-suffixed form from the root of ἐλέω. It is thus possible that μεγαίρω is derived from μέγας 'great' and not from a lost form *μεγαρ(ος) (Risch 1974:286). If this is so, then the Greek verb cannot be directly compared with Armenian *mecarem*.

There is no reason to envisage any common semantic development of the verbs in Greek and Armenian. The shift from an adjective 'great' to a verb 'regard as great, honour' is relatively common, compare, for example the later Greek derivative μεγαλύνω 'magnify, extol', and the presumption that the meaning 'regard as great' underlies Greek μεγαίρω does not necessitate any close connection with the development of a word for 'honour' from this root in Armenian.

In conclusion, it remains possible that a formation *$meg'(h_2)r$- is common to Greek and Armenian and underlies the verbs μεγαίρω and *mecarem*, but in the absence of any certain evidence for the unenlarged form (i.e. Greek *μεγαρ(ος), Armenian *mecar) this must remain unproven.

4.41   *me-$g^{\prime h}(s)ri$- 'in the hand'

Greek μέχρι(ς) 'up to, as far as' and Armenian *merj* 'near' were first connected by Meillet (*MSL* 7 (1890) p. 165 = 1977:7) and phonetically the connection seems perfect. The Armenian verb *merjenam* 'I approach, I touch' (aorist *merjec'ay*, participle *merjeal* at e.g. *Matt.* 3:2) offers additional support for original *$meg^{\prime h}ri$. The verb must be derived from *$merji$-*anam* because there is no class of verbs with a present formed in **-*enam* (Frisk *GEW* II 222).[207]

However, Hübschmann (1897:473) doubted the comparison because of the difference in meaning between *merj* 'near' and μέχρι 'as far as'. Adontz (1937:10f.) thought that the words both derived from *me-$g^{\prime h}ri$, which he took as the preposition *me- and the locative of the word for 'hand': 'le sens est "à la portée de la main" d'où "jusqu'à" et "près" etc.' Adontz's theory works especially well for Armenian; in the Armenian version of the Gospels *merjenam* translates both ἐγγίζω 'I am near' (*Matthew* 3:2, 4:17, 10:7 etc.) and ἅπτομαι 'I touch' (*Matthew* 9:21, 9:29, 14:36 etc.), both of which usages can be best covered by a base meaning 'be at hand'.[208]

However it is less easy to derive both Greek μέχρι and ἄχρι, which some scholars have seen as the reflex of a zero grade *$mg^{\prime h}(s)ri$, from an original formation meaning 'in the hand'. The adverb μέχρι occurs only twice in

Homer: at *Iliad* 13.143 ἀπείλει μέχρι θαλάσσης 'he drove them back as far as the sea'; and *Iliad* 24.128 τέο μέχρις ὀδυρόμενος 'how long in mourning'. The meanings here are clearly 'as far as' and 'how long' (i.e. 'as long as what'), and could be derived from a meaning 'in the reach of' which is later extended to a temporal as well as spatial meaning. The form ἄχρι(ς) appears four times in Homer, three times in the *Iliad*: *Iliad* 4.522 καὶ ὀστέα λᾶας ἀναιδής / ἄχρις ἀπηλοίησεν 'and the relentless stone crushed (lit. 'threshed') his bones ἄχρις'; *Iliad* 16.323f. πρυμνὸν δὲ βραχίονα δουρὸς ἀκωκή / δρύψ' ἀπὸ μυώνων, ἀπὸ δ' ὀστέον ἄχρις ἄραξε 'and the spear-head tore the end of the arm from the muscles and struck off the bone ἄχρις';[209] *Iliad* 17.590 γράψεν δέ οἱ ὀστέον ἄχρις / αἰχμή 'and the spear scratched his bone ἄχρις'; and at *Od*. 18.370f.: ἵνα πειρησαίμεθα ἔργον / νήστιες ἄχρι μάλα κνέφαος 'so that we attempt the work without food even until dusk'. In the last passage ἄχρι is used like μέχρι in the other Homeric passages, but the adverbial usages of ἄχρι in the *Iliad* are more difficult to explain. The traditional explanation is that ἄχρι means 'utterly' in these passages, but this certainly does not fit the context of *Iliad* 17.590 nor explain why the word is always used in conjunction with ὀστέον. It is possible that the phrase at 17.590 originally meant 'and the spear scratched as far as the bone'. Such phrases may have been misinterpreted and led to the extension of ἄχρι to other phrases with ὀστέον.

However, it may be that the etymological connection between ἄχρι and μέχρι is a mirage, and that the meaning 'as far as' of ἄχρι may have arisen from a connection with μέχρι(ς) as the only other adverb ending in -χρι(ς): ἄχρι also serves as a useful variant to μέχρι as it will not make a preceding closed light syllable heavy. It is possible that ἄχρι is in some way connected to the verb ἐγχρίμπτω 'bring near to, strike, dash';[210] at *Iliad* 5.662 the verb is found in a context similar to those in which we saw ἀχρι used above: αἰχμὴ δὲ διέσσυτο μαιμώωσα, / ὀστέῳ ἐγχριμφθεῖσα, 'the eager spearhead rushed through, driven to the bone'. The formation of the adverb may be paralleled by another adverb built from a verbal root, ὑπόδρα 'looking from under the brows', which derives from the neuter accusative of a verbal adjective *(upo)-dr̥k' (Frisk *GEW* II 927). By this analysis ἄχρι would derive from a formation *(sm̥?)-gʰri(m)p.

If one separates ἄχρι from μέχρι the connection of the latter with Armenian *merj* becomes easier, because Adontz's theory of the base meaning 'in the hand' can be maintained. Furthermore, one need not explain how the zero grade *mg̑ʰ(s)ri arose, which would be unexpected if the two words derive from an earlier prepositional phrase.

Adontz's posited zero grade locative of the word for 'hand' must still be justified. The word for 'hand' is better reconstructed not as *g̑ʰer- as he thought, but *g̑ʰes(e/o)r- in order to account for Hittite *keššar* 'hand', and the locative would originally have been *g̑ʰes(e)r-i (cf. the Hittite locative *kiš(še)ri*). A double zero-grade *g̑ʰsri in the locative would be unusual.[211] The zero grade of the locative in this syntagm could be explained if it were seen to have developed at a stage of Proto-Indo-European where the vocalic grades depended on accent; a phrase *mé g$^{'h}$es(e)ri would at that time develop to *még$^{'h}$sri. An exact parallel to this development is found in the syntagm for 'last year', reconstructed as *peruti from the comparison of Sanskrit parut, Greek πέρυσι and Armenian herow. This formation also derives from an earlier phrase with the locative *pér weti which has been reduced to *uti when not under the accent.[212]

The preposition (originally adverb) *me- is found only in Germanic and Greek (Pokorny IEW 702f.) and possibly also in the Proto-Indo-European word for 'middle' *med^{h}yo-. The fact that the preposition does not survive into Armenian except in merj supports the theory of *me-g$^{'h}$sri as an archaism rather than innovation.

Therefore one can reconstruct an archaic formation *mé g$^{'h}$es(e)ri 'in the hand' for the Greek and Armenian forms. Latin mox 'soon' and Vedic makṣu 'soon' may also be connected if they are derived from a Proto-Indo-European syntagm using an original locative plural rather than locative singular *me/o g$^{'h}$(e)s(e)rsu 'in the hands' which would have developed to *me/oksu. The semantic connection of 'soon' and 'at hand' is clearly possible, compare the development of French maintenant to 'now' via 'soon'.[213]

4.42 *mosg$^{'h}$o- 'young ox, cow'

Arutjunjan (1983:298f.) considers the correspondence between Greek μοσχίον 'young calf' and Armenian mozi 'bullock' to be significant. Certainly the phonetic and morphological agreement seems striking. The only parallel for the treatment of *-sg$^{'h}$- in Armenian is the dubious derivation of ozor 'branch' from *osg$^{'h}$o- made by Ačaṝyan (HAB III² 550), who connected the Armenian term (which does not occur in the Classical language) with Greek ὄσχος 'branch' (sic, the actual form attested is the gloss ὄσχαι · κλήματα βοτρεύων γέμοντα (Hesychius) 'vine branches loaded with grapes', note also compound forms with ὦσχο-) and Pahlavi azg 'branch'. Intervocalic *-g$^{'h}$- develops to z, so the development of *-sg$^{'h}$- to -z- seems plausible, but the divergent reflexes of *-k'- > Armenian -s- and *-sk'- > Armenian -c'- show that the straightforward development of the cluster is not certain.

A closer look at the history of the two terms also suggests caution for the etymologist. Greek μοσχίον is a rare word occurring in Ephippus, Theocritus and a papyrus (see LSJ s.v.) and is clearly a diminutive of μόσχος 'calf' (also used of a boy, girl, or bird; see LSJ and LSJ suppl. s.v.), which is attested from the fifth century onwards.

However, in its only occurrence in Homer (Il. 11.105) μόσχος is used as an adjective 'young' applied to a plant, or, following LSJ s.v. λύγος, as a noun 'young shoot' in apposition: ὦ ποτ' Ἀχιλλεύς / Ἴδης ἐν κνημοῖσι δίδη μόσχοισι λύγοισιν 'whom once Achilles bound in the foot-hills of Ida with young withies'. This use of μόσχος to mean 'young (of plants)' or 'young shoot', and the cognate μοσχεύω 'plant a sucker', μόσχευμα 'sucker', offers some support for the old connection of the word with Lithuanian *mãzgas* 'bud' (cf. Solta 1960:319). However, more recent scholarship has rejected this comparison on the grounds that the Lithuanian word can be explained as a derivative from the verb *mègzti* 'knot' (Fraenkel *LEW* s.v. *mègzti*, Frisk *GEW* II 256). It is possible that the Greek meanings 'young (shoot)' and 'young animal' are connected by a common metaphorical transfer.[214]

Other Indo-European connections for the Greek word were given by Szemerényi,[215] who derived the Greek word from **mogʰ-sko-* from a root **mogʰ-* also continued in Avestan *mayava-* 'caelebs', Vedic *mahiṣa-* 'buffalo' and Gothic *magus* 'youth, servant'. He derives the Armenian word *mozi* from a form with a palatal **mogʹʰiyo-*.

Armenian *mozi* first occurs in the late (probably 11th century) commentary of Grigor Magistros on the Armenian translation of Dionysios Thrax (Adontz 1915:240f.), and then only in the works of other grammarians although (according to Ačaṙyan *HAB* s.v.) it has survived into the modern dialects, and has spread to Greek dialects of Turkey and to Caucasian languages. The passage of Grigor Magistros (which abounds in rare words) shows *mozi* to have been a neutered bovine, as it is contrasted to the masculine *ezn* 'bull' and feminine *kov* 'cow'. If a word first occurs late, and denotes an object for which another term was used in earlier texts, it is very likely that the later form is a borrowing, not an inherited word. Armenian uses a number of different terms for cattle in the Bible and shows considerable variation in the translation of the Greek terms as shown by the following examples (drawn mostly from the NT):[216]

ARMENIAN TERM	GREEK TERM	SPECIMEN PASSAGE(S)
ezn	μόσχος	*Lk* 15:23, 27, 30
ezn	βοῦς	*Lk* 13:15
arjaṙ	βοῦς	*Jo.* 2:14, 15
zowarak	μόσχος	*Heb.* 9:12, *Ex.* 29:14
zowarak	ταῦρος	*Mt.* 22:4
[*c'owl*	μόσχος	*Heb.* 9:19. Greek text doubtful]
c'owl	ταῦρος	*Heb.* 9:13, *Acts* 14:13 (14:12 in the Armenian text)
erinj	δάμαλις	*Heb.* 9:13
erinj	βοῦς	1 *Kings* 6:7
ort'	μοσχάριον	*Gen.* 18:7
andi	βοῦς	*Numb.* 7:15
kov	βοῦς	*Gen.* 32:16 (32:15 in the Armenian text).

It should also be noted that μόσχος is used with sense 'bullock' (i.e. castrated male) in the Septuagint and New Testament (for example *Luke* 15:23 where the word refers to the 'fatted calf') although this meaning is not given by *LSJ*.

The fact that *mozi* occurs nowhere in the Bible translation, when such a number of other terms are used, makes it very likely that the word was unknown to the Bible translators. It seems therefore that *mozi* is of later origin in Armenian, and it may even be a loan from Greek.[217]

The exclusive connection of μόσχος and *mozi* looks very uncertain in the light of the late attestation of the words in the literature of the two languages. The connection of μόσχος with other forms (either Lithuanian *mãzgas* or the words derived from **mog^h-* by Szemerényi) seems possible, and lessens the chance that this word pair results from a Greek-Armenian shared innovation.

4.43   **nāg^{wh}-* 'not drinking, eating'

Bugge (1889:22) first made the connection between Greek νήπτης 'sober' and Armenian *nawt'i* 'fasting' which translates νῆστις 'fasting' at *Matt.* 15:32, *Mark* 8:3 etc.; the form *anawt'i* occurs in later Armenian literature. The Greek adjective is derived from νήφω 'abstain from drink' which could continue earlier **nāb^h-*. Frisk (*GEW* II 319) sees the only cognate to this verbal root in Armenian *nawt'i*, which could show the root with the addition of an adjectival **-ti-* suffix. Frisk rightly does not mention the Tocharian A word *nätsw-* (B *mätsts-*) 'starve' which was connected by van Windekens (1941:73), and accepted as a cognate by Solta (1960:356) and Jahowkyan (1987:140); and he also doubts the connection with German *nüchtern* 'fast',[218] which, if connected, would necessitate the reconstruction **nāg^{wh}-*.

There are other possible etymologies for both the Greek and the Armenian terms. Klingenschmitt (1982:167) derives *nawt'i* from **n-h_1d-ti-*, the same form which gives rise to Greek νῆστις 'fasting'. This etymology rests on a peculiar development of the sequence of sonant followed by laryngeal (the traditionally reconstructed 'long sonant') to **naw-* when in initial position. The development of the 'long sonants' in Armenian was discussed at **2.3.1**, and there are no certain parallels for Klingenschmitt's proposed development of *nawt'i*. However, the reconstruction may be right. It is possible that the medial *-a-* of *nawt'i* continues the Proto-Indo-European 'schwa' (with vocalisation of the 'laryngeal', not the sonant, by analogy to the verbal root) and *-wt'-* is the regular reflex of **-tt-* (assuming that the original sequence **-dt-* had already become assimilated to **-tt-* in this root by the time of the parent language).

The question of the development of **-dt-*, **-d^ht-* and **-tt-* was fully discussed by Pedersen (1906:429–432), who could find no secure examples of their reflexes in Armenian,[219] and dismissed the earlier theory of a development to *-st-. Johansson (1902:271) proposed that *-tt- develops to -c- in Armenian on the basis of the comparison of *kayc* 'spark' with Lithuanian *kaistù* 'get hot', etc., and *macown* 'sour milk' with Sanskrit *mastu-* 'sour cream'. However, neither of these comparisons is acceptable; the correspondence between Armenian *k-* and Lithuanian *k-* is not regular in inherited words, and the Armenian word for 'sour milk' seems rather to contain the same root as the verb *macanim* 'curdle' < **mag'-*.[220]

Winter (1962:261) argued for a development of *-dt-* to -wt-, which explained *giwt* 'discovery' from **wid-ti-*, and also *mawt* 'near' beside *matč'im* 'approach'. Winter's explanation of these words is preferable both to the mysterious process of 'epenthesis' resorted to by Hübschmann (*IF* 12 *Anz.* (1901) p. 56, reprinted in 1976:400), Pedersen (1906:409f.) and Godel (1975:88), and to Meillet's theory of *-w-* from **-n-* (1936:44). The development of *-tt-* to -wt'- would parallel Winter's derivation of -wt- from **-dt-*.[221] As **-t-* develops to -w- before **-r-* medially (as *hawr* 'of a father' < **pǝtre/ os*), a development of *-tt-* to -wt'- is not objectionable on phonetic grounds, and it can be compared to the development of **-kt-* to -wt'- envisaged by Pedersen (1906:348f.) and Godel (1975:80).

Klingenschmitt (1982:167) envisages a change of **-tt-* to -t'- in Armenian on the basis of *nawt'i* and *p'oyt'* 'zeal' which he derives from **(s)peut'sto-* or **(s)pout'sto-*, from the root **(s)peud-* 'zeal' with cognates in Greek σπεύδω 'hasten' and Manichaean Parthian *pwd-* 'hasten'. Klingenschmitt's derivation of *p'oyt'*, which was connected to the Greek verb by Meillet, is very attractive, and could be retained to support my revised theory that **-tt-* develops to Armenian -wt'-, since the sequence **-e/owwt'-* is very likely to have been simplified to **-e/owt'-* from which Armenian -oyt'- would develop regularly.

A derivation of Armenian *nawt'i* 'fasting' from **n-h₁d-ti-* 'not eating' seems, therefore, to explain its phonology and semantics adequately. The form *anawt'i*, with initial *a-*, next to *nawt'i* probably arises by analogy with the negative prefix *an-*.[222] If Armenian *nawt'i* does derive from a form **n-h₁d-ti-*, it shares the same process of composition as is found in Greek νῆστις 'fasting', but which has no direct expression in any other Indo-European language. It thus offers the possibility of another Armenian-Greek exclusive lexical agreement. However, the agreement probably represents an archaism. The Greek word has recently been analysed as an old compound meaning 'having nothing to eat', the second member of which, **h₁d-ti-* 'food', may also survive in Iranian and Luvian (Meier-Brügger 1990b:33, with reference to articles on the Iranian and Luvian forms in note 1).

This leaves the Greek verb νήφω, which was derived by Winter (1955b:174f.) from a syntagm **ne ēg^{wh}et* 'does not drink'. Semantically this is preferable to a connection with the Armenian word which refers to food, and not to drink alone. The root **ēg^{wh}-* 'drink' is reconstructed from Latin *ēbrius* 'drunk', Hittite *ekuzi* 'drink' and Tocharian *yok-* 'drink'.[223]

Hence both the Armenian and Greek terms can be explained without recourse to the root envisaged by Frisk and these etymologies account better for the semantic ranges of the two terms. If Armenian *nawt'i* does derive from a form *n-h_1d-ti-, it shares the same process of composition of an inherited root as is found in Greek νῆστις 'fasting'.

4.44 *nuso- 'daughter-in-law'

The Greek and Armenian terms for 'daughter-in-law' (Greek νυός, *Iliad* 22.65 etc.; Armenian *now*, gen. sing. *nowoy*, irregular plural *nowank'*, translating νύμφη 'daughter-in-law' in the Bible) agree in following the *o*-declension as against the *u*-declension of Latin *nurus* and the *ā*-declension of Sanskrit (*snuṣā*), Old Church Slavonic (*snŭcha*) and Germanic (Old English *snoru* etc.; see Pokorny *IEW* 978). Szemerényi (1977a:68) takes the original form to be a *u*-stem, which is preserved in Latin, and sees a common Greek and Armenian dissimilation to *snuso-.[224] However, the Latin *u*-stem can be explained by analogy to *socrus* 'mother-in-law', so it is possible that the *o*-stem declension is original. Even if the original declension form is not an *o*-stem, it is possible that Armenian attraction of the word into the *o*-stem is independent to the Greek declension transfer. All Armenian monosyllabic words ending in -*ow* are declined as *o*-stems (Godel 1975:29), and the declension of the Armenian word may have arisen by analogy to other words of this shape.

4.45 *ob^hel- (*h_3b^hel-) 'increase, sweep'

One of the most remarkable Greek-Armenian isoglosses is the correspondence between forms in the two languages with the two meanings 'sweep' and 'increase'.[224A] The Greek verb ὀφέλλω means both 'increase' (attested from Homer) and 'sweep' (only at Hipponax frag. 51 (Bergk = frag. 79 Masson)). The root is also found in the nouns ὄφελος 'help, advantage' (neuter *s*-stem attested since Homer, note also Mycenaean *o-pe-ro* 'deficit'), ὄφελμα 'broom' (Hipponax *loc. cit.*, Hesychius and Eustathius), ὄφελμος 'broom' (an inscription in Lydia) and ὄφελτρον 'broom' (Hesychius) (denominative ὀφελτρεύω in Lycophron). Greek ὠφελέω 'help, be of use' is also from this root.[225]

Armenian *awel* 'broom' occurs in the Bible in the phrase *acem awel* which translates σαρόω 'sweep' at *Luke* 15:8. The verb *awelem* 'sweep' is a later formation, clearly denominative from *awel*. The adverb *aweli* 'more' is frequent in the Bible translation and later Armenian literature. The verb *awelowm* 'increase' is also well attested from the earliest literature in the compounds *aṙ-awelowm* 'increase' (aorist *aṙ-aweli*) and *y-awelowm* 'add to' (aorist *y-aweli*).[226]

Phonetically the comparison is reasonably straightforward. The root should probably be reconstructed with an initial laryngeal,[227] not only on the grounds of the common 'prothesis' in Greek and Armenian, but also to explain the negative formation Mycenaean *no-pe-re-a₂* (= *nōpʰeleha*; compare later Greek ἀνωφελής 'useless' with secondary ἀ-). For the correspondence between initial *o-* and *a-* we may adduce the comparisons of Armenian *anêck'* 'curse' with Greek ὄνειδος 'reproach', and *atamn* 'tooth' with Greek ὀδούς 'tooth'.

Morphologically the verbal forms in the two languages seem to have developed in separate ways.[228] The sequence -λλ- of Greek ὀφέλλω could represent *-l-ye/o-* or an Aeolic treatment of *-l-ne/o-* or *-l-se/o-*. The *-owm* declension of Armenian *yawelowm* is most likely secondary, and represents a reformation of the present to oppose the root aorist by analogy to *gelowm* 'turn' (aorist *geli*) and other verbs of this class.[229]

The relationship of the Greek and Armenian terms is further complicated by Greek ὀφείλω 'owe' (and the later ὀφλισκάνω 'owe'). Hamp (1982c:230) reconstructs three separate roots meaning 'owe', 'sweep' and 'increase' to account for the different meanings. This reconstruction clearly calls for some pruning. Pedersen (1906:336) had already connected ὀφείλω with ὀφέλλω 'increase' arguing that 'ὀφείλειν τινί τι ist also eigentlich "augere aliquem aliqua re"', a theory which was reformulated by Ruijgh (1986:385 with n. 26) to take account of Mycenaean *o-pe-ro* 'deficit'. Ruijgh argued that the original meaning of the root was 'increase, make prosper'. The neuter noun ὄφελος, Mycenaean *o-pe-ro*, in his opinion originally meant 'increase, surplus' and thence 'profit, utility'; *o-pe-ro* thus meant the increase which would be realised, and thus the amount still due. Slings (1975:9) reckons that in Mycenaean ὄφελος had the meanings of deficit (*o-pe-ro*) and utility (*no-pe-re-a₂*), which he derived from a base meaning 'that which is needed'; he compares the semantic relation between the verbs ὀφείλω 'owe' and ὠφελέω 'be of use' to German *Forderung* 'claim, charge' and *Förderung* 'advancement, promotion'. The connection of the terms is tentatively supported by Lejeune (1956a:20), Ventris and Chadwick (1973:565) and Chantraine (*DELG* 842).[230]

Ruijgh also attempts to derive the meaning 'sweep' from this semantic base, arguing that the phrase 'sweep a room' is an extension from 'améliorer l'état de la chambre', but this is less convincing. It might be better to see the meaning 'sweep together, heap up' as the original (thus Olsen 1985:8). A passage in a Homeric simile might provide support for the semantic development: *Iliad* 15.383 ἷς ἀνέμου · ἥ γάρ τε μάλιστά γε κύματ' ὀφέλλει 'the force of the wind which greatly increases the waves'. In this context a base meaning of 'sweep' could clearly be used metaphorically to mean 'increase'.

This correspondence may therefore represent an important Greek-Armenian isogloss. If ὀφείλω 'owe' is also derived from the same root, the two languages may also show agreement on the aorist formation. Greek ὄφελε, the augmentless aorist of ὀφείλω,[231] can be directly equated with the Armenian aorist (y-)awel. It should be noted, however, that the verbs and nouns from the root with the meaning 'sweep' in Greek are of very uncertain status, as they all probably stem from a passage of Hipponax (mentioned above), an author notorious for his use of foreign vocabulary.[232]

4.46 *o(w)kʷi 'not'

Greek and Armenian have both lost the Proto-Indo-European negation particle *ne and show innovatory particles, οὐ(κ) (Myc. o-u, o-u-qe and o-u-ki) in Greek and oč' or č'- in Armenian. Several scholars have tried to show that this is a shared innovation, but the phonetic divergence of the two terms is difficult to explain (as realised by Hübschmann 1897:481).

Pisani (1950a:166) derived both the forms from *okʷi which developed regularly to (o)č' in Armenian, but underwent an irregular change to *oukʷi in Pre-Greek which gave the attested form o-u-ki.[233] Cowgill (1960) derived the Greek word from a syntagm *Aóyu kʷid with an original meaning 'ever'. The semantic change from 'ever' to 'not' was explained by Cowgill through a stage where *Aóyu kʷid was used in combination with *ne, which was later lost altogether. The process has parallels in the history of many languages; a familiar example is the development from Latin iam to French jamais.

However, Cowgill's derivation of the Armenian form is ad hoc. He sees a development of *Aóyu kʷid to *Aokʷi to oč'. The first stage of this change is unacceptable because the preceding *u would have caused *kʷ to merge with the palatal stops, and the complete loss of *-yu- in this sequence is unparalleled.[234]

Cowgill may be right to derive the Greek and Armenian negatives from a syntagm containing *kʷid which originally functioned as support for the negative *ne with ensuing loss of *ne. Yet the irreconcilable phonetic divergences between the two terms imply that the rest of the syntagm was different; Greek οὐκ(ι) may have derived from *(h₂)oyu kʷi(d), as Cowgill suggested, but this cannot be the ancestor of oč'. Hence the new negative formations seem to result from separate innovations which took place along the same lines. A similar change may have also occurred in Albanian to give the negative s; Albanian also retains a reflex of *ne in the negative nuk.

4.47 *ped- 'after'

The comparison of the Greek (dialectal) preposition πεδά 'after, with'[235] with Armenian yet 'after' has been made by a number of scholars,[236] yet only Hamp (1983e) sees the correspondence as evidence for a specific Greek-Armenian innovation.[237]

Hamp thinks that both forms stem from an old neuter plural *peda or *pedā < *ped()Hₐ (sic) meaning 'traces', with a semantic shift to 'after'. This theory was already proposed in essence for Greek πεδά by Meillet (1931a), but he accounted for Armenian yet differently. In Armenian there exists an o-stem noun het 'footprint', and the initial y- of yet clearly represents the Armenian preposition i 'in' in its prevocalic form. The Armenian preposition yet, which takes the genitive case, is thus clearly a fossilised nominal phrase i het meaning originally 'in the track of'.²³⁸ The loss of h- in this form is not unusual, compare the Armenian prefixed verb yatanem 'I cut off' from hatanem 'I cut'.

Meillet's explanation of the Armenian word is preferable to that given by Hamp, who fails to account for the initial y- of the Armenian word. The two forms therefore most probably represent separate developments of *pedo- 'footprint' (cf. Sanskrit padám 'footstep'). The semantic shift from 'in the footprint (of)' to 'after' is found in other languages,²³⁹ and has most likely taken place independently in Armenian and Greek.

4.48   *per(i)on- 'awl'

Meillet (1936:142) lists the correspondence between Armenian heriwn (gen. herean) 'awl' which translates ὀπήτιον 'awl' at Exodus 21:6 and Deut. 15:17, and Greek περόνη 'anything pointed for piercing or pinning' among his lexical isoglosses. Both are clearly related to the widespread Indo-European root *per- 'pierce' (Pokorny IEW 816). The suffixes are not identical in the two languages; the Armenian suffix -iwn cannot be derived from *-ono/ā-.²⁴⁰

Moreover the Greek suffix -όνη is found in several 'tool-names', for example, βελόνη 'needle' and ἀκόνη 'whetstone'. Greek περόνη can thus be derived from πείρω 'I pierce' within the history of Greek. Hence there is no need to see a common process of suffixation and semantic extension in the two languages.

4.49   *pok̂- 'fleece'

The Greek word for 'fleece' πόκος was linked with Armenian asr 'fleece' as a special isogloss by Meillet (1936:142). The Armenian word translates Greek ἔριον 'fleece' at Daniel 7:8 and elsewhere in the Bible.

The two words agree in meaning, but show different declensions. Armenian asr belongs to the small declension class of words with genitive singular in -ow (thus asow). Other words in this class are reflexes of Proto-Indo-European neuter *u stems. The form asr can be derived from the neuter noun *pek̂'u- with lowering of *-e- to -a- before -u- in the following syllable (de Lamberterie 1978:275, see also 4.3).

Many scholars see the original vocalism of the Armenian word as *pokʿ-.[241] Support for this theory comes from the 'rule' that *p- developed to h- in Armenian except before *-o-, where it was lost completely.[242] The change of *o- to a- would be in accordance with the law that *o- changes to a- in unaccented, open, initial syllables (see **2.2** above). By this analysis a prehistoric paradigm:

nominative   *osr
genitive   *(h)asow,

would have been levelled as follows:

nominative   asr
genitive   asow.

However, the absence of h- in this word does not prove that the vocalism was originally o. Despite the attempts of Greppin (1973b:37ff.), Kortlandt (1983) and Hamp (1985a) to find regularity in the behaviour of initial h- in Armenian, there are clear cases of unexplainable aspiration or lack of it.[243]

The meaning of the reconstructed term *pekʿu-, and the meanings of the cognate terms in Sanskrit (paśu-), Avestan (pasu-), Latin (pecus) and Gothic (faihu), etc., have been made the subject of a thorough study by Benveniste (1969a:47–61).[244] Benveniste argued that *pekʿu is not derived from the root *pekʿ- 'comb, card' (Greek πέκω 'I comb', Lithuanian pešù), with subsequent semantic developments to 'sheep' and 'livestock', as earlier scholars had thought, but that it originally meant 'possession mobilière personelle' (1969a:59f.), which develops secondarily to 'sheep' in some languages. Benveniste parallels the development of meaning from 'property' through 'livestock' to 'sheep' or 'cow' for a number of different terms from a number of different languages, including Greek πρόβατα and English cattle which Benveniste derives ultimately from (late) Latin capitale 'principal sum of money'.[245] Benveniste claims that whereas the change from 'chattel' to 'cattle' is common, there are no examples of the reverse process.[246]

Benveniste's parallels to support his argument are certainly impressive, but it is possible that he is mistaken is projecting historical changes in meaning back into prehistory. In the culture of the Proto-Indo-Europeans there might not have been a rigid distinction between the concepts 'cattle' and 'property' or 'wealth'. For societies primarily concerned with stock-rearing a person's possessions consisted of little more than his cattle. There are a number of examples from the earliest stages of the attested Indo-European languages where wealth, or the value of something, is reckoned in terms of cattle; the most famous example is possibly the passage in the Iliad where Diomedes and Glaucon swap armour χρύσεα χαλκείων, ἑκατόμβοι᾽ ἐννεαβοίων (Iliad 6.236) 'gold for bronze, a hundred oxen's worth for nine oxen's worth'. Parallel examples of the use of cattle as a description of wealth or value are found in Indo-Iranian and Old Irish.[247]

The reason why the term for 'possession, property' develops to mean 'cattle' in so many different languages in the historical period may be connected with this earlier identification of the concepts 'cattle' and 'property'. As cattle-rearing becomes a less dominant part of the economy, so other terms for 'property' arise in different languages based on terms for 'to possess' or 'one's own' or 'good' (cf. Buck 1949:769f.). The semantic shift from 'property' to 'cattle' represents a restriction in meaning due to the introduction of a new term for 'property'. The fact that the Indo-European terms for 'property' listed by Buck in his *Dictionary of Selected Synonyms* (1949:769) nearly all represent separate innovations made by individual languages may reflect the fact that the specific notion of 'property' is in fact a recent concept, arising from a change in the economy. The change in economic values may, of course, have taken place independently at different stages in history.

Consequently, the absence of any shift in meaning from 'cattle' to 'property', may not, as Benveniste implies, reflect a universal semantic law, but merely the fact that in historical times there are no true parallels to the prehistoric situation where (moveable) property consisted almost entirely of livestock.

It is thus possible that the earlier theory, by which the original meaning of *pek'u-* is 'sheep' may still be correct. The generalisation of the term for 'sheep' to denote all livestock could have arisen from the fact that the sheep was the livestock animal *par excellence*. The meaning 'sheep' in turn could represent a metonymic development from 'fleece'.[248] By this analysis the Armenian term *asr* is an archaism, and shows the base meaning of this term which has been lost in the other languages.

If Benveniste's argument is accepted, however, the Armenian form can be explained in two different ways. Either two separate roots *pek'u-* must be reconstructed for the parent language, with meaning 'moveable property' and 'fleece' respectively, or (following Solta 1960:125) the Armenian term could arise out of a contamination of two originally distinct forms, *pok'-* and *pek'u-* (compare the *r/u*-stem *meŕ* 'honey' which reflects a contamination of original *meli-* 'honey' and *medʰu-* 'mead').

Greek πόκος 'fleece' only occurs once in its simple form in Homer, at *Iliad* 12.451, where Hector picks up a stone with the ease of a shepherd carrying πόκον ἄρσενος οἰός 'the fleece of a male sheep'. Other words for 'fleece' are also found in Homer; the term κῶας is used to describe fleeces when they form the covering of a bed (*Iliad* 9.661) or a chair (*Odyssey* 16.47) or spread on the ground (*Odyssey* 3.38, see further *LfrgE* II 1602f. for κῶας in the Homeric poems). This word probably originally denoted a 'sheepskin' to judge from the use of the HIDE ideogram with the Mycenaean form *ko-wo*. Another term for 'fleece' is μαλλός, which first occurs in the simple form in Hesiod, but in Homer is only found in the compounds δασύμαλλος (only at *Odyssey* 9.425 in Homer) 'thick-fleeced' and πηγεσίμαλλος 'thick-fleeced' (only at *Iliad* 3.197). The meaning of μαλλός in these compounds seems equivalent to the meaning of πόκος in the compound εἰροπόκος 'wool-fleeced' (twice in Homer at *Iliad* 5.137 and *Odyssey* 9.443) and indeed at Hesiod *Works and Days* 234 the two terms coincide: εἰροπόκοι δ' ὄιες μαλλοῖς καταβεβρίθασιν 'wool-fleeced sheep weighed down with their fleeces'.

The exact distinction between μαλλός and πόκος cannot be ascertained, nor is it clear which term is the earlier. An ā-stem noun, *πόκᾱ (or perhaps *ποκά), may have existed at the time of the Linear B tablets, if this is the correct interpretation of Mycenaean *po-ka* which seems to mean 'wool' or 'fleece' (Killen 1962 and 1963).[249] This form may have survived in the phrase εἰς ὄνου πόκας, literally 'to an ass's fleece' (or 'to an ass's shearing'), which is used to mean 'nowhere' (Aristophanes *Frogs* 186). The term μαλλός is not found in the Mycenaean documents, although there is speculation that it could underlie the ideogram WOOL, which may be a ligature of the signs *ma* and *ru* (Ventris and Chadwick 1973:434f., Melena 1987:400f.). The etymology of the two terms sheds little light on their meaning or their respective age. The origin of μαλλός is uncertain, but it may be a derivative of a root *mel- 'wool' (cf. Lithuanian *mìlas* 'cloth').[250] The forms *πόκᾱ and πόκος could have been derived from the verb πέκω 'I comb' within the individual history of Greek by a regular inherited process (Chantraine *DELG* 872, see Risch 1974:8f. for examples of this process from Homer) and refer to wool gathered through plucking with a comb (cf. Melena 1987:412–413 and 443 and *passim* for discussion of this method of wool gathering), or they may continue inherited formations. Derivatives from the root *pe/okʹ- with meaning 'fleece' or 'hair' are also found in other Indo-European languages, for example, Old English *feax* '(head)hair' and *fieht* 'fleece'.

There are no compelling reasons for seeing a shared Greek and Armenian development of a word meaning 'fleece' from the root *pe/okʹ-. The Greek and Armenian words present no agreement in formation, except in the possible presence of *o in the root syllable, and this reconstruction is not certain for the Armenian term. Neither of the two languages, it is true, shows a reflex of a form *pekʹu- with meaning 'moveable property' or 'sheep', but, as we have seen, it is possible that the Armenian word *asr* derives directly from *pekʹu- and retains the earlier meaning of the term, or that the meaning was changed by the association with the root *pe/okʹ- 'comb'. The development of a term for 'fleece' from this root is also found in other Indo-European languages. The significance of this Greek-Armenian correspondence is therefore very small.

4.50 *poli-yo- 'white hair, waves'

The Armenian word *alik'* (*plurale tantum*, *ea*-stem, genitive *aleac'*) means both 'grey hair' and 'waves' (it translates κύματα 'waves' at e.g. *Matthew* 8:24, and πολιαί 'grey hair' at e.g. *Proverbs* 20:29). The Armenian word is clearly, like Greek πολιός 'grey, grey hair', derived from the widespread Proto-Indo-European root for 'grey', *pel-* (Pokorny *IEW* 804f.). Solta (1960:19f.) sees a close link between the two terms on grounds that they both derive from *polio-* and because the Greek word is also used with reference to 'the sea' (as in the Homeric formula πολιῆς ἁλός 'of the grey sea' at *Iliad* 1.359 etc.).

The semantic agreement between the two terms cannot be taken to be significant. The application of the two terms to 'grey hair' may represent the original usage of the root *pel-*; the Vedic adjective from the same root, *palitá-* 'grey, old, aged', shows the same semantic spread. The extension of the term to describe the sea is also found in Kurdish where *pēl* means 'wave' (cited by Ačaryan *HAB* I² 93), and so this may also have been part of the terms of reference of the Proto-Indo-European root. It is equally possible that the semantic extension may have been made separately in the three languages.

Solta's comparison is further called into question by the Mycenaean adjective *po-ri-wa* (KN *Ld* 587) which is used to describe textiles and has been connected with later Greek πολιός (Ventris and Chadwick 1973:573, note also the personal name *Po-ri-wo*). The reconstruction of a form with a *-wo-* suffix for the Greek term is unobjectionable on comparative grounds. Lithuanian *palvas*, Old Church Slavonic *plavŭ* 'pale', Old English *fealu*, etc. show the same root with the addition of the *-wo-* suffix, which also marks colour adjectives in other Indo-European languages (Risch 1974:169, Buck 1933:318f.).[251]

Armenian *alik'* must however derive from *poli-yo-* not *poli-wo-*, which would probably give *aliw(k')* (compare *tiw* 'day' from *diw-*).[252] For the phonetic development of *al-* from *pol-* see *asr* **4.49** above.

The suffix of *alik'* can be seen as a development within Armenian. The common Armenian suffix *-i* has many uses,[253] which have been detailed by Gjandschezian (1903). One use, which is not isolated by Gjandschezian, is the formation of substantives from adjectives: for example, *dalari* 'verdure, grass' from *dalar* 'green'; *ahekik'* 'adversity (i.e. things on the left)' from *aheak* 'left'; *hastik'* 'stability, firmness' from *hast* 'firm, solid', etc.[254] The word *alik'* is always used as a substantive in the Bible translation, and the *-ik'* ending may be of the same origin. The loss of the adjective from which *alik'* was derived (*al*) is not surprising. Nearly all the adjectives denoting colours in Armenian have been borrowed from Iranian or other languages (Meillet *REArm* 3 (1923) p. 6, reprinted in 1977:208). Consequently, the Armenian noun *alik'* may show a suffix of recent date and the word can be derived from an inherited adjective **pel-* 'grey'.

Thus the semantic correspondence between the two languages may be due to chance, and they show no agreement on the suffixation of a common Indo-European root.

4.51   **pork'o-* 'fishnet'

Solta (1960:428), following Patrubány (1904:428), sees a significant isogloss between the rare Greek word πόρκος 'a kind of fish-trap' (first in Plato) and the Armenian noun *ors* (*o*-stem, gen. *orsoy*) which he glosses as 'Fischer-netze, Schlinge'. Phonetically and morphologically the correspondence is perfect. However, *ors* is used nowhere in the Bible translation with the meaning of 'fishnet', nor is this meaning listed in the *NBHL*; *ors* translates ἄγρα 'catch' at its two occurrences in the Gospels (*Luke* 5:4, 5:9), and is used elsewhere in the Bible to translate θήρα 'game' (*Genesis* 25:28 etc.). The denominative verb *orsam* means 'I hunt'; it translates ἀγρεύω at *Mark* 12:13 etc. The basic meaning of the Armenian term is thus 'game' and the significa-tion is by no means limited to fish; indeed to translate ἁλιεύς 'fisherman' a compound *jknors* 'fish-catcher' (*jowkn* = 'fish') is used at *Matthew* 4:18.

The meaning of the Armenian term argues strongly against a direct connection. The semantic extension, whether from 'trap' to 'game' (as suggested by Solta *loc. cit.*), or from 'game' to 'trap' (Arutjunjan 1983:299), is unlikely. The most probable etymology of the Armenian term is that suggested by Ačaṝyan (*HAB* III² 588), who connected Latin *porcus* 'pig', etc., and saw an extension in meaning from 'pig' to 'animal for hunting'. It is also possible that the Proto-Indo-European word originally meant 'game', a usage preserved by Armenian, and was restricted in meaning to '(young) pig', in the ancestors of the other Indo-European languages (compare the restriction of the English term *deer* from its original meaning of 'wild animal'). Ačaṝyan reports that he offered this explanation to Meillet, who rejected it on the grounds that the Proto-Indo-European term **pork'os* meant 'domestic pig', and that the term was unknown in the Eastern Indo-European languages. Subsequent research (see in particular Benveniste 1969a:27–36) has shown that Meillet was wrong on both counts;[255] **pork'os* may originally have meant 'young pig' (as *porcus* does in early Latin) not 'domestic pig'; and the term does survive in the Eastern languages, notably in Khotanese *pāsa* 'pig' (Bailey 1979:235).

The origin of Greek πόρκος must therefore remain uncertain, but a connection with the technical term πόρκης 'ring or hoop' (twice in the *Iliad*, at 6.320 and 8.495) seems likely (suggested by Frisk *GEW* II 581 and Chantraine *DELG* 929). Connections outside Greek are unknown.

Therefore this correspondence is uncertain.

4.52 *pre(i)s-gʷu-* 'elder'

De Lamberterie has recently presented a detailed survey of the formation, meaning and use of the Greek term πρέσβυς 'old man'[256] (1990:II.909–926), and of *erêc'* (*u*-stem in the singular, *n*-stem in the plural) 'priest, elder' in Armenian (1990:II.929 f.). He derives the two terms from an Indo-European compound *preis-gʷu-* with meaning 'go in advance, be born in advance' (1990:II.935–937), which is only attested in Greek and Armenian.

De Lamberterie rejects the close connection of both terms with Latin *prīscus* 'ancient' (1990:II.931), but this remains a possibility. The adjectival use of the formation in Latin has parallels in Greek and Armenian: for Greek see de Lamberterie (1990:II.910 f.); for Armenian, note the use of the term *erêc'* to translate πρεσβύτερος and μείζων in the sense 'elder' in the Bible, thus *zordi iwr zerêc'* 'his elder son' at *Genesis* 27:1, and *dowstr im erêc'* 'my elder daughter' at 1 *Kings* 18:17, etc. The *o-/ā*-stem declension of the Latin term may be an innovation replacing an original *u*-stem.[257] Phonetically, as de Lamberterie admits, the Latin and Armenian terms correspond closely: both show the reflex of a form *preiskʷ-* or *preiskʿ-*, rather than *preis-gʷ-*. The claim that *-sgʷ-* would develop to Armenian -*cʿ*- made by Klingenschmitt (1982:191) and de Lamberterie (1990:932 following Bugge 1889:12) is doubtful as it rests on only this comparison. The combination *-sd-* develops to -*st-* in Armenian (cf. *nist* 'seat' < *nisd-*, *ost* 'branch' < *osd-*), and one would thereby expect *-sgʷ-* to develop to -*c*- rather than the aspirate -*cʿ*-.

The Greek and Armenian formations therefore agree only in preserving the ancient usage and meaning of this compound. The formation of compounds of this type is also found in other Indo-European languages, in particular in formations in -*gu-* in Sanskrit, and perhaps also Lithuanian *žmogùs* 'man' (lit. 'he who goes on the earth', Fraenkel *LEW* 1318 f.), and the anomalous inflection of the Greek and Armenian terms marks them out as archaic.

4.53 *prep-* 'appear'

Meillet (1936:142) included the correspondence of Greek πρέπω 'to be conspicuous, clearly distinguishable' and Armenian *erewim* 'I seem' among his Greek-Armenian isoglosses.[258] The Greek verb is usually found compounded with μέτα in Homer, although the simplex does occur (e.g. *Il.* 12.104). Since Hübschmann (1897:444) many scholars have taken the two forms to derive from a root *prep-*,[259] which is also supposed to be found in Old Irish *richt* 'form, shape' and Welsh *rhith* 'species' < *pr̥p-to-*, and perhaps also in Old High German *furban* 'to make good to see' (originally a causative, cf. Pokorny *IEW* 845).[260]

A root *prep- shows repetition of the same stop which is very rare in Proto-Indo-European roots and may have been 'disallowed' in Proto-Indo-European (Szemerényi 1990:103, Penney 1988:368). Bailey (1971:xvf.) takes *prep- to be an enlargement of a root *per-, which is found with a different enlargement in *pr-ek's-, the ancestor of Sanskrit prakṣ- and Avestan fraša- 'conspicuous'. In the absence of the unenlarged form *per- this must remain unproven.

An alternative way out of the problem would be to derive the Armenian and Greek forms, but not the Celtic, from a root *kʷrep-, which would develop regularly to πρεπ- in Greek and probably also to erew- in Armenian. There are no other secure examples of the development of initial *kʷr- in Armenian,[261] but the loss of *kʷ- before *r would be paralleled by the loss of initial *p-, *t- and *kʻ- before *r and *l.[262]

The derivation of Greek πρέπω from *kʷrep- was first made by Schindler (1972:67) who saw the Greek verb as preserving the verbal usage of a root otherwise only known through a root noun *kʷr̥p- 'shape, appearance' reconstructed from Vedic kr̥p– 'beauty, beautiful appearance' (only found in the instrumental kr̥pā).[263]

The decision whether the Greek and Armenian terms derive from *kʷrep- or *prep- ultimately depends upon the investigation of the posited cognates from *prep- in Celtic and the relation of Latin corpus and Old English hrif to Vedic kr̥p-. Whichever explanation is correct, Greek and Armenian agree on the unique formation of a verb from this root.

4.54 *pr̥k't- (*pr̥h₃k't-) 'anus, buttocks'

The Greek word πρωκτός 'anus', beloved of Aristophanes (Wasps 604, Peace 758 etc. and in compounds), has long been connected with Armenian erastank' 'anus, buttocks' which is used to translate ἕδραι at 1 Kings 5:3, etc., and has genitive erastanac'.

Most scholars see the Armenian term deriving from an original zero grade, while πρωκτός derives from a full grade.[264] However the zero grade to *prōk'to- (or *pre/oh₃k'to-) should be *pr̥k'to- not *prək'to-.[265] The Armenian reflex of a long sonant *r̥̄ is not certain, but the development to ra has no firm parallels (see 2.3.1), and therefore an alternative explanation for the Armenian form is preferable.

Several scholars have attempted to explain the phonetic divergences between the two forms with the aid of the laryngeal theory. Beekes derives the Armenian word from *perh₃k't- with vocalisation of h₃ and complete loss of initial *p- before *e (1988:77). However the development of laryngeals in non-initial syllables in Armenian is not certain. Meillet thought that non-initial interconsonantal 'schwa' was lost completely, from the evidence of dowstr 'daughter' beside Greek θυγάτηρ, etc., and he is followed by Lindeman (1982:38).[266] Other scholars have seen a regular reflex of all interconsonantal laryngeals as -*a*-.[267] Muller (1984)[268] detected a twofold reflex of laryngeals in this position, either complete loss before single consonants, or vocalisation of the laryngeal as -*a*- before clusters. De Lamberterie also saw a double reflex, but thought that the vocalisation occurred only after resonants (1982a:41). The paucity of etymologically certain materials means that the question cannot be decisively settled. However, by either Muller's or de Lamberterie's theory the development of *$perh_3k't$*- to *erast*- would be acceptable.[269]

Morphologically the connection is less difficult. The -*ank'* ending of the Armenian form is taken by Hamp (1983d:65) to be the plural of the 'additional' -*n* which is found in other body parts, such as *otn* 'foot', *jeřn* 'hand', etc.[270] However, those terms with 'additional' -*n*, which do not have irregular plurals, have their plurals in -*ownk'* (gen. -*anc'*), for example:

	PLURAL
matn 'finger'	*matownk'*, *matanc'*
t'êkn 'back'	*t'ikownk'*, *t'ikanc'*
řowngn 'nostril'	*řngownk'*, *řnganc'*,

note also the secondary plurals of *akn* 'eye' and *ownkn* 'ear', *akownk'* (with the (Semitic) extension of meaning to 'sources') and *ownkownk'* ('handles').

Clearly *erastank'* (genitive *erastanac'*) cannot have been formed in this way; *erastank'* must in fact show an -*an* suffix which is found in a few other body parts, such as *srban* 'anus' and *erank'* 'loins' (see **4.14**).

If the two words are cognate, they show different ablaut forms of the original formation. The Sanskrit word for 'back' *pṛṣthám* could also be related.[271] A way of reconciling these ablaut differences was tentatively proposed by Beekes in his earlier work (1969:247); he reconstructed an ablauting noun with nominative *$prōk't$-s*, genitive *$pṛk'tos$*, and thereby avoided the difficulties caused by the reconstruction of the internal laryngeal.[272] Unfortunately, this reconstruction does not help to explain the Armenian form, since *ṛ* regularly develops to Armenian *ař* not *ra*. There are, however, two possible ways of accounting for the Armenian form. Either the medial -*a*- could be an epenthetic vowel, inserted to avoid a cluster -*rst*- which may have violated Armenian phonotactic rules which disallowed medial clusters of greater complexity than -*CC*- (Winter 1965a:106); or the original ablaut pattern *$prōk't$-s/ *$pṛk'tos$*, may have been altered in the early stages of the language to *$prōk't$-s/ *$prak'to$-.[273]

In summary, the Greek and Armenian terms agree closely in their semantics, but seem to represent different morphological reformations of a noun which may also be continued in Sanskrit.

4.55 **ps(e)ud–* 'lie'

The Armenian word *sowt* (*o*-stem, gen. *stoy*) 'false' is used in the Bible translation to translate Greek ψευδής 'false', ψεῦδος 'lie', Greek compounds with
first member ψευδ-, and, in conjunction with an appropriate verb, ψεύδομαι
'I lie'.[274] The Greek forms are already the standard terms for 'false' and 'lie' in
the Homeric epics.[275] Given the exact semantic correlation and the closeness
of the phonetic correspondence it seems almost certain that the two terms are
related. The only problem with this comparison is the development of **ps-* to
s- in Armenian, for which see the discussion at **4.6**.[276]

Hence both the Armenian and Greek words can be derived from a root
*psud-. Morphologically the two languages have developed separately. The
Armenian adjective seems to derive from a zero-grade, thematic stem form
*psudo-. Other inherited radical *o*-stem adjectives in Armenian derive from
*e grade forms, such as *hin* 'old' < **seno-* and *jerm* 'warm' < **gʷʰermo-*, and
I can find no parallel for the zero-grade. However the word *sowtak* 'lying'
(three occurrences in the Bible translation), which is formed by the addition
of the Iranian suffix *-ak*, does not show the regular reduction of *-ow-* to
schwa when not under the accent. The adjective *sowtak* can therefore be
derived from a radical **soyt*, which in turn could derive from **psoud-* or
possibly **pseud-*.[277] It is possible, therefore, that the adjective *sowt* shows an
irregular reduction from **soyt*; the reduced forms of *sowt*, such as instrumental *stovk'* (e.g. 2 *Thessalonians* 2:9), show a double reduction by this
theory, but they could be by analogy to *sowt*. This irregular reduction of the
diphthong *-oy-* to *-ow-* may be paralleled by other monosyllabic forms, for
example *k'own* 'sleep' < **swe/opno-* (note the verb *k'ownem* 'I sleep').[278]
Armenian does not show a verbal form of the root.

Taillardat (1977:352f.) related the Greek forms to the rare noun ψύδραξ
'pimple, blister',[279] and the verb ψύχω 'breathe, blow'. He sees a metaphorical
development from 'breath, wind, air' to 'lie', for which he finds parallels in
French (*vendre du vent* 'lie'), German (*windige*), Italian (*buffare* 'blow, talk
idly'), English (*windy*, compare also *hot air*) and Homeric Greek (ἀνεμώλια
βάζειν 'talk words of wind' at *Iliad* 4.355, see further *LfrgE* I 816). Although
Taillardat's examples are open to question (a *windy* speaker is not necessarily a liar), the transfer of meaning is fairly plausible, and the Indo-
European cognates to **psu-* 'blow' are respectable (*psu-* 'breath' is found as
the second member of compounds in Sanskrit).

Taillardat's theory presents a better explanation of the origin of ψευδής
than those given elsewhere (such as for example Schwyzer 1939:329, Frisk
GEW II 1132f.) and, if correct, argues strongly for an important Greek-
Armenian isogloss. For both languages have made the same enlargement
*-d- to an Indo-European root **psu-* (itself no doubt derived from **bʰes-*
'blow', Pokorny *IEW* 146, Mayrhofer *KEWA* II 388–9) and have also made

an innovation in the semantics. The Greek and Armenian derivatives may
have been made separately.

4.56 *ptak– (*pt(e)h₂-k-) 'shy (?)'

Solta (1960:445 f.) included among his list of isoglosses the correspondence
of the Armenian verb t'ak'č'im (aor. t'ak'eay) 'be hidden' (translates κρύπτω
at *Matthew* 5:14, *John* 12:36) and the noun t'ak'owst 'concealment, hiding
place' with the Greek verbs πτώσσω 'shrink from in fear' (e.g. *Iliad* 4.371),
πτήσσω 'cower',[280] and the nouns πτώξ 'cowering (animal)' (accusative
πτώκα at *Iliad* 22.310) and πτάξ 'cowering animal' (only the accusative
πτάκα is found, at Aeschylus *Agamemnon* 137).[281] It is possible that the
Homeric Greek perfect participle πεπτηώς 'cowering' (*Iliad* 2.312 etc.) and
aorist dual (κατα)πτήτην 'cowered' (*Iliad* 8.136) belong to the same original
paradigm as πτήσσω.[281A]

The first problem with this connection is the development of Armenian t'-
from *pt-. Despite the doubts of Hübschmann (1897:449), this sound
change may be valid. Note the following examples:

(a) t'ew 'wing', t'řč'im 'fly' and other forms which might be derived from the
    root *pet- in zero grade (Pokorny *IEW* 825 f.);[282]
(b) t'ełi 'elm tree' connected with Greek πτελέα 'elm', Latin *tilia* 'lime
    tree';[283]
(c) t'i 'shovel, blade of an oar' with Greek πτέον and πτύον 'winnowing fan',
    Lithuanian *petŷs* 'shoulder blade';[284]
(d) Greppin (1982:351) adds a further example in the correspondence
    between t'k'anem 'I spit' and Greek πτύω 'I spit', but the two languages
    have most likely made separate onomatopoeic creations or reforma-
    tions.[285]

None of these examples is conclusive, but the change of *pt- to t'- in
Armenian is phonetically not unlikely. It is comparable to the development of
medial *-pt- to -wt'- (for example, ewt'n 'seven' < *septm̥), and the development of initial *ps- to s- (see **4.6**).

A root *ptak- may not be limited to Greek and Armenian. Meillet (*MSL*
15 (1909) p. 356 = 1977:135) connected the Armenian word to Latin
tacēre, Gothic *þahan* 'be quiet' but did not mention the Greek forms.
Sommer went further and directly equated *tacēre* with the root of Greek
πτήσσω (1914:240), citing the parallel of *tilia* beside πτελέα for the
development of initial *t-* from *pt- (this word may be loaned into the two
languages, see above). Despite Arutjunjan's doubts (1983:284) the development of *pt- to *t-* in Latin does not seem objectionable. The fact that Latin *p-*
corresponds to Greek *pt-* in other words is not significant, because Greek
initial *pt-* can stem from various origins (see Szemerényi 1979). Indeed,

morphologically the Latin verb is closer to *t'ak'č'im* than πτήσσω is. The two Greek present formations derive from a *-ye/o-* suffix, but Latin shows an *-ē-* formation, which Klingenschmitt plausibly sees behind the *-č'im* presents and the corresponding aorists in *-eay*.[286] The root may have originally been a guttural enlargement of the disyllabic root **peth₂-* 'fly, fall' (Frisk *GEW* II 613f.).[287] The Greek forms πεπτηώς and (κατα)πτήτην suggest that the guttural element may originally have been a present-forming suffix, which was later extended through the whole paradigm.

Hence the root is probably found in other languages. As the Armenian and Greek words show no agreement on their formation, the comparison is not of significance.

4.57   **sad-* (**s(e)h₂d-*) 'enough, full'

Frisk (1944:16ff.) first made the connection between Armenian *atok'* 'full, fat' and the Greek family of words comprising the adverb ἄδην 'enough', ἄδος 'satiety' (*hapax* at *Il.* 11.88), ἀδρός 'thick, fat' (also used of grains) and ἀδινός 'thick, compact'. The Armenian word is used with reference to seeds and corn, and translates Greek πληρής (referring to ears of corn) at *Mark* 4:28 and *Genesis* 41:7. The connection is not mentioned by Solta (1960) or Arutjunjan (1983).

The Armenian word shows an *-ok'* suffix, which, although not common, can be found in other Armenian adjectives.[288] Frisk wonders (p. 19f.) whether the meaning 'grain' of the Armenian noun *hat* (translates κόκκος 'grain' at *John* 12:24) could in fact reflect an earlier unsuffixed noun **at* 'grain' which has gained an additional *h-* by analogy to the root of *hatanem* 'I cut'. Greek ἄδην is taken by Frisk as an accusative from a noun **ἄδη* which survives in the compound ἀδήφαγος 'gluttonous'.

Frisk takes these words to be derivatives of the widely attested Indo-European **sā-* (**s(e)h₂-* in laryngeal terms) root, reconstructed from the comparison of Latin *sat*, German *satt*, etc. (Pokorny *IEW* 876). Greek and Armenian show the extension of the root by a *-d-* suffix which is not found elsewhere. The semantic development made by Armenian from 'satisfied, enough' to 'ripe, full' does not seem unlikely; and Frisk gives German parallels for the Greek change of meaning to 'close, thick'. There is no cause to believe that the semantic changes represent a common development of Greek and Armenian since Greek ἄδην preserves the original meaning of 'enough'. Frisk judiciously limits the isogloss between Greek and Armenian to their sharing the addition of a *-d-* suffix to the root.

However, the terms in both languages can equally well be explained differently. Greek ἄδην might derive from the addition of the productive adverbial suffix -δην to the root of ἄμεναι 'be satisfied' (Risch 1974:365) which may have led to the other forms ἄδος and ἀδινός, etc.

The limitation of the Armenian word to contexts where it describes ears of grain and seed, and the putative connection with *hat* 'grain' mentioned above, might lead one to propose an alternative etymology for the Armenian word and connect it with the family of words referring to a type of grain coming from a root **ad-* (Pokorny *IEW* 3, Gamkrelidze and Ivanov 1984:II.655) most clearly represented by Latin *ador* 'type of grain', Gothic *atisk* 'cornfield'. Or one might see a connection with the root *(h)at-* of *hatanem* 'cut' and gloss the original meaning as 'ready to be cut, harvested'.

In conclusion, Frisk's etymology, which would presuppose a unique extension of the root **sā-* with **-d-* in Greek and Armenian, remains a possibility. However, since the connection rests on a correspondence of only two phonemes and both the Greek and Armenian words can be explained otherwise, the etymology cannot be judged to be certain.

4.58 **sak'-/ *sēk'- (*s(e)h₁k'-)* 'arrive'

Klingenschmitt and de Lamberterie have independently proposed a new etymology for the Armenian verb *hasanem* 'I reach, arrive, ripen' (aorist *hasi*),[289] connecting it with Greek ἥκω 'I have come' (twice in Homer at *Il.* 5.478 and *Od.* 13.325 *nisi leg.* ἵκω; ἥκω frequently stands as a variant reading to ἵκω, see *LfrgE* II 903), and reconstructing a full grade **seh₁k'-* for the Greek verb but zero grade **sh₁k'-* for Armenian.[290] The Armenian verb is usually connected with the widespread family **(h₁)ṇk'-* 'reach' (Sanskrit *aśnóti* 'reach', etc., see Pokorny *IEW* 316 f.).[291]

De Lamberterie argues that the derivation of *has-* from **(h₁)ṇk'-* is uncertain on the grounds that it relies upon the unparalleled phonetic change of **-ṇk'-* to *-as-*. The sequence **-ns-* is known to have passed to Armenian *-s-*, but de Lamberterie thinks a convergence between **-nk'-* and **-ns-* is unlikely, given that in other environments, such as after **-r-*, **-k'-* and **-s-* do not merge (1990:I.294 n. 6). The two sounds do, nevertheless, merge as *-s-* before **-t-*.

However, there are two other Armenian words which appear to support a change of **-nk'-* to *-s-*, although unfortunately neither of these is completely certain. The first, cited by Klingenschmitt in his discussion of the history of the sequence **-nk'-* (1982:212), is Meillet's derivation of the accusative of the first person pronoun *z-is* 'me' from a form similar to Greek ἐμέγε with intervening stages **inc* > **ins* (1936:92). A second parallel for the change might be found in the word for 'fifty' *yisown* which may stem from **penkʷē-k'omt-* via **hingisun* > **hingsun* > **hinsun* (Meillet 1936:40).[292]

Neither the derivation of *hasanem* from **sh₁k'-* nor from **(h₁)ṇk'-* offers an adequate explanation for the initial *h-* of the Armenian word,[293] which may have arisen secondarily, or reflect a lost preverb (Pedersen 1906:435).

The Greek verb ἥκω has long resisted a secure etymological explanation.

The semantic connection with ἵκω 'I come' has led to the speculative reconstruction of a root with a 'long diphthong' *sēik- (e.g. Frisk *GEW* I 628), to which may be related the Lithuanian verb *siekti* 'reach' and Tocharian B *sik-, saik-* 'place the foot, walk'.[294]

The etymology of *hasanem* is not certain. The two alternative explanations given here both have points in their favour, and points against. The derivation from *(h_1)n̥k- has the advantage of connecting the Armenian verb with a widespread Indo-European verbal root, but relies upon a sound change for which there are no watertight parallels. The connection with Greek ἧκω is phonetically more satisfying, but apparently related Greek forms cast doubt upon the reconstruction of a straightforward verbal root *s(e)h_1k-.

4.59   *seps-* 'boil, cook'

In the Armenian Bible *ep'em* 'I cook' translates πέσσω 'I cook' (e.g. *Leviticus* 26:26), and it is also used to translate 'boiled' as opposed to 'roasted' in the phrase *pax ep'eal* 'cooked boiled' (*Exodus* 12:9). The Greek verb ἕψω, which is not found in Homer, means 'I boil'; and can be used of the smelting or refining of metal as well as for the cooking of food.[295] The semantic correspondence between the two terms is clearly close and it is natural that scholars (as, for example, Solta 1960:445) should see their agreement as significant.

However, it is less easy to reconstruct a root from which both terms could derive. The situation is complicated by the confusion over the treatment of *-ps- in Armenian, which was discussed above at **4.6** and **4.55**. It was there decided that, despite the lack of conclusive evidence, a development of medial *-ps- to Armenian -p- is possible.[296]

The Greek verb could derive from *seps- or *sep^h-s-; for the derivation of -ψ- from *-φσ- compare the pair δέφω and δέψω, both meaning 'soften, knead'. The 'participle' form ἑφθός unfortunately proves nothing as it could derive from *ἐφ-το- or *ἐψ-το- (Schwyzer 1939:326).[297] The aspirated Greek form of the participle ἑφθός also needs clarification; one expects *ἐφθός by Grassmann's law. Schwyzer (*loc. cit.*) noted that the compound ἄπεφθος occurs in Thucydides and Herodotus, which appears to show an unaspirated form, and deduced that the aspirated form ἑφθός was a later remodelling based on the verb. However, the form ἄπεφθος may have been dissimilated from *ἀφεφθος. The question is not settled.

The two terms can thus be derived from a root either *seps- or *sep^h-. The root shape *seps-, with a final cluster of consonant and sibilant, is unparalleled in Proto-Indo-European,[298] and it is perhaps not surprising that cognate terms have not been found in other Indo-European languages. The Greek and Armenian words for 'boil' could be loan-words from a lost language or languages. The Proto-Indo-European root *pekʷ- appears to have referred to the cooking of food by any means (compare the meanings of Sanskrit *pac-* 'cook, boil, bake, roast' and Latin *coquo* 'I cook, boil, bake'), and many of the Indo-European languages have innovated or borrowed new terms in order to differentiate the semantic field (see Buck 1949:336–339 for details). The divergent phonology of the Greek and Armenian terms could be explained through the loan hypothesis.[299]

4.60 *s[h₂-sk'e/o-* 'appease'

Klingenschmitt (1970) derives Greek ἱλάσκομαι 'appease' from a root *selh₂-* which, he thinks, also survives in the Armenian verb *ałač'em* (aor. *ałač'ec'i*) 'I ask, request' (translates παρακαλέω, δέομαι and ἐρωτάω in the Gospels). Klingenschmitt sees unique parallels in the formation of the verbal paradigms of the two languages.

Klingenschmitt explains the different Greek forms in great detail, and concludes that the present stem formation of ἱλάσκομαι, which he derives from *si-s[h₂-sk'e/o-*, parallels that of γιγνώσκω from *g'i-g'n̥h₃-sk'e/o-*; ἱλάσκομαι shows a short medial vowel by analogy with an original aorist *ε-hελασ-* from *e-selh₂-s-* (1970:82), which has itself been remodelled to ἱλασ(σ)- by analogy with the present stem (1970:79).

If one accepts this explanation one can see a parallelism between the Greek and Armenian pairs of verbs:

GREEK VERB	ARMENIAN VERB
ἱλάσκομαι	*ałač'em*
γιγνώσκω	*čanač'em* (< *canač'em*) 'know'

However, demonstration of a parallelism does not prove that both sets of forms can be derived by regular sound change from the same prototype. Either language may have undergone a process of morphological innovation for the whole class of verbs. Klingenschmitt himself accepts that the reduplication seen in the Greek verbs is a morphological innovation, but still derives the Armenian verbs directly from *s[h₂-sk'e/o-*, etc., which entails two uncertain sound changes.

The first of these is the development of *sk'* to *č'*. The reflex of *sk'* in Armenian is usually taken as *c'* (Meillet 1936:32f. and 40). But Klingenschmitt derives *-č'-* from intervocalic *-sk'-* (1982:84). The examples of the development of *-sk'-* to *-c'-* in medial position which were put forward by Meillet, such as *harc'anem* 'I ask' < *pr̥k'-sk'-*, *ayc'em* 'I want' < *ais-sk'-*, and *hac'i* 'ash' beside Old English *æsc*, are taken by Klingenschmitt either to show special developments of more complex clusters (thus *harc'anem* and *ayc'em*), or to be reflexes of original clusters other than *sk'*.[300]

Klingenschmitt's principal reasons for deriving *č'* from *sk'* is to simplify the explanation of the *-č'im* (and *-č'em*) class of presents. He rejects Meillet's doctrine (1936:109) that this class derives from a combination of *-sk⊥- and *-ye/o-, seeing this as an unlikely combination of suffixes (1970:81 and 1982:83). But this is no less likely than a combination of *-sk⊥- and *-no- (as in harc'anem and Greek ὀφλισκάνω), or a combination of *-sk⊥- and reduplication (as Greek γιγνώσκω), or of *-sk⊥- and a stative suffix *-ē- (as Latin tacēsco). The doubling up of suffixes is a separate development in each language, but the underlying process of (re-)marking the present tense is the same. Klingenschmitt's derivation of č' directly from *sk' is therefore unnecessary and must remain uncertain.

Secondly, the posited change of *l̥h₂ to ała- is not certain (see the discussion of the Armenian treatment of the 'long sonants' at **2.3.1**). The formation of the noun aławt'k' (plurale tantum, i-stem) 'prayer'[301] resembles the nouns canawt' 'knowledge' (i-stem, also used as an adjective 'knowing'), and amawt' 'shame' (an o-stem).[302] The easiest explanation of these pairs of nouns in -awt' beside verbs in -ač'em is that they derive from a root with a labio-velar suffix, which develops to -w- before *-t-, but to č' before the present stem formant *-y-.[303]

In view of this, it is interesting to note Pedersen's connection of ałač'em to the noun ołok' (o-stem) 'supplication'. Pedersen explained both forms from different assimilations of an original *ałok⊥- (1906:389). He further connected the forms to Latin loquor 'speak'; by this analysis, the final guttural is the regular reflex of the root-final labio-velar.

Another explanation of ałač'em is that it is built on a root ał- with guttural suffix.[304] This interpretation may be supported by the noun ałers 'supplication',[305] which could show the root ał- with a different suffix. The root may also underlie the particle ałê which is used with the imperative (e.g. Luke 11:41).

Now that the formal connection between the two roots has been shown to be uncertain, it is worth saying a few words about the semantic connection. The two forms are not as close in meaning as they might at first appear; the earliest attested use of the Greek verb is in the sense of appeasing a god (see LfrgE II 1186), whereas the Armenian verb is used for requests and appeals to other people. It is only the derived noun which has the specific sense of 'requests to God' (i.e. prayer) and this could equally be a later limitation in meaning, or a preservation of the original sense.

Hence Klingenschmitt's direct connection of the two words is not wholly certain. It is possible, indeed likely, that there is a root connection between the two words but the Armenian forms have undergone too many later transformations to make their direct connection with ἱλάσκομαι certain. The root may also be found in Gothic sels 'good', Latin sōlor 'console' (Frisk GEW I 722, Meillet DELL 634, Lehmann 1986 s.v. sels) and perhaps Hittite šalleš- 'become big' and šalḥiyanti- 'belief' (Bader 1990:13 n. 37).

4.61 *smi(h₂)*- 'one'

Greek and Armenian agree in using a reflex of the root *sem-* (Pokorny *IEW* 902) for the numeral 'one'. In Greek an original paradigm *sems, *smia, *sem* has undergone phonetic and analogical changes to give the familiar εἷς, μία, ἕν.[306] Armenian has eliminated gender distinctions; the only form is nominative *mi* with *o*-stem declension, genitive *mioy*, etc.[307]

Most Indo-European languages use a reflex of a root *oi-* for 'one'; thus Sanskrit *eka-*, Latin *unus*, Gothic *ains*, etc. (cf. Pokorny *IEW* 286). However Tocharian also uses the root *sem-* for the numeral: Tocharian A *sas*, Tocharian B *ṣe*, masculine; A *säṃ*, B *sana*, feminine. Albanian may have inherited a similar form for 'one', if we accept Huld's theory (1984:101) that *një* 'one' (from 'Proto-Albanian' *ni-*) is a back-formation from the feminine *smyā* with assimilation of *m* to *n* before following *y*. A relic of the numeral may also survive in Latin *mīlle* 'thousand', if this derives from *smi(h₂)-gʰsli*.[308] Hence the use of *sem-* as a numeral cannot be taken as an exclusive Greek-Armenian innovation.

Peters (1980:131f. n. 79 and 80) thought that the Greek and Armenian numerals were evidence that the two languages had undergone a common phonetic development. He took both forms to derive from *smih₂, which has developed in both languages to *smya and thence to *smiya. However, the development of *ih₂ to *ya in Armenian is unproven (see **2.3.2**). Armenian *mi* must be derived from an earlier paradigm with masculine *smiyo-* and feminine *smī or *smiyā in order to explain the *o*-stem declension. A paradigm with masculine *smiyo-* and feminine *smī, or *smiyā, could reflect analogical reshaping of an original paradigm of masculine *sem-* and feminine *smī.[309]

Both Waanders (1992:386 n. 1) and Meier-Brügger (1992:I.60) have recently postulated that the original Proto-Indo-European feminine singular form of the numeral must have been *semih₂, not *smih₂. Meier-Brügger reconstructs the original paradigm of the feminine as follows:

nom. sing.   *sémih₂
gen. sing.   *sm(i)yéh₂s.

He proposes that the nominative *smih₂ arose by analogy to the genitive. If these two scholars are correct in their reconstruction, the replacement of the original nominative singular *semih₂ by *smih₂ in the prehistory of Greek and Armenian might be considered to be a significant common innovation. The reconstruction of the original form *semih₂, and hence the theory of a common Greek-Armenian innovation, cannot be disproved, but there is no direct evidence for this form. It may have been true at an early stage of the parent language that every word must have a full vowel (that is, *e or *o), but this is certainly not true of the last stage of Proto-Indo-European, as the reconstruction of *$trih_2$, the neuter of the numeral 'three' from Greek τρία and Vedic *$tr\acute{i}$ makes clear.[310]

The ablaut of the root vowel shown by the forms *sem- and *$smih_2$, reconstructed to explain the Greek paradigm, marks the declension out as archaic. And this conclusion is supported by Darms's connection (1976 passim) of the Indo-European words for 'half' (Greek ἡμι-, Latin sēmi-, etc.) which he thinks derive from the original locative *$sēmi$ 'on one side'. It appears, therefore, that the Greek and Armenian usage of the root *sem- to form the numeral 'one' continues an archaic formation. It is possible that the two languages have made a joint replacement of the original feminine nominative singular *$semih_2$ by *$smih_2$, but in the absence of any direct evidence for a form *$semih_2$ this cannot be proven.

4.62   *$srung^h$- 'snout'

Greek ῥύγχος (neuter, gen. ῥύγχεος) 'snout, muzzle' (first in Stesichorus, and after restricted mainly to Comedy and prose) and Armenian r̄ngownk' (plurale tantum, gen. r̄nganc') 'nostrils' appear to share a root not found elsewhere. The Armenian word occurs six times in the Bible translation and is used to translate Greek μυκτήρ and ῥίς (e.g. Numbers 11:20, Job 40:19, 40:24 in the Greek text).

If the two words are cognate, they show the only example of an inherited pair of words with initial ῥ- in Greek and initial r̄- in Armenian.[311] Classical Armenian phonology disallowed words with initials *r-. Words which appear to have initial r- or r̄-, are all (excepting the word under discussion) loan words (Hübschmann 1897:486f.), and they seem to have been pronounced with a schwa preceding the sonant. Thus at Genesis 7:22 the Armenian Bible translates the Greek phrase πνοὴν ζωῆς 'breath of life' by šownč' kendani yr̄ngowns iwr (literally 'living breath in their nostrils'); the orthography yr̄ngowns rather than i r̄ngowns shows that the word was pronounced with an initial schwa, since the preposition i takes the form y- only before vowels.[312]

All other Armenian words inherited from Proto-Indo-European which had initial *r- at an earlier period of the language have undergone a vocalic prothesis. This process also affects words where the r- is of secondary origin, for example erek' 'three' < *$treyes$.[313]

If the pair of words under discussion are inherited they cannot therefore derive from a form with original initial *r-. In order to avoid this difficulty one could reconstruct a cluster *sr- which would account for the Greek form. This would still leave the Armenian word inadequately explained; the only other Armenian words which are plausibly derived from a root with an initial *sr- cluster also appear to have undergone prothesis; for example, oroganem 'I water, irrigate', and perhaps ar̄ow 'canal' (see Solta 1960:77f.) from the root *$srew$-.

Winter (1962:260) tried to rescue the comparison by reconstructing initial *$s_u ru$- for the Armenian word, with a subsequent development of the epenthetic *u to schwa before *r. It is not clear, however, why Winter's epenthetic u does not develop to a full vowel. The reduction of unaccented u to schwa does not normally take place when the vowel stands word-initially.[314] Under Winter's explanation the $\bar{r}$ of the Armenian word is also unexplained.

The Armenian word is thus most easily seen as a borrowing. It has been adopted into the n-declension because this is the standard declension class for body-parts (see **4.54**). The Armenian word may have been borrowed from Greek or from a non-Indo-European language.[315]

4.63 *$twaw$- (*$tweh_2$-wo-) 'whole'

Godel (1984:291–3) gave a new connection of Greek σῶς 'safe' (contracted from *$σαϝος$)[316] with the Armenian adverb k'aw.

Godel tries to elucidate the original meaning of k'aw in the Armenian Bible translation; k'aw usually occurs in conjunction with the verb linim 'become' in the phrase k'aw lic'i which is used with approximate meaning 'Heaven help us!' (or similar). The phrase translates the Greek deprecatory formulae μηδαμῶς (e.g. Genesis 18:25), μὴ γένοιτο (e.g. Romans 6:2), and ἵλεως (in the phrases ἵλεώς μοι or σοι e.g. Matthew 16:22).

The derivative verb k'awem means 'atone, expiate' and translates ἱλάσκομαι at Luke 18:13, 4 Kings 5:18. In other Old Testament passages k'awem translates ἐξιλάσκομαι (e.g. Leviticus 4:26 etc.). At Matthew 27:24 k'aweal em es y-arenê renders the words of Pilate ἀθῷός εἰμι ἀπὸ τοῦ αἵματος 'I am innocent of the blood'. The verbal noun k'awič' also translates ἵλεως (e.g. Jeremiah 5:1).

Having exemplified the Biblical usages, Godel gives an interpretation of k'awem as '"rétablir (ou maintenir) l'intégrité; (re)mettre en état de grace" d'où "pardonner"', and hence k'aw as 'intact, non altéré'. This allows him to make a connection directly with σῶς; deriving both forms from *tw^oA^w-o- 'whole' (sic, following Martinet 1955:228, see further below). Godel's interpretation of the base meaning of k'aw as 'intact' is open to doubt; the Bible citations point rather to 'propitious'. Moreover, the meaning 'whole' in Greek appears to be a development from the primary sense glossed by LSJ s.v. as 'safe and sound', itself no doubt a development from 'strong' (cf. the cognate Sanskrit tavīti 'be strong'). When Agamemnon says (Iliad 1.117) βούλομ' ἐγὼ λαὸν σόον ἔμμεναι ἢ ἀπολέσθαι 'I prefer the army to be safe rather than to perish' clearly σόον could be interpreted 'strong'; in heroic terms not to be strong is not to survive. The semantic equation is therefore uncertain.[317]

Godel, as shown above, follows Martinet in deriving the Greek family of words from an original *tw^oA^w-os* (*sic*). However the grounds for reconstructing a laryngeal *A^w* (i.e. *h_3*, the *o*-colouring laryngeal) in this root are extremely tenuous. Beekes (1969:249) reconstructs an original *u*-stem adjective *tw_eH_2-us*, which has been transferred to the thematic declension to give *$\sigma\alpha\digamma o$-*.[318] The original *u*-stem form is preserved in the Hesychian gloss ταῦς · μέγας, which is also restored by Madvig in Plato.[319] This theory seems inherently more likely than Godel's reconstruction, which, as he himself admits (p. 293), shows a structure of root in zero-grade followed directly by the thematic vowel for which parallels are hard to find. Armenian *k'aw* is unlikely to continue an original *u*-stem adjective. In Armenian the ancient *u*-stem adjectives are, in general, retained and follow a peculiar declension with a nominative singular marker -*r* (see **4.17**).

Hence the semantic and morphological development of *k'aw* and σῶς is not certain, and this casts doubt on Godel's etymology.[320]

4.64 *wes-nu-* 'clothe'

Greek and Armenian alone among Indo-European languages form the present tense of the verb from the root *wes-* 'clothe' by the addition of a *-new-/-nu-* suffix.

Greek ἔννυμι (not found in the uncompounded form), middle ἔννυμαι 'I clothe' is attested from Homer onwards. In Homer ἔννυμαι co-exists with forms from an athematic root present *wes-mai* (e.g. ἕσσαι Od. 24.250) which were synchronically re-interpreted as perfects (Chantraine 1973:303). Greek ἔννυμαι refers to the process of clothing oneself (French *s'habiller*) whereas εἷμαι, like Sanskrit *váste*, refers to the wearing of clothes (French *être habillé*).[321]

The Attic form ἔννυμι shows a development of the cluster *-εσν-* to -εννυ- which, in the face of the expected development to -ειν- (compare εἰμί 'I am' < *esmi*), led Chantraine to see the -νυ- form as a recent creation (1973:175);[322] by his analysis the cluster *-σν-* in this word must first have developed after the changes affecting original *-σν-*. However, the expected -ειν- form is found in the *Iliad* (23.135 καταείνυσαν) and in Ionic, which makes Chantraine's theory seem less likely. In order to follow Chantraine's theory, one would have to envisage two developments of the sequence *-εσν-* in both Ionic and Attic, as follows:

1. Common simplification of *-εσν-* to -ειν-.
2. Later independent simplification to -εν ν- in Attic, but -ειν- in Ionic.

It seems preferable to follow the theory given by Schwyzer to explain ἔννυμαι (1939:322 and 697): the sequence developed differently here because a form with -εσ- was preserved longer in Attic by analogy to ἐσθής, etc.[323] Hence the phonetic history of ἔννυμαι cannot be used as evidence to show that the verb was a recent creation.

Armenian *zgenowm*, aorist *zgec'ay*, is the standard word for 'be clothed' in the Armenian Bible translation (e.g. *Matthew* 6:29); for the transitive 'clothe' the causative *zgec'owc'anem* is used (e.g. *Matthew* 6:30). Apart from the addition of a preverb *z-*,[324] the Armenian present *zgenowm* can be directly derived from an earlier form **wes-nu-*. The medial vowel of the Armenian word, *-e-*, has not undergone the expected development to *-i-* before following *-n-*. This is because of the regular process of lowering of front vowels before *-u-* in the following syllable (see **4.3**).

Klingenschmitt thinks it possible that Armenian and Greek also agree in their aorist formation of this verb, comparing *zgec'ay* directly with Greek ἐσ(σ)άμην (1982:287). This phonetic development of **-ss-* to Armenian *-c'-* is difficult to justify, as this word would be the only example for it, and it contradicts the evidence of *es* 'you are' < **essi*. The existence of the form *astowacazgeac'* 'clothed in God' (in Agat'angełos) suggests that *zgec'ay* is the regular vocalic reduction of an earlier form **zgeac'ay*, and thus not directly derivable from **wes-s-* (de Lamberterie 1985:130).

The comparison of ἔννυμαι and *zgenowm* appears to show strong evidence for a common Greek-Armenian innovation. There is no other form from this root in other Indo-European languages with a **-u-* extension, so it appears that the two languages have made a common morphological innovation in using **-new-/-nu-*, which was abstracted from verbs with root final **u* and nasal infixed present tense, to form a new present stem suffix. Both languages attach the suffix to the root in **e* grade. A nasal infix present would normally show zero grade before the infix in Proto-Indo-European.

An abstracted **-nu-* suffix is found as a present suffix for other Indo-European roots, for example Greek ὄρνυμι and Vedic *ṛnómi*; Armenian *jeřnowm* 'I warm' and Sanskrit *ghṛnoti* 'he warms' (only attested from lexicographers). As seen above, ἔννυμαι has a different usage from the old athematic present εἶμαι in Homer. The suffix **-nu-* is thus used for recharacterising the existing root; this is comparable to the use of the *-nu-* suffix in Hittite which is used to create factitive, denominative, deverbative, causative and '*hypercaractérisant*' verbs.[325]

The replacement of the original zero (or *o*-grade) of the root could have taken place separately in the two languages. Both Greek and Armenian, like the majority of Indo-European languages, show a tendency to replace old ablaut patterns. Indeed in Armenian the ablaut of present and aorist is always the same (excepting anomalous verbs as *tam* 'I give' aorist *etow*). In Greek the *-νυμι* verbs in particular seem to have a predilection for the *e* grade, such as ζεύγνυμι etc. The *e*-grade in this root could also be analogous to nominal forms in the two languages: Greek ἐσθής 'clothing' and Armenian *zgest* 'clothing'.

However, it may be possible to explain the **e* grade of Greek ἔννυμαι and Armenian *zgenowm* through Indo-European morphological processes. Strunk (1985:236) has recently reconciled the differences in vocalism of the pair Greek πτάρνυμαι 'I sneeze' and Latin *sternuo* 'I sneeze' by reconstructing an original '*amphidynamisch*' ablauting present indicative paradigm with the form $*(p)stér-nu-x$ (x = the personal ending) in the singular active but $*(p)st\acute{r}-nu-\acute{x}$ in the plural active and middle. A similar paradigm could be reconstructed for the pair ἕννυμαι and *zgenowm* and also for the pair *jeřnowm* and *ghṛnoti*.

But, given that the root $*wes$- show a '*proterodynamisch*' athematic present tense conjugation with full grade of the root in the weak forms (thus $*westoi$ for the third singular middle rather than $*ustoi$; see Narten (1968:10 and *passim*) for the reconstruction of this conjugation type),[326] it is more likely that the root also formed a '*proterodynamisch*' conjugation with the $*$-*nu*- suffix. A parallel extension of the vocalism of the athematic root present to a $*$-*nu*- present is seen in Vedic *dāśnóti* 'honour, offer a gift' and Homeric Greek δεικνύμενος (for $*\delta\eta\kappa\nu\acute{u}\mu\epsilon\nu\sigma$) 'greeting' (*Iliad* 9.196 etc.), beside the '*proterodynamisch*' root present $*d\acute{e}k'ti$ continued by Vedic *dā́ṣṭi* 'honour', from the root $*dek$-.[327]

The parallel extensions of the vocalic grade of the athematic root present to the derived $*$-*nu*- present may, of course, reflect independent developments in Greek, Vedic and Armenian, rather than the continuation of a morphological process of Proto-Indo-European. But, since the cognate pair of Vedic *dāśnóti* and Homeric Greek $*\delta\eta\kappa\nu\acute{u}\mu\epsilon\nu\sigma$ seem to show exactly the same relationship as Greek ἕννυμαι and Armenian *zgenowm*, it is difficult to explain the Greek and Armenian verbs as the result of a specific Greek-Armenian innovation. The same morphological processes seem to have been utilised by Vedic, Greek and Armenian to 'recharacterise' existing verbal roots.

4.65 $*wi(n)d$- $*g^{\cdot h}(\bar{e})ri$- 'find favour'

The last Greek-Armenian lexical correspondence which I shall consider involves a phrasal similarity which de Lamberterie has posited between the two languages. De Lamberterie (1978–9) connected the Greek phrase χάριν ἴδε 'see recompense' or 'find favour' (used of a warrior who is killed before he can enjoy the return for his bride-price at *Iliad* 11.243) with the Armenian phrase *gtanem šnorhs* 'find favour' (translates εὗρες χάριν 'you have found favour' at *Luke* 1:30 etc.). De Lamberterie thinks that in the Armenian phrase the Iranian loanword *šnorhk῾* 'grace, favour' is a replacement for the inherited noun *jir* 'gift, grace', which first occurs in Eznik with the meaning 'gift'; in the Bible only the derivative *jri* 'freely' (translating δωρεάν 'freely') is found.

This connection is highly uncertain. As de Lamberterie himself notes (1978–9:34–36) the root $*wid$- is also used to mean 'find, obtain' in Vedic and Avestan and in the latter is frequently conjoined with the noun *yāna*- 'favour' parallel to Armenian *gtanem šnorhs* and de Lamberterie's interpretation of χάριν ἴδε. The only way in which Armenian differs from Avestan is that it has retained a noun derived from the root *gʷ'ʰ(ē)ri- which has been lost in Avestan. Armenian thus shows no more evidence for an original syntagm *wi(n)d- *gʷ'ʰ(ē)ri- than Avestan does.[328]

De Lamberterie also mentions the similarity beween the Greek phrase χάριν ἄροιο (*Iliad* 4.95) 'gain favour' and *jir* ... *aṙnowc'ow* 'take a gift' (Eznik), but the two phrases are more likely to agree through chance. The Armenian verb *aṙnowm* 'take, receive' is very common, and the conjunction with a word for 'gift' not surprising.

Finally, Greek χάρις and Armenian *jir* are taken by de Lamberterie as the remnants of an earlier paradigm with ablaut grades *gʷ'ʰēri-, *gʷ'ʰoréy- and *gʷ'ʰori- (1978-9:38-39), from which Armenian generalised the form with the lengthened grade, and Greek the forms with the reduced grade. This ingenious connection of the two forms suffers from the fact that the reduced form *gʷ'ʰor- rather than *gʷ'ʰr- is difficult to explain; the parallel forms which de Lamberterie presents for this reduction show laryngeals in medial position (such as ταυεῖαι 'long, fine' (feminine plural) < *tᵒnh₂ew-). The two nouns may reflect independent derivations from the same root *gʷ'ʰer-, which is widespread in Indo-European languages (Pokorny *IEW* 440-441), but if de Lamberterie's derivation is correct, it shows once again an archaic nominal formation which is preserved in Greek and Armenian but not in other languages.

4.66   Other Greek-Armenian lexical isoglosses

The following is a list of the Greek and Armenian words which some scholars have seen as showing support for a close Greek-Armenian connection, but which have not been discussed in this chapter. These correspondences have not been fully discussed for the following reasons. In most cases I have followed the doubts of Hübschmann (1897), Chantraine *DELG* or Frisk *GEW*, and reference to these works will give the precise reasons for my decision.[329]

(a) doubtful etymology:

ἀκούω 'hear' and *ansam* 'agree' (Haas 1939:235f.)

ἀριθμός 'number' and *hariwr* 'hundred' (van Windekens 1987:610);

ἄφενος 'wealth' and *awnoy* 'property' (Lindeman 1978-9);

ἀφρός 'foam' and *p'rp'owrk'* 'foam' (Solta 1960:434);

βόρβορος 'filth' and *kork* 'dung' (Bugge 1893:12);

δενδίλλω 'turn the eyes' and *tłem* 'move' (*HAB* IV² 413);

δονέω 'shake' and *tatanem* 'shake' (*HAB* IV² 380);

ἕλιξ 'spiral' and *gełj* 'convolvulus' (Arutjunjan 1983:278);

ἐμπίς 'gnat' and *əmpem* 'I drink' (van Windekens 1987:609-610);

ἔρις 'strife' and *heṙ* 'strife' (Hübschmann 1897:466);

ἔρχομαι 'come' and *ert'am* 'come' (Solta 1960:375f.);

ἵημι 'send' and *himn* 'basis' (Frisk 1943:49f.);

λαγνεύω 'copulate' and *lknem* 'be shameless' (Adontz 1937:11);

λάρος 'sea-bird' and *lor* 'quail' (Solta 1960:421f.);

λωΐων 'better' and *law* 'good' (Hübschmann 1897:451);

μαλλός 'fleece' and *mal* 'sheep' (Greppin 1981);[330]

μέριμνα 'care' and *imanam* 'understand' (van Windekens 1987:610);

μολεύω 'transplant shoots' and *mol* 'shoot' (*HAB* III^2 338);

μυχός 'corner' and *mxem* 'pierce' (Solta 1960:188);

μῶλυ 'mythical herb' and *mlowkn* 'bug' (de Lamberterie 1990:I.389f.);

νεβρός 'fawn' and *nerk* 'colour' (Frisk 1944:14f.);[331]

ξηρός 'dry' and *č'or* 'dry' (Solta 1960:234);

ὀλοφύρομαι 'wail' and *otb* 'lament' (Solta 1960:196);

πενία 'poverty' and *p'inat* 'poor' (*HAB* IV^2 505);

πίνος 'dirt' and *p'in* 'excrement' (*HAB* IV^2 504);

πόλεμος 'war' and *atmowk* 'confusion' (*HAB* I^2 133);

πόλις 'city' and *k'atak'* 'city' (Winter 1955a:8);[332]

πτέον 'winnowing-fan' and *t'i* 'shovel, oar' (*HAB* II^2 181);[333]

πτερόν 'wing' and *t'er* 'side' (Solta 1960:65);

ῥόμβος 'bull-roarer' and *r̄owmb* 'missile' (Jahowkyan 1976:49);

σκύλαξ 'puppy' and *c'owl* 'bull' (Solta 1960:433);

σπάνιος 'scarce' and *p'anak'i* 'weak' (*HAB* IV^2 479);

στενός 'narrow' and *stng-* 'spasm' (de Lamberterie 1990:I.263);

στύραξ 'storax' and *t'orem* 'flow down, drop' (van Windekens 1987:610–611);

φάγρος 'whetstone' and *bark* 'bitter' (Lidén 1906: 57f.).

(b) the two languages show no significant differences in form and meaning from a third Indo-European language (or more):

ἄρνυμαι 'win' and *ar̄nowm* 'take' (Solta 1960:367f.);

γέρων 'old man' and *cer* 'old man' (Solta 1960:164f.);

γόνυ 'knee' and *cownr* 'knee' (Solta 1960:165f.);

(ϝ)έξ 'six' and *vec'* 'six' (Solta 1960:109f.);

ἔποψ 'hoopoe' and *yopop* 'hoopoe' (Solta 1960:428);

θεός 'god' and *dik'* 'gods' (Hübschmann 1897:439);

κῆρ/καρδία 'heart' and *sirt* 'heart' (Solta 1960:205f., 465);

λύγξ 'lynx' and *lowsanownk'* 'lynxes' (Solta 1960:161f.);

μύλλω 'copulate' and *malem* 'crush' (Solta 1960:99f.);[334]

νεαρός 'new' and *nor* 'new' (Hübschmann 1897:466);

ὄναρ 'dream' and *anowrj* 'dream' (Solta 1960:287);

ὄνομα 'name' and *anown* 'name' (Solta 1960:23f.);[335]

-οπη ('-eye') and *-akn* ('-eye') (Solta 1960:20f.);

ὄφρα 'that, until' and *erb* 'when' (Solta 1960:396);

πλύνω 'wash' and *lowanam* 'wash' (Solta 1960:94);

πτύω 'spit' and *t'k'anem* 'spit' (Solta 1960:156f.);[336]

πῶλος 'foal' and *owl* 'kid' (Hamp 1985a:135);
ταρσός 'frame for drying cheese' and *t'aṙ* 'perch' (Arutjunjan 1983:284f.);
τρώγω 'gnaw' and *aracem* 'graze' (*HAB* I² 293);
φερνή 'dowry' and *beṙn* 'burden' (Solta 1960:79);
φημί 'say' and *bam* 'say' (Solta 1960:136);
φύω 'grow' and *bowsanim* 'grow' (Solta 1960:79f.).

(c) the correspondence probably represents a common borrowing from a lost source:

πτελέα 'elm' and *t'ełi* 'elm' (Solta 1960:420);[337]
σπόγγος 'sponge' and *sownk* 'mushroom' (Solta 1960:430);
τάρπη 'basket' and *t'arp'* 'creel' (*HAB* II² 162).

(d) the two forms only agree in showing 'vocalic prothesis' which was discussed at **2.2**:

ἀνήρ 'man' and *ayr* 'man' (Solta 1960:121);
ἀστήρ 'star' and *astł* 'star' (Solta 1960:123f.);
ἔρεβος 'darkness' and *erek* 'evening' (Solta 1960:148f.);
ἐρεύγομαι 'belch' and *orcam* 'belch' (Solta 1960:264);
ὀδούς 'tooth' and *atamn* 'tooth' (Solta 1960:26f.);
ὄνειδος 'reproach' and *anêck'* 'curse' (Solta 1960:239).

(e) the specific connection rests on individual interpretations of the Greek or Armenian forms and cannot be taken to be certain:

ἁρμός 'fastening' and *armowkn* 'elbow' (Hamp 1982d:189);[338]
βέομαι 'live' and *keam* 'live' (Hamp 1976:197);
ἔντερα 'entrails' and *ənderk'* 'entrails' (Solta 1960:152);
ἵππος 'horse' and *êš* 'donkey' (Hamp 1973–4:24f.);
τέτορες 'four' and *č'ork'* 'four' (Solta 1960:109).

Wyatt (1982 *passim*) lists further isoglosses, which arise through Armenian borrowings of Greek terms or joint borrowings from other languages.

4.67 Summary and conclusion

The preceding lengthy survey of Greek-Armenian lexical isoglosses can be summarised by the following table, where for each comparison three questions are asked:

1. Is the root confined to Greek and Armenian or is it found in other Indo-European languages?
2. Do Greek and Armenian show the same unique pattern of formation and suffixation of the root derivation?
3. Do Greek and Armenian share a semantic use or range of uses of the item not found when it occurs in other languages?

For each item the answer given to these questions depends on the preceding discussion. In order to save space the answers are coded as follows:

y = 'yes'; there are good grounds for believing this to be the case.

n = 'no' the root/form/meaning is found elsewhere.

? = the answer to the question is uncertain or not proven.

* Items marked with an asterisk are likely to have been borrowed by both languages from a third language or from one language to the other.

A 'blank' in the table means that the correspondence is too uncertain to be given any weight (as for example number 5 *antro-) or that the question cannot be satisfactorily answered.

ITEM	ROOT IN ONLY GREEK AND ARMENIAN	FORM IN ONLY GREEK AND ARMENIAN	MEANING IN ONLY GREEK AND ARMENIAN
1. *aig'- 'goat'	n	y	n
2. *alh₁- 'grind'	n	?	n
3. *alōwpek'- 'fox'	n	n	n
4. *ām-r/n 'day'	?	y	y
5. *antro- 'cave'			
6. *aps- 'limb'	n	n	n
7. *ar- 'fit'	n	y	n
8. *ar- 'deny'			
9. *ard- 'dirt'			
10. *arti 'just now'	n	n	y
11. *au- 'spend the night'	n	?	n
12. *augʰ- 'neck'	?	n	n
13. *bʰrēw- 'source'	n	n	n

ITEM	ROOT IN ONLY GREEK AND ARMENIAN	FORM IN ONLY GREEK AND ARMENIAN	MEANING IN ONLY GREEK AND ARMENIAN
14. *drepan- 'sickle'	*?	*?	n
15. *dwāro- 'long'	n	y	n
16. *dwei- 'fear'	n	n	n
17. *dʰāg- 'cut'	?	n	n
18. *dʰal- 'sprout'	n	?	?
19. *dʰembʰ- 'bury'	?	n	n
20. *dʰr̥bʰu- 'thick'	n	?	n
21. *dʰregʰ- 'turn'	n	n	?
22. *dʰrew- 'cry aloud'			
23. *edun- 'pain'	n	n	n
24. *e/og'ʰīn- 'hedgehog'	n	?	n
25. *enewn̩ 'nine'	n	?	n
26. *g'elh₂- 'laugh'	?	n	y
27. *g'ūr- 'curved'	n	?	n
28. *g'm̩bʰel- 'jaw'	n	n	n
29. *gʷebʰuryā- 'bridge'	*?	*?	*?
30. *gʷl̩no- 'acorn'	n	?	n
31. *gʷnai- 'woman'	n	?	n
32. *g'ʰiyom- 'snow'	n	n	?

ITEM	ROOT IN ONLY GREEK AND ARMENIAN	FORM IN ONLY GREEK AND ARMENIAN	MEANING IN ONLY GREEK AND ARMENIAN
33. *k̕enw- 'empty'	y	n	y
34. *k̕er- 'cord'			
35. *k̕īwon- 'pillar'	*y	*y	*y
36. *kᶿīno- 'kite'	n	?	n
37. *kʰḷ- 'loose'	?	n	?
38. *mātruwyā- 'step-mother'	n	n	y
39. *mēd- 'plans'	n	?	?
40. *meg̕ar- 'great'	n	?	n
41. *me-g̕ʰsri 'in the hand'	n	y	y
42. *mosg̕ʰo- 'young ox, cow'	?	n	?
43. *nāgʷh- 'not drinking, eating'			
44. *nuso- 'daughter-in-law'	n	?	n
45. *obʰel- 'sweep'	y	n	y
46. *owkʷi 'not'			
47. *ped- 'after'	n	n	y
48. *perion- 'awl'	n	n	y
49. *pok̕- 'fleece'	n	n	?
50. *poli-yo- 'white hair, waves'	n	n	y

ITEM	ROOT IN ONLY GREEK AND ARMENIAN	FORM IN ONLY GREEK AND ARMENIAN	MEANING IN ONLY GREEK AND ARMENIAN
51. *pork'o- 'fishnet'			
52. *preis-gʷu- 'elder'	n	y	y
53. *prep- 'appear'	n	y	y
54. *pṛk't- 'anus'	?	n	y
55. *pseud- 'lie'	y	n	y
56. *ptāk- 'shy'	n	n	n
57. *sad- 'enough'	n	?	n
58. *sak'- 'arrive'	?	?	?
59. *seps- 'boil'	*?	*?	*?
60. *sḷh₂-sk'e/o- 'appease'	?	?	?
61. *smih₂- 'one'	n	y	n
62. *srungʰ- 'snout'	*?	*?	*?
63. *twaw- 'whole'	n	?	n
64. *wes-nu- 'clothe'	n	y	n
65. *wind- *g'h(ē)ri 'find favour'	n	?	n

The results can be further summarised by placing the items in several broad categories.

A Roots found only in the two languages:
   (a) well established cases:
      33. *k'en-

45. *ob^hel-
55. *$pseud$-

The root *$pseud$- may arise from an extension of the root *b^hes- 'blow' (see further below). Of these three cases, none shows exact morphological correspondences between the two languages, but they all show close semantic connections. The range of meanings 'sweep' and 'increase' for the root *ob^hel- presents a striking semantic agreement between the two languages.

(b) less certain cases:
- 4. *$ām$-
- 12. *$aug^{·h}$-
- 14. *$drepan$-
- 17. *$d^hāg$-
- 19. *d^hemb^h-
- 22. *d^hrew-
- 26. *$g'elh_2$-
- 35. *$k'īwon$-
- 37. *$k^h\!\!\downarrow$-
- 42. *$mosg^{·h}o$-
- 54. *$p\underset{.}{r}k't$-
- 58. *sak'-
- 59. *$seps$-
- 60. *$s\underset{.}{l}h_2$-
- 62. *$srung^h$-

The roots *$drepan$-, *$k'īwon$-, *$seps$- and *$srung^h$- might reflect words borrowed jointly by Greek and Armenian from a non-Indo-European language or languages, and are discussed under **C** below. Discounting these four roots, the only other root in this list for which the Greek and Armenian derivatives show a close morphological agreement is the root *$ām$- where both forms arise from an earlier *-r/n declension, with different ablaut forms in the nominative singular. The only roots for which the Greek and Armenian derivatives show a close semantic correspondence are *$ām$- 'day', *$g'elh_2$- 'laugh' and *sak' 'arrive'. For several of the roots listed here the Greek-Armenian correspondence is very uncertain. Some of the items in this class are also discussed under class **B**.

B Roots found in other Indo-European languages.
- **(a)** Roots which show well-established exclusive agreement in morphology or meaning in Greek and Armenian.
    - (i) exclusive agreement in morphology and semantics:
        - 1. *aig'-
        - 4. *$ām$-
        - 7. *ar-

41. *me-g$^{\prime h}$sri
52. *preis-g^{w}u-
53. *prep-
55. *pseud-

(ii) exclusive agreement in morphology alone:
15. *dwāro-
30. *g^{w}Īno-
39. *mēd-
61. *smih$_2$-
64. *wes-

(iii) exclusive agreement in semantics alone:
10. *arti
26. *g'elh$_2$-
38. *mātruwyā-
47. *ped-
48. *perion-
50. *poli-

The correspondences in this class are very important for the assessment of the relationship between the two languages, since they might result from a joint semantic or morphological extension made exclusively by Greek and Armenian, and thus provide clear evidence of a common innovation. The most important correspondences are those which show both morphological and semantic agreement. For these correspondences it is essential to ascertain whether the agreement represents an archaism or innovation. It was maintained in the full discussion of the correspondences earlier in this chapter that the agreements between the correspondences *aig'-, *ām-, *ar-, *me-g$^{\prime h}$sri and *preis-g^{w}u- most likely reflected archaisms in morphology and in semantics. The other two correspondences listed here, *prep- (better *k^{w}rep-) 'appear' and *pseud- 'lie' (if derived from *b^{h}es- 'blow'), might represent innovations.

The correspondences which show exclusive morphological formations are more likely to represent innovations, although the peculiar ablaut of *smih$_2$-, originally the feminine form of the numeral 'one', and the long *ē of *mēd- might be archaic. Both languages have innovated in their reshaping of the originally athematic noun for 'acorn', *g^{w}Īno-, but this might have been a shared choice from a set of options; compare the anomalous forms with an *-nd- suffix in Latin and Slavic. The extension of the full grade into the positive form of the adjective *dwāro- (*dweh$_2$ro-) 'long-lasting', and the spread of the *-nu- suffix to form the present of the verb 'to clothe' *wes-nu-, are both innovations, but innovations which are also found in other Indo-European languages, and which might have taken place in the final stage of the parent language.

The exclusive semantic agreement shown by the Greek and Armenian derivatives of *arti, *ped-, *perion- and *poli- are most likely the result of separate, independent innovations made by the two languages, and the meaning 'step-mother' for *mātruwyā- could also have arisen independently. The meaning 'laugh' for the root *g'elh₂- (originally 'shine') looks like an innovation, but for both languages the declension pattern of the derived noun is of an archaic character.

(b) Less certain cases of exclusive semantic or morphological agreement.

    (i) exclusive agreement in morphology and semantics:
        18. *dʰal-
        27. *g'ūr-

    (ii) exclusive agreement in morphology alone:
        2. *alh₁-
       11. *au-
      20. *dʰṛbʰu-
      24. *e/og'ʰīn-
      25. *enewn̥
      31. *gʷnai-
      36. *kᵘīno-
      40. *meg'ar-
      44. *nuso-
      57. *sad-
      63. *twaw-
      65. *g'ʰēri-

    (iii) exclusive agreement in semantics alone:
      21. *dʰregʰ-
      32. *g'ʰiyom-
      49. *pok'-

The posited agreements here are all uncertain. The morphological agreement of *au-, *gʷnai-, *nuso- and *g'ʰēri- might be archaisms, as also the semantic agreements of *dʰal-, *g'ūr-, *dʰregʰ-, *g'ʰiyom- and *pok'-,

C Roots found only in the two languages which might be loans.
    14. *drepan-
    29. *gʷebʰuryā-
    35. *kīwon-
    59. *seps-

The form *drepan- may have been borrowed into an early stage of Armenian from Greek with the meaning 'sickle'. The other three words may have been borrowed by both languages from a common Near-Eastern source. The aberrant shape of the roots *kīwon- and *seps- supports this hypothesis. All four words describe 'culture-specific' objects or activities and so a loan hypothesis is not unlikely.

In conclusion it can be stated that the number of lexical correspondences between Greek and Armenian is not as large as has been previously thought. Many of the correspondences rely on doubtful etymologies, and some have cognates in other languages. There are only three certain cases of roots which are shared by the two languages alone, and five cases where they appear to have made the same innovations in the morphological and semantic development of Indo-European roots which are found in other languages. These lexical correspondences show no limitation to specific semantic fields.

For the majority of the lexical correspondences discussed, the derivational and inflectional morphology of the cognates either does not agree, or is of an archaic character. The number of archaisms shared by the two languages, although not necessarily proof of a close relationship between earlier stages of the two languages, is not without significance.[339] It is possible that the earliest stages of Greek and Armenian did not participate in some of the changes which affected other Indo-European languages.

The few agreements which appear to reflect innovations made by both Greek and Armenian allow various conclusions to be drawn. By one interpretation these agreements could reflect the remnant of a much larger number of agreements made in common by the two languages, most of which were subsequently lost in the later but pre-literate period of the Armenian language during which a large proportion of the inherited vocabulary was replaced. But a different interpretation might be that the number of lexical agreements between Greek and Armenian is merely due to other factors, such as the loss of cognate forms in other Indo-European languages or the loss of other Indo-European languages with cognate forms; the same innovations made separately in the prehistory of Greek and Armenian; influence on the two languages by another language or languages now lost; or chance agreement of unrelated forms. For any Indo-European language there are a number of roots or lexical forms or meanings which are shared exclusively with just one other language which must have arisen in this way. Furthermore, languages which are spoken in neighbouring geographical areas are particularly prone to show a higher level of lexical agreement. The lexical agreements between Armenian and Greek may therefore be no more significant than the lexical agreements between Greek and Latin, for example, or Armenian and Indo-Iranian.[340]

It is true that very many lexical agreements have been proposed between Armenian and Greek (I have mentioned 136 in this chapter, 71 of them in summary), and some scholars may feel that the sheer weight of numbers provides an irresistible argument for a specific relationship between Greek and Armenian, on the lexical level at least. However, it is possible that this is a circular process, and that previous scholars have searched for further Greek and Armenian correspondences, at the expense of correspondences with other languages, in the belief that there was a special relationship between the two languages. The theory of a close relationship between the two languages, and the number of lexical correspondences between them was strongly supported in the earlier half of this century by the belief that the two languages had undergone a common process of 'vocalic prothesis'. However, as was argued at **2.2**, this can no longer be seen as a significant innovation between the two languages, and merely represents independent treatment of an original pre-consonantal laryngeal.

In summary, the existence of a number of exclusive lexical agreements between Armenian and Greek cannot be denied, and the archaic nature of many of these lexical correspondences suggests that the languages did not participate in later innovations which took place in other Indo-European languages. However, the lexical agreements are not of themselves sufficient to support a hypothesis that Greek and Armenian underwent a period of exclusive common development.

5

THE RELATIONSHIP BETWEEN
THE ARMENIAN AND GREEK
VOCABULARIES

The possibility of using large scale lexical surveys to investigate the relationship between two languages in the same family has already been discussed in the first chapter. I mentioned there that the methods used by the glottochronologists for the selection and comparison of the basic vocabularies of languages require considerable refinement, and that their assumption that the rate of lexical replacement over time is constant for all languages is unproven.

Furthermore, large scale comparisons of the lexica of two or more languages are not able to separate shared innovations from parallel, but independent innovations or from common retentions, and consequently do not necessarily indicate whether two languages at one time underwent a period of common development. As I attempted to show in the first chapter, in cases where the languages under comparison have replaced their inherited vocabulary at varying rates, or where they are attested from different historical periods, the results of a lexical comparison which does not distinguish innovations from common retentions may be at odds with the genetic relationship between the languages. In the hypothetical example I gave there (at **1.2.9**), two extremely conservative languages, A and B, showed a far greater number of lexical correspondences with each other than with a third language, C, which had replaced a large proportion of its inherited vocabulary, despite the fact that the B and C had in fact undergone a period of common development.

The drawbacks involved with large scale lexical comparisons mean that the results of these surveys are not of prime importance for the assessment of the genetic relationship between two languages. However, the large scale comparison of lexical items does have a few advantages. I mentioned in the first chapter one of these advantages, the fact that the lexical comparison does not entail the reconstruction of the parent language, and thereby avoids many of the problems which beset the researcher in the investigation of phonological or morphological agreements. Another possible advantage is the ability to uncover a series of agreements between two languages which are also shared in part by other languages in the family. Thus, for example, one could consider the following sets of agreement between languages M, N, O, P and Q, where items denoted by the same letter are cognate:

M	N	O	P	Q
v_1	v_2	v_3	a_1	a_2
w_1	w_2	b_1	w_3	b_2
x_1	x_2	c_1	c_2	x_3
y_1	y_2	y_3	y_4	d_1
z_1	z_2	e_1	z_3	e_2

Thus for the first lexical item languages, M, N and O show forms v_1, v_2 and v_3 respectively, which are cognate terms, and languages P and Q show the cognate terms a_1 and a_2 respectively and so forth. For the five lexical items under consideration, M and N show no exclusive cognate pair of terms; every lexical item which occurs in languages M and N also occur in another language. Yet for each of these five lexical items the terms in M and N are cognate, whereas for no other pair of languages are more than three of the five terms cognate. This agreement between M and N will not emerge from consideration of the exclusive lexical agreements between the languages.

There have been a number of previous studies of the relationships between the lexica of the Indo-European languages, and of the specific relationships of the Greek lexicon and the Armenian lexicon to other languages. As I have already stated, the results of a comparison of the lexical agreements between languages are not necessarily indicative for their genetic relationship, and in consequence I do not think that I need do more here than present a summary of the findings of these studies.

A lexico-statistical investigation into the agreements between the 'basic vocabularies' of eleven Indo-European languages (Vedic/Sanskrit, Avestan, Hittite, Armenian, Greek, Latin, Old Irish, Gothic, Old Church Slavonic, Lithuanian and Albanian) was undertaken by Tischler as an example and test case of the methods of glottochronology (Tischler 1973:45–97). Tischler gives, where possible, the equivalent for each item on the 200 item 'basic vocabulary' list of Swadesh in each of these languages, and further includes what he takes to be the original expression of the item in Proto-Indo-European. Using this material he constructs a table showing the presence or absence of cognate terms in the languages (not dissimilar to the hypothetical table given above) which he then summarises as a table of figures which shows the number of shared cognates for each language pair (1973:95, the figures are expressed as a percentage of the total possible number of cognates on p. 96).

The results which interest us here are those which concern Greek and Armenian. According to Tischler 25% of the items in the 200 word list of Swadesh have cognate forms in Greek and Armenian. For Armenian, which Tischler reckons has inherited 32% of its basic vocabulary from Indo-European, this percentage is quite high; Armenian only has a higher percentage of cognates with Vedic (28%). For Greek, which has inherited 47% of its basic vocabulary, the figure is less impressive; Greek has a higher percentage of cognates with Vedic (31%), Sanskrit (29%), Latin (30%) and Gothic (29%).

Tischler's results must be treated with some caution, however, since a cursory glance at his material reveals some errors and omissions. For example, for item 85 'laugh' Tischler correctly gives the Armenian equivalent cicał- and Greek γελᾶν (1973:64), but he does not recognise the forms as cognate in his table on p. 90 (for full discussion of the Greek and Armenian terms see **4.26**). For item 94 'man' he gives the Armenian equivalent *mard* which is not cognate to the Greek equivalent ἀνήρ (1973:66), but the Armenian word does not mean 'man' but 'human', and is the semantic equivalent of Greek ἄνθρωπος; the actual Armenian word for 'man', *ayr*, is an exact cognate with Greek ἀνήρ and Vedic *nar-* which are given as the words for 'man' by Tischler.

I undertook to repeat Tischler's survey (using Swadesh's 215-item basic vocabulary list) with corrections to the vocabulary items given in the list. I included only vocabulary lists for Greek, Vedic, Gothic, Latin, Old Church Slavonic and Armenian. The results for Greek and Armenian were not far dissimilar to those given by Tischler. In my survey Greek and Armenian had exactly the same number of cognates as Armenian and Vedic (39); the next highest number of cognates with the Armenian vocabulary was 30, which was shown by both Latin and Old Church Slavonic. Greek, however, had a higher number of cognates with Vedic (51) and Latin (47), although in my survey there were only 29 Greek-Gothic cognates.

The results of my survey are similar to those arrived at by Coleman in a recent investigation into the relationship between the Greek vocabulary and the vocabularies of six other Indo-European languages: Vedic, Latin, Armenian, Gothic, Old Irish and Old Church Slavonic (Coleman 1992). Coleman's comparison of the vocabulary lists for these languages is far more sophisticated than previous lexicological surveys of this type. Coleman includes in his survey cognates to a given item in the vocabulary list which do not occur in the vocabulary list for other languages. Thus, for example, for the vocabulary item 'brother' the Greek term is ἀδελφός and the Gothic *broþar*; the method of comparison used by Tischler rightly sees no connection between these two lexical items. However, it does not take account of the fact that Greek has a cognate to the Gothic term, which has undergone a semantic shift, φράτηρ 'member of a fraternity', and the Greek term is a compound of a root found in Gothic (with a shift of meaning) *kalbo* 'calf'. Coleman includes this material in his survey by assigning a ranking to each cognate pair which denotes their semantic and morphological proximity.

Coleman is then able to construct a table which gives several different indices for the lexical agreements between the languages involved (1992:176). Without going into the significance of each of these different indices, it suffices to say that Coleman's results for Greek agree with my separately conducted survey. In all of Coleman's indices (except for that

which lists the incidence of word-pairs which are not cognate) Armenian
shows a smaller percentage of cognates with Greek than are found in Latin
and Vedic.

Other scholars have carried out large-scale investigations of the cognates
to the Armenian inherited vocabulary from a different methodological stand-
point. The work of Solta (1960) and Jahowkyan (1980, 1983b and
1987:105–204) stands out in this respect. These two scholars have
attempted to gather the cognates to the Armenian inherited vocabulary in all
the other Indo-European language groups and then count which language
has the most cognates to Armenian. Solta attempted to list all the inherited
vocabulary of Armenian which he divided into four groups: words which
could be taken as '*gemeinindogermanisch*'; words with cognates in a majority
of other Indo-European language groups; words with cognates in a minority
of Indo-European language groups; words with cognates in only one Indo-
European language group. Solta gives a table listing the languages with
cognates to the Armenian words in numerical order for words in the first
group (1960:116) and for words in the fourth group (1960:482). In both of
these lists Greek is top and Vedic/Sanskrit second. Unfortunately, Solta does
not give the figures on which the lists are based, and consequently it is not
possible to tell how great the gap between first-place Greek and second-place
Indian is. I have not attempted to use the material provided by Solta to count
up the cognates in Greek and Vedic/Sanskrit, because, as became apparent
in the last chapter, there are numerous points where I believe that Solta's
etymologies are at fault.

Jahowkyan attempted a survey of the Armenian inherited vocabulary from
a different basis. He tabulated a list of the Armenian equivalents to the
vocabulary items listed in Buck's *Dictionary of Selected Synonyms in the
Principal Indo-European Languages* (1949) and then listed the Indo-
European roots from which the Armenian words could be derived (following
Pokorny *IEW*) and the presence or absence of the root and equivalent
formations in the other Indo-European languages.[1]

Jahowkyan's survey shows that Greek has the highest number of cognates
to the Armenian words which he lists.[2] In the 1980 article he reckons that
Greek has 812.5 cognates to the 1360 Armenian words in the survey,
whereas the Indian group has only 653.5 cognates (1980:8). The refined
survey of 1400 words shows 878 cognates with Greek and 661.5 cognates
with Indian (1987:203); surprisingly, the number of cognates with Germanic
in this latter survey is considerably higher than the figure for Indian with
783.5 cognates.[3]

However, Jahowkyan's results suffer from the same criticism as those of
Solta; a number of his etymologies would not find general acceptance.
Moreover, for the reconstruction of the root forms and families he follows
the formulations of Pokorny *IEW*, which contains some uncertain or
debatable material. To take an example at random, Jahowkyan (1987:183f.)

connects the Armenian word for 'stomach, womb' *orovayn* from a root **orew-* 'gut' (*IEW* 782) reconstructed from only the highly questionable comparison of Greek ὀρύα 'gut' and Latin *arvīna* 'fat, lard'.

Jahowkyan's survey is further affected by the fact that the Greek vocabulary is better represented in Pokorny's dictionary than any other single language.[4] Bird (1982) carries out a similar experiment to Jahowkyan's based on Pokorny's dictionary. He analyses all the entries in the *IEW* and tabulates which language groups are cited for each of Pokorny's 2044 entries. In a set of three tables at the end of his book (1982:119f.), Bird sets out the 'proportional relationship' of each of the language groups to each other. He gives three tables, the first showing the number of times each language group is cited in the same article as every other language group, and the second showing the figure in the first table expressed as a proportion of the total number of times each language group is cited in all the articles in the *IEW*. Thus Greek and Armenian are both cited in 365 articles in Pokorny *IEW*, this represents 30% of the 1235 Greek entries, and 77% of the 472 Armenian entries. Bird's third table expresses the average of these percentages as a decimal (in the Greek-Armenian case 0.534).

Bird's result that 77% of the Armenian vocabulary (listed in Pokorny *IEW*) has cognates in Greek, a higher percentage than for any other language, seems at first impressive support for Jahowkyan's results; but further investigation reveals that this result is not unusual among the languages which have a smaller number of entries in Pokorny's dictionary; the figures for other language groups is as follows:

LANGUAGE GROUP	COGNATES IN GREEK AS PERCENTAGE OF TOTAL	COGNATES IN GERMANIC AS PERCENTAGE OF TOTAL
Iranian	73	73
Armenian	77	73
Albanian	82	80
Tocharian	80	82
Hittite	84	77
'Phrygian/Dacian'	84	79
'Illyrian'	78	79

The only case where a language group other than Greek or Germanic has a higher proportion of cognates to any of these six language groups is provided by the number of Indian cognates to Iranian words (85%). There is a remarkable consistency for the high percentage of Greek and Germanic cognates to these languages, and it is perhaps not surprising that these languages score so well in comparison to other Indo-European languages, since they have second largest and largest number of entries in Pokorny's dictionary respectively. The results of Bird's survey, if they have any significance at all, show that Greek and Germanic have a larger and more conservative vocabulary than other Indo-European language groups, or at least that their vocabularies have been more extensively researched and utilised for the reconstruction of the Indo-European vocabularies. Bird's survey, therefore, rather than confirming Jahowkyan's results, merely casts doubt on the usefulness of the method.

The findings of Solta and Jahowkyan should therefore be treated with caution, but they do agree with the lexico-statistic data presented above in the conclusion that Armenian does have a high proportion of cognates in Greek and Vedic/Sanskrit. This conclusion is perhaps not surprising, since Greek and Sanskrit are the two Indo-European languages which are earliest attested after Hittite, and both have an extremely large and well-studied inherited vocabulary.

The results of the large-scale comparison of the lexicon consequently are of little use in the assessment of the relationship between Armenian and Greek. Armenian appears to share a large proportion of its cognates with Greek, but it is not certain whether this reflects anything other than the conservatism of the Greek vocabulary. Greek shows a larger proportion of agreements with Latin and Vedic than with Armenian, but this may in turn be due to the fact that these languages are more conservative than Armenian. As we have seen, the comparison of lexical features does not separate innovations from agreements which have arisen through other causes and its importance for the assessment of the relationship between any two languages is limited.

6

CONCLUSION

The aim of this work has been to examine the relationship between Greek and Armenian within the Indo-European family. The classification of closely related languages into sub-groups within a family has always accompanied the construction of language families, and the model of the linguistic family tree will be familiar to most people with some awareness of language relationships. The question which prompted this work may therefore be one which will have occurred to others and which needs to be answered first: did Greek and Armenian form a sub-group of Indo-European?

The answer to this question of course requires a preliminary definition of the term 'sub-group'. I hope to have presented my understanding of the term in the first chapter, and here I shall merely summarise the interpretation I have adopted, which I scarcely think controversial. Two genetically related languages form a sub-group of a language family if they have undergone a period of common development and mutual intelligibility following the period of common development and mutual intelligibility of all the languages in the family. It follows that the only secure ground for assigning two languages to a sub-group is positive evidence that they did undergo a period of common development, in the form of shared linguistic innovations. In the first chapter I argued that the firmest support for the hypothesis that two languages derive from a sub-group is a number of innovations in inflectional morphology.

The examination of the morphological developments of Greek and Armenian which might belong to the category of exclusive innovations in chapter 3 revealed little evidence in favour of the sub-group hypothesis. The material in some cases did not admit a straightforward interpretation, and there was no account of the development of the majority of the Greek and Armenian morphological formations under discussion which could be said to be free from all possibility of criticism. But despite this, there was no development that was better explained through the supposition of a common Greek-Armenian innovation. The absence of any compelling explanation of a morphological development of either language which depends upon a stage of common innovation with the other language suggests strongly that the languages did not form a sub-group.

Close scrutiny of the phonological and lexical agreements between Greek and Armenian in Chapters 2, 4 and 5 did not provide sufficient evidence to refute the conclusion of Chapter 3. The two languages had certainly undergone the same or similar phonological developments: a vocalic reflex of an original initial 'laryngeal' in pre-consonantal position; the aspiration and loss of *s in initial and intervocalic position; the loss of *y in intervocalic position and others. But none of these developments could be shown to have been made jointly by the two languages, and not to reflect independent parallel processes. It is possible that some of the phonological developments made by the two languages could reflect areal developments, since they are found in other languages in Anatolia and the surrounding area. The loss of *s (also found in Iranian) and the development of a prothetic vowel before initial *r (also found in other Anatolian languages and Turkish) are two possible examples of areal developments.

The lexical agreements between Armenian and Greek have long been considered to be the strongest evidence for their close relationship,[1] and they have attracted far more scholarly interest than the phonological or morphological agreements. Consequently they occupy the greater part of this work, Chapter 4, where I have examined 65 supposedly exclusive lexical agreements in detail and mentioned a further 71 in summary (at **4.66**). It is here that my findings may be seen to be more controversial, for of these 136 possible lexical correspondences there were only five cases where the agreement between the cognate pair of words might reflect a common innovation made jointly by Greek and Armenian.[2] The majority of the lexical agreements examined proved either to be unreliable, or to show no significant difference from related terms in other Indo-European languages, and a substantial number seemed to derive from archaic formations which might have been replaced in other Indo-European languages. There is also a small number of Greek-Armenian lexical correspondences which might have arisen through early borrowings from a third language or from each other.

As I have stated in the conclusion to Chapter 4 (**4.67**), the exact interpretation of this small number of lexical agreements which appear to represent innovations made in common by the two languages is difficult. They could be the remnant of a larger number of lexical innovations, or they could have arisen independently, or within the period of the parent language. It seems to me that the first explanation is less likely than the second, and these apparent joint innovations in the form and meaning of lexical items need not contradict the conclusion that the two languages did not form a sub-group.

The lexico-statistical material presented in Chapter 5 carries less weight than anything else in this work. The large-scale comparison of vocabularies is not able to distinguish between archaisms and innovations and consequently a high proportion of cognate terms in the vocabularies of two languages is not necessarily indicative that they at one time formed a sub-group. The comparison of the Armenian and Greek vocabularies, which, as we saw in Chapter 4, might have preserved a number of archaic terms in common, is therefore of little worth for the decision on the sub-group question.

In Chapter 5 I presented the findings of some scholars who had endeavoured to compare the Greek and Armenian vocabularies with those of other Indo-European languages. In these lexical surveys the Armenian vocabulary was found to have more cognates in the Greek vocabulary than in those of other Indo-European languages, whereas the Greek 'basic' vocabulary was found to have more cognates in Latin and Sanskrit than in Armenian. I endeavoured to show that the large number of Greek cognates to the Armenian vocabulary may have been due to the size and conservatism of the Greek vocabulary, and was matched by an equally high proportion of Greek cognates to the Albanian, Tocharian and Hittite vocabularies.

On the basis of the evidence examined in this work, Greek and Armenian do not form a sub-group of Indo-European. This conclusion leads to a second question: are there any grounds for supposing a 'close relationship' between Greek and Armenian, which might, for example, be due to proximity of the Indo-European dialects from which the language developed? The need to separate the situation where two languages derive from a sub-group of a language family from that where they derive from contiguous dialects of the parent language was discussed at **1.2.3**, and the distinguishing features of the two models were decided to be as follows. Languages which derive from sub-groups will show exclusive common innovations, whereas languages which derive from contiguous dialects will share innovations which date from the period of unity of the parent language, and which may also be found in other languages of the family.

The proposal that Greek and Armenian derived from neighbouring dialects of the parent language would account well for the morphological agreements which unite Greek, Armenian and Indo-Iranian which were mentioned at **3.8** (the augment, the case forms in *-osyo* and *-bʰi*), and may well explain the small number of lexical innovations which, as we have seen, may correspond to other developments which have occurred in other Indo-European languages, and consequently are likely to have taken place within the period of the parent speech. The presence of a number of archaic forms retained in Greek and Armenian but not in other Indo-European might also be due to their dialectal proximity in Proto-Indo-European if innovations which took place in other dialects did not affect the Greek-Armenian dialect area; however this argument cannot be used to support the hypothesis of dialectal proximity, since archaisms can also be preserved in completely separate dialects.

The final question which needs to be answered again follows from the last conclusion: were the dialects ancestral to Greek and Armenian closer to each other than to any other dialect? This would correspond to the 'weak' special relationship hypothesis which seems to be advocated by those scholars who see some sort of special relationship between Greek and Armenian without wishing to commit themselves to the construction of a Greek-Armenian sub-group. However, the morphological evidence which suggests that Greek and Armenian stem from neighbouring Proto-Indo-European dialectal areas connects them as closely to the Indo-Iranian languages, and we have also discussed in Chapter 4 a number of possible lexical agreements between the three language groups,[3] which might augment the list of lexical agreements between the languages presented by Porzig (1954:162–164) and others.[4] Scholars have also observed the close relationship between the morphological systems of Greek and Indo-Iranian,[5] and a few exclusive agreements, between Armenian and Indo-Iranian especially, in vocabulary.[6] These various factors all support the reconstruction of a dialectal group of the parent language comprising the speech forms which later developed to give the Armenian, Greek and Indo-Iranian languages, as has recently been argued by K. H. Schmidt (1980) and others.

In my opinion there is not sufficient evidence to suppose any closer link between Greek and Armenian than between either language and Indo-Iranian, and the reconstruction of a Greek-Armenian-Indo-Iranian dialect area is sufficient to account for these agreements.

NOTES

Notes for Chapter 1

1. For more detailed surveys of the different groupings and the methodology behind them, see Schrader (1907:53–76), Porzig (1954:17–52) and Morpurgo Davies (1975). I have relied upon these sources for information on the minor works of the nineteenth century, and for interpretation of the trends in scholarship at that time.

2. A brief survey of the scholars who had recognised the close relationships between Welsh and Irish, between the Germanic languages and between the Romance languages is given by Ruhlen (1991: 28–35).

3. The similarity of the two enterprises is made explicit by Curtius (1858:22) (cited by Timpanaro (1963:76), who discusses the relationship between the two disciplines).

4. Other scholars, notably Pictet, Ebel and Schuchardt, had already anticipated some of Schmidt's ideas.

5. 'Überall sehen wir continuierliche übergänge aus einer sprache in die andere' (1872:26).

6. See Porzig (1954:25f.) for a summary of the principal reviews and replies to Schmidt.

7. The influence of Leskien on Brugmann is clearly seen in the latter's article on sub-grouping (Brugmann 1884), discussed below. As Morpurgo Davies puts it 'the neogrammarians, as often, took their cue from Leskien' (1975:650).

8. 'Die Kriterien einer engeren Gemeinschaft können nur in positiven Uebereinstimmungen der betreffenden Sprachen, die zugleich Abweichungen von den übrigen sind, gefunden werden' (1876:vii).

9. 'Neubildungen in der Flexion gelten mit vollem Recht als Hauptkriterien engerer Verwandtschaft: da die Mittel eine verlorne oder sich verlierende alte Form zu ersetzen sehr mannichfaltig sind und keine allgemeinen sprachlichen Gesetze nothwendig auch auf verschiedenem Boden zur Anwendung dieses oder jenes bestimmten Mittels führen, ist immer die grösste Wahrscheinlichkeit dafür, dass die Anwendung gleicher Mittel auf historischem Zusammenhang beruhe. Dasselbe lässt sich von der besonderen Ausbildung und Anwendung der stammbildenden Suffixe sagen' (1876:xxvii–xxviii).

10. The credit for this discovery was claimed by (and for) a number of scholars (see Collinge 1987) including Verner, Collitz, Thomsen and Schmidt.

11. 'Es ist hier nicht eine einzelne und sind nicht einige wenige auf zweien oder mehreren Gebieten zugleich auftretende Spracherscheinungen, die den Beweis der näheren Gemeinschaft erbringen, sondern nur die grosse Masse von Übereinstimmungen in lautlichen, flexivischen, syntaktischen und lexicalischen Neuerungen, die grosse Masse, die den Gedanken an Zufall ausschliesst' (1884:253).

12. Meillet's concept of the 'unité commune' is not, however, very clear; for he suggests (1908:12) that in the Indo-Iranian group Iranian may show differences from Indo-Aryan which arise from earlier dialectal features of the parent language. In that case, why may not the dialect ancestral to Iranian differ from the dialect ancestral to Indian in the marker of the first person singular of the present thematic conjugation?

13. 'La contestation des domaines dialectaux continus de l'indo-européen est facilitée par ceci que la séparation des langues indo-européennes ne semble pas avoir entrainé de dislocations: l'une des principales conclusions de la présente étude sera que le domaine occupé par la famille a été élargi sans que la position respective des dialectes ait changé d'une manière essentielle' (Meillet 1908:10–11).

14. This criticism is given by Hall (1950:23 n.43).

15. Most notably Bonfante, see, for example Bonfante (1982) and (1987).

16. See, for example, Jahowkyan (1982:202–203), who examines the agreements between

Armenian and other Indo-European languages in a list of 27 phonetic and 35 grammatical features in an attempt to find the dialectal position of Armenian.

17. The glottochronologists' methods and principles are set out in Swadesh (1952), and a full description of the history of the subject is given by Tischler (1973).

18. The inadequacy of this theory was shown by Bergsland and Vogt (1962:125).

19. Greenberg's methods for constructing genetic sub-groups are largely repeated by Ruhlen (1991:14–16 and 252–257). Ruhlen stresses the importance of weighting the significance of agreements between languages (lexical correspondences are of more significance than a shared phonetic change found in many languages, for example), and advocates the use of both lexico-statistical methods and investigation of shared innovations for greater certainty in the reconstruction of sub-groups.

20. Similarly, Tischler (1973:45–107) investigates the fate of the 200 item word-list of the glottochronologists in the Indo-European languages, as a demonstration of the shortcomings of the method.

21. Thus Cowgill wrote on Greek dialects, Emeneau on Indo-Aryan, Lehmann on the groupings of the Germanic languages, Birnbaum on the Slavic languages, Lane on Tocharian and Winter looked for traces of earlier dialectal diversity in Armenian.

22. He thus enlarges on his earlier discussion of these issues (Hoenigswald 1960:144–160), which offers a largely traditional account of the methods and difficulties in constructing language sub-groups.

23. These criticisms of Watkins's criteria are given by K. H. Schmidt (1992:45–47).

24. 'The sub-grouping question is partly one of relative chronology' (1966:32).

25. For example, in a recent volume of papers concerned with Austronesian languages (Geraghty, Carrington and Wurm 1986), discussion of sub-grouping and sub-groups occupied 7 out of 21 papers. Ruhlen's (1991) classification of world languages (largely following the work of Greenberg) organises most of the world's language families into sub-groups.

26. Pedersen (1925:52) had earlier used this shared feature as evidence that these languages had developed from the same dialect of the parent language.

27. The principal criticisms of Meid's theory have come from Schlerath (1981 and 1982–3) and Eichner (1988a), who maintain that the comparative method can only be used to reconstruct a language system free of variation. This point will be discussed in more detail below. Support for Meid has come from several different quarters; note in particular Neu (1976), who applies Meid's model to the reconstruction of the Proto-Indo-European verbal system, and (1984) where he replies to Schlerath (1981 and 1982–3), and Gusmani (1989), who replies to Eichner (1988a). Models of Proto-Indo-European very similar to Meid's are independently constructed by Adrados (1982) and Schmid (1978:10). Southworth (1964, summarised by Anttila 1989:308–309, and imitated by Hock 1986:452) had previously attempted to construct tree-diagrams which allowed the possibility of shared innovations taking place between dialects which had already become differentiated; the resulting triangular diagram is strikingly similar to Meid's.

28. Meid (1989:29–39) gives an overview of the initial reviews of and reactions to Renfrew's book; note in particular the articles in *Current Anthropology* 29.1, 1988, 437–468, and *Antiquity* Vol. 62, No. 236, 1988, 563–595. Mallory (1989) presents in full an alternative model to Renfrew, based largely on the current orthodoxy.

29. See, for example, Palmer (1954:13), who, although no supporter of an Italo-Celtic sub-group, advocates the theory that *-ī in Latin and Celtic represents an innovatory replacement of earlier *-osyo.

30. It will be noticed from the discussion of the earlier literature connected with the interrelationships between the Indo-European languages that some scholars use the term 'sub-group' to refer to what other scholars mean by 'dialect of the parent language'. Thus, for example, Hoenigswald (1966:11) speaks of 'those who think Mycenaean is to be sub-grouped with Arcado-Cypriot', while Cowgill (1966a), writing in the same volume, avoids any reference to 'sub-grouping' the Greek dialects.

31. 'Dialekte sind logischerweise nachurindogermanisch' (Schlerath 1981:186); 'stellt man bei der vergleichenden Rekonstruktion dialektale Differenzen fest, so muss man die Grundsprache weiter zurück in die Vergangenheit ansetzen, in die Zeit, zu der diese dialektalen Differenzen noch nicht ausgebildet waren' (Eichner 1988a:14).

32. These examples are taken from Morpurgo Davies (1985:76 and 101–102).

33. Hoenigswald (1966:12) makes the same point but with a different example.
34. As argued by Gamkrelidze (1985).
35. Greenberg (1957:50).
36. Hence the description of Proto-Indo-European comparative morphology as 'morphology as applied phonology' (Allen 1953:80 (citing Trnka) and Anttila 1989:351).
37. For internal reconstruction, see the discussion of Hock (1986:532–555).
38. cf. Porzig (1954:56).
39. Cowgill (1966b). However, Cowgill sees an early tendency in the Indo-European languages towards more synthesis followed by a decline (1966b:127).
40. The late spread of the thematic forms in Indo-European was noted by Meillet (1931b).
41. The Meglenite Rumanian example is cited by Sandfeld (1938:59), Weinreich (1953:32) and others.
42. Watkins (1976).
43. In the particular case of the relationship between Greek and Armenian, extremely few shared syntactic features have been put forward by scholars. Apart from the agreement noted by Schwyzer presented in the text, the only other possible exclusive syntactic agreement between Armenian and Greek which I know of was suggested by Wackernagel (1924:211), who related the use of the Armenian preposition ǝnd 'with' with the dative (singular) case of some o- and a-stem nouns rather than with the regular locative (Jensen 1959:127f. gives textual examples) to the Greek use of ἐν with the inherited dative singular rather than locative in the o-stems (thus ἐν οἴκῳ rather than ἐν οἴκοι).
44. The root might have been created by an individual Greek extension of an existing formation if the theory deriving the word from *eks-tro-'outside' (see Frisk GEW I 600f. for references to earlier scholars who suggested this etymology) is correct.
45. For example, Kroeber and Chrétien (1937). If the investigation is limited to a field where the data are more comparable (for example the Greek dialects as studied by Coleman 1963), studies of this type meet with less objection. Allen (1953:92f.) gives a method for establishing an index of relationship between two languages which avoids the faults of Kroeber and Chrétien. However, as he points out (p. 101) the index is descriptive not historical and consequently it does not attempt to provide information on how the relationship between the languages has arisen.
46. This method is advocated by Greenberg and his followers.
47. See Schmitt (1972a:38f.) (published in 1974) for a survey of the literature concerning Greek and Armenian affinities since Meillet (1936). Since Schmitt's article Hamp has published a number of articles supporting his thesis that 'the time is approaching when we should speak of Helleno-Armenian' (1976:91); other articles will be mentioned throughout the present work. It is interesting to note that many scholars now seek to explain Armenian phenomena through analogy to developments which took place in Greek, for example, Szemerényi (1960b:22), Peters (1980:132 n. 80), Olsen (1989b:7 n. 7.).
48. Meillet's Esquisse (1936) is still the most readable and attractive of these. Godel's (1975) work gives fuller discussions on a few points, but lacks the scope of the earlier work. The grammar of Schmitt (1981) provides useful reference in a readily accessible form, but does not attempt to enlarge the discussion of its predecessors. The comparative grammar of Jahowkyan (1982, in Russian) is likewise important, often shedding a different perspective on the material.

Notes for Chapter 2

1. Hübschmann (1895:2) transliterates ⟨ow⟩ as v when prevocalic, except in the imperfect of the u-conjugation verbs and in certain names; Jensen (1959, substituting w for v) and Hammalian (1984:26) follow in this practice.
2. Attempts to explain these anomalies have been made by Godel (1975:23) and Feydit (1982:184).

3. Feydit (1982:187), Hammalian (1984:27).

4. Certain pronominal forms, etc., are excepted from this rule; see Meillet (1913:16 f.).

5. A number of scholars have suggested that the Armenian consonants transcribed as *b*, etc., were in fact voiced aspirates, (Pedersen 1906:336–341, Allen 1950, Benveniste 1959:53 f., Vogt 1958:159, de Lamberterie 1974 and others).

6. The vowel [u] is of course normally represented by the digraph ⟨*ow*⟩ in the Armenian script.

7. See especially Meillet (*BSL* 27 (1927) p. 129–135, reprinted in 1977:233–239), Messing (1947:190 f.), Lazzeroni (1958), Cowgill (1965), Winter (1965a), Hovdhaugen (1968), Beekes (1969:18–98 and 1987), Wyatt (1972), Greppin (1973b), Kuryłowicz (1977), Polomé (1980), Lindeman (1982:57 f. and 1987:75–86), Mayrhofer (1982 and 1986:124 f., 134 f. and 142), Olsen (1985), Peters (1986), and Kortlandt (1987a).

8. Szemerényi (1964:112) also denies 'prothesis' as an act of common innovation, against Schwyzer (1939:57, 412), and Porzig (1954:155); cf. also Meillet (*BSL* 27 (1927), p. 135, reprinted in 1977:239, 1936:142 f.).

9. Messing (1947:191), Lazzeroni (1958), Hovdhaugen (1968:131), Peters (1986:370 f.); cf. also on **srungᵸ*- at **4.62**.

10. For example Mayrhofer (1986:126) (**h₁neh₃men-*) and Beekes (1987:1–7) (nominative **h₃neh₃mn̥*), both with references to earlier literature.

11. For further discussion and references to recent publications on this word, see Mayrhofer (1986:126 and n. 114 and n. 116).

12. Other explanations for the origin of the Armenian paradigm are given by Ritter (1985:198) (nominative *anown* < **anuman*), Jahowkyan (1982:108) (*anown* < **anóman* < **onomn̥, anowan* < **anomán*) and Lindeman (1986) (genitive from **-mn̥tos*, with **t* extension as in Greek, followed tentatively by Stempel 1990:49).

13. As given by Szemerényi (1964:240), Olsen (1985:13) and Kortlandt (1987a:62).

14. Crossland (1958:84), Ruijgh (1988:445), Olsen (1988–9:481 f.), and others.

15. Watkins (1974:12 f.) thinks that the Hittite, Greek and Armenian forms have generalised an **o*-grade form of the noun.

16. For example Vedic *sūnára*- 'youthful' and Avestan *kamnānar*- 'with few men' (Mayrhofer 1982:188).

17. For the correspondence between ὀφέλλω 'sweep' and *awel* 'broom', see further **4.45**.

18. The Leiden school see a triple reflex of initial laryngeal in Armenian as well as Greek (cf. Kortlandt 1987a, Beekes 1987:7–8). Their only example of **h₁*- > *e*- which I have not yet discussed involves the very doubtful comparison of the Armenian causative *elowzanem* 'cause to go out' with Greek ἐλεύσομαι 'I shall go' (see also Klingenschmitt 1982:206, 263, and Olsen 1985:11). For **h₃* there is no example of a development to *o*- which could not arise from **(h₃)o*- (as admitted by Kortlandt 1987a:62).

19. See, for example, Mayrhofer (1986:124 f., 134 f., and 142).

20. This is the theory of Pedersen (1906:336 and 416) with the corrections and enlargements of Grammont (1916:223) and Kortlandt (1983:10). The development of **o* in Armenian has received a fairly large amount of scholarly attention. A survey of the principal treatments of the question is given by Considine (1978–9). Articles since Considine's survey which deal with the problem include Kortlandt (1983) and Jahowkyan (1983a and 1990).

21. For example *tasn* '10' < **tasan* < **tesan* (Szemerényi 1960c:21), *vat'sown* '60' < **vec'sown* (Meillet 1936:55; see also **4.3** and **4.26**). But *anown* (see discussion above) cannot derive from **enown* by this lowering rule as Winter suggests (1965a:101); the lowering appears to have occurred after the raising of the **e* before a nasal (or the two processes have counteracted each other), thus giving *zgenowm* 'I wear' not ***zganowm* (see **4.64**).

22. The word is thus taken as a present participle from the root **ed-* (= **h₁ed-*) 'eat', cf. Frisk *GEW* II 353.

23. Klingenschmitt's derivation of *ansam* 'I put up with, agree, obey' from a formation **h₁nēk'ah₂ye/o*, comparing Latvian *nēšāju* 'I carry back and forth' (1982:92) might provide an example of **h₁*- > Armenian *a*-, but the semantic connection is open to doubt.

24. Summarised in Rix (1976:71 f.).

25. See below. Olsen (1988–9:481) presents the same argument for *a*- being the Armenian reflex of initial laryngeal.

26. As shown by the correspondence of Greek ἄημι 'I blow' and Hittite *ḫuwanteš* 'winds'; Mayrhofer (1982:182) also cites evidence for lengthening before the Vedic cognate *vā*-.

27. cf. Phrygian αναρ 'man(?)', and Hittite *ašanzi* 'they are' if from *$h_1$sonti.
28. Using the cover symbols as in Peters (1980:ix) etc.; $R = r\,l\,m\,n$, H = any reconstructed 'laryngeal consonant', T = any obstruent, E = any vowel, $U = u$ or i.
29. Hamp (1983c:102) derives the Armenian word from a root without an internal laryngeal. Szemerényi thinks that the Latin and Sanskrit words are borrowed from Semitic (1989:170f.).
30. Hamp (1982d:188) again derives the Armenian word from a root without an internal laryngeal. The second element of the Armenian word has been connected with the word *mowkn* 'mouse' (Klingenschmitt 1982:68 n. 11, Greppin 1983b s.v.).
31. This was already realised by Hübschmann (*IF* 19 (1906) p. 475, reprinted in 1976:431) who found a parallel to the change from *garin* to *garn* > *gaŕn* in the Armenian word for the Antichrist *neŕn* < Νέρων.
32. The Armenian word was separated from the Greek and Latin forms by Peters (1980:49), on the grounds that *wl- would develop to *etg-, just as *wr- develops to *erg-; but his objections were already anticipated by the proposer of the etymology, Lidén (1906:100), who notes that this is the only example of the sequence *wl- and that since initial *r-receives a prothetic vowel in Armenian, while initial *l- does not, one should not expect the clusters with them to develop in the same way.
33. I discuss some of the more controversial points assumed here in greater detail elsewhere: for the theory of the late productivity of the *-t- suffix in Armenian see **4.11**; for discussion of Klingenschmitt's theory of the development of *-sk'- see **4.60**; for the development of the sequence *-tt- see **4.43**. My account of the sound changes involved here roughly agrees with those sketched by Kortlandt (1980) although I am by no means in total agreement with his theories.
34. The word for 'step-father' seems to show the same suffix -*ay* as other words of relationship, such as *skesreay* 'mother-in-law', *p'esay* 'son-in-law, bride-groom', and so forth, which is discussed by Asmanguljan (1983:35f.). For *erastank'* see **4.54**.
35. Klein (1988:258–260) gives other Indo-European derivatives of this formation.
36. I have rewritten Normier's reconstructions to conform with a more widely recognised notation.
37. e.g. Klein (1988:261–267) and Olsen (1989b:7 n. 17). For scholars who accept similar changes in Tocharian, see the references given by Peters (1988:377). J. H. W. Penney has drawn my attention to a full discussion of the Tocharian evidence by Ringe (1988–90:70–75).
37A. Olsen (1992) has now discussed the Armenian development of the sequences *-iH- and *-uH- more fully, and concludes that *-ih_1- and *-uh_1- developed to pre-Armenian *-$\bar{\imath}$- and *-$\bar{u}$- (1992:132–133) and that *-ih_2- and *-uh_2- developed to pre-Armenian *-(*i*)*ya*- and *-(*u*)*wa*- (1992:133–138). She also proposes, that *-ih_3- > *-(*i*)*ya*- (1992:138–143).
38. Peters also notes that there are no certain examples of another development of *-iH and *-uH (1980:128 n. 175), rejecting the derivation of instrumentals in -*ī* from *-ih_1.
39. See Eichner (1978:146 n. 17), Peters (1980:132 n. 80) and de Lamberterie (1990:I.177 and 491 n. 26). De Lamberterie agrees with the many scholars who consider the change to be morphologically, not phonetically, conditioned.
40. For Vedic *sthūra*- see also Bader (1989:16f.).
41. See further the discussion of *k'aw* at **4.63**.
42. I argue at **4.63** that the Armenian word should not be connected to this root on morphological and semantic grounds.
43. Hamp's reconstruction for the Greek verb is uncertain; the common explanation (Frisk *GEW* II 565, Chantraine *DELG* 919) is that the Greek present derives from *πλυν-yω.
44. Eichner (1978:152 n. 34, following Klingenschmitt) gives an alternative explanation of the *-k-; he suggests that the form *mowkn* may have emerged through contamination of an accusative *mekan < *mewsṃ and genitive *muheh < *muses.
45. This led Meillet (*DELL* 236) to declare the correspondence as 'phonétiquement impossible'.
45A. After this was written, I discovered that Olsen has now proposed several new etymologies which rely on the change of *-iH- to pre-Armenian *-ya-. Olsen derives *cawi* 'clear-eyed' from *dih_2-tiyo*-, comparing Sanskrit *dīti*- 'brightness' (1992:136), and *cacanim* (misprinted as *cananim*) 'I wave, ripple', *cal* 'fold, wave' and *cat* 'ripple' all from the root *dih_2*- 'spin, hasten' comparing Greek δῑνέω 'I spin' etc. (1992:137). Neither of these etymologies is without

phonetic, semantic or morphological problems. Olsen's derivation of *keank'* 'life' < **g"ih₃-wn̥-* via **kiyawant-* > **keawant-* (1992:137) and of the suffix *-ean* from **-ih₃no-* also have little to recommend them. Olsen also puts forward a new example of the change **-uH-* > **-wa-* with her derivation of *k'am* 'squeezing, pressing' < **swamo-* < **suH-mo-*, comparing Sanskrit *sunóti* 'press out' (1992:135); unfortunately there is no direct evidence from Indo-Iranian for a root **suH-* with final laryngeal.

46. See also **4.46** for *oč'*. Cowgill (1960:349) considers a development of **-k"i(d)* to **-k"y* also to be possible in these words. Jahowkyan (1967:168) takes *č'* in these words to derive from **k"e*.

47. Hamp sees a regular development of **-wy-* to *-ǰ-* (1972), but Klingenschmitt thinks that **-wy-* may have merged with **-y-* (1982:105), see also note 58 at **2.4**.

48. For the Armenian reflex of **-ws-* see **4.11**, especially notes 97 and 98. Note also that Eichner is not happy that the syllabification of the reconstructions of *cowngk'* and *akanjk'* should disagree.

49. For Armenian *o*-stems see Tumanjan (1978:151–161).

50. A similar explanation is given by Meillet (*REArm* 5 (1925) p. 1f., reprinted in 1977:225f.); see also Darms (1976:29 n. 15). Note also Rasmussen's derivation of *mimeans* 'each other' from **smih₂-smiah₂-m* (1987:46), with **smih₂-* > *mi*. The original paradigm of this word is further discussed at **4.61**.

51. See further **4.3** and especially note 47.

52. This explanation of *artasowk'* was previously proposed by Godel (1972:54) and Eichner (1978:146 n. 17, following Klingenschmitt). Another example of an old neuter plural extended with **-a* might be *mawrowk'* (or *morowk'*) 'beard'. Klingenschmitt (1992:126) takes *cowngk'* 'knees' < **g'onwh₂* but *artasowk'* < **artasua* < **-uh₂* and *morowk'* < **morua* < **smok'ru-h₂*; he attributes the different treatments of the cluster **-uh₂* to the preceding consonant or consonants, and draws parallels for the alternation from Greek and Tocharian.

53. This led Pedersen to reconstruct **sterdʰyo-* for *sterǰ* (1905:224, followed by Pisani 1950a:178 and Solta 1960:234f.).

54. The reason for the avoidance of *sterǰ* in the Bible seems to be that the Armenian word could only be used of animals (like its cognates στεῖρα in early Greek and *starī-* in Sanskrit), unlike στεῖρος in the Septuagint and its usual Armenian equivalent *amowl* which could be used for humans. All of the Biblical instances of στεῖρα are used with reference to women.

55. Other scholars had previously argued for such a change in Greek, for example Ruijgh (1988:459).

56. The discrepancy between the different forms was noted by Pedersen (1926:32f.) who mentions the suggestion of Per Slomann that **-iH-* etc. before or under the original accent developed to **-ī-* but after the accent to **-yɔ-*.

57. Hoenigswald (1966:12) emphasises the importance of this distinction for language sub-grouping.

58. Bonfante gives only the example of Armenian *kogi* 'butter' and Greek ἐννεάβοιος 'nine cows' worth' as evidence of the common retention of **-wy-*. Meillet, who first drew attention to the isogloss (*MSL* 9 (1896) p. 152, reprinted in 1977:27), also gave the example of (*h*)*ogi* 'soul, spirit' which he derived from **owyo-* and compared to Greek οὖρος 'fair wind', αὖρα 'breeze' and ἄ(ϝ)ελλα 'whirlwind'. Meillet's etymology of *hogi* has not been accepted by other scholars, but Ačaṙyan takes *hogi* from a form **powyo-* (*HAB* III² 107; compare also Pokorny *IEW* 847 who reconstructs **powi-*). These Armenian words cannot be used as direct evidence as a treatment of **-wy-* comparable to Greek *-βοιος* and Sanskrit *gavya-* in any case; the final *-i* cannot derive from **y*. They must rather show the very common Armenian derivative adjective suffix *-i* which may reflect a generalised Sievers variant of the **-ye/o-* suffix, **-iye/o-*. There are, in fact, no certain examples of the treatment of original **-wy-* in Armenian. (Eichner's suggestion that *jow* 'egg' derives from **ōwyo-m* (1978:146 n. 17), Hamp's theory that **-wy-* passes to *ǰ* (1972, repeated at Jahowkyan 1982:71) and Olsen's proposed derivation of *č* < **-wy-* (1985:13 and 14 n. 17) hardly clarify the situation.)

59. See also the discussion under **4.6** and **4.37**.

60. All of Bonfante's examples can be explained in other ways: for *kaṫin* 'acorn' see **4.30**; *gaṙink'* 'lambs' and *amaṙn* 'summer' may arise from analogy to other *n-* stems and to *am* 'year' respectively; *al* (or *ali*) is compared by Bonfante to Sanskrit *śilā* 'rock' and glossed as 'enclume' ('anvil'), but the word only occurs once in Armenian, in Philo's *Quaestiones et solutiones in*

Exodum: *ali holovelov oč' p'oxê ztełin* 'the *ali* in turning does not change its position', a context which suits the meaning 'axle, millstone, pulley' (as given in the *NBHL* and Ačaȓyan *HAB* I² 93).

61. Pisani (1961:174) first put forward the theory that Armenian showed a special affinity to the ancestor of the Aeolic dialect.

62. See O'Neil (1969:45f.) for a summary of the developments.

63. Morani (1981b:14) thinks that the dialectal difference in treatments of syllabic resonants in Greek can be compared to a double reflex in Armenian as both *-owr-* and *-ar-* (for the posited development of syllabic resonants to Armenian *-owr-*, etc., see Meillet *BSL* 36 (1935) pp. 121–123, reprinted in 1977:286f.). However it is doubtful whether any cases of *-owr-* etc. in Armenian can be best explained as the reflexes of syllabic resonants; they may rather reflect extended grade forms from earlier root nouns. Hence *dowrgn* 'potter's wheel' can be derived from *$*d^h\bar{o}rg^h$-* not *$*d^h\r{r}g^h$-* (Eichner 1978:147 n. 19 and Létoublon and de Lamberterie 1980:315).

64. See García-Ramón (1985) for recent arguments for the theory, and Leukart (1987:360) and Meier-Brügger (1992:II.116f.) for arguments against and literature.

65. Other examples may be the formula Ἐνυαλίῳ ἀνδρεϊφόντῃ (used at line endings) if this epithet continues *$*anr̥g^{wh}ontāi$* 'man-slaying', and ἀβρότη (epithet of νύξ at *Iliad* 14:78) < *$*amr̥tā$,* see most recently Janko (1992:11) for further possible examples and literature, and Tichy (1981:53–55) for criticism of the theory (with very full indications of the earlier literature at n. 58 to page 53).

66. Albanian *tre* 'three' < *$*treyes$* indicates that intervocalic *$*y$* was lost (Huld 1984:117).

67. A parallel situation is seen in the development of the Vulgar Latin vowel system, where the diphthong *ae* was monophthongised to a long vowel which differed in quality from inherited *ē*, and later merged with inherited *e*, while *$*\bar{e}$* merged with *i*; see Coleman (1971, especially p. 190f.).

68. On this development in Armenian see also Pedersen (1906:404), Pisani (1950a:178f.), Godel (1975:87f.), Schmitt (1980:427f.), Morani (1981b:15), Klingenschmitt (1982:133f.), Olsen (1985:6 n. 6) and below under **4.4**.

69. e.g. βαίνω < *$*g^w m̥-ye/o-$.* The interpretation of the Mycenaean signs *ra₂* and *ro₂* as *rya* and *ryo* (note the alternation between *-ti-ri-ja* and *-ti-ra₂*) suggests that the process has not yet fully taken place at this date (see further Ruijgh 1967:29f., Lejeune 1972:156, Ventris and Chadwick 1973:386 and 395f., and Meier-Brügger 1992:I.48). If Jahowkyan's etymologies (1967:223) of *p'ayl* 'flash' < *$*p^h l̥yo-$* etc. are correct then this suggests that the change occurs after the development of the vocalic resonants in Armenian as well. Grammont (1916:237) used the example of *gayl* 'wolf' < *$*w l̥k^w o-$* as evidence for this chronology (followed by Winter 1962:261, and Kortlandt 1980:103), but the etymology is not certain (see Solta 1960:32f.). Winter's other example *jayn* 'voice' (1962:261, see also Olsen 1989a:222 n. 8) need not stem from a form with a syllabic nasal (Solta 1960:316 takes *$*g^h won-y-$* as the prototype), moreover, the syllabic nasals need not have developed at the same time as the syllabic liquids.

70. Similar developments are found elsewhere, for example in Romance (French *cuir* < *corium*). Pisani (1950a:179f.) thinks that the development of affricates from clusters of stop + *$*y$* in both Greek and Armenian is significant, but again the same change is widely attested elsewhere, for example in Proto-Romance.

71. See, for example, Rix (1976:70) for the theory that Greek ζ- is the result of laryngeal followed by *$*y$-,* and Peters (1976) for the opposite view that laryngeal followed by *$*y$-* develops to *h-*.

72. This theory has received support from Greppin (1972:69f. and 1978) and Morani (1981b:14); note also Minshall's derivation of initial *ǰ-* from *$*Hy$-* (1955). Pisani's theory was perhaps anticipated by Benveniste, who, according to Dumézil (1938:192), had thought that the Greek and Armenian words which appeared to show ζ- and *l-* from initial *$*y$-* might perhaps have conserved the traces of a lost initial consonant.

73. In support of each development, see respectively Meillet (1936:52), Pedersen (1906:406), Hamp (1982b:190) and Pisani (1950a:180f.) (followed by Mawet 1986:84f.).

74. Lejeune (1972:153) and Slings (1975:4f.) restrict the sound change to Lesbian and Thessalian; *$*-ln-$* developed to single -λ- with compensatory lengthening of the preceding vowel in the other dialects.

75. This sound change was first proposed by Pedersen (1906:354) to explain the verbs

hełowm 'I pour' and *t'ołowm* 'I let'; Klingenschmitt sees further support for the change in the derivation of nouns with final *-ł* from *-ln- (1982:242).

76. The same change may have taken place in Latin, for example, if the derivation of e.g. *stella* from *stel-nā* is correct (cf. Ernout-Meillet *DELL* 646).

77. The development of the inherited diphthong *-eu- is not clear enough to make certain Meillet's theory (1936:39, followed by Ravnæs 1988:234) that *-esō developed to *-ehu- and then merged with inherited *-eu- to develop to -oy-. De Lamberterie (1982c:81) finds evidence for a change of *eu to iw (see further note 277 at **4.55**); by this theory either the loss of *-h- < *-s- is after the development of inherited *-eu- or the combinations *-eu- and *-eō- developed differently.

78. Initial *σμ- seems to have been retained in certain words, as shown by the doublets σμικρός and μικρός (see further Schwyzer 1939:311 and Lejeune 1972:120f.).

79. See Ringe (1984:49f.) for discussion of the reconstruction of the initial vowel in this word.

80. Lejeune's theory of a metathesis of *-ns- etc., to *-sn- etc., in Greek (1972:128f.) is unnecessary, see Miller (1976:165).

81. For earlier proponents of this view see Szemerényi (1966:191f.), and for Pisani's earlier views Szemerényi (1968).

82. Szemerényi dates the Armenian change to the same period as the Iranian change on no firmer evidence than the fact that the languages were in contact (1985:785).

83. Hock (1986:392). A striking example of this process is found in the Old Irish substitution of *q* for *p* in loanwords.

84. Hence the pre-Euclidean Attic spelling with -χσ- and -φσ- for -ξ- and -ψ-, and the Armenian transcription of Greek ξ and ψ by *k*'s and *p*'s (Allen 1987:60, Schmitt 1980:421f. and Schwink 1991:120–121).

85. The change of *s* to *h* occurred again in Sparta during the historical period (Thumb & Kieckers 1932:84f.).

86. See the full discussion by Miller (1976), who follows Wackernagel's theory that the divergent Greek development is dependent on the position of the accent. Miller supports the theory with the derivations of οὐρά 'tail' < *orsá, οὐρέω 'urinate' < *worséyō, and κουρεύς 'barber' < *kors-eús. The last word, which shows the innovatory Greek noun suffix -εύς, suggests that if Miller's theory is correct, the development has taken place relatively recently in Greek.

87. For discussion of the *centum/satəm* problem and the velar series of Proto-Indo-European see Allen (1978).

88. The merger may also have taken place before *u, see **4.17** and **4.23**.

89. See further **4.12** for discussion.

90. See further **4.35** and note 186.

91. See Pisani (1950a:165), Jahowkyan (1975) and Kortlandt (1975) for different theories.

92. Allen (1957:121f.) explains this selective palatalisation from general principles.

93. Pisani (1950a:168f.), and Kortlandt (1975) provide elaborate alternative theories for the Armenian phenomena.

94. Schindler (1974:5) puts forward this theory for final *-n, so also Hamp (1988–9:25), who thinks the analogical restoration of the nasal a shared Greek-Armenian innovation.

95. Godel (1975:99–102) gives a full discussion of the problem and review of the scholarly treatments; he sees the different treatments as the result of morphological, not phonological, changes. Stempel (1990) follows and clarifies Pisani's theory.

96. M. Wheeler points out to me that in Romance final -*m* also develops to -*n* as for example (Old) French *rien* 'nothing' < Latin *rem*, and that where a language has only one word-final nasal it is nearly always the dental or alveolar nasal.

97. There have been many attempts to elucidate the development of the word *leard*; see, for example, Arbeitman (1980) who tries to derive the word from an early collocation 'fat liver'; for *neard* see the information on the Indo-European family garnered by Szemerényi (1989:61f.).

98. *MSL* 7 (1890) p. 162, reprinted in Meillet (1977:4 n. 1); note also Pisani (1950a:167) who derives the Armenian form from *kʷim-kʷe. The Armenian form cannot have been directly inherited from the parent language since *(kʷ)-im-kʷi/e- would develop to **inǰ, compare *drand* 'door post' beside Latin *antae*.

99. Bolognesi (1954:127) and de Lamberterie (1978:245) give similar accounts for the

double development, as also Olsen, in an earlier work (1985:11 n. 13), who limits the change of *-nt-* > *-nd-* to initial syllables in order to allow Schindler's derivation of *atamn* 'tooth' < *h_1dntm (Schindler 1975b:61).
100. The Latin reflexes of the voiced aspirates may also have undergone a voiceless aspirate stage (Allen 1958:100f.) but this is not certain.
101. De Lamberterie has argued that some developments of the Armenian consonant shift took place after the introduction of the earliest Iranian loans (1978:250f.).
102. See the above discussion and Grammont (1916:214–219) and Meillet (1936:39f.).

Notes for Chapter 3

1. A distinctive vocative form is found for some Greek names in translation literature.
2. Meillet (*MSL* 17 (1911) pp. 12–35, reprinted in 1962:134–157) has investigated the semantic properties of both these types of nouns in detail.
3. Several of these will be discussed in detail later.
4. Lyonnet (1933) undertook a full survey of the use of this formation in the Armenian Gospels and in Eznik and came to the conclusion that it represented a true perfect of state.
5. Meillet (*MSL* 11 (1900) pp. 369–377, reprinted in 1962:39–47) showed that mono-syllabic adjectives tend to be declined, and that polysyllabic adjectives tend to be declined when following the noun (the marked order), but not when preceding it.
6. A list of morphological isoglosses between Greek and Armenian is given by Bonfante (1981), see also Meillet (1936:142f.), Schwyzer (1939:57), K. H. Schmidt (1980 and 1984), Solta (1990:15).
7. Also Brugmann (1907–8:172), Meillet *BSL* 33 (1932), p. 51, reprinted in (1977:270), Bonfante (1981:64) and Solta (1990:10).
8. Pedersen's reconstruction (1905:223) of *-$g^{wh}i$/ for the two forms (and for Sanskrit -*hi*) is untenable in the light of the fact that *g^{wh}/ in Greek has developed to ϕ not θ before *i* in ὄφις 'snake' < *$og^{wh}i$- (cf. Sanskrit *áhi-*); see also Allen (1957:121f.).
9. The phonetic development is not exactly comparable, because there is a change of the preceding *e* to *ê* in *mêj* (elsewhere in Armenian *ê* can be derived from *ey*). Winter (1962:261) therefore sees a regular change of *d^hy to *yj*. However, the change of *e* to *ê* seems to have been a regular development before affricates and sibilants of the *š* series (Pedersen 1906:404; de Lamberterie 1978:262–268). A similar development does not seem to have affected *o* before these sounds, cf. *goč'em* 'I call' < *wok^w-ye/o- (this etymology is doubted by Hübschmann 1897:436, Ačaṙyan *HAB* s.v. and Solta 1960:382, although in form and meaning the equation is unobjectionable).
10. For Indo-European *d^h forms see Brugmann (1911:728f.), and Lejeune (1939:251–257, 285–290, 386–396). Vedic has extended *-d^h forms from the pronouns to some adjectives, such as *viśvaha* or *viśvadha* 'überall' (Thumb & Hauschild 1959: 182). An extended form *-d^hi may also have survived into Indo-Aryan, cf. Lejeune (1939:285f.).
11. Thus *i diwroj* for κατ᾽ εὐθύ 3 *Kings* 20:25 (21:25 in the Greek text) cited by Jensen (1959:53). Note that κατ᾽ εὐθύ is rendered by *i diwri* two verses earlier in exactly the same context. Elsewhere in the Bible *diwr* is declined as an *a*-stem. Marr (1903:72) cites a locative form *jermoj* (*jerm* 'warm', *o*-stem) from Ełišê (see further Weitenberg 1984:206f.), and also the forms *jioj* (from *ji* 'horse') and *mardoj* (from *mard* 'man'), but without textual references.
12. Following Meillet's observations (*MSL* 8 (1892) p. 157, reprinted in 1977:12 and *Banasêr* II (1900) p. 112, reprinted in 1977:83).
13. Thus Meillet (1913:47), Jensen (1959:52f.), Thomson (1975:25), Godel (1975:30), Šilak'adze (1975:111), Schmitt (1981:95), and Tumanjan (1971:208, 213f.), who cites dative forms in *-oj* following Jahowkyan (1959:96) and the native Armenian grammatical tradition which does not separate the dative and locative cases in the singular.
14. As realised by Marr (1903:72) and Abrahamyan (1964:52) (citing *jori*). Mann (1968:71) cites *i tarwoj* 'in the year' (frequent in the Bible) as a *wo*-stem; but *tari* 'year' is an *ea*-stem noun, genitive plural *tareac'* at *Wisd*. 7:19.
15. It is noteworthy that in Hübschmann's article (*ZDMG* 36 (1882) p. 122f., reprinted in

1976:130 f.), which first elucidated the use of the -oǰ as a locative marker in the Bible translation, all the forms with -oǰ occur after the preposition *i*, except one after *ař*.

16. Abrahamyan (1964:52) and Tumanjan (1971:14) note the existence of nouns in the *ea*-class with locative in -*i*.

17. See Mariès & Mercier (1959:729 n. 435) for details of the previous attempts to explain this phrase; Mariès chooses to separate *i miowm* from *tełi* and translates 's'arranger une place dans un (réceptacle) unique' (1959:606).

18. See further Meillet (1913:49), and Jensen (1959:50).

19. This form is discussed by Meillet (*Banasêr* 1 (1899) pp. 144–146, reprinted in 1977:54–56, and translated from Armenian into French in Meillet 1979), with examples of its uses in the Bible translation.

20. And the adjectives *ayl* 'other' and *mi* 'one'; Meillet (1913:66).

21. Schmitt (1981:119) for the phonetic change of **-osm-* to *-owm-* compare the change of **-esm-* to *-im* (see Klingenschmitt 1982:234 for discussion).

22. Meillet (*MSL* 12 (1901–3) p. 420, reprinted in 1962:74) sees the development of a distinct locative singular case arising from influence from 'les langues caucasiques du Sud a riche flexion casuelle'; however, in Old Georgian there is no distinct locative case, although modern Georgian does have a locative. There is, however, a large array of local cases in the East Caucasian languages (Deeters 1963:69–72).

23. Meillet (*MSL* 12 (1901–3) p. 419, reprinted in 1962:73).

24. A list of occurrences of *mioǰ* in the Bible functioning as genitive and dative is given by Weitenberg (1984:205). His citation of *dangi mioǰ* at 1 *Cor.* 2:36 should be corrected to 1 *Kings* 2:36. Other examples of *mioǰ* used as a genitive in the Bible (in the Venice 1805 Zōhrab edition) can be added to Weitenberg's list, e.g. *žamow mioǰ* (*Judith* 13:11), and *ařn mioǰ* (*Judith* 14:5); as dative e.g. *tarwoy mioǰ* (1 *Macc.* 3:28).

25. A theory influenced by the theory that the locative -*oǰ* is limited to the *ea*-declension, which we have seen to be incorrect. Abrahamyan (1964:74) already realised that the two declensions depended on whether the form occurred before or after the noun with which it agrees that this difference in position entailed a difference in meaning: my rules for the position of *mi* given below provide support for this view.

26. (1984:207 f.).

27. Note also that Weitenberg includes the long central portion of Agat'angełos's *History* known as *The Teaching of St Gregory* 'qui n'est qu'une énorme interpolation' (Meillet *JA* (1910) II p. 461, reprinted in 1977:362).

28. The use of postposed *mi* as an indefinite has already been noted by a number of scholars, for example Meillet (*MSL* 10 (1898) p. 266, reprinted in 1962:30), Cuendet (1929:95–98) and Künzle (1984:II.464).

29. A similar idiom is found in Old Georgian e.g. *siaves ertes* (*siav* 'pot', *ert* 'one') translates λέβητα at *Jer.* 1:13.

30. Turner (1963:195 f.). At *Matt.* 13:46 the Zōhrab Bible and Künzle's manuscript E read *gteal mi patowakan margarit* 'finding one pearl of great price' for Greek εὑρὼν δὲ ἕνα πολύτιμον μαργαρίτην, as expected, but Künzle's manuscript M has *gteal margarit mi patowakan*, taking Greek εἷς as an indefinite article.

31. The form *mioǰ* is found preceding the noun at P'awstos Bowzand *The Epic Histories* 5.43 (p. 256 of the 1933 Venice edition).

32. Bagratuni (1852:42 cited by Weitenberg 1984:205) cites 2 *Cor.* 11:2 as *ařn mioǰ* not *ařn mioy* or *ařn miowm*, although this reading is not noted by Zōhrab in the 1805 Bible edition. By whatever reading, the position of *mi* in this passage appears to contradict the rules given above, but this might be explainable on closer consideration of the Armenian text. The sentence reads *zi xawsec'ay* (or *xawsec'ayc'*) *zjez ařn miowm, ibrew zkoys mi sowrb* 'for I have espoused' (or 'shall espouse') 'you to *one* [*miowm*] husband, like a [*mi*] holy virgin' (Greek text: ἡρμοσάμην γὰρ ὑμᾶς ἑνὶ ἀνδρὶ παρθένον ἁγνήν). By the rules which I have set out the Armenian translation should read *miowm ařn, ibrew zkoys mi sowrb*. It seems not unlikely that the word order has been changed from *miowm ařn* to *ařn miowm* by association with the parallel phrase *zkoys mi*.

33. This brief survey of the Greek -θι forms is based on Lejeune (1939) (especially 187–209 and 258–290), Debrunner (1937), Chantraine (1973:244–246) and Risch (1974:356 f.).

34. *Hapax* at *Od.* 14.352; on this form see Lejeune (1939:194 f.).

35. Lejeune (1939:200 and 270). He considers πόθι to be the starting point of the forms.

36. This is the opinion of Debrunner (1937) and Lejeune (1939:202–209, where the forms are subjected to a rigorous analysis); the phrase ἠῶθι πρό may contain a true locative (Lejeune *loc. cit.*). Note also that of the five occurrences of the -όθι πρό formula two occur in similes and a third in a late passage (Shipp 1972:70f.).

37. Pisani (1950a:182ff., 1976:279–283) explains *knoǰ* through the addition of dative and genitive markers *-yās/*-yāi to a stem *knay- (with development of *-yy- to *ǰ*). Kortlandt (1984:100) derives -*ǰ* from the addition of a genitive-dative marker *-yos to a stem final resonant. The original formation is preserved in *geǰ* the genitive-dative singular of *gewt* 'village'; (this explanation of *geǰ* was also proposed by Meillet (*MSL* 8 (1892) p. 158, reprinted in 1977:13)), and in other relic forms, such as *towənǰean*, gen.-dat.-loc. of *tiw* 'day'. The marker -*ǰ* was later abstracted and added to the thematic declension by this theory. Schmalstieg's connection of -*oǰ* with the *o*-stem genitive-dative-ablative -*oy* (1982) does not merit serious consideration.

38. Meillet (*MSL* 8 (1892) p. 157, reprinted in 1977:12) connected -*oǰ* with the Vedic infinitives in -*adhyai*.

39. Brugmann (1907–8:172) thought that the -*oǰ* of *knoǰ* had been transferred from the locative *tetwoǰ*. However the Armenian case system has been moving away from syncretic and towards analytic formations throughout the history of the language, and this extension of a case morph to a wider function would be unique in the development of the language.

40. Meillet (1936:143), Schwyzer (1939:57), Porzig (1954:90), K. H. Schmidt (1980:47, 1987:40) Bonfante (1981:64), Gamkrelidze and Ivanov (1984:I.381) and Solta (1990:9). Brugmann's theory (1911:186) that a reflex of *-bʰi is to be found in the dative singular of Old Irish neuter *n*-stems is to be rejected on phonetic grounds (Thurneysen 1946:213).

41. For example, *feraib* dative plural of *fer* 'man' < *vir-o-bʰi- (K. H. Schmidt 1963:1f.). Note also the extension of -*ebhis* from the pronominal declension into the thematic stems in Vedic, and the thematic forms in -*aibis* in Old Persian (Thumb & Hauschild 1959:36).

42. Thurneysen (1946:182), and K. H. Schmidt (1963:2 n. 4).

43. Porzig (1954:90), and Lazzeroni (1970).

44. The dialectal evidence for the suffix is limited to a few scattered forms; see Morpurgo Davies (1970) and Meier-Brügger (1992:II.67).

45. The case system of Mycenaean is still imperfectly known; for a survey of recent literature see Nieto Hernández (1987:277f.) and Meier-Brügger (1992:II.65). A majority of scholars favour a syncretic case of instrumental and locative, and a separate dative case and genitive case.

46. In the much larger Homeric corpus there are only 192 examples of -φι (Lejeune 1956b:187).

47. Chadwick (1958:291), and Ruijgh (1967:83 and 1979:81).

48. See Nieto Hernández (1987:279f.) and Meier-Brügger (1992:II.67).

49. Compare the Armenian genitive-dative-ablative plural marker -*c* which probably derives from an adjectival formation in *-sk- (Meillet 1936:72).

50. Note also the frequent use of -φι with nouns in Homer which have both a plural and singular form (Lejeune 1956b:205). Ruijgh thinks a reason for the spread of the singular -ηφι forms in Homer may be that the ending is metrically more convenient than the dative -η (1979:81).

51. The interpretation of the noun *o-mo-pi* is not certain enough to decide whether it is an *o*-stem or not (Ventris and Chadwick 1973:369 and Ruijgh 1967:242 offer an identification with οἶμος 'band' and ὅρμος 'chain' respectively); the place names *ma-ro-pi* and *mo-ro-ko-wo-wo-pi* are likewise obscure. Note that the graph -*o-pi* may reflect the addition of -φι to an *n*-stem, such as *ki-to-pi* 'tunics' for /kʰitompʰi/, or to a consonant stem such as *po-pi* 'feet' most likely written for *poppʰi* (assimilated from *podpʰi*).

52. The use of thematic adjectives in -*o* agreeing with forms in -*pi* is common in the *Ta* series at Pylos, e.g. *e-re-pa-te-jo ka-ra-a-pi* at *Ta* 722.

53. Shipp (1961:40) observes that 'in a woefully inadequate writing system -*pi* would have considerable value indicating case with a clarity otherwise so often lacking'. Some small support for the theory that *e-re-pa-te-jo-pi* is anomalous at Knossos is given by *e-re-pa-te-jo o-po-qo* KN *Sd* 4403 'ivory cheek-straps' in a list of instrumental plurals and perhaps the reading *e-re-pa-te-o o-mo|* at *Se* 1007.

54. Note in particular that the only inscriptional evidence for the extension of -οφι to the athematic declension (*ΚΑΡΟΦΙ* from Cyrene) has now been read differently (Meier-Brügger

1992:II.67, citing M. Bile, C. Brixhe *et al*. 'Bulletin de dialectologie grecque', *REG* 101 (1988), p. 103 (section 81)).

55. Meillet (*MSL* 11 (1900) p. 372, reprinted in 1962:42). The construction of singular adjective agreeing with plural noun is found in other cases as well, but Meillet remarks (*MSL* 11 (1900) p. 381, reprinted in 1962:51) that it is most frequent for instrumental and nominative.

56. See further the discussion at **4.31**. Pedersen (1905:211) also cited the example of the adjectives of the class of *canr* 'heavy' which have singular genitive-dative-locative *canow* and nominative plural *canownk'* etc. Pedersen stated that the instrumental singular of this class is *canowmb*, thus following the *n*-stem declension of the plural. However I have been unable to trace any such forms in the Armenian Bible, and the regular instrumental singular seems to be *-ow* for this class, e.g. *canow* at 3 *Kings* 10:2, 4 *Kings* 18:17, *barjow* (from *barjr* 'high') at *Deut*. 11:30 etc. For *k'ar* 'stone' (gen.-dat.-loc. sing. *k'ari*, nom. plur. *k'arink'*, gen.-dat.-abl. plur. *k'aranc'*), Jensen (1959:59) cites alternative inst. sing. forms *k'ariw* and *k'aramb*, of which the latter appears to contain the plural stem; however, I have only been able to locate an instrumental singular *k'ariw* in the Bible (*Exod*. 21:18).

57. This form occurs in the Bible translation at *Jude* 18, *Hebrews* 7:8 etc. The more common plural form is the irregular collective *mardik*.

58. Scholars are divided on the origin of the *-k'* marker. Essentially there are two separate camps (for brief surveys of the theories and discussions see Deeters 1927:88–90, Schmitt 1972a:15f., and de Lamberterie 1979:321–326):

(a) *-k'* derives from final **-s* (note also the discussions of Godel 1975:162f., Pisani 1975, Klingenschmitt 1982:23, and Kortlandt 1984:98f.).

(b) *-k'* is an additional particle (see most recently Dowsett 1989).

As the example of **mr̥tos > mard* shows, it is difficult to see a direct continuation of **-s* as *-k'* in all cases (note also that the *i*- and *u*-stem genitives *-i* and *-u* are plausibly derived from **-ie/os* and **-ue/os* where the final *-s* also seems to have been lost (Meillet 1936:72, Godel 1975:104f., de Lamberterie 1979:327f. and Schmitt 1981:113)). There must therefore have been some degree of morphological pressure in the spread of *-k'* rather than pure phonetic derivation, whatever the ultimate origin (see further de Lamberterie 1979:325f.).

59. See note 58.

60. For the Greek forms see also Meillet (1932), Solta (1970:51f.), and Chantraine (1974:126). For the Armenian see also Meillet (*JA* (1903) II pp. 502–503, reprinted in 1977:316–317), Stempel (1983:32–35, 88f.), and Minassian (1986); the last-named article gives details on the formation and occurrence of *-oł* participles in the earliest Armenian texts.

61. The forms are μαινόλης 'raving', φαινόλης 'light-giving', σκωπτόλης 'mocker', κορυπτόλης 'one that butts with the head', ὀπυιόλης glossed in Hesychius as 'married', οἰφόλης 'lewd', and the tribe name Ὀζόλαι. For the late extension of the suffix in Γενειόλης (epithet of Hermes in Callimachus fr. 199) and other late forms see Chantraine (1974:126f.).

62. Unless Schwyzer is right to derive the name Μιδιόλης from μειδιάω 'smile' (1946:56).

63. From the present stem, *t'šnamunoł* (*Rom*. 1:30 etc.) from *t'šnamanem* 'I offend'; from the aorist, *keroł* from *keray* 'I ate' (suppletive aorist of *owtem*) and *arbec'oł* from *arbec'ay*, aorist to *arbenam* 'I get drunk', both of which occur at *Matt*. 11:19 and *Luke* 7:34.

64. The **l*-formations of Indo-European are discussed by Brugmann (1906:360f.), Benveniste (1935: Chapter 3), Lazzeroni (1966:69–71), Zucchelli (1970:111–114), Solta (1970), and Stempel (1983:40–45).

65. Lejeune (1967:84f.), Zucchelli (1970:35f. and *passim*), and Leumann (1977:311).

66. Krause & Thomas (1960:186).

67. For example Gothic *sakuls* from *sakan* 'rebuke'. De Lamberterie (1982a:44) notes that at 1 *Tim*. 3:3 Greek ἄμαχον 'not contentious' is translated by *ni sakuls* in Gothic and *mi kr̄owoł* (from *kr̄owem* 'dispute') in Armenian, both languages using reflexes of the **-ol-* suffix.

68. Note also the existence of some forms of Phrygian (inscriptional |*kupolas*, the name Μαιόλη and river name Πεγκαλας) which Neumann (1988:8) interprets as evidence for a Phrygian suffix *-lā*.

69. Jensen (1959:104f.).

70. Meillet (1936:75), and Stempel (1983:90). Klingenschmitt derived *-ič'* from **-iskā*, with a development of **s* to **š* after *i* in this position (1970:87). In his 1982 work he implicitly rejects his earlier views on the phonetic developments of **-sk'-* and **-sk-* (pp. 83f.), and takes *č'* to be the

regular intervocalic reflex of *-sk ⌐. The point being made is not altered if the forms derive from *-isk-.

71. The distinction between the suffixes -oł and -awł was first made clear by Meillet (*JA* (1903) II pp. 502 f., reprinted in 1977:316 f.), and is further discussed by de Lamberterie (1982a:38–42).

72. De Lamberterie (1982a:51) interprets the preservation of the two forms in Greek and Armenian as an archaism.

73. In Celtic, Baltic, Slavonic and Germanic, and for one Latin verb (*posco*), verbs which contain a reflex of the suffix have generalised it throughout the paradigm. For the use and development of the suffix in Indo-European I have principally followed the treatments of Brugmann (1913:350–361), Porzig (1927), Meillet (1937:220 f.), Kuryłowicz (1964:106–109), Watkins (1969:56 f.), Keller (1985), Rix (1986), and Szemerényi (1990:293 f.); for Hittite, Bechtel (1936), Couvreur (1938), and Oettinger (1979); for Tocharian, Couvreur (1938) and Krause & Thomas (1960); for Latin, Berrettoni (1971); for Indo-Iranian, Vendryes (1911).

74. A causative function is also associated with the suffix in certain Greek verbs, for example μεθύσκω 'I intoxicate' alongside μεθύω 'I get drunk'; Szemerényi has argued that these verbs are a secondary development of Greek (1964:67).

75. For example, Benveniste (1936:231) ('itératif-intensif'); Ramat (1967:122 f.); Rix (1986:13) ('iterativum'); and Szemerényi (1990:293) ('iterativ-durativ'). But Meillet (1937:221) and Kuryłowicz (1964:109) are reluctant to ascribe a precise meaning to the suffix in the parent language.

76. An extended form of the suffix *-isk ⌐ is probably not to be reconstructed for the parent language (despite Brugmann 1913:353 and Watkins 1969:57); see Klingenschmitt (1982:72 f., especially p. 73 n. 17).

77. The Greek and Armenian forms are compared by Pedersen (1905:207), Meillet (1936:115), Bonfante (1942:104), Solta (1963:118 and 1990:12), Barton (1965:74), Godel (1969:257), Watkins (1969:57), Chantraine (1973:323 n. 2), Wathelet (1973:404), Negri (1976:241), Jasanoff (1979:133 n. 3), K. H. Schmidt (1980:45), Morani (1981c:102 n. 20), Schmitt (1981:145) and Jahowkyan (1982:190).

78. I have used the discussions of the Ionic iteratives by Kluge (1911), Schwyzer (1939:710–712), Ramat (1967:115–122), Bottin (1969:116–124), Wathelet (1973), Chantraine (1973:316–325), Risch (1974:276–278), Negri (1976), Kimball (1980), Keller (1985:35 f.), and Ruijgh (1985:145 f.). Bottin gives a list of all the iterative forms and all their occurrences in Homer and Herodotus; however, some of his material is questionable (e.g. he cites κικλήσκω as an iterative formation) and the figures for frequency of occurrence of forms etc. in Homer are from my own researches, checked against Bottin's list.

79. For Herodotus's usage see Rosén (1962:125 f.).

80. The intensive meaning is found at e.g. *Il.* 3.388 μάλιστα δέ μιν φιλέεσκε (see further Ramat 1967:117); this is the less common use of the suffix.

81. The iterative ἐμισγέσκοντο at *Od.* 20.7 is the only case where the augment is necessary for the metre; it may be due to Attic influence (Wackernagel 1916:118 f.).

82. Chantraine (1973:323). For example, in Book 24 of the *Iliad* there are three such groups (more than in any other book of the *Iliad*), lines 11–24 (7 iteratives), lines 454–6 (3 iteratives), and lines 751–6 (3 iteratives). Bottin provides examples of all the iterative formations which occur in groups in Homer and in Herodotus, where the phenomenon is also noticeable (1969:120 f.).

83. See Wathelet (1973:395) for an analysis of the occurrence of this and other late or Ionic features in conjunction with iterative forms.

84. See Schwyzer (1939:711) and Ramat (1967:118 f.) for further criticisms of Brugmann's theory.

85. Chantraine (1973:319–321), and Negri (1976:236). Kluge's hypothesis that augmentless φάσκε always has an iterative force (1911:26) is unconvincing as he has to 'correct' one of the four occurrences of φάσκε to ἔφασκε, and one of ἔφασκε to φάσκε, and excuses another non-iterative φάσκε as being at the beginning of the line.

86. This explanation is based on Keller (1985:36 f.). Chantraine (1973:320 f.) gives examples of the difference in meaning of ἔσκε, ἦν and γένετο. Chantraine underestimates the metrical convenience of ἔσκε, which, unlike ἔην, can be followed by a word with initial consonant and still be scanned as a trochee (Shipp 1972:88).

87. Rix puts forward this theory with the sole example of καλέσκετο (1976:229); Ruijgh (1985:147) adds the derivation of ἔασκε.

88. The accent would have originally been on the thematic vowel following the *-sk ʾ- suffix, as Vedic pṛccháti, so -λη- not -ελε- is the expected result of *lh₁ by the rules set out by Rix (1976:73f.).

89. The quality of the vowel alternates between -a- or -ā- for non-causative, and -ä- for causative use of -sk- in Tocharian B (Krause & Thomas 1960:210f.). Van Windekens (1982:19f.) finds evidence to suggest that the link-vowel derives from *e.

90. Wathelet (1973:383) also notes the presence of -a- before some occurrences of -s- (< *-sk ʾ-) in Avestan, such as išasa– 'desire' beside Sanskrit icchati; but unfortunately the evidence for this formation is very uncertain, see Humbach (1956:66f.).

91. This form has prompted a certain amount of discussion. Meillet (JA (1903) II pp. 500f., reprinted in 1977:314–316) thought ê was original, and that the present tense was ənkenowm rather than the expected *ənkinowm because of the rule that *i was lowered to e when u occurred in the following syllable (see further the discussion of ałowês at 4.3 and zgenowm at 4.64). Frisk (1944:24f.) considered the writing ənkêc' to be a later scribal corruption of ənkec' when the two vowels no longer differed in pronunciation, and he is followed by Godel (1969:256) and Klingenschmitt (1982:249 n. 6, citing in support the word ełegn 'reed', which in later manuscripts is written ełegn). However, in early manuscripts, where the difference between ê and e is still observed, ənkêc' is written (de Lamberterie 1982a:26. n. 18, and Künzle 1984:II.264 citing ənkêc' at John 21:7 in the earliest manuscripts), and this supports Meillet's hypothesis.

92. Ačaṙyan HAB s.v. had already derived ənkenowm from *sengʷ-. Kortlandt (1987b:52 n. 1) tries to connect the word to βάλλω. Possible etymologies of the other three words of the -nowm class with aorists in -c ʾ- are discussed by Klingenschmitt (1982:249–252).

93. keam 'I live' and lam 'I cry' could also derive from athematic verbs in the parent language; see Klingenschmitt (1982:85 and 104f.).

94. Klingenschmitt (1982:122f.) discusses this word and the origin of the -anam class.

95. Pisani (1950a:181) connected asem to Sanskrit yaśa- 'glory'.

96. See note 91 above.

97. Godel's objection that the vowels *-e-a- contracted to -a- in 'pre-Armenian' (as garown 'spring' < *wesar-, and ariwn 'blood' < *esar-, see also Schmitt 1981:78) is not relevant because the spread of -ac ʾ- may have occurred at a later stage of the language. Moreover, the fact that in these two forms cited the vowel in the following syllable is [u] casts some doubt over this law of contraction; in other words [u] has a lowering effect on the vowel in the preceding syllable (see also 4.3 and 4.26).

98. Pedersen (1905:212), Mariès (1930:168), Karstien (1956:221f.), and K. H. Schmidt (1980:44 and 1985:227) all take *-āsk ʾ- as the productive morph, but see different processes of extension. My analysis follows that of Schmidt.

99. The theory that Armenian merged aorist and imperfect to form a single preterite at some stage in its prehistory is necessary to explain the presence of ancient imperfects functioning as aorists, for example, eber 'he carried', cognate with Greek ἔφερε (see further Godel 1965:24f.).

100. But see Pedersen (1905:206) and (1906:423f.), Bonfante (1942), Kortlandt (1987b), Barton (1989 and the citation of Barton's unpublished 1965 PhD thesis by Solta 1987:633) for attempts to find reflexes of the sigmatic aorists in Armenian.

101. Pisani (1950b:529, 1951:66, 1959:177). At (1951:66) he attributes the change to phonetic causes, but he later reverts to a morphological explanation.

102. Watkins (1969:57, 1971:70f.).

103. The posited change of *-sk ʾ- to č' is also unproven, see further 4.60 for discussion, and 4.64 for discussion of zgec'ay the aorist of zgenowm 'I clothe'.

104. Jahowkyan (1982:231 n. 69) notes the existence of Tocharian preterites in -ṣ- and -ṣṣ- (Krause & Thomas's Class IV, 1960:251f.) which derive from palatalised *-sk ʾ-; these preterites are invariably associated with presents in -sk- and so probably should be considered separately from the Greek and Armenian use of a reflex of *-sk ʾ- to mark past forms (I am indebted to J. H. W. Penney for clarification on this point).

105. For the nasal affix in the Indo-European verbal system see Brugmann (1913:272–336), Kuiper (1937), Strunk (1967) and Szemerényi (1990:290–293).

106. Hamp (1975a:108) derives əmpem 'I drink' from *pi-m-b-e/o, i.e. a nasal infix

secondarily inserted in the reduplication syllable of the original word for 'drink' *pi-b-e/o-
(from *pi-ph₃-e/o-?). He compares the Greek present formations of the type of πίμπλημι. This
cannot be used as support for a morphological isogloss between the two languages, because
əmpem is the only formation of this type in Armenian. There are also other derivations of
əmpem; Meillet (MSL 9 (1896) p. 155, reprinted in 1977:30) reconstructed *ənd-hipem, and
other theories are listed by Ačařyan HAB s.v. owmp.

107. Greek replaced the original alternation pattern of strong grade *-neu- and weak grade
*-nu-, by -νῡ-/-νυ-. The Armenian first singular -nowm can derive from *-nūmi or *-numi,
either generalising the weak grade or making the same innovation as Greek; it is impossible to tell
which. Pedersen (1906:358) and Klingenschmitt (1982:11) also see the influence of a middle
form *-um(h₂)ai in 'Proto-Armenian' which would show an innovatory first person singular
middle form *-m(h₂)ai for the Proto-Indo-European form *-(h₂)ai (Vedic -e etc.). This would
be a shared innovation with Greek and Tocharian (cf. Krause & Thomas 1960:255), but, again, it
is impossible to verify this hypothetical development.

108. Schwyzer (1939:697) and Rix (1976:210).

109. A fourth example may be ῥήγνυμι 'I break' if this can be compared to Latin frango 'I
break', reconstructing initial *sr-. But see Pokorny IEW 165 and 1181 for different explanations.

110. Meillet (1937:216).

111. For the possibility of a formation *pleh₁-nu- inherited into Celtic see Klingenschmitt
(1982:253f.); see also 3.5.2 for lnowm in Armenian.

112. This etymology is uncertain; see de Lamberterie (1978:266–269).

113. See 3.5.2 and Klingenschmitt (1982:242–259) for other verbs of the -nowm class.

114. For the Greek formation of the type -άνω see Kuiper (1937:152ff.), Schwyzer
(1939:699f.), and Chantraine (1973:314f.).

115. The Armenian present class in -anem is very fully discussed by Klingenschmitt
(1982:159–229).

116. Note also the Hittite durative stems formed from the addition of a suffix -annāi-
connected to the Greek and Armenian suffixes by Bonfante (1939:387) and Morani
(1981c:102).

117. For discussion of this Armenian sound change see 4.12.

118. See Pokorny IEW 114f., 779 and Klingenschmitt (1982:180f., 184f.) for reconstruction of *e/ongʷ- and *bʰeg-.

119. See further the discussion of the -an- suffix at 4.14.

120. This isogloss is also discussed by Rocca (1985); see also 4.56 for discussion of a verbal
formation common to Greek, Latin, Gothic and Armenian (*pt(e)h₂-k-) the final guttural of
which may have originated as a present stem suffix.

121. The verb lsem is derived from an *-sk̑- present *k̑'lusk'ō by Hübschmann (1897:454),
an *-s- present by Solta (1960:95) and Barton (1965:44), and from *k̑'lu-n-s- by Kortlandt
(1987b:50). Sanskrit śloka- may also show a *-k- extension to this root (Klingenschmitt
1982:189).

122. See Klingenschmitt (1982:229f.) for the Proto-Indo-European verbal *u extension.

123. See note 99.

124. The restriction of the present imperative (with mi) to prohibitive and of the aorist
imperative to imperative may also be due to Caucasian influence; cf. K. H. Schmidt (1967). The
extent of convergence in the morphology of the two languages is discussed by Deeters (1927:63–
107) and Vogt (1988:181–183, reprinted from Studia Septentrionalia II (1945) pp. 217–219).

125. For example, the root πενθ- in Homer forms two present stems (πυνθάνομαι and
πεύθομαι) and two aorist stems πυθόμην and πεπυθ-.

Notes for Chapter 4

1. Chief amongst these studies and lists are Meillet (1936:142f.), Schwyzer (1939:57), Porzig
(1954:155f.), Solta (1960:462–466 and passim), Makaev (1967:456–457), Širokov (1980),
Klingenschmitt (1982:61 n. 2), Wyatt (1982), Arutjunjan (1983) and Jahowkyan (1987:107 and
300f.).

2. The comparison is included in all the lists cited in note 1 except those of Porzig and Klingenschmitt. Not all scholars agree on the importance of the correspondence.

3. Kortlandt sees a regular development of *h_2e- to *ha*- in Armenian (1986:38f.). Hence he rejects the derivation of *ayc* from *h_2eig- but proposes two alternative explanations: either *ayc* derives from *h_2ig- (following Peters who envisages a possible original paradigm with ablaut grades *h_2eig- and *h_2ig- (1980:83)); or *ayc* is an 'orientalisches Kulturwort' (following Specht 1939:13). But Kortlandt's rule that *h_2e- goes to Armenian *ha*- does not explain *acem* 'I bring' < *h_2eg- (Latin *ago*) which shows no initial *h*-. There seems to have been a fluctuation between initial *h*- and Ø- in Classical Armenian; for example *ogi* and *hogi* are both used in the Armenian Bible to translate either Greek πνεῦμα or ψυχή (see Considine 1978–9:362f.). Therefore attempts to etymologise initial *h*- in all occurrences are probably futile.

4. The Greek text has ἔριφος and ἐρίφιον in this passage, literally 'kid'. At *Luke* 15:29 ἔριφος is translated by *owl*, the normal Armenian word for 'kid'.

5. In the Bible translation the genitive plural *ayceac'* is in fact more common, and will be discussed later. The form *aycic'* always occurs in the phrase *eramak aycic'* 'herd of goats' used to translate Greek ἀγέλη τῶν αἰγῶν (*Song of S.* 4:1 etc.), and is also found at *Genesis* 31:10 (Zōhrab edition).

6. Meillet himself explained the plural form *aycik'* by supposing that it reflected the addition of a collective suffix *-ik'* also present in *awdik'* 'flock of sheep' and *andik'* 'herd of cattle' (*MSL* 17 (1911) p. 22, reprinted in 1962:144). However, in the Gospel passages cited the meaning is certainly 'goats' not 'flock of goats'. The restriction of the meaning to 'flock of goats' may have occurred later in accordance with Kuryłowicz's fourth 'law' of analogical change: the chronologically older form is restricted to a secondary function.

7. See also Szemerényi (1990:201f.).

8. Klingenschmitt (1982:25 n. 19) derives *ayceamn* thus, and connects the suffix with the Slavic suffix for animal names *-ęt-*. Jahowkyan (1982:116) gives other examples of Armenian animal and plant names formed with the suffix.

9. Brugmann (1906:170–175) saw a close relationship between *i-stems and consonant stems in the parent language.

10. Note also Mycenaean *a_3-za*, in *di-pte-ra a_3-za* (PY *Ub* 1318.7) which Perpillou thinks may represent a genitive *αἴζᾱς (1972:122) but which Ruijgh (1985:115) takes to be a nominative in apposition to *di-pte-ra* 'skin'.

11. Cases where αἰγι- shows the dative case of the noun, such as in αἰγίβοτος 'browsed by goats' (Risch 1974:219) form a separate class. The connection of other forms such as αἴγιθος 'a kind of bird' (Mannessy-Guitton 1988:423), αἰγίλιψ 'steep (?)' (Manessy-Guitton 1988:428), αἰγίοχος epithet of Zeus etc. (West 1978:366f.), to this root remains doubtful.

12. Schwyzer (1939:447f.), Perpillou (1972:119) and Manessy-Guitton (1988:423) all explain the compositional form αἰγι- as an archaic form. But Meier-Brügger (1992:II.38) suggests that the medial *-i-* represents a liaison vowel, modelled on compounds with the first element *owi*- 'sheep'.

13. Specht thought that the term was borrowed by Greek and Armenian from a non-Indo-European language (1939:13); he is followed by Kortlandt, see note 3 above.

14. Compare the separate replacements of the inherited term *ek'wo*- 'horse' in European languages (detailed by Buck 1949:167f.). Lidén (1906:13) thought that the parent language may have had a number of terms for different types of goats. Schrader & Nehring (1917–29:II.692f.) suggest that the goat was already domesticated at the time of the Proto-Indo-Europeans.

15. The suffix *-aēna*- is usually used in Avestan to characterise adjectives of material, although it can have a wider meaning (Hoffmann 1967:36; I am indebted to Mr P. Khoroche for this reference).

16. Thieme (1953:43); the Sanskrit word is explained through the addition of the *-aka*- suffix to *eǵ-*, which arose through the false analysis of original case-forms such as instrumental *eǵbhis* < *aigʰi*- (compare the instrumental *rādbhis* from *rāj-* 'king'); this explanation seems rather tenuous, although favoured by Mayrhofer *EWA* I 264. Greek αἴξ is also connected with the Vedic verb *éjati* 'move, jump' (cf. Boisacq 1950:20, not accepted by Chantraine *DELG* or Frisk *GEW* s.v.). The connection is supported by Thieme (1953:43, citing *RV* I 10.2 *yūthéna vṛṣnír ejati* 'as a ram with his flock he leaps'), and Manessy-Guitton (1988:421), who compares the putative connection of Gothic *gaits*, English *goat* with the Lithuanian verb *žáisti* 'play' (*ejati* may be cognate with Russian *igrat'* 'play', Pokorny *IEW* 13f.). But Mayrhofer (*EWA* s.v.) takes

ejati from the same root as *iṅg-* 'move, agitate' which entails the reconstruction of a root **aig-* or **aigʷ-*, not **aigʰ-*.

17. The 'Dacian' etc. cognates cited by Jahowkyan (1959:36, 57, 63, 110) and Haas (1959:46–48) are not conclusive evidence since they rest on onomastic material (but cf. also the Mycenaean personal names with first element *a₃-ki-*, Ventris and Chadwick 1973:536f.). Also of little worth is Rumanian (from 'Dacian'?) *aiṭ* cited by Jahowkyan (1987:298), which is glossed by Băltăceanu (1980:21) as an 'interjection for calling goats'.

18. Possible explanations for the fluctuation of the root vocalism are noted by Neumann at *LfrgE* I 325 (citing a suggestion that the genitive **aig'os* represents metathesised **ag'yos*) and Szemerényi (1971:652, citing Porru's theory that **aigʰ-* represents a blend of **ag'-* and **gʰaido-*).

19. For Greek root-nouns see Schwyzer (1939:422–425), Chantraine (1933:2), Schindler (1972).

20. For the Indo-Iranian cognates see Pokorny *IEW* 28, Bailey (1933:60) and, most fully, (1979:22). Hamp (1965:130) also connected Albanian *hollë* 'fine, thin'. Although this etymology was termed 'semantically weak' by Huld (1984:76), it relies upon the same development in meaning as the derivation of Vedic *áṇu-* 'fine, minute' from **al-nu-* which Mayrhofer (*EWA* s.v.) thinks plausible despite the lack of secure evidence for the sound change.

21. Meillet had earlier derived Greek ἀλέω from an athematic present (*REArm* 4 (1924) p. 5, reprinted in 1977:213).

22. The only other possible parallel is *hark'* 'fathers', the plural of *hayr* 'father' from an original plural **pɔteres* via **ha(y)erk'* (Godel 1972:56), but the accusative *hars* (from **pɔtṛns*) may have influenced the nominative (Hamp 1969b:17).

23. Beekes (1987:5 n. 5) rejects his earlier view and takes the reflex of **HR̥HC-* to be *vRvC-* in Greek on the basis of ὄνομα 'name' < **h₃ṇh₃m-*.

24. Rix (1991:194) dismisses Peters' theory as 'nicht sehr wahrscheinlich' and argues that in Greek the word for 'duck' was reshaped from **h₂ṇh₂-t-* to **sṇh₂-t-*.

25. Ruijgh (1988:458f.) argues that since an ablaut of the type full grade **ἔλα-* < **h₁elh₂-*, zero grade **ἐλᾱ-* < **h₁ḷh₂-* would be anomalous within Greek the zero grades were reformed to agree with the full grade.

26. Francis, in his unpublished PhD dissertation (1970:290f.), argues that the aorist ἄλεσ(σ)αι requires the reconstruction **h₂elh₁-*. Following the theories of Anttila (1969), he rejects a *Schwebeablaut* form **h₂leh₁-* for the root, and explains the above forms as secondary developments.

27. First proposed by Meillet (*REArm* 4 (1924) p. 4, reprinted in 1977:212). Parallels for the sound change of **-ln-* to *-ł-* are given by Pedersen (1906:354f.) and Meillet (1936:48).

28. This derivation of *ałam* was suggested by Lindeman (1982:40). A parallel to the re-marking of the present by **-na-* is seen by the verb *baṙnam* 'I raise' (from **barjnam* cf. aorist *barji*) where the present conjugation in *-nam* is a development peculiar to Armenian (see Klingenschmitt 1982:107ff.).

29. For the late development of the thematic type in Indo-European see Meillet (1931b), Watkins (1969:62f.).

30. As shown by Greppin (1983a).

31. The *NBHL* gives only two other citations of *aławri* with meaning 'mill', from the Pseudo-Ełišē commentary on *Judges* (*yaławris hamakeal*, of Samson) and the late *Tōnakan Matean* (*aławreōk'* or *aławriwk' maleal*). If *aławriwk'* is read in the second passage, and *yaławris* is interpreted as *yaławri-s* (i.e. an *i-* or *a-*stem genitive-dative-locative singular (or an *o-*stem locative singular, cf. Meillet 1913:49) with the article) these two citations could be taken as evidence for a noun *aławr* 'mill', comparable to *arawr* 'plough' (*o-*stem in the Classical language, later *i-* or *a-*stem), for which see further below. However, they may arise from a misinterpretation of the Biblical passage cited above.

32. Greek ἀλετρίς is a feminine to ἀλέτης 'grinder' (attested in inscriptions, cf. also ὄνος ἀλέτης 'millstone') which may replace a form **ἀλέτηρ* (Schwyzer 1939:499).

33. For the phonetic development of these forms see de Lamberterie (1982a:43f.). Olsen (1988:16 and 36) proposes that the choice between the suffixes **-tr-* and **-tl-* is governed by whether the root contains a liquid or not, which would explain the difference between *aławri* and *cnawł*.

34. The different uses of the suffix *-i* are discussed by Gjandschezian (1903).

35. See Ačaṙyan *HAB* s.v. *ayri* for discussion of this etymology. Note also the derivatives

arn-i 'virile' and *aramb-i* 'married woman' from the genitive and instrumental respectively of *ayr*.

36. The declension of *alewr* as an *o*-stem is first found in post-Classical texts (see *NBHL* s.v.), and probably arises from comparison with the Greek form (compare the later form *t'eatron* 'theatre', reformed to match Greek θέατρον from earlier *t'atr*; Hübschmann 1897:350).

37. A paradigm for this noun class is given by Meillet (1913:52) and Jensen (1959:62). However the formation of the instrumental plural and singular is not as certain as Meillet and Jensen suggest. In the Bible translation, the instrumental forms *-erb(k')*, *-eraw(k')*, *-erov(k')* and *-ereaw(k')* are found for *atbewr* and *etjewr* (only these two nouns provide examples); thus *atberbk'* at 3 *Kings* 18:5, *etjereaw* at 1 *Chroncles* 25:5, *etjerovk'* at *Ezekiel* 34:21. In the genitive-dative-locative plural there is a fluctuation between *-erac'* and *-iwrac'*, for example *atberac'* at 2 *Chronicles* 32:4 but *atbiwrac'* at 2 *Chronicles* 32:3 in the Zōhrab edition (with some of Zōhrab's manuscripts reading *atberac'*).

38. Meillet (*JA* (1903) II p. 493, reprinted in 1977:307), but see Feydit (1982:99) for a different interpretation.

39. The connection of *etjewr* with Hittite *karawar* (? for *garawar*) 'horn' (Normier 1980, Hilmarsson 1985), is at first sight attractive; but the posited Armenian phonetic development relies upon the secondary palatalisation of the original velar after the metathesis of **gr-* to **rg-* which contradicts other Armenian evidence suggesting that the palatalisation preceded the metathesis (see Job 1986:28f. and Weitenberg 1992:138ff. for full discussion). The Hittite word has also been connected with the family of Greek κέρας 'horn', etc. (cf. especially Nussbaum 1986:31–36). Etymologies given for *atewr/etewr* since Ačaryan *HAB* II² 24f. have connected it (a) to Sanskrit *drávati* 'run' (Mann 1963:144, followed by Eichner 1978:153 n. 38); (b) to Latin *palūs* 'marsh' (Pisani 1976:273f.); (c) to Greek δροίτη 'bath-tub' (Greppin 1984a). None of these is fully satisfactory both semantically and morphologically. Hübschmann (1897:415) reconstructed a form **drewr* for this word.

40. This possibility is noted by Irigoin *LfrgE* I 465, Francis (1970:291) and Eichner (1978:153 n. 37), and is all but confirmed by the existence of the metathesised genitive form βασιλέως and ἱερέως in the same inscription (published in Schwyzer 1923:352 n. 725).

41. See above note 26.

42. Eichner (1978:153 n. 37) wonders whether the different ablaut types may have originated from a present/aorist distinction.

43. Only words appearing in the Bible translation or in Eznik are given here. Words with initial *l-* are not listed as Armenian tended to avoid *t* in initial position.

44. It is worth noting that Meillet seems to have favoured the explanation of *alewr* as a loan from Greek (personal communication to Ačaryan recorded at *HAB* I² 94, and note published by Minassian 1978–9:21).

45. Note also the irregular accusative plural *atowesowns* at *Song of S.* 2:15. On the fluctuation between *e* and *ê* see below.

46. Furlan (1984) connected Hittite *ḫwelpi-* 'young, fresh, tender' (note also Hittite *ḫwelpi* 'young animal') with the Greek and Armenian words and also with words for 'fox' in other Indo-European languages, such as Latin *volpēs*. He thinks that the word has undergone taboo deformation and derives ἀλώπηξ from **Hwlōp-ek'-* and *atowês* from **Hlupek'-*. However it is not certain that **Hwl-* would have given Greek ἀλ- and it is preferable to follow Olsen (1985:7) and derive Greek ἀλώπηξ, Armenian *atowês* and Sanskrit *lopāśá-* from **h₂lōwpēk'-* and Latin *volpēs* and so forth from **h₂w(e/o)lp-*; this theory entails fewer metatheses.

47. For this rule see Meillet (*MSL* 8 (1892) p. 164, reprinted in 1977:19, *MSL* 11 (1900) p. 400, reprinted in 1977:67, *Banasêr* 2 (1900) p. 113, reprinted in 1977:84, *JA* (1903) II pp. 500–501, reprinted in 1977:314–315, and 1936:55); Grammont (1916:246f.) (who attempts to explain the exceptions to this rule: most can be dealt with by paradigm analogy); de Lamberterie (1978:269, 271); Klingenschmitt (1982:234 n. 7) and Peters (1986:378). It is possible that the Armenian genitive *atowesow* derives from an original form with ending **-ēk'-* with the normal development of **ē* to *i* disrupted by the lowering effect of the following **-u-*. Klingenschmitt (*loc. cit.*) denies that **ē* or **i* is affected by |u| in the following syllable but Meillet gave the parallels of *skesowr* 'step-mother' < **swek'urā* (although this is very uncertain) and *eresown* 'thirty' < **trī-k'omt-* (*MSL* 11 (1900) p. 400, reprinted in 1977:67f.).

48. So Hübschmann (1897:415). See Meillet (*JA* (1903) II p. 491, reprinted in 1977:305 and 1913:19) for other examples of the later writing of *ê* for *e*; Klingenschmitt (1982:249 n. 6) adds *etêgn* 'reed' which is written *etegn* in the earliest manuscripts of the Gospels.

49. Tumanjan (1968:60); see also the list of u-stem nouns in Schmitt (1981:98), most of which denote animals.

50. It is possible that the vocalism of the Vedic word has been altered by analogy to the root *lup*- 'steal, plunder'.

⸰ 51. Rix derives the alternation from earlier *-ōk's, *-ék'os (1976:143).

52. So also Hübschmann (*ZDMG* 35 (1881) p. 654f., reprinted in 1976:112f.), Meillet (1977:153).

53. See Meillet *loc. cit.* and Jasanoff (1979:136) for further posited occurrences of the change; but Klingenschmitt (1982:24ff.) remains sceptical.

54. The principal discussions of 'u-epenthesis' and 'i-epenthesis' in Armenian are Pedersen (1906:404–411), Godel (1975:87f.), and Olsen (1985:6 n. 6).

55. This theory does not account for forms such as *giwt* (i-stem) 'discovery' next to *gtanem* 'I find', which are explained through 'epenthetical' developments by Pedersen (1906:409f.) and Klingenschmitt (1982:179f.), but there is no certain evidence that this word ever contained *w or *u. See **4.43** for another explanation of *giwt*.

56. See Oettinger (1982:233f.) for discussion of the dental enlargement and Eichner (1978:154) for the phonetic derivation. It is possible that the Armenian form derives from a form with final *-ti, see **2.4.6**.

57. See also Hamp (1983a:7f.) and Jahowkyan (1982:106) for much more complicated derivations of the paradigm.

58. First proposed by J. Schmidt (1889:195) and followed by Schindler (1975a:3 and *passim*) and others.

59. Peters' theory is followed and enlarged upon by Leukart (1987:357–361), who discusses the Mycenaean form in some detail.

60. Benveniste (1935:27), Schwyzer (1939:518).

61. Dressler (1969:21). Note also Klingenschmitt's link with Latin *āreō* 'be dry' (1982:24 n. 15, 61 n. 2). The Armenian phrase *awr awowr* 'from day to day' need not show the same formation as Mycenaean *a-mo-ra-ma*, as Dressler proposes; the Armenian phrase may be a reduction of **awowr awowr* (Szemerényi 1978:282f.) and thus continue the same inherited formation which is also found in Vedic *divé-dive* 'from day to day', with repetition of the dative case.

62. See Ačaṙyan *HAB* I² 174f. for citation of earlier connections of the Greek and Armenian forms.

63. Feydit (1982:93) saw a development of *-nT- to -y- as likely on the evidence of doublets such as k'ayk'ayel and k'andel (both 'destroy'), and because of the parallel fate of original *-nK-,
⸰ for example in *yisown* 'fifty'. However he does not have any secure etymologies for the 'doublet' forms, and the derivation of *yisown* is notoriously vexed; see Hamp (1986a) for a different explanation.

64. Scholion PQ at *Od.* 4:794 τὰς συναφὰς τῶν μελῶν οὐ τὰ μέλη 'the joints of the limbs, not the limbs'; Hesychius gloss α 8948 (Latte's edition) ἄψεα · αἱ συναφαὶ τῶν μελῶν, οὐχὶ τὰ μέλη 'ἄψεα, the joints of the limbs, not the limbs'; *Etymologicum Magnum* ἄψεα κύριως αἱ συναφαὶ τῶν μελῶν, καταχρηστικῶς δὲ, καὶ τὰ μέλη, παρὰ τὸ ἅπτω, ἄψω, ἄψον, 'ἄψεα correctly the joints of the limbs, but also the limbs by catachresis, from the verb ἅπτω ["I touch"].' The interpretation 'joint' is defended by R. van Bennekom *LfgrE* I 1786–7, who discusses the difference between ἄψεα, γυῖα and μέλη. The word ἄψις 'felloe' (Hes. *Works and Days* 426, cf. *LfgrE* I 1788–1790 for full bibliography and discussion of this word and also ἄψις 'loop, mesh') might derive from ἄψος; a semantic parallel is given by Ilievski (1987:307) who cites a term for 'felloe' in Macedonian Slav dialects which derives from 'elbow', and gives other Indo-European terms which he takes to show a semantic connection between 'arm, joint of an arm' and 'felloe, spoke of a wheel' (although he does not mention the connection between ἄψος and ἄψις). If this connection is correct, and the semantic distance between the two terms makes it uncertain, it will offer some support for a meaning 'joint' for ἄψος.

65. Compare also the Scholion V at *Od.* 4:794 ἄψεα δὲ τὰ μέλη φησὶν, ἀπὸ τοῦ συνῆφθαι 'he calls the limbs ἄψεα from their conjunction'; the passage in the *Etymologicum Magnum* cited in the above note; the *Etymologicum Gudianum* (in Stefani's edition I 254) ἄψεα παρὰ τὸ συνῆφθαι αὐτὰ εἰς σύστασιν ὅλου τοῦ σώματος 'ἄψεα, from the conjunction of them to the structure of the whole body'; the *Etymologicum Gudianum* I 254 1.20 ἄψεα τὰ μέλη ἀπὸ τοῦ ἐφάπτεσθαι ἀλλήλων 'ἄψεα, the limbs, from their attachment to each other'; and Hesychius gloss α 2211 αἴψεα · τὰ μέλη, οἱ δὲ ἄψεα 'αἴψεα, limbs, others ἄψεα'.

66. The phrase *ənd ap'* is only found in Künzle's manuscript E (1984:II.120).

67. The other etymologies given by Pedersen are even more tenuous: *p'etem* 'pluck' linked with Greek ψεδνός 'thin, bald'; *p'ap'owk* 'soft' with Greek ψαφαρός 'friable'; *p'owx(r)* 'friable' with Greek ψώχω 'rub'; and *cep'* 'mortar, cement' with Greek γύψος. None of these are accepted in the etymological works and dictionaries of Hübschmann, Ačaṙyan, Frisk or Chantraine.

68. Normier (1981:24 f.) follows Pedersen, and gives further etymological support: *top'em* 'I beat' alongside Greek δέψω 'I knead'; *lap'em* 'I lick' alongside Greek λάψοντες at *Iliad* 16.161 (taken by Normier as originally a present and not as future to λάπτω 'I lick'); and *op'i* 'white poplar' < *ops-*. However *top'em* and *lap'em* could derive their aspirate consonants from earlier 'voiceless aspirates' (cf. Greek δέφω and λαφύσσω), and *op'i* may derive from a form *osp-*.

69. A less likely etymology for *eres* is proposed by Hamp, who attempts to derive the word from *protiH₀kʷik'a-* (1982e:53).

70. Brugmann (1906:520), Meillet (1936:74).

71. Neither μῖσος 'hate' nor ὕψος 'height' need show an original *-se/os-* suffix, and the isolated forms μύσος, 'uncleanness', πῖσος 'meadow', ἄλσος 'grove' and ἄρσος 'meadow' are all etymologically too uncertain to carry any weight (they are all declared obscure or uncertain by Frisk *GEW* and Chantraine *DELG* s.vv.). The only other example which seems to be inherited is φάρσος.

72. Kretschmer (1916:352). The only evidence for the existence of the unaspirated form ἀφή cited by Meillet is a marginal note to Hipponax frag. 9 (Bergk = frag. 8 Masson) which states that the word is psilotic in Ionic; the Hipponax fragment begins κἀφῆ παρέξειν ἰσχάδας 'to provide figs with the hand' which shows a unique sense of 'hand' for ἀφή which would match *ap'* perfectly. Solta's (1960:411) ἄφος and Bailey's (1969:145) τὸ ἄφος 'joint' are ghost-words.

73. Witczak glosses the Tocharian word as '(minor) limbs' following van Windekens (1976:166) who glosses 'membres secondaires, membres saillants du corps'. Bailey (1969:144) shows that the Tocharian 'cliché' *lyā āpsā lyiyā āpsā* translates Buddhist Sanskrit *anga-pratyanga-* explained by the Buddhist commentaries as the major and minor limbs. A translation 'limb, part of the body' would seem to suffice for the Tocharian word.

74. Bailey (1969:141-144) presents the passages in the Veda in which *ápsas-* occurs and attempts to elucidate the meanings. It may be significant that in three of the four occurrences of *ápsas-* meaning 'front part of the body' in the Veda it is applied to females (twice in the formula *ni riṇīte ápsaḥ* of obscure meaning), which recalls the use of ἄψεα restricted to Penelope in the *Odyssey*.

75. Bailey had previously connected the Sanskrit and Tocharian words (1969:144), and Eichner connected the Hittite, Sanskrit and Tocharian forms (see Mayrhofer *EWA* I 90).

76. It is possible that there is some connection to another reconstructed Proto-Indo-European term for a body-part: *pesos-* 'penis' (*IEW* 824). A transfer of meaning from 'limb' to 'penis' is very possible (compare German 'männliches Glied') and it is possible that the two forms were originally related but have been altered by 'taboo deformation'. Witczak cites *pesos-* in connection with Hittite *ḫapušaš* (neuter *s-*stem) which he explains, following a suggestion made by I. R. Danka, as a contamination between *apsos-* and *pesos* (1989:30-31). Bailey (1969:144f.) reconstructed a root *ap-* 'point' for *ápsas-* etc. to which he ascribed Hittite *ḫapušaš* 'penis' and a number of Iranian forms.

77. This is taken as a significant isogloss by Meillet (1936:142), Arutjunjan (1983:270), Risch (1985:183), and others.

78. Meier-Brügger (1992:I.65 and II.58) takes the peculiar Mycenaean participle *a-ra-ro-mo-te-me-na* 'fitted out' as evidence that this type of aorist formation was already present in Mycenaean, but this Mycenaean formation seems to represent a perfect participle rather than an aorist (Ventris and Chadwick 1973:533, Ruijgh 1979:88, etc.).

79. Rix (1976:205) connects the Greek reduplicated aorist with the 'intensives' but sees this as a Greek innovation. The Armenian and Vedic parallels make this unlikely. Bonfante (1939:383 n. 4), Morani (1981c:102) and Oettinger (1979:431) connect the total reduplication for the Hittite root *eš-* 'sit' which has a causative *ašaš-* (or *ašeš-*) with the Vedic, Greek and Armenian processes. Szemerényi (1990:289 n. 5) adds further cases of reduplication of this type citing the example of the Luvian 3rd singular present (of uncertain meaning) *el-elḫaiti* but 3rd singular imperative *elḫadu*.

80. Pokorny *IEW* 55-61; see also **4.10**. Oettinger has also connected Luvian *ḫirud-* and *ḫirun-* 'oath' < *h₂ēr-w-* (suggestion recorded at Mayrhofer 1986:133).

81. The Vedic forms are discussed by Klingenschmitt (1982:162f.); he gives as an example *ṚV* I 30.14 *ṛṇór ákṣaṃ ná cakryòḥ* 'you fasten like an axle onto the two wheels'.

82. But the connection is not accepted by Bailey (1979:23) who links *aŕnem* with an Iranian verbal base **ar-* meaning 'work', a distinct (but homophonous) root to **ar-* 'fit', and **ar-* 'grant, provide'. The evidence rests primarily on nominal forms in Iranian languages.

83. The connection of the Greek and Armenian words with Albanian *nërrój* 'deny' (supposedly metathesised from **rrënój*, Pokorny *IEW* 62) and Latin *ōrō* 'I pray' (Meillet *BSL* 26 (1925) p. 19f. = 1977:222f.) seems unlikely.

84. Following Hübschmann (1897:478) who is doubtful about the connection. An alternative etymology for the Old English word is given by Holthausen (1963:233) who connects it to the family of Latin *nervus* 'sinew'.

85. For the root see Pokorny *IEW* 55–61, and **4.7**.

86. It first occurs at Theognis 998.

87. The Homeric compound adjectives with first member ἀρτι- are fully discussed by Calame (1977) and Haudry (1983); the same sense of ἄρτι is found in some post-Homeric compounds such as ἀρτίκολλος 'well-joined'.

88. Calame (1977:219), whose arguments I have largely followed, thinks that the adverb originally had local meaning, and developed a temporal signification in the post-Homeric period.

89. Solta (1960:127). Pokorny *IEW* 57 derives the Lithuanian form from the locative of a *ti*-stem, whereas Greek ἄρτι appears to derive from a consonant stem. However, the Lithuanian form may equally well continue the locative of a consonant stem (so Specht 1924:51). If Pokorny is right, it is not a serious problem for the connection of *arti* with ἄρτι since the Baltic *i*-stem has replaced a consonant stem elsewhere (Brugmann 1906:170ff.). Bader (1970:109) thinks that the adverb may continue a fossilised neuter noun in **-ti*.

90. So Hübschmann (1897:411f.), Ačaṙyan *HAB* I² 76, Arutjunjan (1983:256f.), Frisk *GEW* I 186, Chantraine *DELG* 24, Barton (1988), and others. Solta (1960:442f.) sees the isogloss as especially important.

91. De Lamberterie (1990:II.799–820, especially p. 817) reconstructs two separate roots; **h₂wes-* 'spend the night' and **h₁wes-* 'live' for these forms.

92. See Peters (1980:34–38) and Klingenschmitt (1982:203) for full analysis and rejection of reconstructions **iawe/o-* and **iawye/o-*. Klingenschmitt parallels the formation of the reconstruction of **h₂-i-h₂(a)ws-ye/o-* to the reconstruction **li-las-ye/o-* ancestor of λιλαίομαι 'long for' (1982:203 n. 50). Seiler *LfrgE* I 181 also derives the present from **h₂ews-*.

93. See Seiler *LfrgE* I 182, O'Sullivan *LfrgE* II 1109f. and Peters (1980:34–36) for full presentation of the Homeric material. The aorist ἴαυσα is a recent creation (Chantraine 1973:313).

94. Frisk *GEW* I 25 s.v. ἄεσα (citing Bechtel); note that ἀέσσαμεν, if the correct reading, would be the only occurrence of the aorist ἄεσα in Homer not conjoined with νύκτα(ς).

95. Peters (1980:52) lists other possible *Schwebeablaut* variations in Greek verbal paradigms.

96. Armenian *gom* must be derived from an ancient perfect form (cf. Gothic *was*, English *was*), see further Meillet (1936:112), Klingenschmitt (1982:260).

97. Pisani (1950a:167 followed by Eichner 1978:151 and 152 n. 34) thinks that **-ws-* develops to *-k-* in Armenian on the basis of *akanjk'* 'ears' < **awsṇ-*. Eichner (1978:152) also cites the opinion of Klingenschmitt that **-ws-* passes to *-w-* in *aṙawawt* 'morning', which Klingenschmitt derives from **h₂ews-* 'dawn' (Ačaṙyan *HAB* I² 256 cites an earlier attempt to link *aṙawawt* and **h₂ews-* 'dawn' by Patrubány in *HA* 1906 p. 341).

98. A possible parallel is the word for 'dawn' *ayg* which before now has received no satisfactory etymology (cf. Ačaṙyan *HAB* I² 163). The word may derive from the locative of the Indo-European term for dawn **h₂(e)ws-(e/o)s-* (Greek ἕως, Vedic *uṣás*, Latin *aurōra*) which can be reconstructed as **h₂(e)usi* (by simplification of **h₂eus-s-i*) from the comparison of Greek **ἦι* (in ἠικανός (Hesychius) 'cock' i.e. 'one who sings at dawn') and Avestan **uši* (in the name *Ušidā*, see Pokorny *IEW* 86f.). The Armenian form *ayg* would derive regularly from **h₂ewsi* by the process of 'epenthesis' described at **4.4**. The generalisation of the vocalism of the locative may be due to the widespread use of locutions such as *ənd ayg* 'at dawn' (e.g. *Mark* 1:35). Compare also the two words for 'evening' in Classical Armenian, *erek* and *erekoy* (more frequent), the second of which is an original genitive of time which has been reinterpreted as a

nominative (de Lamberterie 1990:I.162 n. 21). The stem *ag*- from other cases may survive in *anagan* 'late' and *agan* (post-classical) 'early'. The change of *-ws- > -g- must have proceeded via *w, so *aŕawawt* 'morning' may continue another form of this root with development of *-w- to -w- not -g- in a different phonetic environment; see note 97.

99. As evidence Frisk cited *awd* 'shoe' which he took to show the same formation as Avestan *aōθra-* 'shoe', i.e. a *-t- suffix, thereby proving that *awt- develops to *awd*, and *awtʰ- to *awt'*, just as *ort'* 'calf' can be derived from *portʰu-*, but *ard* from *arti*. However, the Avestan word proves little as it contains a *-tro- suffix, and *awd* cannot stem from *aw-tro-*. It is possible that *awd* actually contains the reflex of a *-dʰ- suffix, also found in Greek ἐσθής 'clothing' (Klingenschmitt 1982:174).

100. So Hübschmann (*KZ* 32 (1877) p. 401, reprinted in 1976:78), Pedersen (1905:218), Meillet (1936:76f.), Godel (1975:66), Klingenschmitt (1982:100), and Stempel (1983:95f.).

101. Pedersen (1905:219) also argued for the late productivity of the suffix *-ti- in Armenian, and so also Peters (1980:40f.) for this word.

102. The Theocritus passage gives the accusative τὸν ἄμφενα; the nominative ἄμφην is glossed as αὐχήν, τράχηλος by Hesychius. The Hesychius gloss ἀμφήν · αὐλήν is probably a corruption of this gloss. The word αὔφην 'neck' which is cited as an Aeolic form by Philoponus (Johannes Grammaticus), probably arises from a confusion of αὐχήν and ἄμφην; Pisani (1950a:188f.) gives a full discussion of the older literature on the Greek forms.

103. A root *augʰ- is reconstructed by Pokorny (*IEW* 87) who also connects Sanskrit *uṣṇíhā* 'nape of the neck'; this is highly doubtful, because it involves a concatenation of suffixes (*ugʰ-s-n-igʰā-) and then dissimilation of the first *-gʰ-.

104. For other explanations of *giwt* see note 55 at **4.4** above and **4.43**.

105. Pisani believed that Greek αὐχήν might have arisen from a prehistoric contact with the ancestor to Armenian, which had already undergone the change of *-nKʷ- to -wK- (1950a:191).

106. See **4.2** for the -*i* suffix; this derivation of *awjik'* is suggested by the *NBHL* and Y. Hiwnk'earpêyêntean (only known to me through the reference given by Ačaŕyan *HAB* IV² 612) who cites a parallel range of meanings 'snake' and 'necklace' for the Persian word which he transcribes into Armenian script as *t'iyb*; unfortunately, I can find no other evidence for this word.

107. Lehmann (1986:60) connects Gothic *hals-aggan* 'neck' (correction for *balsaggan* at *Mark* 9:42) and Old High German *ancha*.

108. Further examples of the suffix -*ayn* are given by Lidén (1906:23).

109. My account of the suffix in Iranian loan-words in Armenian is largely based on Bolognesi (1962:105–117).

110. A disadvantage of Olsen's theory is that there are no other certain reflexes of the *-nt-participle inherited into Armenian. Stempel (1983:91f.) derived the Armenian suffix -*own*, which forms verbal adjectives on some roots in the classical language (on the Biblical usage see de Lamberterie 1982a:35f.), from the Proto-Indo-European *-ont- participle. Meillet (1936:48) and de Lamberterie *loc. cit.* derive the suffix from *-omno-. Even if Stempel's derivation is correct, it offers little support for Olsen's theory, because the participle here develops to a verbal adjective, not an action noun.

111. See Meillet (*REArm* 3 (1923) pp. 3–6, reprinted in 1977:205f.) and Schmitt (1983:98–100), for a summary of the different Armenian declension classes for Iranian loans.

112. The verb *top'em* has been compared to Greek δέφω 'I knead' (Solta 1960:389), *xt'em* to Vedic *khidáti* 'press down' (Ačaŕyan *HAB* II² 325), *jnjem* 'wipe, efface' (from which *jnjan* 'duster, rubber') to Greek θείνω, etc. (Solta 1960:80f.); none of these etymologies is completely certain.

113. See Meillet (*REArm* 4 (1924) p. 3f., reprinted in 1977:211f.) for examples of the Biblical usage of *erkar, erkayn* and the denominative verb *yerkarem*.

114. Francis (1970:280f.) connected the Latin word and envisaged a semantic development from the meaning 'long-lasting' cf. Plautus *Amph.* 166 *servitus dūra*, and the verb *dūrāre* 'endure'.

115. See Kortlandt (1989) for references to the views of the other scholars mentioned.

116. Klein (1988:258–260) gives other Indo-European derivatives of this formation.

117. Monro (1891:24). Evidence for the stem δειδικ- is given by the imperative δείδιχθι at Nicander *Alex.* 443.

118. This etymology is rejected by Meillet (*MSL* 15 (1909) p. 354 = 1977:133) and de

Lamberterie (1988:232 n. 33) on the grounds that the reflex of *perg- would have initial h-. As there was a fluctuation between initial aspirate and zero in Classical Armenian this is not conclusive (see note 3 at **4.1** above and also Kortlandt (1989:48) who defends Pedersen's etymology).

119. The earliest citation recorded in the *NBHL* is from the Armenian translation of Chrysostom.

120. For Pindar's θήξαις (*O.* 10.20) see Forssman (1966:129 f.).

121. For the voicing of *k after a nasal, compare dr-and 'door-post' alongside Latin *antae*.

122. See Meillet (1913:50 f., 1936:82); Hamp (1983b, especially p. 4 f.); and de Lamberterie (1990:I.192), for a fuller discussion of the Armenian development of *u*-stem adjectives and their derivatives.

123. Omitted in the Zōhrab text, but cited (as *Sirach* 24:41) in the *NHBL* s.v. *acow*.

124. Gjandschezian connected the Armenian -*ow* suffix with the perfect participle in *-*we*/*os*-, but this theory, unobjectionable if one derives the Armenian form from the feminine stem *-*usyā*- (as Jahowkyan 1987:241, comparing *acow* with Greek ἄγυια 'street'), has found little favour outside Armenia; neither the comparative grammars of Meillet, Godel or Schmitt nor Klingenschmitt's or Stempel's (1983) works on the Armenian verb adopt it. An alternative explanation for the origin of the suffix, which explains its prevalent use in compound forms, is that it has been extended from the compounds with final -*tow* '-giver' (e.g. *lowsatow* 'light-giving') < *-*doh₃*- (cf. Vedic *aśva-dā*- 'giving horses') which have been re-analysed as -*t-ow*.

125. Similarly none of the terms for 'knife' (Buck 1949:558), 'spear' (Buck 1949:1390) or 'sword' (Buck 1949:1392) is derived from 'sharpen' apart from Rumanian *cuṭit* 'knife' < 'sharpened'.

126. Considine (1979:226 n. 12) considers the possibility that *ardar* is a loan from Iranian *artaδā (cf. Hesychius ἀρτάδες 'the just (δίκαιοι) among the Magi'), but decides that the form *ard*- rather than *art*- is better explained if the word is inherited. It is possible that the word may have been influenced in meaning by the Iranian form.

127. Pokorny (*IEW* 234) gives parallel roots *dʰal- and *dʰel-. De Lamberterie (1990:II.663) derives the Armenian *det*- forms from the Indo-European colour root *gʰel- with an irregular change of the expected *jet*- to *det*- arising through contamination with the *dʰal-root.

128. See also **4.17** above and **4.33** below. The origin of -*k*- in *mowkn* and *jowkn* has prompted some discussion owing to the fact that some scholars have explained it as the reflex of an earlier laryngeal (Winter 1965a:104 f., Kortlandt 1985:9).

129. The derived adjective *dambanakan* and verb *dambaranem* are also found in post-fifth-century Armenian; the adjective *dambanakan* is used in the Armenian translation of the *Ars Grammatica* of Dionysios Thrax (which may be as old as the sixth century) to translate Greek ἐλεγεῖα 'elegiac' (Adontz 1915:2, line 21). The Armenian commentators gloss *dambanakan* as *gerezman(an)akan* 'sepulchral' (Adontz 1915:57 line 22, 1915:128, and 1970:317).

130. A possible semantic route might be 'cry aloud' > 'curse' > 'swear'. The Armenian word consistently translates ὀμνύω in the New Testament.

131. For the meaning 'labour pains' the plural *erkownk'* is used, except at I *Thess.* 5:3 where the singular is found.

132. Schindler also discusses other possible origins for the nominative singular.

133. I follow Szemerényi's (1964:112) rejection of this hypothesis. Szemerényi (1964:106–118) also gives and rejects other theories which have been proposed to link the Greek and Armenian numerals, and gives a full discussion of the problems of the Greek and Armenian forms.

134. For this reconstruction see Godel (1982:13), Eichner (1978:152 n. 35), and **2.3.2**. Normier (1981:27 n. 40) argues that *-*nw*- develops to Armenian -*n* if the preceding vowel is not *u, citing *erkan* 'mill' < **gʷrh₂/₃nuh₂* as a parallel, but this reconstruction is open to doubt; other explanations of *erkan* are given by Meillet (1925b:8) and Eichner (1978:152 n. 35), who derive it from a form without *-*w*-. Hamp (1975b) thinks that it may have undergone a morphological reshaping peculiar to Armenian.

134A. J. H. W. Penney has brought to my attention Peters' article on the numeral '9' in Greek and Armenian (Peters 1991). Peters derives the Armenian form *inn* from *h₁newṇ via pre-Armenian *enōn the result of a contraction (for which there are no parallels) of *enoan <

*enowan with irregular loss of *-w-; *enowan in turn stems from *enewan by a regular sound change, but the initial vowel of *enewan is the result of an irregular assimilation of original *anewan < *h₁newn̥ (Peters 1991:304–305). One could be forgiven for treating this derivation with some scepticism.

135. See **4.3** and note 47 for this rule. Grammont's observation that the change does not occur over the sequence *-elu- (1916:246f.) is not certain because all his examples are verbs with present tense in -owm, in which the -e- may be preserved by analogy to the aorist (as c'elowm 'I split', aorist c'eli). The -e- of meɫow 'bee' may likewise be retained through analogy to meɫr 'honey'.

136. The noun k'irtn 'sweat' may have originally followed this declension (cf. Greek ἴδρως and Latin sudor) but it has been transferred to the Armenian n-stem declension, perhaps by analogy to the declension in -n of terms denoting body-parts. Pisani (1951:52 n. 1) suggested that k'irtn derived from an old *-r/n stem. In note 98 at **4.11** above it was suggested that the Armenian word for 'dawn', ayg, may be derived from the same formation as Greek ἔως, etc.; ayg is twice in the Bible (Old Testament) declined as an o-stem, and six times (thrice in the Gospels) as a u-stem. The u-declension of ayg may be secondary, since many nouns with stem-final *w are transferred to the u-declension in Armenian (Meillet 1936:76), or it may arise from a reinterpretation of *awuh (< *awōs), as a u-stem nominative. The o-stem declension can be compared to the Armenian o-stem declension of Proto-Indo-European neuters in *-os. If this etymology is correct, it provides a strong argument against Klingenschmitt's derivation of catr, since it shows that a Proto-Indo-European noun with nominative singular in *-ōs would not have developed to an Armenian noun of the asr type.

137. Chadwick (1992) shows that the inscriptional form ΗΡΥΣ should be read differently and that there is consequently no reason to believe that ἥρως was ever a u-stem.

138. The following scholars are among those who have assumed an earlier form *γελασ- as the base of verbal or nominal forms: Brugmann (1906:533), Frisk GEW I 294f., Chantraine DELG 214, Francis (1970:170), Manessy-Guitton (1972:93), Risch (1974:320), Peters (1980:144) and Tucker (1990:251); Schwyzer (1939:680) and Szemerényi (1967:78–84, reprinted in 1987:II.1305–1310) offer alternative explanations, which will be discussed below.

139. Note also J. Schmidt (1889:386f.) for the connection of forms in -ως/-ας with the alternation between forms in -ās/-iṣ- in Sanskrit.

140. Blanc (1985) connects the second part of ἀπηνής and προσηνής with the verb αἰνέω 'praise'.

141. Gregory of Corinth and Meermannianus both have the same wording: λέγεται δὲ παρ' αὐτοῖς (i.e. the Aeolians) ὁ ἔρως ἔρος, ὁ γέλως γέλος 'they (the Aeolians) say ἔρως as ἔρος, γέλως as γέλος.' They both stem from the same archetype derived from a compendium περὶ διαλέκτων by Philoponus (Johannes Grammaticus) (Hoffmann 1893:212) but the other source for this work omits the section (section 42 in Hoffmann 1893:221) and gives an alternative 'Aeolic' form γέλων for the accusative τὸν γέλωτα, which is clearly corrupt. It is not certain that the form γέλος can be attributed to Philoponus.

142. Compare also W. Beck's comments on the meaning of γελάω in early Greek epic (LfrgE II 124f.): the analogy of the human countenance in laughter to 'brightening' can often suffice for γελάω.

143. The Latin forms are also connected by Stanford (1936:115) and de Lamberterie (1978).

144. The unmarked term seems to be t'ewr (translates σκολιός at Deut. 32:5, Prov. 28:18]; kamakor (literally 'with crooked will') is used for σκολιός when it is applied metaphorically to the 'unrighteous' and xotoreal (past participle of xotorem 'I bend') translates διεστραμμένη (Deut. 32:5). However, the semantic distinction between the three terms is very slight; note the translation of (γενεὰ) σκολιὰ καὶ διεστραμμένη by t'ewr ew xotoreal at Deut. 32:5 but kamakor ew xeɫat'ewr at Phil. 2:15, and (γενεὰ) σκολιά by xotoreal at Acts 2:40.

145. The unexpected ř in meřanim 'I die' might offer a parallel for ř in place of expected r.

146. The words kowr 'skiff' and kowřn 'back', which Lidén cites as derivations from the same root *geu- and as evidence against the merger of velars and palatals, may rather be related to the same root as kerem 'I carry' and may derive their vocalism from an ancient lengthened grade ō; kowřn 'back' ('that which carries') may therefore stand in the same relation to kerem 'I carry' as bowřn 'fist, violence' to berem 'I carry', dowrgn 'potter's wheel' to dařnam (aorist darjay) 'I turn' and owřn 'hammer' to hari (aorist) 'I hit' (cf. Eichner 1978:147 and Létoublon and de Lamberterie 1980:317).

147. Mayrhofer is tempted to assign *gola-* a non-Indo-European etymology (*KEWA* I 349), but note also the cognate Iranian forms given by Bailey (1979:88) s.v. Khotanese *gūla-* 'ball', for example, Ossetic (Iron) *qul* 'eyeball'.

148. Another example may be *damban* see **4.19**. The development of **-mbʰ-* to **-mb-* is considered regular by Hübschmann (1976:332, reprinted from *IF Anz*. 10 (1899) p. 48) and Lidén (1906:42f.). Pedersen (1906:361) argues for the development of **-mbʰ-* to *-m-* and sees the instrumental case in *-mb* as the result of analogy.

149. The Greek suffix is discussed by Chantraine (1933:242) and Risch (1974:109). The suffix may have been added to γόμφος 'tooth' to form γαμφηλαί (*LfrgE* II 120); analogy with the word γόμφος could also account for the form γαμφ- in place of the expected *γαφ- from *g'ṃbʰ-.

150. This derivational process is discussed and exemplified by Gjandschezian (1903:55–57).

151. See Lejeune (1972:45) for the 'dissimilation' theory, who expresses some doubt over it in footnote 11.

152. The meaning of γέφυρα in Homer has been fully discussed by Puhvel (1976) and Hooker (1979:387f.).

153. In the latter passage a spear is compared to the ξύλον διαβάθρας, Armenian *p'ayt kamrǰi*; unfortunately the passage is not in the received Hebrew text so one cannot be sure whether a ladder, gangplank or wooden bridge is referred to. The passage does show that a *kamowrǰ* could be a construction of wood.

154. There have been numerous attempts to find etymologies for either or both of the words; for Armenian see the material collected by Ačaryan *HAB* s.v. and Schmitt (1972a:25), to which can be added Knobloch (1975) and van Windekens (1987). For the Greek word new explanations since Frisk *GEW* are given by Puhvel (1976) (on the Homeric formula πολέμοιο γέφυραι; see the criticism of Hooker 1979), Knobloch (1975), and Hooker (1979) (a loan-word from Semitic).

155. Frisk writes the Albanian form as *lênd* and gives also Tosk *lëndë*, but Huld (1984:37) writes *lende*, glossing *lëndë* as 'timber, material' (so also Mann 1977:37). Orel (1988:111) gives *len, lend* and *lende* as the standard forms and also cites Tosk *lëndë*.

156. The comparable cluster *-tm* is retained in the nominative of *hotm* (genitive *hotmoy*) 'wind'.

157. Morani (1987:680) has offered a similar explanation for *lowsin*.

158. The Armenian word is usually compared with Greek οὐδας 'ground' and Hittite *utne* 'land', which are derived from *n-suffixed forms by Hamp (1969a); the troublesome phonetic correspondence between Hittite initial *ut-*, Armenian *get-* < **wet-*, and Greek οὐδ- is discussed by Peters (1980:57f.) who considers it possible that they derive from **h₃u(e)d-*.

159. Further examples of transfers of this type are given by Godel (1975:96), Stempel (1990:51f.).

160. So Brugmann (1907–8:180f.), Schwyzer (1939:583), Arutjunjan (1983:294f.), and Lühr (1991:171).

161. Most recently Harðarson (1987:129f.), who derives the nominative plural *kanayk'* from **g"ṇna(h₂)ik-es* and the accusative and locative plural *kanays* from earlier **-ayk'(a)s* and **-aik's(u)* with remodelling after the nominative.

162. For other examples of original consonant stems attracted to the Armenian *i*-stem declension see **4.1**. The *i*-declension of this root has parallels in other Indo-European languages, for instance, Gothic *qens*, Vedic *jani-* 'wife' (if this last does not reflect an original nominative **g"enh₂*; see Szemerényi 1960b:14 for discussion).

163. Other etymologies for the Tocharian word are not compelling: van Windekens (1976: s.v.) compares Modern Irish *caile* 'girl' and Schindler connects the root **gul-* 'lie' (Tocharian *kul-* 'subside', Lithuanian *gulti* 'lie') with the same semantic extension as in Greek ἄλοχος 'wife' (personal communication to Jasanoff recorded at Jasanoff 1978:39). I am indebted to J. H. W. Penney for clarification of the Tocharian material.

164. See **2.4.6** for discussion of whether the change of final **-m* to *-n* reflects a common phonological innovation made by the two languages.

165. The interpretation of Homeric δῶ as a neuter noun is confirmed by Mycenaean *do-de* (TH *Of* 25, and elsewhere in the Thebes tablets) 'to the house'. Szemerényi (1980:220–225) discusses the Mycenaean form, and the relationship between the words δῶ and δῶμα; he takes the latter as the result of the addition of a 'prop-vowel' *-a* to original **δῶμ*.

166. The original paradigm of this word is reconstructed by Szemerényi (1960a:121) and Schindler (1972:34), who agree on the nominative *$g^{\cdot h}i\bar{o}m$, genitive *$g^{\cdot h}imos$ and locative *$g^{\cdot h}iemi$, but disagree on the accusative, for which Schindler reconstructs *$g^{\cdot h}iom\eta$ but Szemerényi *$g^{\cdot h}iem\eta$. The variation between *$g^{\cdot h}y$- and *$g^{\cdot h}iy$- is paralleled in the reconstruction of *$k\,'w\bar{o}$ (Vedic śvā́) and *$k\,'uw\bar{o}$ (Greek κύων) for the Proto-Indo-European word for 'dog' (Mayrhofer 1986:166f.).

167. For example Szemerényi (1960a:123).

168. Greek χίων is used seven times in the Homeric epics. Sometimes it refers explicitly to fallen snow (e.g. Od. 19.205), but it can also be used to refer to falling snow; for example at Il. 12.278 νιφάδες χίονος means 'snowflakes'.

169. Solta (1960:441) and Jahowkyan (1987:131).

170. Other examples of this transfer are given by Schwyzer (1939:472), Risch (1974:168) and de Lamberterie (1990:I.187f.). De Lamberterie does not, however, include *κενύς in his survey of Greek u-stem adjectives (1990). Ruijgh (1987:536–537) proposes that the transfer originates from the reinterpretation of neuter plurals in -α as thematic stems.

171. Evidence for the original u-stem declension is given by the suffixed form ἔτυμος 'true'. De Lamberterie does not include *ἐτύς in his survey of Greek u-stem adjectives (1990). The connection, first made by Meillet (MSL 22 (1920) pp. 61–63, reprinted in 1977:177f.), and repeated by de Lamberterie (1990:I.480), between Greek ἐτεός and Armenian stoyg 'true' (< *stewwā), is difficult; the gemination of *w in the ancestor of the Armenian form is irregular, as is the complete loss of h- from *s- in all dialects of Greek. Ruijgh (1987:537), who accepts that κενεός and κενός derive from an earlier u-stem adjective, cites (n. 12) the pair οὖλος 'destructive' (from *ολϝο-) and ὀλοός 'destructive' (from *ολεϝο-, refashioned after θοός) as parallel forms.

172. For the treatment of u-stem adjectives in Armenian see 4.17.

173. I consider Poucha's connection of Tocharian A akäṃtsune 'res, pecunia' < *ṇ-k'en- (1955:1) extremely unlikely. The Sanskrit word for 'empty' śūnya- (from śūna- 'emptiness') could be derived from a root *k'ūn- which would have the same consonantism as the Greek-Armenian root, but a different vowel.

174. The word is also used at [Pʻawstos] 5.7 alongside other words for metal fetters and chains which are used to bind Aršak.

175. For example čʻowan 'rope' translates σχοινίον at Ezek. 27:24; kap 'bond' translates δεσμός at Numb. 30:14; kapan 'bond' translates σειρα at 2 Pet. 2:4, δεσμός at Luke 8:29; toṙn 'rope' translates δεσμός at Prov. 7:22, σειρα at Prov. 5:22; štʻay 'chain' translates ἅλυσις at Luke 8:29; eriz- 'cord' translates κειρία at Prov. 7:16; and malowx 'rope' translates κάμιλος (not κάμηλος!) at Mark 10:25 etc.

176. Solta (1960:330f.) also connected the Sanskrit word, which Mayrhofer (KEWA III 368) derives from a root *k'er-.

177. Pedersen (1924:224), Meillet (1936:142), Schwyzer (1939:57), Porzig (1954:156), Solta (1960:430), Frisk GEW I 863, Chantraine DELG 537, Klingenschmitt (1982:61 n. 2), Arutjunjan (1983:303) and others.

178. Mycenaean ki-wo (κίων) is opposed to ta-to-mo (= σταθμός) in this tablet (PY V 46). In Homer σταθμός means 'pillar' or 'door-post' (also 'stable' or 'pen') while κίων means 'column', and refers to a free-standing construction inside a building. The two terms occur within fifteen lines of each other at Od. 8.458 and 473, both with reference to Alcinous's palace. At 1.458 Nausicaa stands παρὰ σταθμὸν τέγεος to bid farewell to Odysseus, and at 1.473 Demodocus takes up position in the hall πρὸς κίονα μακρόν (see further LfrgE II 1430 for other occurrences of κίων in early Greek epic).

179. Since Schmitt's (1972a) survey, the fullest treatments of the fate of *-w- are given by Greppin (1972), Eichner (1978:148–156), Godel (1982) and Olsen (1984 and 1986). I shall not discuss these theories and their shortcomings here except where they relate directly to siwn.

180. Eichner takes areg to be the old genitive of arew, on the grounds that in the Bible areg kʻałakʻ translates ἡλίου πόλις (e.g. Exodus 1:11) and areg atber translates πηγῆς ἡλίου (Josh. 15:7). He also cites other place names incorporating areg in Classical authors. However, arewow is used as a genitive already in the translation of the Gospels (e.g. Matt. 13:6). The form areg in areg kʻałakʻ can be explained as a development from earlier *aregi kʻałakʻ if this phrase was treated as a compound and accented only on the final syllable of kʻałakʻ. In this case the final -i of aregi would drop by regular vocalic reduction (Godel 1982:10).

181. Followed by Olsen (1984:222).

182. For *erkan* see note 134 at **4.25**.

183. At *Ezekiel* 43:8 *seamk'* is used in opposition to *drand* 'threshold', translating Greek φλία and πρόθυρον respectively.

184. Schindler also mentions the Indo-Iranian use of the suffix to form agent nouns from verbal roots.

185. So Arutjunjan (1983:303).

186. Further possibilities of early Armenian loans made before the sound-shift are given by de Lamberterie (1978:245–262) who takes *arcat'* 'silver', *partêz* 'garden' and *arciw* 'eagle' to be loans from Iranian, Morani (1981a:22), and Jahowkyan (1987:307) who adds *t'owz* 'fig' from the same prototype as Greek σῦκον (Boeotian τῦκον) and Latin *ficus*; see also **2.4.5** and **4.14**.

187. It also translates ἴβις at *Isaiah* 34:11.

188. For the metathesis compare τίκτω 'I beget, give birth to' from the root τεκ-.

189. Meillet's theory is rejected by Hiersche (1964:232–253), de Lamberterie (1974:41), Greppin (1984b) and Lindeman (1987:87). However Klingenschmitt (1982:168–170), Mayrhofer (1986:98f.) and Szemerényi (1990:69f.) follow Meillet's analysis. Note however that the only parallels for the reconstruction of initial *k^h- are onomatopoeic or 'expressive' formations (Pokorny *IEW* 634).

190. Compare *joyl* 'smelted, cast', an *-l* participle from the root *$g'hew$-* 'pour' (Klingenschmitt 1982:57).

191. The semantic discrepancy between *xałam* 'I march' and *xałał* 'peace' argues against Leroy's theory (1986:73) that *xałał* can be derived from a reduplicated formation from *xał* 'game'. Leroy compares Greek γελάω and γαλήνη for the semantic relationship between 'game' and 'peace', but as was shown above at **4.26**, the Greek words may both be derived from a base meaning 'shine'.

192. Francis posited that *k^hḷ$h_2$enti* might give χόλαισι in Aeolic by regular sound change (1974:24 n. 32), but this is highly questionable.

193. Masson (1987:46f.) connects Greek χαλάω and derivatives with the Semitic root ḪLL 'loosen, relax'. Armenian *xałał* may also be plausibly connected with the Semitic words (note, for example Arabic *ḥalal* 'slackening of the tendons').

194. The word μητρυιά 'step-mother' is not found in the Greek Bible, which may explain the absence of Armenian *mawrow*. The phrase γυνή πατρός 'father's wife' (or possibly 'father's concubine') at *Lev.* 18:8 is translated by a periphrasis *kin hawr* (lit. 'father's wife') rather than by *mawrow*; but this probably arises from a close rendering of the text.

195. In the form *mowrow mêr*, etc.; see Ačaṙyan *HAB* s.v.

196. For the phonetic developments compare *marb* < *$m\bar{a}trb^hi(s)$*, instrumental of *mayr*, and *cowngk'* 'knees' < *$g'onw\bar{\i}$* (with final *g* < *w* perhaps by analogy to genitive *cowngac'*).

197. The Armenian reflex of *-wy-* is uncertain; see note 58 at **2.4**; *mawrow* could derive from *$m\bar{a}truy$-* or *$m\bar{a}truwy$-* in any case (so also Klingenschmitt 1982:105).

198. G. Schmidt proposes (1973:74f.) that the form *maHtruyo-* (*sic*) has replaced earlier and regular *maHtrwyo-* by analogy to regular *pHtruyo-*, which itself was replaced by *pHtrwyo-* in the ancestor of Sanskrit by analogy to *maHtrwyo-*. It is unfortunate for this theory that there is so little evidence for the 'regular' forms. Mayrhofer (1986:138 n. 172) reconstructs *$ph_1trwiyo$-* and *$m\bar{a}truwiy\bar{a}$-*.

199. Solta (1960:187) and Hamp (1983a:5f.) emphasise the significance of this Greek-Armenian correspondence.

200. The use of the plural is compared by Meillet to other words which describe mental processes which are *pluralia tantum* (*MSL* 17 (1911) p. 30, reprinted in 1962:152); Meillet also noted the use of the singular in set phrases.

201. See also Isebaert (1992:201), who reconstructs a present *$m\acute{e}d$-$t(i)$* (third person singular), *$m\acute{e}d$-$nt(i)$* (third person plural) for this root.

202. Armenian usually continues inherited *s*-stems as *o*-stems, for example *erek* (*o*-stem) 'evening' beside Greek ἔρεβος 'darkness', but the *a*-stem declension of *mitk'* may be, as Hamp (1983a:6) suggests, built upon the neuter plural. Armenian has lost the neuter gender, and the plural marker *-a* may have been reinterpreted as an *a*-stem morph at some time in the prehistory of the language; compare the *a*-stem *artasowk'* 'tears' which has replaced an earlier neuter plural.

203. Schindler lists the following examples: Vedic *ágas*- 'sin' (: Greek ἄγος 'pollution, guilt'), Vedic *vásas*- 'clothing', Vedic *váhas*- 'offering', Greek γῆρας 'old age' (: γέρας 'honour'), Greek ἦθος 'custom' (: ἔθος 'custom'), Greek μήδεα and μέδεα both 'genitals', Greek ῥῆγος and ῥέγος both 'rug, blanket', Old Irish *síd* (**sēdos*) 'abode of the gods'; Isebaert (1992:203) considers the possibility that roots which show this ablaut pattern for the *s*-stem noun also form present tense conjugations of the '*proterodynamisch*' type.

204. As noted at **4.4** above, many Armenian nouns have generalised the original nominative formation and ablaut throughout the paradigm at the expense of the oblique cases.

205. See Pokorny *IEW* 705f. and Benveniste (1969b:122–132) for the Indo-European forms.

206. The Armenian verb renders Greek δοξάζω 'honour' (at e.g. 1 *Kings* 15:30) and τιμάω (*Prov.* 4:8) in the Armenian Bible translation, and the derived noun *mecarank'* translates Greek τιμή 'honour' (note *Sirach* 3:11 where *mecarank'* = τιμή is opposed to *p'aṙk'* 'glory' = δόξα).

207. De Lamberterie (1990:I.160f.) explains the present *merjenam* as a new formation derived from the aorist *merjec'ay*, and posits that the older present is *merjim* (*Psalms* 103:32 etc.). However, the textual evidence is against this. There are ten present-stem forms from *merjenam* in the oldest Armenian manuscripts of the Gospels (edited by Künzle 1984; the figures are taken from his *Lexikon* to the edition), and none from *merjim*, although the participle *merjeal* does occur five times. Moreover, there are only three other verbs of the pattern: present -*enam*, aorist -*ec'ay*, *arbenam* 'I get drunk' (compare *arbi* 'I drank' suppletive aorist of *ǝmpem* 'I drink'), *yagenam* 'I am sated', by-form of *yagim*, and *yamenam* 'I linger', whereas the pattern: present -*im*, aorist -*ec'ay*, is common. It is therefore more probable that the -*im* form stems from the attraction of the anomalous verb into a larger class. This is demonstrably the case for the form *arbim* which is first attested in the Armenian translation of Plato, while *arbenam* is used in the Bible translation. Note also that *arbeal* 'drunk' is used in the Bible as a participle for *arbenam* 'I get drunk' as well as *ǝmpem* 'I drink' (for example at *Acts* 2:15 *arbeal ic'en* translates μεθύουσιν) and that consequently the participle *merjeal* need not imply a present stem *merj*-.

208. It is interesting to note that the Authorised Version translates ἐγγίζω by 'be at hand', and that ἐγγύς itself may be derived from **en gu-s* 'in the hand' (Frisk *GEW* I 437) or **en gus(i)* 'in the hands' (Szemerényi 1971:666).

209. *LSJ* gloss ἀπαράσσω as 'crush' here, but the meaning 'strike off' is recommended by the *LfrgE* I 1184.

210. Compare the connection of ἄχρι with the verb χραύω 'I scrape' (Schwyzer & Debrunner 1950:487 n. 7), cited by Mader (*LfrgE* I 1780) who proposes a basic meaning of 'reaching' or 'touching' for the adverb.

211. See Schindler (1967a:244–249) for the reconstruction of the original paradigm of this word and explanation of the Greek, Armenian and Tocharian anomalies.

212. Pokorny *IEW* 1175, Schindler (1967b:300 n. 1) and Nussbaum (1986:82f.). Nussbaum gives further examples of vowel reduction in set prepositional phrases (e.g. ἐπικάρ 'head-first').

213. Bader (1982:132ff.) also connects *mox* and μέχρι, but derives the forms from a pronominal base **me-g'ʰ*- with different suffixes. The Armenian word seems to show the same semantic development at *Romans* 16:20 where *merj ǝnd merj* translates Greek ἐν τάχει (the passage is noted by de Lamberterie 1990:I.161, who uses it to support his hypothesis that *merj* is actually cognate with Greek βραχύς, etc., with original meaning 'at a short distance'; this theory suffers from the need to posit an ablaut **merg'ʰ*- to explain the Armenian form as against **mr̥g'ʰ*- in Greek, Indo-Iranian and Germanic, and perhaps **mreg'ʰw*- for Latin *brevis* (cf. Frisk *GEW* s.v. βραχύς and Ernout & Meillet *DELL* s.v. *brevis*)).

214. Compare English *sucker*, first of an animal, later extended to plants, and *scion*, first meaning 'shoot'; a further example may be Greek πόρθος 'calf' if related to Hittite *paršdu*- 'shoot'. Further examples of the metaphorical connection of 'young animal' and 'young plant' from French (*élève*), Latin (*pullus*), Armenian (*ort* 'calf, vine', and *erinj*, 'heifer, vine'), together with a discussion of the Greek derivatives μοσχεύω and μόσχευμα, are given by Perpillou (1981).

215. In *Egyetemes Philologiae Közlöny* 61 (1937), 1–23; the article is only known to me through Szemerényi's summary in (1977b:4).

216. On the Greek and Hebrew terms for cattle in the Bible see Hastings (1898–1904) s.v. 'calf', 'ox' and 'food' (in particular vol. II, p. 35 col. b).

217. Băltăceanu (1980:22) connected *mozi* to Rumanian *muşcoi* 'mule', which, like

Albanian *mushk* 'mule' is likely to derive from the 'Mediterranean' word which lies behind Greek μυχλός 'mule' and Latin *mūlus* 'mule' (< **mukslo-* ?) with metathesis of **-ks-* > **-sk-* (Pisani 1950a:187).

218. The German word may be a loan from Latin *nocturnus* (cf. Frisk *GEW* II 319).

219. Pedersen's derivation of *hac'* 'bread' from **pat-ti-* has not met with general acceptance; see Charpentier (1909:241 f.) and Ačaṙyan *HAB* s.v. for over ten other etymologies of the word.

220. The comparisons are also dismissed by Olsen (1985:8 n. 10), but for different reasons. For the root **mag'-* in Armenian see Meillet (*MSL* 19 (1914) p. 122, reprinted in 1977:159), and de Lamberterie (1980:30 f.).

221. In Proto-Indo-European the cluster **-t-t-* appears to have had a phonetic representation **-t͡st-* (discussed most recently by Mayrhofer 1986:110 f. and Szemerényi 1990:108 f.). If the theory of the development of **-tt-* to Armenian *-wt'-* given here is correct, it implies that **-t͡st-* was simplified to **-tt-* at an early stage of Armenian. The same development took place (independently) in the ancestor of the Indo-Aryan language group.

222. Klingenschmitt (1982:167 n. 13); compare the later spread of form with a secondary privative α- in Greek, such as ἀνωφελής 'useless' beside earlier (Mycenaean) *no-pe-re-a₂*.

223. Mayrhofer (1986:109) with references to earlier literature.

224. Szemerényi's explanation is motivated by his desire to derive the Proto-Indo-European term for 'sister-in-law' from a compound **sunu-sūs*.

224A. De Lamberterie's article on the Greek verbs ὀφέλλω and their semantic and formal relationship to the Armenian forms (de Lamberterie 1992) only became available to me after this was written. De Lamberterie accepts the connection of the Greek and Armenian forms and relates them all to the same root, which he reconstructs as **h₃bʰel-*.

225. Leumann (1950:120 f.) explains the formal and semantic development of ὠφελέω.

226. Armenian *aweli* translates πλεῖον 'more', etc., for example *Matt.* 20:10; *aṙawelowm* translates περισσεύω 'be abundant' at *Matt.* 5:20, 2 *Corinthians* 9:12; *yawelowm* translates προστίθημι 'add to' at *Matt.* 6:27, *Luke* 3:20.

227. Hamp (1982c:230), Klingenschmitt (1982:105 n. 27), Mayrhofer (1986:142), Ruijgh (1986:385), Beekes (1988:76) and others reconstruct an original root **h₃bʰel-*.

228. Hamp (1983a:11 f.) compares (*y*)*awelowm* directly to Greek ὀφέλλω by deriving Greek *-λλ-* from **-lw-*, thus showing a thematic **-we/o-* suffix beside athematic **-u-* in Armenian. This rests on an irregular change of **-lw-* to *-λλ-*, for which Hamp parallels πολλός from **polwo-*. This is by no means certain; Szemerényi (1974) has pointed out the shortcomings of this and other explanations of πολλός, and derives the form from πολλά < **πολγά < **πολέα, although de Lamberterie (1990:II.632 f.), reverts to the earlier derivation from the feminine **πολϝγα. The sequence **-lw-* developed differently elsewhere; compare (Attic) ὅλος from **holwo-* (Lejeune 1972:159).

229. Klingenschmitt (1982:235) discusses the origins of the Armenian *-owm* conjugation. Meillet interpreted *awelowm* as a denominative to a lost noun **awel* (1936:112), but there is little evidence to support the theory of denominatives in the *-owm* class, as the only other possible example seems to be *argelowm* 'I hinder' from *argel* 'hindrance'. Note also that verbs with stem-final *-l* show a particular affinity for the *-owm* conjugation.

230. The Arcadian form ϝοφληκόσι (*IG* V 262 line 18, from Mantinea) cannot be taken as proof of an initial **w-* in ὀφείλω in the light of Mycenaean (see Szemerényi 1964:201, Strunk 1978:209 f.). On the development of ὀφείλω and ὀφλισκάνω in Greek see Szemerényi (1964:199 ff.) and Hamp (1982c:227 f.).

231. Slings (1975:6) takes ὤφλον (with Mycenaean *jo-o-po-ro* (MY Ge 602) interpreted as yω-ώφλον) as the original aorist formation and ὄφελε as the original imperfect, later reinterpreted as an aorist. Since several Armenian aorists continue earlier imperfect formations (e.g. *eber* 'he carried'), it does not affect the argument if the equation is between ὄφελε and *awel* as original imperfects.

232. Jahowkyan (1970:21) connected *yawelowm* with the Urartian word *abilidu* 'join, increase', and Arutjunjan (1983:272) thinks Greek and Armenian may have both borrowed a Near-Eastern word. The anomalous shape of the root offers some support for this theory.

233. Pisani also connected Albanian *s* 'not', following Pedersen (1982:2, reprinted from *KZ* 36 (1900) p. 341).

234. Cowgill compares the development of **-ayemi* to *-am* in the Armenian *-am* conjugation for the change of **oyu kʷ-* to **okʷ*, but this is not a conclusive parallel. Analogy to athematic

verbs in *-ā- and to the other conjugations is likely to have played a large part in the creation of the Armenian -am conjugation (Klingenschmitt 1982:91).

235. The preposition is found principally in Lesbian, Boeotian, Arcadian (as πε(τ)) and Argolic (see further Schwyzer & Debrunner 1950:498f.), and possibly also in Mycenaean pe-da (in pe-da wa-tu which can be interpreted as peda wastu 'to the town' KN V 114, Ventris and Chadwick 1973:569).

236. Hübschmann (1897:467), Meillet (1931a:43), Schwyzer & Debrunner (1950:499), Frisk GEW II 485, Chantraine DELG 867 and others.

237. Note also that de Lamberterie (1988:230 n. 16) remarks that 'l'isoglosse gréco-arménienne est frappante'.

238. The form het can be nominative, accusative or locative; the form yetoy 'behind' (trans-lates ὄπισθεν at Gen. 18:10) continues a phrase with the ablative i hetoy 'from the footprint of'.

239. Meillet (1931a:43) cites Latvian pêc 'after' from pēdis 'on the footprints', from the same root as the Armenian and Greek forms, and Hamp (1983e) mentions a similar semantic shift for Old Irish éis 'track'.

240. Szemerényi (1964:103 n. 3) and de Lamberterie (1982b:67).

241. Thus Hübschmann (1897:422), Pokorny IEW 797, Solta (1960:125), Greppin (1973b:30 n. 17), Hamp (1983a:9), and others.

242. First formulated by Pedersen (1906:370f.), and defended most recently by Hamp (1985a).

243. See note 3 at **4.1**.

244. A slightly enlarged version of the essay is given in Benveniste (1970).

245. Benveniste (1970:319) cites further examples such as Arabic māl 'possession, sheep' and others but some of his etymologies are open to question. A further example from a modern Armenian dialect is provided by Ačaṙyan HAB III² 224, who cites the Łarabał dialect word aprank' 'possessions, cattle', which derives from Classical Armenian aprank' 'life, livelihood'.

246. Buck (1949:770) connects Modern Irish ealbh 'flock, herd' with Welsh elw 'profit' with the gloss 'referring originally to property in cattle'; this would appear to present a counter to Benveniste's hypothesis.

247. Schrader & Nehring (1917–29:I.370f.) give a survey of the practice in Indo-European societies. Benveniste himself does not deny that 'possession mobilière personelle' in practice would amount to no more than cattle (1969a:59).

248. De Lamberterie (1978:276) gives this as one possible explanation of the Armenian word. Other scholars have also rejected Benveniste's theory, for example Gamkrelidze and Ivanov (1984:II.580), who reconstruct an original meaning of 'sheep' for *pek'u- and explain the connection with *pek'- 'comb, etc.' through the fact that *pek'u- originally referred to sheep kept for their wool; they explain the extension in meaning to 'livestock' from the fact that the sheep was the first animal domesticated by the Indo-Europeans. Meid (1989:27 n. 20) also rejects Benveniste's theory.

249. Melena (1987:443f.) also connects the obscure Mycenaean term po-ku-ta which he interprets as pokurtās (p. 455) 'wool plucker, washer'.

250. Pokorny IEW 721, Frisk GEW II 168, Chantraine DELG 663; Hamp connects the Greek word to Welsh blew 'hair' < *mles-wo- (most recently Hamp 1982a:61). Greppin (1981) attempts to relate μαλλός to the Armenian hapax mal 'male sheep' which only occurs in the commentary of Grigor Magistros on the Armenian translation of Dionysios Thrax (Adontz 1915:239), but, as Hamp has shown (Hamp 1982a:61f.), Greppin never fully clarifies the exact semantic and morphological relations between the terms. The Armenian word is better explained as a borrowing from Arabic māl 'possession' with its transferred meaning 'sheep' (so Ačaṙyan HAB III² 224).

251. The Greek form *πολιϝος rather than *πολϝος may be due to influence of πελιτνός 'livid' which has replaced *πελιτός by analogy to a feminine *πελιτνι-, cf. Sanskrit palitá-, feminine páliknī (for *pálitnī) cited by grammarians.

252. Other examples of Armenian reflexes of forms in *-iwo- (such as t'iw 'number' and c'iw 'roof') are given by Eichner (1978:153).

253. For this suffix see also **4.2** and **4.12**.

254. See also Meillet (MSL 17 (1911) p. 34f., reprinted in 1962:156f.), who thinks the suffix indicates a collective or abstract nuance; he also gives the examples of č'arik' 'evil' < č'ar 'bad' and kełcik' 'dissimulation' < kełc 'false'.

255. Meillet's first objection was still seen as valid by Arutjunjan (1983:299).
256. Note also Cretan (Gortyn) πρείγυς.
257. In this connection it is relevant to note that Latin has no *u*-stem adjectives.
258. The comparison is not mentioned by Pedersen (1924:225) or Arutjunjan (1983).
259. So Pokorny *IEW* 845, Solta (1960:374f.), Frisk *GEW* II 591, Chantraine *DELG* 936, Bailey (1971:xvf.), Schmitt (1981:180), Klingenschmitt (1982:143f.) and others.
260. The Celtic and Germanic connections are accepted by Solta (1960:374), but Frisk (*GEW* II 591f.) dismissed the Germanic cognate.
261. Pedersen's connection (1906:343) of *aragil* 'stork' with Sanskrit *krakara-* (or *kṛkara-*) 'partridge' is too uncertain to be of any weight.
262. See Pedersen (1906:343), Winter (1962:259), and Godel (1975:78f.); the comparison of *srownk'* 'leg' with Latin *crūs* does not necessarily, as Schmitt (1981:75) thinks, argue against this. The word *srownk'* may not derive from a form with an initial cluster. Other clusters of the shape **Cr* have been metathesised; *srownk'* could derive from **k'ē/ōr-* (Pedersen *loc. cit.*; see also Kortlandt 1985:10) or **k'ṛr-*, via **sᵤr-* (Winter 1962:260).
263. Schindler further connected Middle Irish *cri* 'body' (1972:67), Old High German *href* 'body' (1967b:298) and Latin *corpus* 'body' < **kʷṛp-os* (1975c:265) with this root noun.
264. Thus Hübschmann (1897:443), Pokorny *IEW* 846, Schmitt (1981:57). Greek πρωκτός may equally well derive from a zero grade **pṛh₃k'to-*.
265. In terms of the laryngeal theory, this means that the resonant is vocalised not the laryngeal; see Mayrhofer (1986:128).
266. Other explanations of the loss of the inter-consonantal laryngeal in *dowstr* are given by Hamp (1970) and Szemerényi (1977a:20 n. 71). The former sees a special development of the sequence **-gHT-* > *-sT-*; the latter derives *dowstr* by syncope from **dusutir*; the internal **u* supposedly preserves a vocalic reflex of the laryngeal which has developed to **u* by 'assimilation'.
267. Thus Klingenschmitt (1970:80 and 86 n. 9).
268. A work only available to me through the summaries of Peters (1986:366 n. 7), Kortlandt (1987a) and Beekes (1988:77).
269. Jahowkyan (1967:165 n. 10) denies that the cluster **-k't-* develops to *-st-* in Armenian, citing the counter-examples of *owt'* 'eight' < **ok'tōw* and *arj* 'bear' < **ark'to-* (*sic*). On the same page, however, he derives *dowstr* 'daughter' < **dhuk'ter* < **dhugɔter*. It is easier to derive *owt'* from a form **optō* (by analogy to **septm̥*, cf. Meillet 1936:32) than to assume that **-k't-* developed to *-wt'-* and to seek a different explanation for *dowstr* (Pedersen (1906:349f.) explained the different treatments of the cluster by the effect of the following vowel).
270. The 'additional' *-n* may derive from an earlier accusative form, or it may reflect a later suffix. The *n*-declension has become the standard declension class for body-parts in Armenian (see the lists of body-parts with additional *-n* given at Jahowkyan 1959:255f., Winter 1986:19 and Stempel 1990:54).
271. This connection is made by Hübschmann (1897:443) and Jahowkyan (1967:165 n. 10).
272. The root noun reconstructed cannot be related to any Indo-European root, but it would seem to correspond to root nouns of the type of **pod-* 'foot' (Schindler 1972:36). The **-t-* may represent a secondary suffix, since the root shape **prek't-* would be unusual.
273. There are other examples of an Armenian ablaut between *-ow-* < **-ō-* and *-a-*, for example *dowrgn* 'potter's wheel' and *darnam* 'I turn'.
274. Examples of each usage are found at *Acts* 6:13, *John* 8:44, *Matthew* 7:15 and *Matthew* 5:11 respectively. Armenian *sowt* translates the Greek noun ψεῦδος (*John* 8:44) in the phrase λάλει τὸ ψεῦδος 'tell a lie', for which the Armenian gives *xawsic'i sowt*; this is probably an adverbial usage of the adjective rather than evidence that *sowt* also means 'lie'.
275. For example, ψεῦδος 'lie' *Il.* 2.81, etc., ψεύδομαι 'I lie' *Il.* 4.404, etc., ψευδής 'false' *Il.* 4.235, ψεύστης 'liar' *Il.* 24.261.
276. There is certainly no need to follow Arutjunjan (1983:313f.) in seeing the development to *s-* as evidence of substrate influence.
277. There are no unambiguous examples of the change **eu* to *oy* and this diphthong may have developed differently; de Lamberterie (1982c:81) sees a regular development of inherited **-eu-* to *-iw-* (as in *hiwcanim* 'be sick' < **seug'-*, *ařiwc* 'lion' < **reug'-* and *hiwsn* 'carpenter' < **peuk'-*; see also Ałabekyan 1981:60f.). But Ravnæs (1988:227f.) dismisses de Lamberterie's

examples, and sees support for the traditional view in the suffix -oyt', which he connects with Greek -ευσις.

278. The development of k'own is discussed by Pisani (1951:57). De Lamberterie (1978:281) gives other examples of possible 'irregular' vocalic reduction, including owt''eight' < *optō, and iž 'snake' < *êž.

279. The connection was also made in ancient times; the scholiast at Theocritus 12.24 relates that a pimple (ψυδράκιον) on the nose is reputedly caused by telling a lie.

280. Apparently transitive at Iliad 14.40, see Janko (1992) ad loc.

281. The co-existence of πτώξ and πτάξ points to an original ablauting athematic noun. For the reconstruction of nouns of this type see Schindler (1972:34f.).

281A. Hackstein has recently proposed a new etymology for the Greek forms, in an article which only became available to me after this was written (Hackstein 1992). He rejects the derivation of πτήσσω etc. from a root *pteh₂k-, which he considers an unlikely root shape for Proto-Indo-European, but proposes to connect the Greek verb with Tocharian B pyāktsi 'hit' and to reconstruct a root *pyeh₂-k- 'shock'. If this etymology is correct, the Greek-Armenian connection will have to be dropped.

282. See Ačaṙyan HAB II² 184f. for a survey of the large number of Armenian words which are derived from a root t'iṙ- and related forms. The connection of the Armenian words with the Indo-European root is doubted by Mayrhofer (KEWA II 204), and Klingenschmitt (1982:71).

283. All these words may be loaned from a 'Mediterranean' source, or else the Armenian word could be loaned from Greek (Hübschmann 1897:374f.) but Ačaṙyan (HAB s.v.), Solta (1960:420) and Arutjunjan (1983:286) include t'ełi among the vocabulary inherited from Indo-European.

284. The connection is not accepted by Frisk (GEW II 615f.) or Chantraine (DELG 950) but is defended by Arutjunjan (1983:287, 1988:172) and de Lamberterie (1990:I.218 n. 1). The three languages appear to have made independent derivations from a root *pet-/*pt- 'flat' (probably connected with *pet- 'spread'; Pokorny IEW 824).

285. See further Klingenschmitt (1982:207) for discussion of this verb. Pedersen (1906:342) reconstructed *spty- 'spit' to account for the divergent Indo-European derivatives of this verbal root. Greppin's theory that Armenian forms in t- afford a 'unique parallel' (1982:347) to Greek πτ- is unfounded. There is no evidence to assume that Armenian has undergone a change of *py- to *pt-. Where Armenian t- corresponds to Greek πτ-, both forms derive from a Proto-Indo-European initial cluster *pt-. This is a straightforward phonetic correspondence and is not indicative of a close relationship.

286. Klingenschmitt (1982:75–79). Watkins (1971) and Jasanoff (1978) trace the function, spread and origin of the verbal suffix *-ē- in Indo-European languages. There is no need to follow Klingenschmitt in equating -č'- directly with *-sk-, see further 4.60.

287. Klingenschmitt (1975:77) also connected Tocharian A tpuk- B tuk- 'be hidden' but he does not mention this connection in his later work on the Armenian verb (1982). K. T. Schmidt, following van Windekens (1976 s.v. ptuk-) connects the Tocharian verbs with the Tocharian A form ptuk(k) 'darkness' and Sanskrit tvac- 'cover' (1987:295f.).

288. For example barwok' 'good' alongside bari 'good', borbok' 'hot' alongside borb 'heat'. On the labio-velar suffixes in Armenian see further Frisk loc. cit., Meillet (MSL 15 (1909) p. 355, reprinted in 1977:134) and Jahowkyan (1987:432).

289. The Armenian verb is very frequent in texts from the earliest period of the literature; note also the derivative hasown 'ripe, powerful', and the synchronically anomalous form hasow which only occurs in the phrase hasow linim 'I have power over', which translates καταλαμβάνω at John 1:5.

290. Klingenschmitt first proposed this etymology in (1975:77 n. 5), and enlarged upon it in (1982:213). De Lamberterie first published his findings in (1990:I.294f.).

291. Hübschmann (1897:464), Meillet (1936:106), Ačaṙyan HAB III² 46f., Pokorny IEW 316, Winter (1962:256), Olsen (1985:15), etc. Klingenschmitt (1982:212) also sees this as a possible explanation for the Armenian verb.

292. This word has prompted many attempts at explanation; the theories of Hübschmann (1897:477), Pedersen (1906:433), Grammont (1916:233), Szemerényi (1960c:26 n. 119) and Hamp (1986a) all rely upon the loss of *-n- before *-s- < *-k-. Winter (1992b:359) envisages a loss of *-n- before *-x- < *-kʷ- and Feydit (1982:93) posits a change of *-nK- > *-hy- > -y-.

293. Greppin (1973a and 1973b) proposed the theory that *HV- regularly gives Armenian hV- (followed by Kortlandt (1983) and others), and compared the initial h- of hasanem with initial ḫ- in Hittite ḫenkzi 'divides' from *(h₁)n̥kʷ- (1973a:71); Greppin's theory has not, however, met with general acceptance (see also note 3 at **4.1**).

294. Van Windekens (1976:427), Klingenschmitt (1982:213 n. 69); de Lamberterie derives the verbal roots from a base *seh₁-/ *sey-, which also underlies Greek ἰθύς 'straight', Vedic sādhú- 'straight', etc. (1990:I.290–299).

295. The term may also occur in Mycenaean with reference to the boiling of cloth, if the reading of e-we-pe-se-so-me-na (MY Oe 127, coming after pa-we-a₂ 'cloth') as eu hepsēsomena 'to be well boiled' is correct (Ventris and Chadwick 1973:547); for criticism of this theory see Beekes (1969:69) who connects the form with the root of ὑφαίνω 'I weave'.

296. Meillet (BSL 36 (1935) p. 111, reprinted in 1977:276, and 1936:39) thought that the Armenian form might derive from *-pʰ-, but, as was discussed at **4.37**, the reconstruction of a 'voiceless aspirate' series for the ancestor of Armenian is very uncertain.

297. For the second development compare ἐχθρός < *eks-tro-.

298. See also Szemerényi (1990:102f.) for possible Indo-European root shapes. Hamp (1983a:11) reconstructs a root *sep- which he thinks received an enlargement *-s- in Greek and *-H- in Armenian.

299. The Armenian word is also seen as an early loan by Arutjunjan (1983:282) and Jahowkyan (1987:302).

300. Thus Klingenschmitt derives hac'i from a root *osk- with a velar. Normier (1981) reconstructs *oks- for this word.

301. y-aławt's kam 'I stand in prayer' regularly translates Greek προσεύχομαι in the Gospels, e.g. at Matthew 6:5–7.

302. The noun amawt' is related to the verb amač'em 'I am ashamed', aorist amač'ec'i. The etymology of this word is uncertain; Klingenschmitt (1982:68f.) tentatively connects Greek μῶμος 'blame'.

303. Thus Godel (1975:80), who follows Pedersen (1906:348) in seeing a development of guttural to w before *t (see also **2.3.1**).

304. See also **4.57** for guttural suffixes in Armenian.

305. The denominative veb ałersem translates ἱκετεύω e.g. at Job 19:17.

306. The Mycenaean dative e-me (PY Ta 641) still retains the original -m-.

307. The form mioj and the usage of the Armenian term as an indefinite article was discussed at **3.2.1.2**.

308. The Latin word has thus been compared to Greek χίλιοι 'thousand' and Vedic sahásram, see Mayrhofer KEWA III 451 f. for discussion and literature.

309. A similar explanation is given by Meillet (REArm 5 (1925) p. 1f., reprinted in 1977:225f.); see also Darms (1976:29 n. 15).

310. Note that Winter (1992a:101) also derives the Tocharian feminine forms from *smih₂.

311. Discounting the highly doubtful connection of Greek ῥόμβος 'bull-roarer' with Armenian r̄owmb 'missile' put forward by Jahowkyan (1976:49).

312. For full discussion of the Classical pronunciation of words with initial r- and r̄- see Feydit (1982:81ff.).

313. A similar process may have taken place in Greek (see **2.2**). Some scholars see all cases of Greek prothesis before *r- as the reflex of an original laryngeal consonant, on the grounds that the parent language itself lacked roots with initial *r- (e.g. Kortlandt 1987a:62f. following Lehmann 1951).

314. Jensen (1959:21); the pair ǝmpem 'I drink', owmp 'drink' does not contradict this. The noun owmp is only attested in the Armenian translation of the τέχνη attributed to Dionysios Thrax (Adontz 1915:12) and is probably an analogous formation from ǝmpem (Vogt 1988:132, reprinted from 1938:337, and Klingenschmitt 1982:156).

315. See Solta (1960:429 fn.) and Jahowkyan (1987:302) for (very doubtful) suggestions of other forms in Mediterranean languages which may be related.

316. See Leumann (1957) for a full history of the Greek words of this family.

317. De Lamberterie (1990:I.174) follows Meillet's tentative connection of Latin tūtus to this root (DELL s.v. tueor), and sees the base meaning of the root as 'être fort, en sécurité' (1990:I.173).

318. Hamp (1988–9:26) gives a similar reconstruction, *twH_a-wo-, but sees the *-wo- suffix

as Indo-European, rather than as a Greek innovation. This theory has the disadvantage of leaving ταῦς unexplained. De Lamberterie (1990:I.171–178), who accepts Godel's connection of σῶς and k'aw, gives a full account of the phonetic and morphological developments of the root in Greek and Indo-Iranian. He derives the form σαϝο- from a zero-grade *twa- formed analogically from the full grade of the *thème II* of the root, *tweH₂- (> *twā-); a reformation which also took place, in his view, in Armenian (1990:I.177). See also the discussion of the posited changes of *-iH-/*-uH- to *-yā-/*-wā-, etc. at **2.3.2**.

319. See on κενός (**4.33**) above for the transfer of u-stems to thematics in Greek.

320. Olsen (1989b:7 n. 7) attempts to connect k'aw to the Proto-Indo-European root *puH- (Pokorny *IEW* 827), with an uncertain sound change of *pw- to kʿ; see also **2.3.2**.

321. Bader (1979:208 and 214 n. 78) gives examples of the Homeric and Vedic usages of εἷμαι and *vaste*; see also *LfrgE* II 602 f. for the Homeric usage. Eichner (1969) gives a survey of all the Indo-European derivatives of the root, and detailed discussion of the Hittite cognate *wešš-/waššiya-* 'wear, put on'.

322. The normal Homeric orthography ἕννυμαι may be an Atticism (Wackernagel 1916:16).

323. Rix thinks that *-συ- developed differently over a 'Morphemgrenze' (1976:79; cf. also Slings 1975:6).

324. For other examples of this preverb see Hübschmann (1976:416–422, reprinted from *IF* 19 (1906) pp. 460–466).

325. See Bader (1979:193 f.) who thinks that the use of a *-nu- suffix was part of the (late) Proto-Indo-European morphological inventory (*passim* and especially 223 f.).

326. The Hittite third singular form *wešta* 'he wears' confirms this reconstruction (Eichner 1969:35).

327. See further Narten (1968:14–15, especially notes 33 and 43).

328. De Lamberterie (1978–9:40) mentions the phrase *or jri egit zastowacatowr šnorhsn* 'who freely found the divine favour' in Ełišê, but here the conjunction of *jri* 'freely' and *egit* 'found' must be a secondary development.

329. If the connection is mentioned in Hübschmann (1897), Solta (1960), Ačaṟyan's *Hayeren armatakan baṟaran* or Arutjunjan (1983), I have given that discussion as the 'source' reference, otherwise I have given a reference to the work in which the connection, or the case for seeing a common development, is first made.

330. See also the discussion of this word at **4.49** above.

331. See Belardi (1950), de Lamberterie (1986:53–54) for criticism of this correspondence.

332. See also the discussion of this word at **2.3.1** above.

333. See also the discussion of this word at **4.56** above.

334. Solta (1960:99 f.) noted that the other Indo-European verbal derivatives of this root meant 'grind', and took the absence of this meaning to be a significant Greek-Armenian agreement. But the Mycenaean term *me-re-ti-ri-ja* 'female grinders of corn' shows that the meaning 'grind' was known early in Greek.

335. See also the discussion of this word at **2.2** above.

336. See also the discussion of this word at **4.56** above.

337. See also the discussion of this word at **4.56** above.

338. See also the discussion of this word at **2.3.1** above.

339. Porzig (1954:157), followed by Makaev (1967:457), also notes that several of the Greek-Armenian correspondences are archaisms. Several other formations which are shared by Greek, Armenian and a minority of other Indo-European languages may also reflect archaisms. For example, the word for 'dream', Greek ὄναρ, Armenian *anowrǰ* and Albanian *ëndërrë*, derives from the archaic *-r/n stem declension class and has been replaced by a derived form *swepn-(i)yom in other languages (Schindler 1966:75–76).

340. For a summary of the exclusive lexical agreements between Greek and Latin see Schwyzer (1939:57–58); between Armenian and Indo-Iranian, Solta (1960:459–460) and Xačaturova (1973).

Notes for Chapter 5

1. Jahowkyan (1983b) (in Russian) lists the Armenian equivalences to the vocabulary items given in Buck (1949) and gives a table showing the relevant Indo-European roots and their presence or absence in the other Indo-European languages. The actual results of the survey are given in Jahowkyan (1980:8). Jahowkyan (1987:105–204) (in Armenian) in essence repeats the material given in Jahowkyan (1983b), but gives a much fuller account of the method and the etymological considerations behind the exercise; the results of the survey are given in (1987:203) and are substantially different from the earlier results owing to 'refinement' of the material.

2. Jahowkyan also counts the 'partial presence (incomplete expression of the feature)' by half a point, while the shared presence is counted as one point (1980:7).

3. Jahowkyan does not give a figure for Indo-Iranian cognates to the Armenian vocabulary, but this can be calculated to be 720 from his table.

4. Bird (1982:9) counts the number of times each of the Indo-European languages is listed in the entries in Pokorny *IEW*. Greek words are cited in 1235 of the 2044 articles in the *IEW* (60.4%) a figure which is only topped by Germanic (1377 entries, or 67.4%); the Germanic figure combines entries from the different Germanic languages.

Notes for Chapter 6

1. Thus Pedersen (1923:225), Meillet (1936:142), Rix (1976:8) and others.

2. See the discussion of *$dw\bar{a}ro$- (*$dweh_2ro$-) 'long-lasting' (**4.15**), *$g^w\!\!\hat{\bar{\jmath}}h_2no$- 'acorn' (**4.30**), *$prep$- 'appear' (**4.53**), *$ps(e)ud$- 'lie' (**4.55**), and *wes-nu- 'clothe' (**4.64**).

3. See **4.1** (*aig'- 'goat'), **4.2** (*$al(h_1)$- 'grind'), **4.3** (*$al\bar{o}wpek$'- 'fox'), **4.7** (*ar- 'fit'), **4.32** (*$g^{'h}iyom$- 'snow'), **4.36** (*$(i)k^u\bar{\imath}no$- 'kite') and **4.54** (*$p\bar{r}k't$- 'anus').

4. The important lexical agreements between the three languages are (excluding those mentioned in the previous note): use of a derived form of *mer- 'die' to denote the concept 'mortal man' (Greek βροτός 'mortal', Armenian *mard* 'man' and Avestan *maš(ii)a*- 'man'); Greek ἀρήν 'lamb', Armenian *gaŕn* 'lamb' and Sanskrit *uraṇa*- 'lamb'; Greek ἄρνυμαι 'win, gain', Armenian *aŕnowm* 'take' and Avestan *ərənauu*- 'grant'; Greek γέρων 'old man', Armenian *cer* 'old man' and Sanskrit *jarant*- 'old man'; Greek στήνιον 'breast', Armenian *stin* 'breast' and Sanskrit *stana*- 'breast'.

5. Euler (1979:18–23) gives a survey of the scholarly literature dealing with the similarities between Greek and Indo-Iranian and supporting their close relationship.

6. In addition to the discussion of the agreements between Armenian and Indo-Iranian by Porzig (1954:161 f.) note also the investigation of Armenian-Sanskrit lexical agreements by Xačaturova (1973), and the new agreements put forward by de Lamberterie (1986) (the preverb *ni-, unique to the two languages, and the syntax of adverbs of place).

REFERENCES

Abbreviations for Greek authors and works follow those used in the *Greek-English Lexicon* of H. G. Liddell and R. Scott, rev. H. Jones (1940) pp. xvi–xxxviii, except for the titles of the books of the Bible, where the abbreviations follow those used in *The Shorter Oxford English Dictionary* 3rd ed. (1944, Oxford: Oxford University Press) p. xxi. All other abbreviations follow those used in the *Bibliographie Linguistique publiée par le Comité International Permanent des Linguistes* (Kluwer: Dordrecht, Boston, London) except for the following:

AnnIPhO   *Annuaire de l'Institut de Philologie et d'Histoire Orientales et Slaves*, Bruxelles.

DELG   *Dictionnaire étymologique de la langue grecque*, P. Chantraine, (1968–1980), 4 vols, Paris: Klincksieck.

DELL   *Dictionnaire étymologique de la langue latine*, 4th ed., A. Ernout and A. Meillet, (1959), Paris: Klincksieck.

EWA   *Etymologisches Wörterbuch des Altindoarischen*, M. Mayrhofer, (1986– in progress), Heidelberg: Winter.

GEW   *Griechisches etymologisches Wörterbuch*, H. Frisk, (1960–1972), 3 vols, Heidelberg: Winter.

HAB   *Hayeren armatakan baṙaran*, H. Ačaṙyan, 1926–1935, second edition reset and published 1971–1979 in 4 vols, Erevan: University Press.

IEW   *Indogermanisches etymologisches Wörterbuch*, J. Pokorny, (1959), 2 vols, Bern: Francke.

KEWA   *Kurzgefasstes etymologisches Wörterbuch des Altindischen*, M. Mayrhofer, (1956–80), 4 vols, Heidelberg: Winter.

LEW   *Litauisches etymologisches Wörterbuch*, E. Fraenkel, (1962–1965), 2 vols, Heidelberg: Winter.

LfrgE   *Lexikon des frühgriechischen Epos*, begründet von B. Snell, (1955– in progress), Göttingen: Vandenhoeck & Ruprecht.

LSJ   *Greek-English Lexicon*, H. G. Liddell and R. Scott, 9th ed., rev. H. Jones, (1940); *Supplement* E. A. Barber, (ed.), (1968), Oxford: University Press.

MSL   *Mémoires de la société de linguistique de Paris*, Paris, 1868f.

NBHL   *Nor baṙgirk' haykazean lezowi*, G. Awetik'ean, X. Siwrmêlean and M. Awgerean, (1836–1837), 2 vols, Venice: St Lazar, (reprinted 1990, Osnabrück: Biblio).

RIA Dict.   *Dictionary of the Irish Language based mainly on Old and Middle Irish Materials*, (1913–1976), Dublin: Royal Irish Academy.

RL   *Ricerche Linguistiche. Bollettino semestrale dell'Istituto di Glottologia dell'Università di Roma*, Roma.

SEG   *Supplementum Epigraphicum Graecum*, (1923– in progress).

Abrahamyan, A. A. (1964) *Grabari jeṙnark*, 3rd ed., Erevan: Haypetowsmank'rat.

Ačaṙyan, H. *HAB* (1971–1979) *Hayeren armatakan baṙaran*, 2nd ed., 4 vols, Erevan: University Press.

Adontz, N. (1915) *Dionisij Θrakijskij i armjanskie tolkovateli*, (*Bibliotheca Armeno-Georgica* VI), Petrograd: Tipografija Imperatorskoj Akademii Nauk.

Adontz, N. (1937) 'Quelques étymologies arméniennes', *Mélanges Émile Boisacq* I, *AnnIPhO* 5, 5–12.

Adontz, N. (1970) *Denys de Thrace et les commentateurs arméniens, traduit du russe (avec un appendice)*, Louvain: Imprimerie Orientaliste.

Adrados, F. R. (1963) *Evolución y estructura del verbo indoeuropeo*, Madrid: Instituto 'Antonio de Nebrija'.

Adrados, F. R. (1982) *Die räumliche und zeitliche Differenzierung des Indoeuropäischen im Lichte der Vor- und Frühgeschichte*, Innsbruck: Inst. für Sprachwiss. d. Univ.

Ałabekyan, M. A. (1981) 'Hndevropakan jaynavor ev jaynord **u*-n hayerenowm', *LHG* 1981.8, 56–63.

Ałayan, E. B. (1974) *Bařak'nnakan ev stowgabanakan hetazotowt'yownner*, Erevan: Haykakan SSH GA hrat.

Allen, W. S. (1950) 'Notes on the phonetics of an Eastern Armenian Speaker', *TPhS* 1950, 180–206.

Allen, W. S. (1953) 'Relationship in comparative linguistics', *TPhS* 1953, 52–108.

Allen, W. S. (1957) 'Some problems of palatalization in Greek', *Lingua* 7, (1957–8), 113–133.

Allen, W. S. (1958) 'Some problems in the phonetic development of the IE voiced aspirates in Latin', *ArchL* 10, 100–116.

Allen, W. S. (1973) 'χθών, "ruki", and related matters: a reappraisal', *TPhS* 1973, 98–126.

Allen, W. S. (1978) 'The PIE velar series: Neogrammarian and other solutions in the light of attested parallels', *TPhS* 1978, 87–110.

Allen, W. S. (1987) *Vox Graeca*, 3rd ed., Cambridge: University Press.

Anttila, R. (1969) *Proto-Indo-European Schwebeablaut*, Berkeley and Los Angeles: University of California Press.

Anttila, R. (1989) *Historical and Comparative Linguistics* (revised edition of *An Introduction to Historical and Comparative Linguistics*, 1972, New York: Macmillan), Amsterdam/ Philadelphia: Benjamins.

Arbeitman, Y. (1980) 'The recovery of an IE collocation', in J. A. C. Greppin (ed.), *First International Conference on Armenian Linguistics: Proceedings*, Delmar, N.Y.: Caravan, 225–231.

Arutjunjan, C. R. |C. R. Harowt'yownyan| (1983) 'Armjano-grečeskie leksičeskie izoglossy', in G. B. Jahowkyan |G. B. Džaukjan| (ed.), *Očerki po sravnitel'noj leksikologii armjanskogo jazyka*, Erevan: Izd-vo AN Armjanskoj SSR, 221–355.

Arutjunjan, C. R. |C. R. Harowt'yownyan| (1988) 'Ob armjano-greko-baltijskix leksičeskix sxoždenijax', *Baltistica* 24(2), 170–177.

Asmanguljan, A. A. (1983) *Istorija armjanskix terminov rodstva*, Erevan: Izd. Erevanskogo universiteta.

Astowacatowrean, T. (1895) *Hamabarbař hin ew nor ktakaranac'*, (Armenian Bible Concordance), Jerusalem: St James.

Bader, F. (1970) 'Neutres grecs en -*ti*: absolutifs et privatifs verbaux', *BSL* 65, 85–136.

Bader, F. (1979) 'Les présents à nasale indo-européens: la classe en **-nu*-', *BSL* 74, 191–235.

Bader, F. (1982) 'Autour du réfléchi anatolien: étymologies pronominales', *BSL* 77, 83–156.

Bader, F. (1989), '*Πάν*', *RPh* 63, 7–46.

Bader, F. (1990) 'Traitement de laryngales en groupe: allongement compensatoire, assimilation, anaptyxe', in J. Kellens and J. Dor (eds.), *La Reconstruction des laryngales*, Liège: Bibliothèque de la Faculté de Philosophie et Lettres de l'Université de Liège, fasc. CCCIII, 1–47.

Bagratuni, A. (1852) *Hayerên k'erakanowt'iwn i pêts zargac'eloc'*, Venice: St Lazar.

Bailey, H. W. (1933) 'Western Iranian dialects', *TPhS* 1933, 46–64.

Bailey, H. W. (1969) 'Arya notes', in *Studia Classica et Orientalia Antonio Pagliaro oblata* I, Roma: Herder, 137–149.

Bailey, H. W. (1971) *Zoroastrian Problems in the Ninth-Century Books*, 2nd ed., Oxford: University Press.

Bailey, H. W. (1979) *Dictionary of Khotan Saka*, Cambridge: University Press.

Bălțăceanu, M.-F. (1980) 'Arménien et daco-mésien', in R. Vulpe (ed.), *Actes du IIe congrès international de thracologie* III, Bucureşti: Editura Academiei Republicii Socialiste România, 14–25.

Bammesberger, A. (1984) *Studien zur Laryngaltheorie*, Göttingen: Vandenhoeck & Ruprecht.

Bartoli, M. (1925) *Introduzione alla neolinguistica*, (Biblioteca dell' 'Archivum Romanicum' II 12), Genève: Olschki.

Barton, C. R. (1965) *A Re-examination of the Historical Morphology of the Old Armenian Verb with a Classification of Stems from the point of view of Comparative Indo-European Linguistics*, unpublished doctoral dissertation, New York University.

Barton, C. R. (1988) 'Gk. *áesa*, Arm. *agay* and PIE **h₁*', in A. Bammesberger (ed.), *Die*

Laryngaltheorie und die Rekonstruktion des indogermanischen Laut- und Formensystems, Heidelberg: Winter, 49–58.

Barton, C. R. (1989) 'PIE **mer-*, Armenian *meṙanim* "die"', *IF* 94, 135–157.

Bechtel, G. (1936) *Hittite Verbs in -sk-*, Ann Arbor: Edwards Brothers.

Beekes, R. S. P. (1969) *The Development of the Proto-Indo-European Laryngeals in Greek*, The Hague: Mouton.

Beekes, R. S. P. (1987) 'The PIE words for "name" and "me"', *Sprache* 33, 1–12.

Beekes, R. S. P. (1988) 'Laryngeal developments: a survey', in A. Bammesberger (ed.), *Die Laryngaltheorie und die Rekonstruktion des indogermanischen Laut- und Formensystems*, Heidelberg: Winter, 59–105.

Belardi, W. (1950) 'Arm. *nerkanem*', *RL* 1, 147–148.

Benveniste, E. (1932) 'Sur le consonantisme *hittite*', *BSL* 33, 136–143.

Benveniste, E. (1935) *Origines de la formation des noms en indo-européen*, Paris: Maisonneuve.

Benveniste, E. (1936) 'Tocharien et indo-européen', in H. Arntz (ed.), *Germanen und Indogermanen: Volkstum, Sprache, Heimat, Kultur; Festschrift für Herman Hirt*, vol. II, Heidelberg: Winter, 227–240.

Benveniste, E. (1954) 'Problèmes sémantiques de la reconstruction', *Word* 10, 251–264.

Benveniste, E. (1956) '"Hiver" et "neige" en indo-européen', in H. Kronasser (ed.), *ΜΝΗΜΗΣ ΧΑΡΙΝ: Gedenkschrift Paul Kretschmer I*, Wien: Wiener Sprachgesellschaft, 31–39.

Benveniste, E. (1959) 'Sur la phonétique et la syntaxe de l'arménien classique', *BSL* 54, 46–68.

Benveniste, E. (1969a) *Le Vocabulaire des institutions indo-européennes: 1. Économie, parenté, société*, Paris: Minuit.

Benveniste, E. (1969b) *Le Vocabulaire des institutions indo-européennes: 2. Pouvoir, droit, religion*, Paris: Minuit.

Benveniste, E. (1970) 'Les valeurs économiques dans le vocabulaire indo-européen', in G. Cardona, H. M. Hoenigswald and A. Senn (eds.), *Indo-European and Indo-Europeans; Papers Presented at the Third Indo-European Conference at the University of Pennsylvania*, Philadelphia: University of Pennsylvania Press, 307–320.

Benveniste, E. (1971) *Problems in General Linguistics*, (translation of E. Benveniste (1966), *Problèmes de linguistique générale*, Paris: Gallimard, by M. E. Meek), Miami: University Press.

Bergsland, K. and Vogt, H. (1962) 'On the validity of glottochronology', *CAnthr* 3, 115–153.

Berrettoni, P. (1971) 'Considerazione sui verbi latini in *-sco*', *SSL* 11, 89–169.

Bird, N. (1982) *The Distribution of Indo-European Root Morphemes: (A Checklist for Philologists)*, Wiesbaden: Harrassowitz.

Birnbaum, H. and Puhvel, J. (eds.), (1966) *Ancient Indo-European Dialects*, Berkeley and Los Angeles: California University Press.

Blanc, A. (1985) 'Étymologie de ἀπηνής et προσηνής', *RPh* 59.2, 255–263.

Boisacq, E. (1950) *Dictionnaire étymologique de la langue grecque*, 4th ed., Heidelberg: Winter.

Bolognesi, G. (1954) 'Ricerche sulla fonetica armena', *RL* 3, 123–154.

Bolognesi, G. (1960) *Le fonti dialettali degli imprestiti iranici in armeno*, Milano: Università Cattolica del Sacro Cuore.

Bolognesi, G. (1962) 'Studi armeni', *RL* 5, 105–147.

Bonfante, G. (1937) 'Les isoglosses gréco-arméniennes I. Faits phonétiques', in L. Hjelmslev, C. Höeg, C. Møller and Ad. Stender-Petersen (eds.), *Mélanges linguistiques offerts à Holger Pedersen*, Aarhus: Universitetsforlaget, 15–33.

Bonfante, G. (1939), 'La position du hittite parmi les langues indo-européennes', *RBPh* 18, 381–392.

Bonfante, G. (1942) 'The Armenian aorist', *JAOS* 62, 102–105.

Bonfante, G. (1981) 'Hayereni dirkʻə hndevropakan lezowneri mej', *IFŽ* 1981.2, 54–67.

Bonfante, G. (1982) 'The place of Armenian among the Indo-European languages' *AIΩN* 4, 151–169.

Bonfante, G. (1987) 'The relative position of the Indo-European languages', *JIES* 15, 77–80.

Bottin, L. (1969) 'Studio dell' aumento in Omero', *SMEA* 10, 69–145.

Brugmann, K. (1884) 'Zur Frage nach den Verwandtschaftverhältnissen der indogermanischen Sprachen', *Internationale Zeitschrift für allgemeine Sprachwissenschaft* 1, 226–256.

Brugmann, K. (1897) *Grundriss der vergleichenden Grammatik der indogermanischen Sprachen*, 2nd ed., vol. 1, Strassburg: Trübner.

Brugmann, K. (1903) 'Die ionische Iterativpräterita auf -σκον', *IF* 13, 267–277.
Brugmann, K. (1906) *Grundriss der vergleichenden Grammatik der indogermanischen Sprachen*, 2nd ed., 2 Band, 1 Teil, Strassburg: Trübner.
Brugmann, K. (1907–8) 'Die Anomalien in der Flexion von griech. γυνή, armen. *kin* und altnord. *kona*', *IF* 22, 171–193.
Brugmann, K. (1911) *Grundriss der vergleichenden Grammatik der indogermanischen Sprachen*, 2nd ed., 2 Band, 2 Teil, Strassburg: Trübner.
Brugmann, K. (1913) *Grundriss der vergleichenden Grammatik der indogermanischen Sprachen*, 2nd ed., 2 Band, 3 Teil, 1 Lieferung, Strassburg: Trübner.
Buck, C. D. (1933) *Comparative Grammar of Greek and Latin*, Chicago: University Press.
Buck, C. D. (1949) *A Dictionary of Selected Synonyms in the Principal Indo-European Languages*, Chicago: University Press.
Bugge, S. (1889) *Beiträge zur etymologischen Erläuterung der armenischen Sprache*, Christiana.
Bugge, S. (1893) 'Beiträge zur etymologischen Erläuterung der armenischen Sprache', *KZ* 32, 1–87.
Calame, C. (1977) 'Die Komposita mit ἀρτι- im frühgriechischen Epos', *MH* 34, 209–220.
Chadwick, J. (1958) 'Error and abnormality in the Mycenean noun declension', *PP* 13, 285–295.
Chadwick, J. (1992) 'ΗΡΥΣ – A Greek ghost-word', in B. Brogyanyi and R. Lipp (eds.), *Historical Philology: Greek, Latin, and Romance. Papers in Honor of Oswald Szemerényi II*, Amsterdam: Benjamins, 99–102.
Chantraine, P. (1933) *La Formation des noms en grec ancien*, Paris: Champion.
Chantraine, P. *DELG* (1968–1980) *Dictionnaire étymologique de la langue grecque*, 4 vols, Paris: Klincksieck.
Chantraine, P. (1973) *Grammaire homérique I. Phonétique et morphologie*, 5th ed., Paris: Klincksieck.
Chantraine, P. (1974) 'Hermès Généiolès - A propos de Callimaque fr. 199 (Pfeiffer)', in *Mélanges d'histoire des religions offerts à Henri-Charles Puech*, Paris: Presses Universitaires de France, 125–128.
Charpentier, J. (1909) 'Kleine Beiträge zur armenischen Wortkunde', *IF* 25, 241–256.
Coleman, R. G. G. (1963) 'The dialect geography of Ancient Greece', *TPhS* 1963, 58–126.
Coleman, R. G. G. (1971) 'The monophthongization of /ae/ and the Vulgar Latin vowel system', *TPhS* 1971, 175–191.
Coleman, R. G. G. (1992) 'Le lexique grec et le lexique indo-européen: étude comparative', in F. Létoublon (ed.), *La Langue et les textes en grec ancien: actes du colloque Pierre Chantraine (Grenoble - 5-8 septembre 1989)*, Amsterdam: Gieben, 169–179.
Collinge, N. E. (1987) 'Who did discover the law of the palatals?', in G. Cardona and N. H. Zide (eds.), *Festschrift for Henry Hoenigswald, On the Occasion of his Seventieth birthday*, Tübingen: Narr, 73–80.
Considine, P. (1978–9) Revue de J. A. C. Greppin (1973), *Initial vowel and aspiration in Classical Armenian*, *REArm* n.s. 13, 355–364.
Considine, P. (1979) 'A semantic approach to the identification of Iranian loan-words in Armenian', in B. Brogyanyi (ed.), *Studies in diachronic, synchronic and typological linguistics: Festschrift for Oswald Szemerényi on the occasion of his 65th birthday*, Amsterdam: Benjamins, 213–228.
Cop, B. (1957) 'Beiträge zur idg. Wortforschung II', *Sprache* 3, 135–149.
Couvreur, W. (1938) 'Les dérivés verbaux en -*ske/o* du hittite et du tocharien', *Revue des Études Indo-Européennes*, Bucarest, 1, 89–101.
Cowgill, W. C. (1960) 'Greek οὐ and Armenian *oč̣*', *Lg* 36, 347–350.
Cowgill, W. C. (1965) 'Evidence in Greek', in W. Winter (ed.), *Evidence for Laryngeals*, 2nd ed., The Hague: Mouton, 142–180.
Cowgill, W. C. (1966a) 'Ancient Greek dialectology in the light of Mycenaean', in H. Birnbaum and J. Puhvel (eds.), *Ancient Indo-European Dialects*, Berkeley and Los Angeles: California University Press, 77–95.
Cowgill, W. C. (1966b) 'A search for universals in Indo-European diachronic morphology', in J. H. Greenberg (ed.), *Universals of Language*, 2nd ed., Cambridge, Mass./London: MIT Press, 114–141.

Cowgill, W. C. (1986) 'Band I/1: Einleitung', in J. Kuryłowicz (founder ed.) and M. Mayrhofer (ed.), *Indogermanische Grammatik*, Heidelberg: Winter.

Crossland, R. A. (1958) 'Remarks on the Indo-European laryngeals', *ArchL* 10, 79–99.

Cuendet, G. (1929) *L'Ordre des mots dans le texte grec et dans les versions gotique, arménienne et vieux slave des Évangiles; Ie partie: les groupes nominaux*, Paris: Champion.

Curtius, G. (1858) *Grundzüge der griechischen Etymologie*, Leipzig: Teubner.

Darms, G. (1976) 'Urindogermanisch **sēmi*', *MSS* 35, 7–32.

Davies, P. and Ross, A. S. C. (1975) '"Close relationship" in the Indo-European languages', *TPhS* 1975, 82–100.

Debrunner, A. (1937) 'Homerica', in L. Hjelmslev, C. Höeg, C. Møller and Ad. Stender-Petersen (eds.), *Mélanges linguistiques offerts à Holger Pedersen*, Aarhus: Universitetsforlaget, 197–204.

Deeters, G. (1927) *Armenisch und Südkaukasisch, ein Beitrag zur Frage der Sprachmischung*, Leipzig: Asia Major.

Deeters, G. (1963) 'Die kaukasischen Sprachen', in B. Spuler (ed.), *Handbuch der Orientalistik I.7*, Leiden: Brill, 1–79.

Delbrück, B. (1889) *Die indogermanischen Verwandtschaftsnamen*, Leipzig: Hirzel.

Dowsett, C. J. F. (1989) 'Some Reflections on *nerk*', etc.', *AArmL* 10, 27–41.

Dressler, W. (1969) 'Altarmenisch *awr awur* "Tag für Tag"', *REArm* n.s. 6, 19–21.

Dumbreck, J. C. and Forbes, N. (1964) *Russian Grammar*, 3rd ed., revised and enlarged, Oxford: University Press.

Dumézil, G. (1938) 'Le plus vieux nom arménien du "jeune homme"', *BSL* 39, 185–193.

Eichner, H. (1969) 'Hethitisch *u̯ešš-/u̯aššiya-* "(Gewänder) tragen; anziehen; bekleiden"', *MSS* 27, 5–44.

Eichner, H. (1978) 'Die urindogermanische Wurzel **H₂reu-* "hell machen"', *Sprache* 24, 144–162.

Eichner, H. (1988a) 'Sprachwandel und Rekonstruktion', in C. Zinko (ed.), *Akten der 13. Österreichischen Linguistentagung*, Graz: Leykam, 10–40.

Eichner, H. (1988b) 'Anatolisch und Trilaryngalismus', in A. Bammesberger (ed.), *Die Laryngaltheorie und die Rekonstruktion des indogermanischen Laut- und Formensystems*, Heidelberg: Winter, 123–151.

Eichner, H. (1992) 'Anatolian', in J. Gvozdanović (ed.), *Indo-European Numerals*, Berlin/New York: Mouton de Gruyter, 29–96.

Ernout, A. and Meillet, A. *DELL* (1959) *Dictionnaire étymologique de la langue latine*, 4th ed., Paris: Klincksieck.

Euler, W. (1979) *Indoiranisch-griechische Gemeinsamkeiten der Nominalbildung und deren indogermanische Grundlagen*, Innsbruck: Inst. für Sprachwiss. d. Univ.

Feydit, F. (1982) *Considérations sur l'alphabet de Saint Mesrop et recherches sur la phonétique de l'arménien*, 2nd ed., Vienna: Mechitharisten.

Forssman, B. (1966) *Untersuchungen zur Sprache Pindars*, Wiesbaden: Harrassowitz.

Forssman, B. (1969) 'Nachlese zu ὄσσε', *MSS* 25, 39–50.

Fraenkel, E. *LEW* (1962–5) *Litauisches etymologisches Wörterbuch*, Heidelberg: Winter.

Francis, E. D. (1970) *Greek disyllabic roots: the aorist formations*, unpublished doctoral dissertation, Yale University.

Francis, E. D. (1974) 'Greek ἔβλην', *Glotta* 52, 11–30.

Frisk, H. (1936), *Suffixales* 'th' *im Indogermanischen*, *Göteborgs Högskolas Arsskrift* 42, Göteborg: Wettergren and Kerber.

Frisk, H. (1943) 'Zur griechischen Wortkunde', *Eranos* 41, 48–64.

Frisk, H. (1944) *Etyma Armeniaca, Göteborgs Högskolas Arsskrift* 50, Göteborg: Wettergren and Kerber.

Frisk, H. *GEW* (1960–72) *Griechisches etymologisches Wörterbuch*, 3 vols., Heidelberg: Winter.

Furlan, M. (1984) 'Hittite *ḫuelpi-* "young, tender, fresh" and IE **Hulp-*, **Hlup-*', *Ling* 24, 455–466.

Gamkrelidze, T. V. (1985) 'The Indo-European "Glottalic Theory" and the system of Old Armenian consonantism', in U. Pieper and G. Stickel (eds.), *Studia linguistica diachronica et synchronica: Werner Winter sexagenario anno oblata*, Berlin: de Gruyter, 281–284.

Gamkrelidze, T. V. and Ivanov, V. V. (1984) *Indoevropejskij jazyk i indoevropejcy*, 2 vols, Tbilisi: Izd-vo Tbilisskogo un-ta.

García-Ramón, J.-L. (1984) 'The spelling *Ta* and *Ta-ra* for inherited *Tr̥ in Mycenaean: sound law, phonetic sequence and morphological factors at work', *Minos* 19, 195–226.

Geraghty, P., Carrington, L. and Wurm, S. A. (eds.) (1986) *FOCAL II: Papers from the Fourth International Conference on Austronesian Linguistics (PL Series C 94)*, Canberra: Department of Linguistics, Australian National University.

Gjandschezian, E. (1903) 'Beiträge zur altarmenischen nominalen Stammbildungslehre', *Zeitschrift für armenische Philologie* 1, 33–63.

Godel, R. (1965) 'Les origines de la conjugaison arménienne', *REArm* n.s. 2, 21–41.

Godel, R. (1969) 'Les aoristes arméniens en *-c̣-*', in *Studia Classica et Orientalia Antonio Pagliaro oblata* II, Roma: Herder, 253–258.

Godel, R. (1972) 'Questions de phonétique et de morphologie arméniennes (II)', *REArm* n.s. 9, 47–67.

Godel, R. (1975) *An Introduction to the Study of Classical Armenian*, Wiesbaden: Reichert.

Godel, R. (1982) 'Une loi phonétique bien difficile à énoncer: **w >* arm. *w(v)/g/zéro*', *REArm* n.s. 16, 9–15.

Godel, R. (1984) 'Une concordance lexicale gréco-arménienne', *CFS* 38, 289–293, reprinted in D. Kouymjian (ed.), (1986) *Armenian studies / Études arméniennes: in memoriam Haig Berbérian*, Lisboa: Gulbenkian, 265–269.

Gow, A. S. F. (1944) 'Ὀφρύς', *CR* 58.2, 38 f.

Grammont, M. (1916) 'Notes de phonétique générale. VI. Arménien classique', *MSL* 20, 213–259.

Greenberg, J. (1957) *Essays in Linguistics*, Chicago: University Press.

Greppin, J. A. C. (1972) 'The Armenian reflexes of IE **w* and **y*', *REArm* n.s. 9, 69–78.

Greppin, J. A. C. (1973a) 'Armenian *h-*, Hittite *h-* and the Indo-European laryngeal', *HA* 87.1–3, 61–80.

Greppin, J. A. C. (1973b) *Initial vowel and aspiration in Classical Armenian*, Vienna: Mechitharisten.

Greppin, J. A. C. (1978) 'On Greek zeta', *JIES* 6, 141 f.

Greppin, J. A. C. (1981) 'Greek μαλλός "fleece, lock of wool"', *Glotta* 59, 70–75.

Greppin, J. A. C. (1982) 'Arm. *t̔-* Gk *πτ-*', *JIES* 10, 347–354.

Greppin, J. A. C. (1983a) 'Gk ἀλέτριος and the modern Armenian Grammarians', *REArm* n.s. 17, 19–20.

Greppin, J. A. C. (1983b) 'An etymological dictionary of the Indo-European components of Armenian (part 1)', *Bazmavêp* 141.1–4, 235–322.

Greppin, J. A. C. (1984a) 'Revisions to the etymologies of Arm. *doyn, noyn, soyn* "same" and *ałtiwr* "marsh", and comments on *VwV* in Armenian', *REArm* n.s. 18, 301–305.

Greppin, J. A. C. (1984b) 'The reflex of the Indo-European "voiceless aspirates" in Armenian', *Miĵazgayin hayerenagitakan gitažołov, Erevan, 21–25 septemberi, 1982 t̔.*, Erevan: Haykakan SSH GA hrat., 35–48.

Greppin, J. A. C. (1988) 'The various aloës in ancient times', *JIES* 16, 33–45.

Gusmani, R. (1989) 'Ursprache, Rekonstrukt, hermeneutische Modelle', in K. Heller, O. Panagl and J. Tischler (eds.), *Indogermanica Europaea; Festschrift für Wolfgang Meid zum 60. Geburtstag am 12.11.1989 (= Grazer Linguistische Monographien 4)*, Graz: Grazer Linguistische Monographien, 69–77.

Haas, O. (1939) 'Ἀκούω – ansam', *HA* 53.7–12, 235–237.

Haas, O. (1959) 'Die Lehre von den indogermanischen Substraten in Griechenland', *BalkE* 1, 29–56.

Hainsworth, J. B. (1988) 'The Epic Dialect', in A. Heubeck, S. West and J. B. Hainsworth, *A Commentary on Homer's* Odyssey: *Volume I, Introduction and Books i–viii*, Oxford: Oxford University Press, 24–32.

Hackstein, O. (1992) 'Eine weitere griechisch-tocharische Gleichung: Griechisch πτῆξαι und tocharisch B *pyāktsi*', *Glotta* 70. 3–4, 136–165.

Hall, R. A. Jr (1950) 'The reconstruction of Proto-Romance', *Lg* 26, 6–27.

Hammalian, S. J. (1984) *A Generative Phonology of Old Armenian*, unpublished PhD dissertation, New York University.

Hamp, E. P. (1965) 'Evidence in Albanian', in W. Winter (ed.), *Evidence for Laryngeals*, 2nd ed., The Hague: Mouton, 123–141.

Hamp, E. P. (1969a), 'Hittite *utne-*, Greek οὖδας', in *Studia Classica et Orientalia Antonio Pagliaro oblata* III, Roma: Herder, 7–16.

Hamp, E. P. (1969b) 'Armenian *harb*, *hars*, *harc'*, *REArm* n.s. 6, 15–17.
Hamp, E. P. (1970) 'Sanskrit *duhitā*, Armenian *dustr*, and IE internal schwa', *JAOS* 90, 228–231.
Hamp, E. P. (1972) 'Occam's razor and explanation in etymology', *PCLS* 8, 470–472.
Hamp, E. P. (1973–4) 'On *$k'w$- in Armenian', *REArm* n.s. 10, 23–25.
Hamp, E. P. (1975a) 'On the nasal presents of Armenian', *KZ* 89, 100–109.
Hamp, E. P. (1975b) 'IE *$g^w reH_u on$-', *MSS* 33, 41–43.
Hamp, E. P. (1976) ' *$g^w eiH_o$- "live"', in A. Morpurgo Davies and W. Meid (eds.), *Studies in Greek, Italic and Indo-European Linguistics offered to Leonard R. Palmer on the occasion of his 70th birthday*, Innsbruck: Inst. für Sprachwiss. d. Univ., 87–91.
Hamp, E. P. (1982a) '$\mu\alpha\lambda\lambda\delta s$: a clarification', *Glotta* 60, 61 f.
Hamp, E. P. (1982b) 'On Greek ζ- : *y-', *JIES* 10, 190 f.
Hamp, E. P. (1982c) 'Two roots *$H_o bhel$-', *Glotta* 60, 227–230.
Hamp, E. P. (1982d) 'Arm, shoulder', *JIES* 10, 187–189.
Hamp, E. P. (1982e) 'Armenian miscellanea, *AArmL* 3, 53–56.
Hamp, E. P. (1983a) 'Philologica varia', *REArm* n.s. 17, 5–12.
Hamp, E. P. (1983b) 'A morphological law', *Lingua* 61, 1–8.
Hamp, E. P. (1983c) 'Skt *ātāḥ'*, *IIJ* 25.2, 102.
Hamp, E. P. (1983d) '*Erastank''*, *AArmL* 4, 64 f.
Hamp, E. P. (1983e) '$\pi\epsilon\delta\acute{a}$', *Glotta* 61, 193.
Hamp, E. P. (1984) 'Armen. *dalar* "green", $\theta\alpha\lambda\epsilon\rho\acute{o}s$ "moist"', *Sprache* 30, 156–159.
Hamp, E. P. (1985a) 'On asymmetric labial loss and Armenian', *TUBA* 9, 133–136.
Hamp, E. P. (1985b) 'Greek *$\pi\tau$*- and Armenian', *AArmL* 6, 51–52.
Hamp, E. P. (1986a) 'Armenian *yisun*', in D. Kouymjian (ed.), *Armenian studies / Études arméniennes: in memoriam Haig Berbérian*, Lisboa: Gulbenkian, 293–294.
Hamp, E. P. (1986b) '*Tellus* ("earth")', *RhM* 129, 360–361.
Hamp, E. P. (1988–9) 'Two Armenian etymologies', *REArm* 21, 25–27.
Harðarson, J. A. (1987) 'Das urindogermanische Wort für "Frau"', *MSS* 48, 115–137.
Harrison, S. P. (1986) 'On the nature of sub-grouping arguments', in P. Geraghty, L. Carrington and S. A. Wurm (eds.), *FOCAL II: Papers from the Fourth International Conference on Austronesian Linguistics* (= *PL*, Series C, No. 94), Canberra: Department of Linguistics, Australian National University, 13–21.
Hastings, J. (ed.), (1898–1904) *A Dictionary of the Bible*, 5 vols, Edinburgh: Clark.
Haudry, J. (1983) 'Les composés homériques en $\acute{a}\rho\tau\iota$-', *LALIES: actes des sessions de linguistique et de littérature*, Paris, 2, 7–12.
Hettrich, H. (1973) Review of E. D. Francis (1970) *Greek disyllabic roots: the aorist formations*, unpublished doctoral dissertation, Yale University, *Kratylos* 18, 147–155.
Heubeck, A. (1972) 'Syllabic *r* in Mycenaean Greek?', *Minos* 12, 55–79.
Hiersche, R. (1964) *Untersuchungen zur Frage der Tenues aspiratae im Indogermanischen*, Wiesbaden: Harrassowitz.
Hilmarsson, J. (1985) 'Tocharian B *krorīyai* (obl. sing.), A *kror* "crescent, horn of the moon" ~ Hittite *karawar* "horn" ~ Arm. *eɫjewr* "horn" < IE *$ghrēwr$', *Sprache* 31, 40–47.
Hock, H. H. (1986) *Principles of Historical Linguistics*, Berlin: Mouton de Gruyter.
Hoenigswald, H. M. (1960) *Language Change and Linguistic Reconstruction*, Chicago: University Press.
Hoenigswald, H. (1966) 'Criteria for the subgrouping of languages', in H. Birnbaum and J. Puhvel (eds.), *Ancient Indo-European Dialects*, Berkeley and Los Angeles: California University Press, 1–12.
Hoffmann, K. (1965) 'Av. *daxma*-', *KZ* 79, 238.
Hoffmann, K. (1967) 'Drei indogermanische Tiernamen in einem Avesta-Fragment', *MSS* 22, 29–38.
Hoffmann, O. (1893) *Die griechischen Dialekte: II Band. Der nord-achäische Dialekte*, Göttingen: Vandenhoeck & Ruprecht.
Holthausen, F. (1963) *Altenglisches etymologisches Wörterbuch*, 2nd ed., Heidelberg: Winter.
Hooker, J. T. (1979) '$\gamma\epsilon\phi\bar{v}\rho a$: a Semitic loan-word?', in B. Brogyanyi (ed.), *Studies in diachronic, synchronic and typological linguistics: Festschrift for Oswald Szemerényi on the occasion of his 65th birthday*, Amsterdam: Benjamins, 387–398.
Hovdhaugen, E. (1968) 'Prothetic vowels in Armenian and Greek and the Laryngeal theory', *NTS* 22, 115–132.

Hübschmann, H. (1875) 'Ueber die stellung des armenischen im kreise der indogermanischen sprachen', *KZ* 23, 5–49.

Hübschmann, H. (1883) *Armenische Studien. I. Grundzüge der armenischen Etymologie. Erster Theil*, Leipzig: Breitkopf & Härtel.

Hübschmann, H. (1895) *Armenische Grammatik. I Band: Armenische Etymologie. I. Theil. Die persischen und arabischen Lehnwörter im Altarmenischen*, Leipzig: Breitkopf & Härtel.

Hübschmann, H. (1897) *Armenische Grammatik. I Theil: Armenische Etymologie. II Abtheilung. Die syrischen und griechischen Lehnwörter im Altarmenischen und die echtarmenischen Wörter*, Leipzig: Breitkopf & Härtel.

Hübschmann, H. (1976) *Kleine Schriften zum Armenischen*, hrsg. R. Schmitt, Hildersheim: Olms.

Huld, M. E. (1984) *Basic Albanian Etymologies*, Columbus, Ohio: Slavica.

Humbach, H. (1956) 'Gathisch-awestische Verbalformen', *MSS* 9, 66–78.

Ilievski, P. H. (1987) 'Mycenaean *a-mo* /(*h*)*armo*-/ and some IE co-radicals', *Minos* 20–22, 295–309.

Isebaert, L. (1992) 'Spuren akrostatischer Präsensflexion im Lateinischen', in O. Panagl and T. Krisch (eds.), *Latein und Indogermanisch. Akten des Kolloquiums der Indogermanischen Gesellschaft, Salzburg, 23.–26. September 1986*, Innsbruck: Inst. für Sprachwiss. d. Univ., 193–205.

Jahowkyan, G. B. (1959) *Hin hayereni holovman sistemɔ ev nra cagowmɔ*, Erevan: University Press.

Jahowkyan, G. B. |G. B. Džaukjan| (1967) *Očerki po istorii dopis'mennogo perioda armjanskogo jazyka*, Erevan: Izd-vo AN Armjanskoj SSR.

Jahowkyan, G. B. (1970) *Hayerenɔ ev hndevropakan hin lezownerɔ*, Erevan: Izd-vo. AN Armjanskoj SSR.

Jahowkyan, G. B. |G. B. Jahukyan| (1975) 'Die Bedeutung der ersten (indogermanischen) und der zweiten (inner-armenischen) Palatalisierung für die Konstituierung des armenischen Konsonanten-Systems', *KZ* 89, 31–41.

Jahowkyan, G. B. (1976) 'Stowgabanowt'yownner', *LHG* 1976.12, 31–51.

Jahowkyan, G. B. |G. B. Džaukjan| (1980), 'On the position of Armenian in the Indo-European languages', in J. A. C. Greppin (ed.), *First International Conference on Armenian Linguistics: Proceedings*, Delmar, N.Y.: Caravan, 3–16.

Jahowkyan, G. B. |G. B. Džaukjan| (1982) *Sravnitel'naja grammatika armjanskogo jazyka*, Erevan: Izd-vo AN Armjanskoj SSR.

Jahowkyan, G. B. |G. B. Džaukjan| (1983a) 'O perexode **o* > *a* v armjanskom jazyke', *Armjanski jazyk i literatura*, Erevan: Izd-vo AN Armjanskoj SSR, 1–2.

Jahowkyan, G. B. |G. B. Džaukjan| (1983b) 'Opyt semantičeskoj klassifikacii i areal'nogo raspredelenija indoevropejskoj leksiki armjanskogo jazyka', in G. B. Jahowkyan |G. B. Džaukjan| (ed.), *Očerki po sravnitel'noj leksikologii armjanskogo jazyka*, Erevan: Izd-vo AN Armjanskoj SSR, 5–116.

Jahowkyan, G. B. (1987) *Hayoc' lezvi patmowt'iown: naxagrayin žamanakašrjan*, Erevan: Izd-vo AN Armjanskoj SSR.

Jahowkyan, G. B. |G. B. Djahukian| (1990) 'Combinatory vowel changes in Armenian', *AArmL* 11, 1–16.

Janko, R. (1992) *The Iliad: a commentary. Vol. IV, books 13–16*, (General ed. G. S. Kirk), Cambridge: Cambridge University Press.

Jasanoff, J. H. (1978) *Stative and Middle in Indo-European*, Innsbruck: Inst. für Sprachwiss. d. Univ.

Jasanoff, J. H. (1979) 'Notes on the Armenian personal endings', *KZ* 93, 133–149.

Jensen, H. (1959) *Altarmenische Grammatik*, Heidelberg: Winter.

Job, M. (1986) 'Les noms des parties du corps dans le vocabulaire de base arménien', in M. Leroy and F. Mawet (eds.), *La Place de l'arménien dans les langues indo-européennes*, Louvain: Peeters, 20–37.

Johansson, K. F. (1902) 'Arische Beiträge', *IF* 14, 265–338.

Karst, J. (1901) *Historische Grammatik des Kilikisch-Armenischen*, Strassburg: Trübner.

Karstien, H. (1956) 'Das slav. Imperf. und der arm. -*aҫe*- Aor.', *Festschrift für Max Vasmer*, Wiesbaden: Harrassowitz, 211–229.

Keller, M. (1985) 'Latin *escit, escunt* a-t-il des correspondants?', *RPh* 59, 27–44.

Killen, J. T. (1962) 'Mycenaean *po-ka*: a suggested interpretation', *PP* 17, 26–31.

Killen, J. T. (1963) 'Mycenaean *po-ka*: a further note', *PP* 18, 447–450.
Kimball, S. E. (1980) 'A Homeric note', *Glotta* 58, 44–46.
Kimball, S. E. (1988) 'Analogy, Secondary Ablaut and *$*oH_2$* in Common Greek', in A. Bammesberger (ed.), *Die Laryngaltheorie und die Rekonstruktion des indogermanischen Laut- und Formensystems*, Heidelberg: Winter, 241–256.
Klein, J. S. (1988) 'Proto-Indo-European *$*g^wiH_3$*- "live" and related problems of laryngeals in Greek', in A. Bammesberger (ed.), *Die Laryngaltheorie und die Rekonstruktion des indogermanischen Laut- und Formensystems*, Heidelberg: Winter, 257–279.
Klingenschmitt, G. (1970) 'Griechisch ἐλάσκεσθαι', *MSS* 28, 75–88.
Klingenschmitt, G. (1975) 'Altindisch *śaśvat-*', *MSS* 33, 67–78.
Klingenschmitt, G. (1982) *Das altarmenische Verbum*, Wiesbaden: Reichert.
Klingenschmitt, G. (1992) 'Die lateinische Nominalflexion', in O. Panagl und T. Krisch (eds.), *Latein und Indogermanisch. Akten des Kolloquiums der Indogermanischen Gesellschaft, Salzburg, 23.–26. September 1986*, Innsbruck: Inst. für Sprachwiss. d. Univ., 89–135.
Kluge, H. (1911) *Syntaxis Graecae quaestiones selectae*, Berlin.
Knobloch, J. (1975) 'Die Brücke – eine armenisch-griechische Isoglosse?', *KZ* 89, 76–79.
Kortlandt, F. (1975) 'A note on the Armenian palatalization', *KZ* 89, 43–45.
Kortlandt, F. (1980) 'The relative chronology of Armenian sound-changes', in J. A. C. Greppin (ed.), *First International Conference on Armenian Linguistics: Proceedings*, Delmar, N.Y.: Caravan, 97–106.
Kortlandt, F. (1983) 'Notes on Armenian historical phonology III: *h*', *SCauc* 5, 9–16.
Kortlandt, F. (1984) 'Proto-Armenian case endings', in *Mijazgayin hayerenagitakan gitažołov, Erevan, 21–25 septemberi, 1982 t'.*, Erevan: Haykakan SSH GA hrat, 97–106.
Kortlandt, F. (1985) 'Notes on Armenian historical phonology IV', *SCauc* 6, 9–11.
Kortlandt, F. (1986) 'Armenian and Albanian', in M. Leroy and F. Mawet (eds.), *La Place de l'arménien dans les langues indo-européennes*, Louvain: Peeters, 38–47.
Kortlandt, F. (1987a) 'Notes on Armenian historical phonology V', *SCauc* 7, 61–65.
Kortlandt, F. (1987b) 'Sigmatic or root aorist?', *AArmL* 8, 49–52.
Kortlandt, F. (1989) 'The making of a puzzle', *AArmL* 10, 43–52.
Kortlandt, F. (1991) 'Arm. *canawt'* "known"', *AArmL* 12, 1–4.
Krause, W. (1952) *Westtocharische Grammatik I*, Heidelberg: Winter.
Krause, W. and Thomas, W. (1960) *Tocharische Elementarbuch I*, Heidelberg: Winter.
Kretschmer, P. (1916) 'Literaturbericht für das Jahr 1913: griechisch', *Glotta* 7, 321–359.
Krishnamurti, Bh., Moses, L. and Danforth, D. G. (1983) 'Unchanged cognates as a criterion in linguistic subgrouping', *Lg* 59.3, 541–568.
Kroeber, A. L. and Chrétien, C. D. (1937) 'Quantitative classification of Indo-European languages', *Lg* 13, 83–103.
Kuiper, F. B. J. (1937) *Die indogermanischen Nasalpräsentia*, Amsterdam: Noord-Hollandsche Uitgeversmaatschrift.
Künzle, B. O. (1984) *Das altarmenische Evangelium/I 'Évangile arménien ancien*, (2 vols) Bern: Lang.
Kuryłowicz, J. (1964) *The Inflectional Categories of Indo-European*, Heidelberg: Winter.
Kuryłowicz, J. (1977) 'Indo-européen *$*ə$* et grec *e, a, o*', *BSL* 72, 69–72.
Lamberterie, C. de (1974) 'Les occlusives sonores aspirées de l'arménien classique', *REArm* n.s. 10, 39–44.
Lamberterie, C. de (1978) 'Armeniaca I–VIII: études lexicales', *BSL* 73, 243–285.
Lamberterie, C. de (1978–9) 'Armeniaca X: une isoglosse gréco-arménienne', *REArm* n.s. 13, 31–40.
Lamberterie, C. de (1979) 'Le signe du pluriel en arménien classique', *BSL* 74, 319–332.
Lamberterie, C. de (1980) 'Échange de gutturales en arménien', *AArmL* 1, 23–37.
Lamberterie, C. de (1982a) 'Poids et force: reconstruction d'une racine verbale indo-européenne', *REArm* n.s. 16, 21–55.
Lamberterie, C. de (1982b) 'La racine *$*(s)per-g'h-$* en arménien', *REArm* n.s. 16, 57–68.
Lamberterie, C. de (1982c) Revue de R. Schmitt, *Grammatik des Klassisch-Armenischen* (1981), *BSL* 77.2, 80–84.
Lamberterie, C. de (1983) 'Une bagatelle étymologique (*artewanunk'/δρεπάνη*)', *REArm* n.s. 17, 21–22.
Lamberterie, C. de (1984) 'Benveniste et la linguistique arménienne', in J. Taillardat et al. (eds.),

E. Benveniste aujourd'hui: Actes du colloque international du CNRS II, Paris: Société pour l'Information Grammaticale, 225-238.

Lamberterie, C. de (1985) Revue de R. Stempel (1983), *Die infiniten Verbalformen des Armenischen, BSL* 80.2, 129-131.

Lamberterie, C. de (1986) 'Deux isoglosses entre l'arménien et l'indo-iranien', in M. Leroy and F. Mawet (eds.), *La Place de l'arménien dans les languges indo-européennes*, Louvain: Peeters, 48-61.

Lamberterie, C. de (1988) 'Meillet et l'arménien', *Histoire, épistémologie, langage: Revue publiée par la Société d'Histoire et d'Épistémologie des Sciences du Langage*, Lille, X-2, 217-234.

Lamberterie, C. de (1990) *Les Adjectifs grecs en -us*, 2 vols, Louvain: Peeters.

Lamberterie, C. de (1992) 'Le problème de l'homonymie: les trois verbes ὀφέλλω en grec ancien', in F. Létoublon (ed.), *La Langue et les textes en grec ancien: actes du colloque Pierre Chantraine (Grenoble – 5-8 septembre 1989)*, Amsterdam: Gieben, 201-217.

Laroche, E. (1956) 'Hittite *-ima-*: indo-européen *-mo-*', *BSL* 52, 72-82.

Lazzeroni, R. (1958) 'Ipotesi sulla vocale protetica davanti a *-r-* in greco e in armeno', *ASNP* 27, 127-136.

Lazzeroni, R. (1966) 'Su alcune isoglosse indoeuropee "centrali"', *SSL* 6, 54-68.

Lazzeroni, R. (1970) 'Fra glottogonia e storia: la desinenza dello strumentale plurale indoeuropeo', *SSL* 10, 53-78.

Lehmann, W. P. (1951) 'The distribution of Proto-Indo-European / **r/*', *Lg* 27, 13-17.

Lehmann, W. P. (1986) *A Gothic Etymological Dictionary*, Leiden: Brill.

Lejeune, M. (1939) *Les Adverbes grecs en -θεν*, Bordeaux: Delmas.

Lejeune, M. (1956a) 'Études de philologie mycénienne', *REA* 58, 5-41.

Lejeune, M. (1956b) 'La désinence *-φι* en mycénien', *BSL* 52, 187-218.

Lejeune, M. (1967) '"Fils" et "fille" dans les langues de l'Italie ancienne', *BSL* 62, 67-86.

Lejeune, M. (1972) *Phonétique historique du mycénien et du grec ancien*, Paris: Klincksieck.

Leroy, M. (1986) 'Le redoublement comme procédé de formation nominale en arménien classique', in M. Leroy and F. Mawet (eds.), *La Place de l'arménien dans les langues indoeuropéennes*, Louvain: Peeters, 62-75.

Leskien, A. (1876) *Die Deklination im Slavisch-Litauischen und Germanischen*, Leipzig: Hirzel.

Létoublon, F. and Lamberterie, C. de (1980) 'La roue tourne', *RPh* 54, 305-326.

Leukart, A. (1987) '*Po-ro-qa-ta-jo, to-sa-pe-mo, a-mo-ra-ma* and others: Further evidence for Proto-Greek collective formations in Mycenaean and early alphabetic Greek', *Minos* 20-22, 343-365.

Leumann, M. (1950) *Homerische Wörter*, Basel: Reinhardt.

Leumann, M. (1957) 'σάος und σῶς', in H. Kronasser (ed.), *ΜΝΗΜΗΣ ΧΑΡΙΝ: Gedenkschrift Paul Kretschmer* II, Wien: Wiener Sprachgesellschaft, 8-14.

Leumann, M. (1977) *Lateinische Grammatik I. Lateinische Laut- und Formenlehre*, 7th ed., München: Beck.

Lidén, E. (1906) *Armenische Studien*, Göteborg: Wald.

Lindeman, F. O. (1978-9) 'Note étymologique', *REArm* n.s. 13, 41-42.

Lindeman, F. O. (1982) *The triple representation of schwa in Greek and some related problems of Indo-European phonology*, Oslo: Universitetsforlaget.

Lindeman, F. O. (1986) 'A note on the morphology of Classical Armenian *anun*', *AArmL* 7, 57-58.

Lindeman, F. O. (1987) *Introduction to the 'Laryngeal Theory'*, Oslo: Norwegian University Press.

Lindeman, F. O. (1989) Review of A. Bammesberger (ed.), *Die Laryngaltheorie und die Rekonstruktion des indogermanischen Laut- und Formensystems* (1988), Heidelberg: Winter, *HS* (= *KZ*) 102, 268-297.

Lowenstam, S. (1979) 'The meaning of IE **dhal-*', *TAPA* 109, 125-135.

Lühr, R. (1991) 'Analogische "formae difficiliores"' *HS* (= *KZ*) 104, 170-185.

Lyonnet, S. (1933) *Le Parfait en arménien classique*, Paris: Champion.

Makaev, E. A. (1967) 'Armjano-indoevropejskie leksičeskie izoglossy i areal'naja lingvistika', *ZPhon* 20, 449-464.

Mallory, J. P. (1989) *In search of the Indo-Europeans: language, archaeology and myth*, London: Thames and Hudson.

Manessy-Guitton, J. (1972) 'Les substantifs neutres à suffixe -nos chez Homère', BSL, 85–108.
Manessy-Guitton, J. (1988) 'Les champs sémantiques de la racine *H₂ei-g- en grec', in M. A.
Jazayery and W. Winter (eds.), Languages and Cultures: Studies in Honour of Edgar C.
Polomé, The Hague: Mouton, 419–437.
Mann, S. E. (1963) Armenian and Indo-European, London: Luzac.
Mann, S. E. (1968) An Armenian Historical Grammar in Latin Characters, London: Luzac.
Mann, S. E. (1977) An Albanian Historical Grammar, Hamburg: Buske.
Mariès, L. (1930) 'Sur la formation de l'aoriste et des subjonctifs en -ç- en arménien', REArm
10, 167–182.
Mariès, L. and Mercier, C. (1959) Eznik de Kołb, De Deo: édition, traduction française, notes et
tables, in F. Graffin (ed.), Patrologia Orientalis. Tome XXVIII fasc. 3–4, Paris: Firmin-Didot.
Marr, N. (1903) Grammatika drevnearmjanskago jazyka, St. Petersburg.
Marr, N. and Brière, M. (1931) La Langue géorgienne, Paris: Firmin-Didot.
Martinet, A. (1955) Économie des changements phonétiques: Traité de phonologie dia-
chronique, Berne: Francke.
Martinet, A. (1964) Économie des changements phonétiques, 2nd ed., Berne: Francke.
Masson, M. (1987) 'Noms de cordes en grec ancien: Problèmes d'étymologie', RPh 61, 37–47.
Mawet, F. (1986) 'Les développements fonctionnels de arménien (e)t'e', in M. Leroy and F.
Mawet (eds.), La Place de l'arménien dans les langues indo-européennes, Louvain: Peeters,
76–89.
Mayrhofer, M. (1953) 'Zwei griechische Wortdeutungen', KZ 71, 74–77.
Mayrhofer, M. KEWA (1956–80) Kurzgefasstes etymologisches Wörterbuch des Altindischen, 4
vols., Heidelberg: Winter.
Mayrhofer, M. (1982) 'Über griechische Vokalprothese, Laryngaltheorie und externe Rekon-
struktion', in J. Tischler (ed.), Serta Indogermanica: Festschrift für Günter Neumann zum 60.
Geburtstag, Innsbruck: Inst. für Sprachwiss. d. Univ., 177–192.
Mayrhofer, M. (1986) 'Band I/2: Lautlehre', in J. Kuryłowicz (founder ed.) and M. Mayrhofer
(ed.), Indogermanische Grammatik, Heidelberg: Winter.
Mayrhofer, M. EWA (1986– in progress) Etymologisches Wörterbuch des Altindoarischen,
Heidelberg: Winter.
Meid, W. (1975) 'Probleme der räumlichen und zeitlichen Gliederung des Indogermanischen',
in H. Rix (ed.), Flexion und Wortbildung: Akten der V Fachtagung der Idg. Gesellschaft,
Wiesbaden: Reichert, 204–219.
Meid, W. (1989) Archäologie und Sprachwissenschaft; Kritisches zu neueren Hypothesen der
Ausbreitung der Indogermanen, Innsbruck: Inst. für Sprachwiss. d. Univ.
Meier-Brügger, M. (1989) 'Griech. θῡμός und seine Sippe', MH 46, 243–246.
Meier-Brügger, M. (1990a) 'Zu griechisch ἀρήν und κρῑός', HS (= KZ) 103, 26–29.
Meier-Brügger, M. (1990b) 'Zu griechisch ἄγρωστις', HS (= KZ) 103, 33–34.
Meier-Brügger, M. (1992) Griechische Sprachwissenschaft, (2 volumes), Berlin/New York:
Sammlung Göschen/de Gruyter.
Meillet, A. (1889) 'Les groupes indo-européennes uk, ug, ugh', MSL 7, 57–60.
Meillet, A. (1900) 'Sur les suffixes verbaux secondaires', MSL 11, 297–323.
Meillet, A. (1908) Les Dialectes indo-européens, Paris: Champion.
Meillet, A. (1913) Altarmenisches Elementarbuch, Heidelberg: Winter.
Meillet, A. (1920) 'Le nom de "pont"', BSL 22, 17 f.
Meillet, A. (1922) Les Dialectes indo-européens, nouveau tirage, Paris: Champion.
Meillet, A. (1925a) La Méthode comparative en linguistique historique, Oslo: Aschehoug.
Meillet, A. (1925b) 'Le nom indo-européen de la meule', Mélanges publiés en l'honneur de Paul
Boyer, Paris: Champion, 1–12.
Meillet, A. (1931a) 'Achéen et Dorien πεδά', BSL 31, 42–44.
Meillet, A. (1931b) 'Caractère secondaire du type thématique indo-européen', BSL 32, 192–202.
Meillet, A. (1932) 'Sur le type du gr. μαινόλης', BSL 33, 130–132.
Meillet, A. (1936) Esquisse d'une grammaire comparée de l'arménien classique, 2nd ed.,
Vienna: Mekhitharistes.
Meillet, A. (1937) Introduction à l'étude comparative des langues indo-européennes, 8th ed.,
Paris: Hachette, repr. 1964, Alabama: University Press.
Meillet, A. (1962) Études de linguistique et de philologie arméniennes I, Lisboa: Librairie
Bertrand.

Meillet, A. (1977) *Études de linguistique et de philologie arméniennes* II, Louvain: Orientaliste.
Meillet, A. (1979) 'Le locatif *yamsean* "dans le mois" en arménien' (French translation by M.
Minassian of 'Hayerêni mêj "yamsean" nergoyakanɔ', *Banasêr* I (1899), 144–146), *BSL* 74,
333–334.
Melena, J. L. (1987) 'On the Linear B ideogrammatic syllabogram *ZE*', *Minos* 20–22, 389–458.
Merlingen, W. (1957) 'Idg. *þ* und Verwandtes', in H. Kronasser (ed.), *MNHMΣ XAPIN*:
Gedenkschrift Paul Kretschmer II, Wien: Wiener Sprachgesellschaft, 49–61.
Messing, G. M. (1947) 'Selected studies in Indo-European Philology', *HSPh* 56–57, 161–232.
Miller, D. G. (1976) 'Liquid plus *s* in Ancient Greek', *Glotta* 54, 159–172.
Minassian, M. (1978–9) 'A. Meillet et l'adaptation inachevée du *Dictionnaire étymologique
arménien* d'Ačařyan', *REArm* n.s. 13, 15–30.
Minassian, M. (1986) 'Formation du participe en *-oł* en arménien classique', *AArmL* 7, 85–98.
Minshall, R. (1955) '"Initial" Indo-European */y/* in Armenian', *Lg* 31, 499–503.
Monro, D. B. (1891) *A Grammar of the Homeric Dialect*, 2nd ed., Oxford: University Press.
Morani, M. (1981a) 'Armeno e problema *satɔm*', *HA* 95.1–12, 13–30.
Morani, M. (1981b) 'In margine a una concordanza greco-armena', *AGI* 66, 1–15.
Morani, M. (1981c) 'Di alcuni rapporti armeno-ittiti', *ASGM* 21, 99–103.
Morani, M. (1987) 'A proposito della vocale composizionale *-a-* in armeno', *HA* 101.1–12,
677–684.
Morpurgo Davies, A. (1970) 'Epigraphical *-φι*', *Glotta* 47, 46–54.
Morpurgo Davies, A. (1975) 'Language classification in the nineteenth century', in T. Sebeok
(ed.), *Current Trends in Linguistics* 13, The Hague, Paris: Mouton, 607–716.
Morpurgo Davies, A. (1985) 'Mycenaean and Greek Language', in A. Morpurgo Davies and Y.
Duhoux (eds.), *Linear B: A 1984 Survey*, (= *BCILL no. 26*), Louvain-la-Neuve: Cabay, 75–
125.
Muller, G. (1984) 'The development of vocalised laryngeals in Old Armenian', *APILKU* 4, 95–
98.
Narten, J. (1968) 'Zum "proterodynamischen" Wurzelpräsens', in J. C. Heesterman, G. H.
Schokker and V. I. Subramoniam (eds.), *Pratidānam: Indian, Iranian and Indo-European
Studies Presented to Franciscus Bernardus Jacobus Kuiper on his Sixtieth Birthday*, The
Hague/Paris: Mouton, 9–19.
Negri, M. (1976) 'Studi sul verbo greco II', *Acme* 29, 233–250.
Neu, E. (1976) 'Zur Rekonstruktion des indogermanischen Verbalsystems', in A. Morpurgo
Davies and W. Meid (eds.), *Studies in Greek, Italic and Indo-European Linguistics offered to
Leonard R. Palmer on the occasion of his 70th birthday*, Innsbruck: Inst. für Sprachwiss. d.
Univ., 239–254.
Neu, E. (1984) 'Konstruieren und Rekonstruieren', *InL* 9, 101–131.
Neumann, G. (1988) *Phrygisch und Griechisch*, (= *SbÖAW* 499), Wien: Österreichische Akad.
d. Wiss.
Nieto Hernández, P. (1987) 'Un problema de lengua homérica: la desinencia *-φι*', *Emerita* 55,
273–306.
Normier, R. (1977) 'Idg. Konsonantismus, germ. "Lautverschiebung" und Verner'sches Gesetz',
KZ 91, 171–218.
Normier, R. (1980) 'Beiträge zur armenischen Etymologie', *AArmL* 1, 19–20.
Normier, R. (1981) 'Zu Esche und Espe', *Sprache* 27, 22–29.
Nussbaum, A. J. (1986) *Head and Horn in Indo-European*, Berlin and New York: de Gruyter.
Oettinger, N. (1979) *Die Stammbildung des hethitischen Verbums*, Nürnberg: Carl.
Oettinger, N. (1982) 'Die Dentalerweiterung von n-Stämmen und Heteroklitika im Griech-
ischen, Anatolischen und Altindischen', in J. Tischler (ed.), *Serta Indogermanica: Festschrift
für Günter Neumann zum 60. Geburtstag*, Innsbruck: Inst. für Sprachwiss. d. Univ., 233–245.
Olsen, B. A. (1984) 'The Armenian reflexes of Indo-European intervocalic **w*', *Mijazgayin
hayerenagitakan gitažołov, Erevan, 21–25 septemberi, 1982 t'.*, Erevan: Haykakan SSH GA
hrat., 219–223.
Olsen, B. A. (1985) 'On the development of Indo-European prothetic vowels in Classical
Armenian', *REArm* n.s. 19, 5–17.
Olsen, B. A. (1986) 'The Armenian continuations of Indo-European intervocalic **w*', *AArmL*
7, 51–56.
Olsen, B. A. (1988) *The Proto-Indo-European Instrument Noun Suffix **-tlom* and its Variants*,

(*Kongelige Danske Videnskabernes Selskab, Historisk-filosofiske Meddelelser* 55), Copenhagen: Munksgaard.

Olsen, B. A. (1988–9) 'A surrejoinder to J. A. C. Greppin's remarks on prothetic vowels in Armenian', *REArm* n.s. 21, 481–483.

Olsen, B. A. (1989a) 'A trace of Indo-European accent in Armenian', *HS* (=*KZ*) 102, 220–240.

Olsen, B. A. (1989b) 'Three notes on Armenian historical phonology', *AArmL* 10, 5–25.

Olsen, B. A. (1992) 'The development of high vowel plus laryngeal in Armenian', in J. A. C. Greppin (ed.), *Proceedings of the Fourth International Conference on Armenian Linguistics. Cleveland State University, Cleveland, Ohio. September 14–18, 1991*, Delmar, N.Y.: Caravan, 129–146.

O'Neil, J. L. (1969) 'The treatment of vocalic *R* and *L* in Greek', *Glotta* 47, 8–46.

Orel, V. E. (1988) 'Albanica parerga', *IF* 93, 102–120.

Osthoff, H. (1901) *Etymologische Parerga*, Leipzig: Hirzel.

Palmer, L. R. (1954) *The Latin Language*, London: Faber and Faber.

Patrubány, L. von (1904) 'Miscellen', *KZ* 37, 427–428.

Pedersen, H. (1900) 'Albanesisch und Armenisch', *KZ* 36, 340–341.

Pedersen, H. (1905) 'Zur armenischen Sprachgeschichte', *KZ* 38, 194–240.

Pedersen, H. (1906) 'Armenisch und die Nachbarsprachen', *KZ* 39, 334–485.

Pedersen, H. (1924) s.v. 'Armenier', in M. Ebert (ed.), *Reallexikon der Vorgeschichte*, vol. 1, Berlin: de Gruyter, 219–226.

Pedersen, H. (1925) *Le Groupement des dialectes indo-européens*, København: Lunos.

Pedersen, H. (1926) *La Cinquième Déclinaison latine*, København: Høst.

Pedersen, H. (1982) *Kleine Schriften zum Armenischen*, hrsg. von. R. Schmitt, Hildersheim: Olms.

Penney, J. H. W. (1988) 'Laryngeals and the Indo-European root', in A. Bammesberger (ed.), *Die Laryngaltheorie und die Rekonstruktion des indogermanischen Laut- und Formensystems*, Heidelberg: Winter, 361–372.

Perpillou, J. L. (1972) 'Notules laconiennes', *BSL* 67, 109–128.

Perpillou, J. L. (1981) 'Vinealia 2; "Marcotte, drageon, plant" et "veau": une métaphore', *RPh* 55, 215–223.

Peters, M. (1976) 'Attisch *hiēmi*', *Sprache* 22, 157–161.

Peters, M. (1980) *Untersuchungen zur Vertretung der indogermanischen Laryngale im Griechischen*, (*SbÖAW* 377), Wien: Österreichische Akad. d. Wiss.

Peters, M. (1986) 'Probleme mit anlautenden Laryngalen', *Sprache* 32, 365–383.

Peters, M. (1988) 'Zur Frage strukturell uneinheitlicher Laryngalreflexe in idg. Einzelsprachen', in A. Bamesberger (ed.), *Die Laryngaltheorie und die Rekonstruktion des indogermanischen Laut- und Formensystems*, Heidelberg: Winter, 373–381.

Peters, M. (1991) 'Idg. "9" im Armenischen und Griechischen', *ZPSK* (= *ZPhon*) 44, 301–310.

Petersson, H. (1916) 'Beiträge zur armenische Wortkunde', *KZ* 47, 240–291.

Pisani, V. (1944) 'Armenische Studien', *KZ* 68, 157–177.

Pisani, V. (1950a) 'Studi sulla fonetica dell'armeno', *RL* 1, 165–193.

Pisani, V. (1950b) 'L'albanais et les autres langues indo-européennes', in ΠΑΓΚΑΡΠΕΙΑ: *Mélanges Henri Grégoire* II, (= *AnnIPhO* 10), 519–538.

Pisani, V. (1951) 'Studi sulla fonetica dell'armeno (cont.)', *RL* 2, 47–74.

Pisani, V. (1959) 'Obiter scripta 7. Gli iterativi ionici e ittiti con "sk" e il suffisso armeno -*ç*-', *Paideia* 14, 176f.

Pisani, V. (1961) Review of Solta (1960) *Die Stellung des Armenischen im Kreise der indogermanischen Sprachen*, *AGI* 66, 172–177.

Pisani, V. (1966) 'Armenische Miszellen', *Sprache* 12, 227–236.

Pisani, V. (1975) 'Zum armenischen Pluralzeichen -*kʻ*', *KZ* 89, 94–99.

Pisani, V. (1976) 'Note di etimologia e morfologia armene', *HA* 90.1–12, 273–286.

Pokorny, J. *IEW* (1959) *Indogermanisches etymologisches Wörterbuch*, Bern: Francke.

Polomé, E. C. (1980) 'Armenian and the Proto-Indo-European laryngeals', in J. A. C. Greppin (ed.), *First International Conference on Armenian Linguistics: Proceedings*, Delmar, N.Y.: Caravan, 17–33.

Porzig, W. (1927) 'Zur Aktionsart indogermanischer Präsensbildung', *IF* 45, 152–167.

Porzig, W. (1954) *Die Gliederung des indogermanischen Sprachgebiets*, Heidelberg: Winter.

Poucha, P. (1955) *Thesaurus Linguae Tocharicae, Dialecti A*, Prague: Státni Pedagogické Nakladatelství.

Puhvel, J. (1976) 'πολέμοιο γέφυραι', *IF* 81, 60–66.

Ramat, A. G. (1967) 'La funzione del suffisso -σκ- nel sistema verbale greco', *AGI* 52, 105–123.

Rasmussen, J. E. (1984) 'Miscellaneous morphological problems in Indo-European languages (III)', *APILKU* 4, 133–149.

Rasmussen, J. E. (1987) 'Miscellaneous morphological problems in Indo-European languages (I–II)', *LPosn* 28, 27–62.

Ravnæs, E. (1988) 'The Prehistory of Armenian *ē* and *oy*', in F. Thordarson (ed.), *Studia Caucasologica I: Proceedings of the Third Caucasian Colloquium, Oslo, July 1986*, Oslo: Norwegian University Press, 225–238.

Renfrew, C. (1987) *Archaeology and Language*, Cambridge: University Press.

Ringe, D. A. (1984) 'Ionic ὀνονημένα', *Glotta* 62, 45–56.

Ringe, D. A. (1988–90) 'Evidence for the position of Tocharian in the Indo-European family?', *Sprache* 34.1, 59–123.

Risch, E. (1974) *Wortbildung der homerischen Sprache*, 2nd ed., Berlin: de Gruyter.

Risch, E. (1985) 'Die Ausbildung des Griechischen im 2. Jahrtausend v. Chr.', *Studien zur Ethnogenese*, (= *ARWAW* 72), Opladen: Westdeutscher Verlag, 165–187.

Ritter, R. P. (1983) 'Eine verkannte Etymologie für armen. *aniw* "Rad"', *MSS* 42, 191–196.

Ritter, R. P. (1985) 'Zum Wandel uridg. **mn* > arm. *wn*', *MSS* 45, 197–199.

Rix, H. (1976) *Historische Grammatik des Griechischen. Laut- und Formenlehre*, Darmstadt: Wissenschaftliche Buchgesellschaft.

Rix, H. (1986) *Zur Entstehung des urindogermanischen Modussystems*, Innsbruck: Inst. für Sprachwiss. d. Univ.

Rix, H. (1991) 'Nochmals griech. νῆττα/νῆσσα/νᾶσσα', *HS*, (= *KZ*) 104, 186–198.

Rocca, G. (1985) 'Una congruenza morfologica greco-armena', *ASGM* 26, 73–79.

Roider, U. (1981) 'Griech. θυμός "Mut" – ai. *dhūmáḥ* "Rauch"', *KZ* 95, 99–109.

Rosén, H. B. (1962) *Laut- und Formenlehre der herodotischen Sprachform*, Heidelberg: Winter.

Ruhlen, M. (1991) *A Guide to the World's Languages, Volume I: Classification* (2nd edition), London: Arnold.

Ruijgh, C. J. (1967) *Études sur la grammaire et le vocabulaire du grec mycénien*, Amsterdam: Hakkert.

Ruijgh, C. J. (1972) 'Le redoublement dit attique dans l'évolution du système morphologique du verbe grec', *Mélanges de linguistique et de philologie grecques offerts à Pierre Chantraine*, Paris: Klincksieck, 211–230.

Ruijgh, C. J. (1979) 'La morphologie du grec', *SMEA* 20, 69–89.

Ruijgh, C. J. (1985) 'Problèmes de philologie mycénienne', *Minos* 19, 105–167.

Ruijgh, C. J. (1986) 'Observations sur κορέσαι, κορέω, myc. *da-ko-ro* δακόρος etc.', in A. Etter (ed.), *O-o-pe-ro-si: Festschrift für Ernst Risch zum 75. Geburtstag*, Berlin: de Gruyter, 376–392.

Ruijgh, C. J. (1987) 'À propos de ϝισϝο- (*wi-si-wo*), ἐϝισυ- (*e-wi-su-*) et hom. ἐ(ϝ)εισάμενος', *Minos* 20–22, 533–544.

Ruijgh, C. J. (1988) 'Observations sur les traitements des laryngales en grec', in A. Bammesberger (ed.), *Die Laryngaltheorie und die Rekonstruktion des indogermanischen Laut- und Formensystems*, Heidelberg: Winter, 443–469.

Sandfeld, K. (1938) 'Problèmes d'interférences linguistiques', *PICL* 4, 59–61.

Schindler J. (1966) 'Bemerkungen zum idg. Wort für "Schlaf"', *Sprache* 12, 67–76.

Schindler, J. (1966–7) 'Idg. **dw-* im Tocharischen', *IF* 71, 236–238.

Schindler, J. (1967a) 'Tocharische Miszellen', *IF* 72, 239–249.

Schindler, J. (1967b) 'Zu hethitisch *nekuz*', *KZ* 81, 290–303.

Schindler, J. (1970) Review of R. Anttila (1969), *Proto-Indo-European Schwebeablaut*, Berkeley and Los Angeles: University of California Press, *Kratylos* 15, 146–152.

Schindler, J. (1972) 'L'apophonie des noms-racines indo-européens', *BSL* 67, 31–38.

Schindler, J. (1974) 'Fragen zum paradigmatischen Ausgleich', *Sprache* 20, 1–9.

Schindler, J. (1975a) 'L'apophonie des thèmes indo-européens en *-r/-n*', *BSL* 70, 1–10.

Schindler, J. (1975b) 'Armenisch *erkn*, griechisch ὀδύνη, irisch *idu*', *KZ* 89, 53–65.

Schindler, J. (1975c) 'Zum ablaut der neutralen *s*-Stämme des Indogermanischen', in H. Rix (ed.), *Flexion und Wortbildung: Akten der V Fachtagung der Idg. Gesellschaft*, Wiesbaden: Reichert, 259–267.

Schindler, J. (1976) 'On the Greek type ἱππεύς', in A. Morpurgo Davies and W. Meid (eds.), *Studies in Greek, Italic and Indo-European Linguistics offered to Leonard R. Palmer on the occasion of his 70th birthday*, Innsbruck: Inst. für Sprachwiss. d. Univ., 349–352.

Schindler, J. (1977) 'A thorny problem', *Sprache* 23, 23–35.

Schleicher, A. (1861) *Compendium der vergleichenden Grammatik des indogermanischen Sprachen I*, Weimer: Böhlau.

Schlerath, B. (1981) 'Ist ein Raum/Zeit-Modell für eine rekonstruierte Sprache möglich?', *KZ* 95, 175–202.

Schlerath, B. (1982–3) 'Sprachvergleich und Rekonstruktion: Methoden und Möglichkeiten', *InL* 8, 53–69.

Schlerath, B. (1987) 'On the reality and status of a reconstructed language', *JIES* 15, 41–46.

Schmalstieg, W. R. (1982) 'A note on the Armenian dative-locative endings -*um*, -*oy*, and -*oj*', *AArmL* 3, 61–64.

Schmid, W. P. (1978) *Indogermanische Modelle und osteuropäische Frühgeschichte*, (= *AAWL* 1978.1), Wiesbaden: Steiner.

Schmidt, G. (1973) 'Die iranischen Wörter für "Tochter" und "Vater" und die Reflexe des interkonsonantischen *H* (ǝ) in den idg. Sprachen', *KZ* 87, 36–83.

Schmidt, G. (1978) *Stammbildung und Flexion der indogermanischen Personalpronomina*, Wiesbaden: Harrassowitz.

Schmidt, J. (1872) *Die Verwantschaftverhältnisse der indogermanischen Sprachen*, Weimar: Böhlau.

Schmidt, J. (1889) *Die Pluralbildungen der indogermanischen Neutra*, Weimar: Böhlau.

Schmidt, K. H. (1963) 'Dativ und Instrumental im Plural', *Glotta* 41, 1–10.

Schmidt, K. H. (1967) 'Beiträge zu einer typologisch-vergleichenden Grammatik der indogermanischen und südkaukasischen Sprachen', *MSS* 22, 81–92.

Schmidt, K. H. (1980) 'Armenian and Indo-European', in J. A. C. Greppin (ed.), *First International Conference on Armenian Linguistics: Proceedings*, Delmar, N.Y.: Caravan, 35–58.

Schmidt, K. H. (1984) 'Hin hayereni bayi hndevropakan himkʻǝ', *IFŽ* 1984.1, 17–37.

Schmidt, K. H. (1985) 'Die indogermanischen Grundlagen des altarmenischen Verbums', *KZ* 98, 214–237.

Schmidt, K. H. (1987) 'Hin hayereni anvanakan holovman hndevropakan himkʻerǝ', *IFŽ* 1987.1, 29–39.

Schmidt, K. H. (1992) 'Latein und Keltisch: Genetische Verwandtschaft und areale Beziehungen', in O. Panagl und T. Krisch (eds.), *Latein und Indogermanisch. Akten des Kolloquiums der Indogermanischen Gesellschaft, Salzburg, 23.–26. September 1986*, Innsbruck: Inst. für Sprachwiss. d. Univ., 29–51.

Schmidt, K. T. (1980) 'Zu Stand und Aufgaben der etymologischen Forschung auf dem Gebiete des Tocharischen', in M. Mayrhofer, M. Peters and O. E. Pfeiffer (eds.), *Lautgeschichte und Etymologie: Akten der VI. Fachtagung der Indogermanischen Gesellschaft*, Wiesbaden: Reichert, 394–411.

Schmidt, K. T. (1987) 'Zu einigen Archäismen in Flexion und Wortschatz des Tocharischen', in W. Meid (ed.), *Studien zum indogermanischen Wortschatz*, Innsbruck: Inst. für Sprachwiss. d. Univ., 287–300.

Schmitt, R. (1972a) 'Die Erforschung des Klassisch-Armenischen seit Meillet (1936)', *Kratylos* 17, 1–68.

Schmitt, R. (1972b) 'Empfehlungen zur Transliteration der armenischen Schrift', *KZ* 86, 296–306.

Schmitt, R. (1980) 'Die Lautgeschichte und ihre Abhängigkeit von der Etymologie, am Beispiel des Armenischen', in M. Mayrhofer, M. Peters und O. E. Pfeiffer (eds.), *Lautgeschichte und Etymologie: Akten der VI. Fachtagung der Indogermanischen Gesellschaft*, Wiesbaden: Reichert, 412–430.

Schmitt, R. (1981) *Grammatik des Klassisch-Armenischen mit sprachvergleichenden Erläuterungen*, Innsbruck: Inst. für Sprachwiss. d. Univ.

Schmitt, R. (1983) 'Iranisches Lehngut im Armenischen', *REArm* n.s. 17, 73–112.

Schrader, O. (1907) *Sprachvergleichung und Urgeschichte, Teil I* (3rd edition), Jena: Costenoble, (reprinted in 1980, Hildersheim/New York: Olms).

Schrader, O. and Nehring, A. (1917-29) *Reallexikon der indogermanischen Altertumskunde*, 2nd ed., 2 vols, Berlin: de Gruyter.

Schwink, F. W. (1991) 'The writing of ancient Greek consonant clusters', *Kadmos* 30, 113-127.

Schwyzer, E. (1923) *Dialectorum Graecarum exempla epigraphica potiora*, 3rd ed., Leipzig: Hirzel.

Schwyzer, E. (1939) *Griechische Grammatik I*, München: Beck.

Schwyzer, E. (1943) *Zum persönlichen Agens beim Passiv, besonders im Griechischen*, (*Abh. der Preuss. Akad.d. Wiss.* 1942:10), Berlin: de Gruyter.

Schwyzer, E. (1946) 'Ein armenisch-griechisches Nominalsuffix', *MH* 3, 49-58.

Schwyzer, E. and Debrunner, A. (1950) *Griechische Grammatik II*, München: Beck.

Shipp, G. P. (1961) *Essays in Mycenaean and Homeric Greek*, Melbourne: University Press.

Shipp, G. P. (1972) *Studies in the language of Homer*, 2nd ed., Cambridge: University Press.

Šilak'adze, I. (1975) *Dzweli somxuri enis grammat'ik'a, krest'omatiita da leksik'onit*, 2nd ed., Tbilisi: Izd-vo Tbilisskogo un-ta.

Širokov, O. (1980) 'Mesto armjanskogo jazyka sredi indoevropejskix i problema armjanskoj prarodiny', *LHG* 1980.5, 80-93.

Slings, S. R. (1975) 'The etymology of βούλομαι and ὀφείλω', *Mn* 28, 1-16.

Solta, G. R. (1960) *Die Stellung des Armenischen im Kreise der indogermanischen Sprachen*, Vienna: Mechitharisten.

Solta, G. R. (1963) 'Die Armenische Sprache', in B. Spuler (ed.), *Handbuch der Orientalistik* I.7, Leiden: Brill, 80-128.

Solta, G. R. (1965-6) 'Palatalisierung und Labialisierung', *IF* 70, 276-315.

Solta, G. R. (1970) 'Der hethitische Imperativ der 1. Person Singular und das idg. *l*-Formans als quasi-desideratives Element', *IF* 75, 44-84.

Solta, G. R. (1987) 'Einige Bemerkungen zu den sigmatischen Formen im Altarmenischen', *HA* 101.1-12, 629-637.

Solta, G. R. (1990) 'Die Stellung des Armenischen im Kreise der indogermanischen Sprachen. Ein Überblick', in E. M. Ruprechtsberger (ed.), *Armenien: Frühzeit bis 1. Jahrtausend; Sprache, Kunst und Geschichte*, Linz: Linzer Archäologische Forschungen Band 18, 7-18.

Sommer, F. (1914) *Handbuch der lateinischen Laut- und Formenlehre*, Heidelberg: Winter.

Southworth, F. C. (1964) 'Family tree diagrams', *Lg* 40, 557-565.

Specht, F. (1924) Rev. of E. Nieminen, *Der uridg. Ausgang -ai des Nominativ-Akkusativ Pluralis des Neutrums im Baltischen, IF Anz.* 42, 48-53.

Specht, F. (1939) 'Sprachliches zur Urheimat der Idg.', *KZ* 66, 1-74.

Stanford, W. B. (1936) *Greek Metaphor*, Oxford: Blackwell.

Stempel, R. (1983) *Die infiniten Verbalformen des Armenischen*, Bern: Lang.

Stempel, R. (1990) 'Die Entwicklung von auslautendem **m* und das Problem sekundärer *n*-Stämme im Armenischen', *IF* 95, 38-62.

Strunk, K. S. (1967) *Nasalpräsentien und Aoriste*, Heidelberg: Winter.

Strunk, K. S. (1978) 'Umstrittenes *ΤΑΣΑΝΟΔΕΑΣΑΣ* im arkadischen Urteil von Mantinea (IG V 2.262,17)', *Glotta* 56, 206-212.

Strunk, K. S. (1985) 'Zum Verhältnis zwischen gr. πτάρνυμαι und lat. *sternuo*', *MSS* 46, 221-242.

Swadesh, M. (1952) 'Lexico-statistic dating of prehistoric ethnic contacts. With special reference to North American Indians and Eskimos', *Proceedings of the American Philosophical Society*, Philadelphia, 96, 452-463.

Szemerényi, O. (1960a) 'Latin *hibernus* and Greek χειμερινός', *Glotta* 38, 107-125.

Szemerényi, O. (1960b) 'Indo-European **tālis*, **kʷālis* and the Greek κ-stems, ἧλιξ, γυνή/ γυναικ-', *AION-L* 2, 1-30.

Szemerényi, O. (1960c) *Studies in the Indo-European system of numerals*, Heidelberg: Winter.

Szemerényi, O. (1964) *Syncope in Greek and Indo-European and the nature of Indo-European accent*, Napoli: Istituto Orientale.

Szemerényi, O. (1966) 'Iranica II (nos. 9-31)', *Sprache* 12, 190-226.

Szemerényi, O. (1967) 'The history of Attic οὖς and some of its compounds', *SMEA* 3, 47-88.

Szemerényi, O. (1968) 'The development *s* > *h* in Indo-European languages', *Sprache* 14, 161-163.

Szemerényi, O. (1971) Review of P. Chantraine, *Dictionnaire étymologique de la langue grecque*, Paris: Klincksieck, *Gnomon* 43, 641-675.

Szemerényi, O. (1974) 'Greek πολύς and πολλός', *KZ* 88, 1–31.

Szemerényi, O. (1977a) 'Studies in the kinship terminology of the Indo-European languages, with special reference to Indian, Iranian, Greek and Latin', in *Varia 1977* (= *Acta Iranica* 16), Téhéran/Liège: Bibliothèque Pahlavi, 1–240.

Szemerényi, O. (1977b) Review of P. Chantraine, *Dictionnaire étymologique de la langue grecque*, Paris: Klincksieck, *Gnomon* 49, 1–10.

Szemerényi, O. (1978) 'On reconstruction in morphology', in M. A. Jazayery, E. C. Polomé and W. Winter (eds.), *Linguistic and Literary Studies in Honor of Archibald A. Hill*, Vol. III, The Hague: Mouton, 267–283.

Szemerényi, O. (1979) 'The consonant alternation *pt-/p-* in early Greek', in E. Risch and H. Mühlestein, (eds.), *Colloquium Mycenaeum: Proceedings of the 6th Mycenaean Colloquium*, Genève: Droz, 323–340.

Szemerényi, O. (1980) 'Etyma Graeca IV (22–29): Homerica et Mycenaica', *SMEA* 20, 207–226.

Szemerényi, O. (1985) 'Armenian between Iran and Greece', in U. Pieper and G. Stickel (eds.), *Studia linguistica diachronica et synchronica Werner Winter sexagenario anno oblata*, Berlin: de Gruyter, 783–799.

Szemerényi, O. (1987) *Scripta Minora I–III*, P. Considine and J. T. Hooker (eds.), Innsbruck: Inst. für Sprachwiss. d. Univ.

Szemerényi, O. (1989) *An den Quellen des lateinischen Wortschatzes*, Innsbruck: Inst. für Sprachwiss. d. Univ.

Szemerényi, O. (1990) *Einführung in die vergleichende Sprachwissenschaft*, 4th ed., Darmstadt: Wissenschaftliche Buchgesellschaft.

Szemerényi, O. (1991) *Scripta Minora IV*, P. Considine and J. T. Hooker (eds.), Innsbruck: Inst. für Sprachwiss. d. Univ.

Taillardat, J. (1977) 'Images et matrices métaphoriques', *Bulletin de l'Association Guillaume Budé*, Paris, 36, 344–354.

Thieme, P. (1953) *Die Heimat der indogermanischen Gemeinsprache*, *AAWL* 1953, Wiesbaden: Steiner.

Thomson, R. W. (1975) *An Introduction to Classical Armenian*, Delmar, N.Y.: Caravan.

Thumb, A. and Kieckers, E. (1932) *Handbuch der griechischen Dialekte: Erster Teil*, 2nd ed., Heidelberg: Winter.

Thumb, A. and Hauschild, R. (1959) *Handbuch des Sanskrit. II Teil: Formenlehre*, 3rd ed., Heidelberg: Winter.

Thurneysen, R. (1946) *A Grammar of Old Irish*, 2nd ed., translated by D. A. Binchy and O. Bergin, Dublin: Institute for Advanced Studies.

Tichy, E. (1991) 'Hom. ἀνδροτῆτα und die Vorgeschichte des daktylischen Hexameters', *Glotta* 49, 28–75.

Timpanaro, S. (1963) *La genesi del metodo del Lachmann*, Firenzi: Felice le Monnier.

Tischler, J. (1973) *Glottochronologie und Lexikostatistik*, Innsbruck: Inst. für Sprachwiss. d. Univ.

Tucker, E. F. (1990) *The Creation of Morphological Regularity: Early Greek verbs in -έω, -άω, -όω, -ύω, -ίω*, Göttingen: Vandenhoeck & Ruprecht.

Tumanjan, E. G. (1968) 'Morfologičeskij analiz indoevropejskix terminov, oboznačajuščix životnyx, v armjanskom jazyke', *VJa* 1968.5, 50–65.

Tumanjan, E. G. (1971) *Drevnearmjanskij jazyk*, Moscow: Nauka.

Tumanan, E. G. (1978) *Struktura indoevropejskix imën v armjanskom jazyke*, Moscow: Nauka.

Turner, N. (1963) *A Grammar of New Testament Greek* (by J. H. Moulton). Vol. III. *Syntax*. Edinburgh: Clark.

Vendryes, J. (1911) 'Le type verbal en *-ske/o-* de l'indo-iranien', *Mélanges d'indianisme offerts à S. Levi*, Paris: Leroux, 173–182.

Ventris, M. and Chadwick, J. (1973) *Documents in Mycenaean Greek*, 2nd ed., Cambridge: University Press.

Vogt, H. (1938) 'Arménien et caucasique du sud', *NTS* 9, 321–338.

Vogt, H. (1958) 'Les occlusives de l'arménien', *NTS* 18, 143–161.

Vogt, H. (1988) *Linguistique caucasienne et arménienne*, E. Hovdhaugen and F. Thordarson (eds.), Oslo: Norwegian University Press.

Waanders, F. M. J. (1992) 'Greek', in J. Gvozdanović (ed.), *Indo-European Numerals*, Berlin/New York: Mouton de Gruyter, 369–388.

Wackernagel, J. (1895) 'Μοῦσα', *KZ* 33, 571–574.
Wackernagel, J. (1916) *Sprachliche Untersuchungen zu Homer*, Göttingen: Vandenhoeck & Ruprecht.
Wackernagel, J. (1924) *Vorlesungen über Syntax*, vol. II, Basel: Birkhäuser.
Wathelet, P. (1973) 'Etudes de linguistique homérique', *AC* 42, 379–405.
Watkins, C. (1966) 'Italo-Celtic revisited', in H. Birnbaum and J. Puhvel (eds), *Ancient Indo-European Dialects*, Berkeley and Los Angeles: California University Press, 29–50.
Watkins, C. (1969) 'Band III/1: Formenlehre. Erster Teil: Geschichte der Indogermanischen Verbalflexion', in J. Kuryłowicz (ed.), *Indogermanische Grammatik*, Heidelberg: Winter.
Watkins, C. (1971) 'Hittite and Indo-European studies: the denominative statives in -ē-', *TPhS* 1971, 51–93.
Watkins, C. (1974) 'I-E "star"', *Sprache* 20.1, 10–14.
Watkins, C. (1976) 'Towards Proto-Indo-European syntax: problems and pseudo-problems', in S. B. Steever, C. A. Walker and S. S. Mufwene (eds.), *Papers from the Parasession on Diachronic Syntax, April 22, 1976*, Chicago: Chicago Linguistic Society, 305–326.
Weinreich, U. (1953) *Languages in Contact*, New York: Linguistic Circle.
Weitenberg, J. J. S. (1984) 'The inflection of *mi* "one" as a trace of Proto-Armenian nominal gender', *Mijazgayin hayerenagitakan gitažołov, Erevan, 21–25 septemberi, 1982 t'.*, Erevan: Haykakan SSH GA hrat., 195–218.
Weitenberg, J. J. S. (1989) 'The inflection of proper names in Armenian', *AArmL* 10, 57–72.
Weitenberg, J. J. S. (1992) 'Aspekte der relativen Chronologie des Klassisch-Armenischen', in R. Beekes, A. Lubotsky and J. Weitenberg (eds.), *Rekonstruktion und relative Chronologie: Akten der VIII. Fachtagung der Indogermanischen Gesellschaft, Leiden, 31 August–4 September 1987*, Innsbruck: Inst. für Sprachwiss. d. Univ., 137–149.
West, M. L. (1978) *Hesiod: Works and Days, edited with Prolegomenon and Commentary*, Oxford: University Press.
Windekens, A. J. van (1941) *Lexique étymologique des dialectes tokhariens*, Louvain: Muséon.
Windekens, A. J. van (1976) *Le Tokharien confronté avec les autres langues indo-européennes. Vol. I. La Phonétique et le vocabulaire*, Louvain: Université Catholique Néerlandaise.
Windekens, A. J. van (1982) *Le Tokharien confronté avec les autres langues indo-européennes. Vol. II, 2. La Morphologie verbale*, Louvain: Université Catholique Néerlandaise.
Windekens, A. J. van (1987) 'Réflexions sur quelques concordances lexicales entre l'arménien et le grec', *HA* 101.1–12, 609–612.
Winter, W. (1955a) 'Problems of Armenian phonology II', *Lg* 31, 4–8.
Winter, W. (1955b) 'Nochmals ved. *aśnáti*', *KZ* 72, 161–175.
Winter, W. (1962) 'Problems of Armenian Phonology III', *Lg* 38, 254–262.
Winter, W. (1965a) 'Armenian evidence', in W. Winter (ed.), *Evidence for Laryngeals*, 2nd ed., The Hague: Mouton, 100–115.
Winter, W. (1965b) 'Tocharian evidence', in W. Winter (ed.), *Evidence for Laryngeals*, 2nd ed., The Hague: Mouton, 190–211.
Winter, W. (1986) 'Hayereni anvanakan t'ek'man mi k'ani harc'er', *IFŽ* 1986.2, 17–24.
Winter, W. (1992a) 'Tocharian', in J. Gvozdanović (ed.), *Indo-European Numerals*, Berlin/New York: Mouton de Gruyter, 97–161.
Winter, W. (1992b) 'Armenian', in J. Gvozdanović (ed.), *Indo-European Numerals*, Berlin/New York: Mouton de Gruyter, 347–359.
Witczak, K. T. (1989) 'Tocharian A *āpsā* (pl.) "(minor) limbs" and its cognates', *TIES* 3, 23–34.
Witczak, K. T. (1991) 'Armenian *op'i* "white poplar, Populus alba L." and the development of **ps* in Armenian', *AArmL* 12, 65–75.
Wyatt, W. F. (1972) *The Greek Prothetic Vowel*, Cleveland, Ohio: Case Western Reserve University Press.
Wyatt, W. F. (1982) 'Lexical correspondences between Armenian and Greek', *AArmL* 3, 19–42.
Xačaturova, E. G. (1973) 'Ob armjano-indijskix leksičeskix izoglossax', *IFŽ* 1973.2, 191–199.
Zōhrab, Y. [Y. Zōhrapean] (1805) *Astowcašownč' matean hin ew nor ktakaranac'*, (Armenian Bible), Venice: St Lazar.
Zucchelli, B. (1970) *Studi sulle formazioni latine in -lo- non diminutive e sui loro rapporti con i diminutivi*, Parma: University Press.

WORD INDEX

Albanian

dal 118
derth 122
drapër 112
dreth 122–123
edh 90
ëndërrë 236
hollë 219
im 340
len 227
lend 227

lende 135, 227
lëndë (Tosk) 227
lênd 227
mushk 231
një 175
nuk 158
s 158, 231
thur 140
tre 209

Anatolian languages
(Hittite unspecified)

ammuk 34
ašanzi 207
ašaš- 222
ašeš- 222
ekuzi 155

el-elḫaiti (Luvian) 222
elḫadu (Luvian) 222
eš- 222
ḫappeššar- 101
ḫapušaš 222

Armenian

Armenian words are listed following the order of the Armenian alphabet, which is as follows: *a b g d e z ê ∂ t' ž i l x c k h j ł č m y n š o č' p ǰ r̄ s v t r c' w p' k'.*

(b) Mycenaean Greek

Indo-Iranian Languages
(a) Sanskrit

The Sanskrit words are listed following the order of the Sanskrit alphabet, which is as follows: a $ā$ i $ī$ u u $ṛ$ $ṝ$ $ḷ$ $ḹ$ e ai o au $ṁ$ k kh g gh $ṅ$ c ch j jh $ñ$ $ṭ$ $ṭh$ $ḍ$ $ḍh$ $ṇ$ t th d dh n p ph b bh m y r l v $ś$ $ṣ$ s $ḥ$.

pṛṣṭhá- 167
prátīka- 42
prātá- 114
makṣu 152
mūrá- 42
lopāśá- 35, 96, 220
vásati 106
váste 236
śū́na- 228
śū́nya- 228
śṛnkhala- 139
śyāvá- 143

śyená- 143
śvā́ 228
siṃha- 13
sūnára- 206
stana- 237
sthāvará- 43
sthūra- 43
snih- 138
svad- 49
hím 138
hyás 143

(b) Iranian Languages
(i) Avestan

The Avestan words are listed following the order of the Avestan alphabet, which is as follows: a ā ə ə̄ e ē o ō å ā̊ i ī u ū k g γ x č j t d δ θ t p b w f n ŋ m y v r s z š ž h xʸ.

ərənauu- 237
izaēna- 90
išasa- 216
kamnānar- 206
daxma- 121
θraŋhi 100

pasu- 160
maš(ii)a- 237
rah- 103
saēna- 143
siiāuua- 143

(ii) Other Iranian languages

ārr- (Khotanese) 92
dr'w- (Manichean Parthian) 123
pēl (Kurdish) 163

stavar (Pahlavi) 43
zəm (Waxī) 138

Italic Languages
(a) Latin

ador 171
anguis 54
antae 36
antrum 98
areo 221
arvina 197
bibulus 74
cicer 54, 143
circus 133
corpus 233
credulus 74
crus 44
curvus 133
daga 118
durare 224

durus 113, 224
ebrius 155
filius 24
fumus 24
gelare 131
gelu 131
glans 135
grandis 113
grando 38
hibernus 137
lavo 44
lorum 39
mille 175
modestus 148
mox 152, 230

(b) Other Italic and Romance languages

Phrygian

Slavonic Languages
(Russian unspecified)

Tocharian A and B